PROJECTION OF POWER

PROJECTION OF POWER
PERSPECTIVES, PERCEPTIONS AND PROBLEMS

Edited by

Uri Ra'anan

Robert L. Pfaltzgraff, Jr.

Geoffrey Kemp

International Security Studies Program
The Fletcher School of Law and Diplomacy
Tufts University
Medford, Massachusetts 02155

ARCHON BOOKS
1982

© 1982   The Fletcher School of Law and Diplomacy of Tufts University
First published 1982 as an Archon Book,
an imprint of THE SHOE STRING PRESS, INC.,
Hamden, Connecticut 06514

Printed in the United States of America

Library of Congress Cataloging in Publication Data
Main entry under title:

Projection of Power.

"An outgrowth of papers and discussions at the ninth
annual conference of the Fletcher School's International
Security Studies Program, held in Cambridge on April
23–25, 1980"—Introd.
Includes bibliographical references and index.
1. Military policy—Addresses, essays, lectures.
2. Strategy—Addresses, essays, lectures. I. Ra'anan,
Uri, 1926–   . II. Pfaltzgraff, Robert L., Jr. III. Kemp,
Geoffrey. IV. Fletcher School of Law and Diplomacy.
International Studies Program.
UA11.P67   355'.0335   82-6697
ISBN 0-208-01954-5   AACR2

Contents

About the Authors

1. General Russell E. Dougherty, USAF (Ret.), is former Commander of the Strategic Air Command and is Executive Director of the Air Force Association in Washington, D.C.

2. Professor Uri Ra'anan is Professor of International Politics at The Fletcher School of Law and Diplomacy, Tufts University, and Chairman of the International Security Studies Program.

3. Dr. Geoffrey Kemp, Associate Professor of International Politics at The Fletcher School of Law and Diplomacy, Tufts University, is now Senior Staff Member for Near East and South Asian Affairs, the National Security Council in Washington, D.C.

   Mr. John Maurer is a Ph.D. candidate at The Fletcher School of Law and Diplomacy, Tufts University.

4. Dr. Fred C. Iklé is Under Secretary of Defense for Policy in the Department of Defense in Washington, D.C. He is former Director of U.S. Arms Control & Disarmament Agency; former Professor of Political Science at Massachusetts Institute of Technology; and former Director of Social Science Research Branch at Rand Corporation.

5. R. James Woolsey, Esq., is former Counsel to the Senate Armed Services Committee; former Under Secretary of the Navy; now with the law firm of Shea & Gardner in Washington, D.C.

6. Dr. Michael Vlahos received his Ph.D. degree from The Fletcher School of Law and Diplomacy, Tufts University, in May 1981. He is former Research Associate Staff Member in Military and Strategic Studies for R & D Associates in Washington, D.C.; and he has been Adjunct Professor at the

School of Advanced International Studies, The Johns Hopkins University.

7.   Dr. Alvin Cottrell is Professor at the Center for Strategic and International Studies at Georgetown University in Washington, D.C.

8.   Dr. Jeffrey Record, former Legislative Assistant for Military Affairs for Senator Sam Nunn (Georgia), is a Senior Research Staff Member of the Institute for Foreign Policy Analysis, Washington, D.C.

9.   Dr. Dov S. Zakheim is Senior Analyst in the Congressional Budget Office.

10. Captain C. Kenneth Allard, USA, is Associate Professor of Social Science at the U.S. Military Academy at West Point and is a Ph.D. candidate at The Fletcher School of Law and Diplomacy, Tufts University.

11. Dr. Barry M. Blechman is former Assistant Director of U.S. Arms Control and Disarmament Agency. He is now a senior associate at the Carnegie Endowment for International Peace in Washington, D.C.

12. Dr. Kenneth A. Myers is Director of European Studies at the Center for Strategic and International Studies at Georgetown University in Washington, D.C.

13. General Zeiner Gundersen, Norwegian Army, is former Chairman of the NATO Military Committee in Brussels, Belgium.

14. Captain James G. Roche, USN, is Senior Deputy Director, Policy Planning Staff, Department of State.

15. Dr. Hisashi Owada, Security Affairs Advisor to the government of Japan, was for two years Visiting Professor at Harvard Law School, and is now a Minister in the Embassy of Japan to the Soviet Union in Moscow.

16. Dr. Roger W. Fontaine is Senior Staff Member for Inter-American Affairs, the National Security Council in Washington, D.C.

17. Dr. Gavriel D. Ra'anan is Research Analyst at the Advanced International Studies Institute, Washington, D.C.

18. Dr. Robert L. Pfaltzgraff, Jr., is Professor of International Politics at The Fletcher School of Law and Diplomacy, Tufts University, and President of the Institute for Foreign Policy Analysis in Cambridge, Massachusetts and Washington, D.C.

Introduction

This book is an outgrowth of papers presented and discussed at the Ninth Annual Conference of the Fletcher School's International Security Studies Program, held in Cambridge on April 23–25, 1980. The Conference theme was "Projection of Power: Perspectives, Perceptions and Logistics," and it brought together prominent experts from academic institutions, research organizations, the U.S. armed services, Congress and the executive branch of government.

The material in the book covers the theoretical and practical aspects of the problem of power projection in its broadest parameters and examines such issues as the nature of power itself, including its sundry emanations and its impact upon political perceptions. It goes on to consider the historical and contemporary uses of military power projection in its various forms and the constraints within which it has to operate. Specific attention is devoted to the problem of logistics as it affects the maritime, naval, and air dimensions of power projection. This is followed by an examination of several geographic regions to which external military forces may have to be sent in the next decade. Finally, conclusions are drawn with respect to planning, mobilization (including the economic sector), and policy formation during the 1980s.

The timeliness of the subject matter was highlighted during the last day of the Conference, when the problems of power projection to Southwest Asia were considered. This session coincided with the news of the abortive U.S. rescue mission in Iran, with resulting media interest in the Conference and its participants.

While the Conference provided a point of departure for the work presented here, its contents have been enlarged and supplemented by relevant material added during the intervening period. Much of the work of editing the chapters of this book was influenced by the discussion periods at the Conference which were of particular intensity, since not all of the participants were able to publish their contributions in view of the sensitivity of their positions.

As editors, we are especially pleased to note that some of the graduates from the International Security Studies Program, who are now working on U.S. defense policy, were able to make very substantial contributions to this work. Thus, a mere nine years after its inception, the Program already is the beneficiary of the products of its own "nursery."

The Program and the School wish to express their gratitude in particular to the Scaife Family Charitable Trusts and the Sarah Scaife Foundation, Inc., whose generous and imaginative support helped to establish the Program and assisted so significantly in its development.

In presenting this book, not only to the defense and foreign affairs "community," but to the interested public at large, the editors hope to arouse discussion about the nature of power and power projection as such, and the ways in which it may be brought to bear, as well as to shed light on the more technical issues of an operational nature. In this way, we hope the work may perform a useful role as a bridge between the theoreticians and the practitioners, in academic institutions and in government.

The Program wishes to express its appreciation to its Administrative Assistant, Mrs. Charlotte C. Wise, and to its Air Force Associate during the academic year 1979–80, Colonel Robert E. Ceruti, for their contributions to this work since its inception.

The Editors
July, 1981
Medford, Massachusetts

1

Power Projection: Historic and Contemporary Perspectives

Russell E. Dougherty

The projection of military power must be examined both from contemporary and historical perspectives if we are to draw inferences for the world of the 1980s. Perceptions of power; air, land and sea capabilities; the economics of power projection; Soviet perceptions and capabilities and regional differences all will be discussed in this volume, but a few fundamental principles must underlie any study of power projection.

First, to be useful in the pursuit of our national objectives, our power must be believable—to us, to our allies, and to our adversaries. Second, to be believable, the power to be projected must be real. Although cover and deception may provide useful adjuncts to our power projection capabilites, in the final analysis, those capabilities must be built on actual forces, tailored to the tasks they are assigned. Uncertainty of use has some value, but only if it is coupled with the certainty of capability. Third, to be real, the force must be realistically projected and fit to fight. Repeated shows of force accompanied by disclaimers that the force is without weapons or ammunition are counterproductive, and will become even more dangerous if shifts in the world balance of power continue. Should the circumstances giving use to the projection of force demand it, the projected force must be capable of sustained, successful operation.

This possibility of having to fight a war should be the leitmotiv of all the chapters in this volume, and of all our decisions and actions in building our military forces. As Secretary of Defense Robert A. Lovett wrote to President Truman in 1952, "The primary purpose of the Department of Defense is, of course, to protect and defend this country. This duty may involve fighting a war. If this becomes necessary, the duty of the Department of Defense is to fight a successful war . . . the better equipped the Department of Defense is to fight, the better it serves its role of a deterrent to war."

We must not make the fatal mistake of thinking that we can somehow develop military forces that project power without being powerful fighting forces. There are many difficulties—the historical, political, psychological difficulties—in building and maintaining power projection forces in our country. It was difficult to do this in the 1950s after Korea, in the 1960s and 1970s when our aggregate superiority was being challenged, but was still comfortably apparent. In the decades ahead, the building and maintaining of such a force may prove to be the single most important—and difficult—action in our government's history. There is no assurance that we will accept the burdens of what Churchill termed the "mantle of history" that has descended on our shoulders—but it is apparent that if we do not accept this responsibility there is no one else in the Western world who will, or can. The test for us is one of wise decisions, long-term resource allocations and national will.

The contributions from this group of intellectually active and influential leaders in our nation's policy and academic circles can be an effective source of responsible influence and advice for our nation. Obviously this is a critical time of transition, a time for national decisions and change. The contributors to this volume reflect on our historical perspectives; undertake thorough analysis of our situation; and offer responsible judgments on our needed policy decisions and actions.

From my view of history, the success of sustained force projection reflected the willingness of the state to support it with resources—manpower, talented leaders and strategists, subsistence and transportation—and the willingness to engage and destroy those who resisted or interfered. Force projection survived and flourished on victories; relative strength was important, but skill, tactics, verve and support were also important, as were reserves and luck.

Force projection was basically offensive—tactical defensive operations were necessary, but these were limited and incidental to the offensive thrust of the projected force. Until very recently in man's history, the speed of force projections was limited to that of a fast horse or a fast sailing boat. Actual firepower was limited to visual ranges, natural barriers were effective, remote logistic bases were effective, redoubts possible—and the relative credibility of force projections was built and established by word-of-mouth and hand-carried messages. Military projection forces were regulars—or mercenaries.

Col. David MacIsaac and Dr. Samuel Wells have thoroughly documented the reluctance of the United States to maintain an army of any consequence, or a navy for any role other than symbolic.

They trace "A 'Minuteman' Tradition" of the United States through the "happy security" of its geography, the devotion of prime energies to continental development and the use of militia and volunteers in its few major conflicts. "The rising business class saw the military professionals as economic parasites . . . alien to an egalitarian unregimented democracy." "To a far greater extent than Americans realized at the time, the Second World War was much like the first . . . after the victory in 1945, some things were forgotten; the early U.S. defeats, the importance of British resistance, the delays in arming and organizing U.S. forces; the preponderant role of Soviet armies in the two-front war against Germany . . . ."[1] Notwithstanding the tremendous stockpiles of military materials remaining after World War II, it was evident that we Americans eschewed the role of "World Policeman," became comfortable and satiated with the occupation duties of our military forces, and made no attempt to develop military forces for power projection. General Arnold's "GHQ Air Force"—the predecessor of today's SAC—was, in General Curtis LeMay's words, "gone to utter hell" and, I suspect, our Navy's sixth and seventh strike fleets were little, if any, better!

So it was until the rapid succession of post-World War II events dramatically changed the nature of our world and the implications for our continued security. On March 5, 1946, at Westminster College in Missouri, Winston Churchill (with President Truman in the audience) spoke of the domination of the nations and peoples of Central Europe as "an iron curtain" that "has descended" across the center of the European continent. Speaking directly to President Truman, the leader of the victorious, intact nation which Churchill described that day as " . . . at the pinnacle of world power," he said: "With primacy in power is also joined an awe-inspiring accountability to the future . . . you must feel not only the sense of duty done, but also anxiety lest you fall below the level of achievement. Opportunity is here now . . . ."[2] Churchill's Westminster College speech is worth rereading as a clarion call for effective power projection!

Pundits of the press and radio interpreted the significance of that day differently; nevertheless, there followed in quick succession the Truman Doctrine of March 11, 1947, the Marshall Plan for restoring the political and economic vitality of Europe; the North Atlantic Treaty of April 4, 1949; and the stalwart stand in Korea in 1950. All these in the aftermath of Mr. Churchill's admonition that we not "take the course of letting events drift along until it is too late." We were on the threshold of building a capability and a framework for power projection.

As MacIsaac and Wells interpret it, "The dramatically altered international situation produced new attitudes in Washington toward military forces. Americans traditionally had divorced war and peace, allowing only limited roles for diplomats during war and for military men during peacetime. Now a postwar consensus developed that embraced the need for the United States to organize its regulars, and use military power, even without actual combat, in the exercise of its new responsibilities as a world leader. America's long epoch of 'free security' had come to an end."[3]

We entered the era of sustained power projection; but power projection for defensive purposes, not for aggression or the offensive thrust of a militaristic foreign policy. We augmented the occupation forces in Europe with defensive air and ground units assigned in war to the international military staff structure of the North Atlantic Treaty Organization—forces to help maintain a forward defense in Allied Command Europe. We stationed strike and antisubmarine warfare naval units in the Mediterranean for defensive purposes. We developed the striking forces of bombers and accompanying fighters of Strategic Air Command to assist in the defensive deterrent to conflict through the reflected offensive capability of its weapon systems. We maintained similar defensive force projections in the Pacific. Through the global mobility of our air, naval and ground forces, and through the expanded capability of our weapons and our delivery systems, we embarked on an entirely new phase of power projection—deterrence through retaliation; damage limitation through offensive counterattacks; forward defense through deployed forces backed up by external strategic forces for interdiction and retardation, later augmented by theater nuclear forces for both retardation and direct defense against engaged forces. We built a respectable defensive environment in and around our continent and enjoyed an uneven but remarkable consensus of the prime movers of national policy.

During this period of consensus, the United States entered the era of political/military fusion predicted by Professor Lincoln of West Point in his classic article "The Debouch of the Scholars". As a result of the changed and dynamic power projection requirements created by evident Soviet aggressive potential, we broadened the scope and consequence of the preparation of military scholars, and provided intense graduate training and associations. The military took to heart the admonition of Sir William Butler that "the nation that will insist on drawing a broad line of demarcation between the fighting man and the thinking man is liable to find its fighting done by fools and its thinking done by cowards."

Professor Albert Wohlstetter's "Delicate Balance of Terror" updated Dohet; Bernard Brodie's "Anatomy of Deterrence" modernized Karl von Clausewitz; *Foreign Affairs* became required reading in every military plans office.

The education of our military officers in the history of war is but one part of the complex, multifaceted process of training professionals to keep our nation—and our allies—alive and free despite a variety of threats ranging from irresponsible, unpredictable terrorist activities to the omnipresent possibility of direct confrontation with the Soviet Union. Clearly, education on war and all its ramifications and uncertainties should not be limited only to our military leaders. The makers of modern strategy, the creators of modern military forces, and the decision makers on military policy include far more than the professional military.

Education in the history of wars—those won, and those lost— should be an imperative for all those who would share in the development, disposition, and the control of military forces. It should be an imperative for our key administrators, legislators, policy consultants, analysts, technical consultants, and the media. The task of preparing power projection forces is shared by so many people that it is inadequate—even naive—to educate only our military leaders in the uncertainties and vicissitudes of war. While they may have to shoulder the ultimate responsibility for the success or failure of employment, they may well have the least influence on the circumstances of the engagement and the structure of the force with which they will engage.

Certainly no modern American commander could address civilian policy makers as Livy reported a Roman Commander suggesting to the Senate just before departing for a campaign in Macedonia: "If there are those among you who would offer advice as to the conduct of the campaign upon which I am embarked, then let him come with me into Macedonia . . . for I will heed no counsel save that given around my campfire." Today many are involved in the preparation and employment of our forces. The security agencies and offices in the Administration and the Congress are involved in the formulation of the missions and purposes of our projection forces. Some few influential principals, staffers, and advisors will conceive and approve the organizational framework. Government agencies, civilian industries and interest groups will influence the size, type of equipment, and capabilities of these forces. Then, given modern communications, we can expect direct high-level attention in the Administration and Congress concerning tactical employment of projection forces. Finally, there are sure to be influential members of the government, the public, and the media who will dispute the need for any plans for force projection.

Power projection requirements create a need for sophisticated understanding of the theory and practice of war across a wide range of civilian and military positions. But historical study alone will not solve many of the thorny problems raised by remote area control, resource availability, control of lines of communication or even identification of the enemy. In the familiar areas of strategic nuclear deterrence and the NATO and Korean areas of confrontation, these questions have been rather clear-cut. Even so, the United States has weathered difficulties in maintaining the necessary consensus for action, both domestically and internationally.

Historically, we have succeeded in projecting power only in those situations where our nation had a well-recognized challenge to its sovereignty, a direct threat to our territory or our people, and an "impulse of fear." We have not done well in those instances where the challenge appeared obscure or remote. The lesson seems clear: if we expect force projection to work, we will have to do it with external forces, and sea or air modes of employment that require minimum fixed logistics. In any situation where we plan to use ground forces in direct confrontations, we must carefully prepare a total supporting environment and engage consequential forces only if we are assured *that our nation is totally and unequivocally involved and cognizant of a clear and present danger, clearly understood by our executive and legislative leaders.* This leads me to the conclusion that—except for Korea and NATO Europe—there are very real limits as to the circumstances and the locations where our ground forces of the Rapid Deployment Force can or should be deployed.

I discussed the prospects of our military force projections in the 1980s with a respected European friend. We considered the great difficulty of obtaining and maintaining the necessary consensus to build such forces, and to employ such forces. I told him of my concern that our nation did not fully appreciate the limitations on our force projection capabilites, nor the imperative need for improvements—of my concern that we not ask our armed forces to take risks that the nation was not willing to take. He asked, "What are your choices—what are your alternatives?"

Those are the right questions. The United States, and its Allies must come to grips with those questions. Do we have the guts for this "mantle of world responsibility"—or, is Pogo right? Could it be that we will meet the enemy of successful force projections in the 1980s only to find out that "the enemy is us"?

NOTES

1. David MacIsaac and Samuel Wells, "A Minuteman Tradition," in *The Wilson Quarterly*, Spring 1979, p. 110.
2. Winston Churchill, *The Sinews of Peace* (Boston: Houghton Mifflin Company, 1949), pp. 94–100.
3. MacIsaac and Wells, p. 113.

2

Power Projection:
The Perception of Power*

Uri Ra'anan

Theorists in the Soviet defense "community" have demonstrated profound awareness of the key psychological effects of power projection, an aspect that they have subsumed usually under the heading of "peacetime use" of military force. It is not surprising, perhaps, that the foremost spokesman for this approach should emanate from the Soviet Navy, which has become the carrier, so to speak, of the imperial dimensions of the Soviet state. The apparently indestructible Admiral Gorshkov graphically described these concepts when he wrote in his now classical series of articles, "Navies in War and Peace," that a major purpose of deploying vast military (particularly naval) power was

> To demonstrate vividly the economic and military power of a country beyond its borders . . . to show readiness for decisive actions, so as to support friendly states . . . to surprise probable enemies with the perfection of the equipment being exhibited, to affect their morale, to intimidate them right up to the outbreak of war, and to

 * This chapter constitutes an extension of *The Changing American-Soviet Strategic Balance: Some Political Implications*, a memorandum written by the author in 1972, at the request of the Subcommittee on National Security and International Operations of the Committee on Government Operations of the U.S. Senate. That work, addressing itself to an analysis of the ingredients of power—which it examined in terms of *perceptions*—was published in 1972 by that Senate Committee and republished, in 1974, in the second edition of *Great Issues of International Politics*, edited by Morton A. Kaplan, where it appeared as Chapter 31. The author noted that, subsequently, work appeared employing very similar concepts and, in some places, terminology.

suggest to them in advance the hopelessness of fighting. . . .
[This] in many cases has permitted the achievement of
political goals without resorting to military operations.[1]

In essence, what the good Admiral has done is to reverse
Clausewitz and to advance the hypothesis that "peace is conflict
carried out by other use of the same [military] means." This
suggestion, of course, is far from revolutionary and follows the
insights of classical political theorists before Gorshkov (or Lenin,
for that matter). Many other members of the Soviet defense
establishment have emphasized the same approach. Professor
Colonel M. P. Skirdo (in the work *People, Army, Military Leader*)
stresses that "[Power should be] aimed at . . . external political
isolation of the enemy and the collapse of his coalition."[2]

The well known V. M. Kulish expresses himself rather neatly
on this issue:

This does not at all mean that a world nuclear missile war
has now ceased to serve as a foreign policy tool . . . . The
very danger of such a war being unleashed . . . exerts an
influence on the foreign policies of a majority of states . . . .
a country which possesses not only stockpiles of nuclear
weapons, but also an adequate amount of conventional
military weapons would be able to impose demands, even
though limited, back them up with a demonstration of force,
and have these demands met without having taken great
risk.[3]

What all of these authors are saying, of course, is that it is not
so much the direct application of (military) power itself, but rather
the disproportionate shadow which it projects, that has impact upon
the political scene—with beneficial or deleterious effect, depending
on which side one supports. Professor Colonel Skirdo refines this
concept, by pointing out that power is not a static element, but rather
that its potential must be utilized in an appropriate manner,
otherwise its existence becomes irrelevant:

There have been many examples in the history of warfare
when a given nation was economically superior to its
adversary and possessed a powerful and large army, but
failed to utilize its forces and resources correctly . . . . If the
leaders are unable to utilize existing capabilities, to
transform them into reality, defeat becomes inevitable.[4]

These texts, and many others like them, demonstrate the
profound understanding on the Soviet side that military power
cannot, or should not, be evaluated except in relation to the overall

political postures that its projection is meant to serve. To take only one example, it is hardly meaningful to treat certain weapons systems as "offensive" or "defensive" without examining the nature of the political goals in the furtherance of which (one hopes) weapons are deployed. It is by no means unusual for party A, in the pursuit of essentially defensive aims, to be obliged to resort to "offensive" tactics, because the rival power B, in its attempt to change the existing territorial and political order, has seized the initiative—perhaps by covert or indirect means—leaving state A little choice but to attempt to restore the situation through a limited application or threat of force. Thus, it is less than "scientific" to ignore the existence of major disparity, or asymmetry, between opposing sets of political concepts and to proceed to deal with the weapons systems themselves in vacuo.

Soviet leaders, to take just one example, are good enough Leninists to think in such terms, dynamically, and, above all, to appreciate the perceptual value of the initiative. Thus, V. V. Larionov's article, "The Transformation of the 'Strategic Sufficiency' Concept," in discussing American behavior, goes out of its way to stress that:

> ... No energetic actions were undertaken ... as a result the United States lost the initiative on the psychological plane ... [the] proposal is to regain this initiative by "intimidating" potential enemies ....[5]

In order to deal coherently with the whole issue of power projection, it may be helpful to reexamine the concept of political impact in a thermonuclear age. All too frequently, it is overlooked that political weight, or influence, is directly proportional not so much to political might, in absolute, objective terms, as to *perceived* power—a subjective factor that can be, and is, manipulated (although, of course, physical might is one of its constituent ingredients). In the case of the superpowers, this means that their relative global impact must be measured in terms of the power each projects, *as perceived* by its own decision-makers, its intelligentsia and its general public, respectively, by its allies and clients, by the decision-makers, intelligentsia and general public of the rival superpower, by that rival's allies and clients, and, finally, by various "third parties." It is this perception (i.e., the impact of power projected), whether accurate or not, that will mold the expectations and the decisions of all the "actors" involved and, therefore, must be regarded as the critical political factor in any given situation. It will determine who is likely to "blink first" in a potential confrontation and who, in anticipation of such a dénouement, will be tempted to precipitate that crisis; it will sway other parties and will play a major role in shaping the global "line-up." (Of course, there may be situations in which the perceptions of the various participants will differ, complicating the picture, but diametrically opposed appraisals of power are far less common nowadays than might be supposed.)

Once again, a Soviet writer, A. Trofimenko has drawn particular attention to this aspect:

> The problem of the psychological effect of nuclear weapons not only on the field of battle (at the time of their physical use) but also under the conditions of "confrontation" undoubtedly is a problem which deserves the specialists' closest attention.[6]

The question arises, then, what are the elements that, cumulatively, create a specific perception of power? Objective physical might, to be sure, is one of these factors, but it is only one, and strategic forces, however awesome, can constitute only a single ingredient of that factor. Consequently, it is misleading to equate political power (i.e., the perception of power projected) almost exclusively with strategic forces, measured in absolute terms, viewed in a static fashion and divorced from the broader and much more complex overall equation—as, regrettably, a major proportion of contemporary Western literature is inclined to do.

The political impact of strategic power cannot be appreciated, in fact, unless viewed in the context of the broader power equation within which it operates. To repeat, political weight, or influence, is proportional to *perceived* power—a subjective, impressionistic projection that results cumulatively from a number of "inputs," of which physical might is one, the latter consisting, in turn, of several distinct ingredients, including strategic forces.

To be precise, the power equation contains the following elements: "Available physical inputs" (such as strategic forces, general purpose forces, geographical propinquity to focal areas of conflict), "potential physical inputs" (such as economic and scientific-technological potential, mobilizable manpower), and "psychological inputs" (such as "mission," i.e., political intentions which, themselves, are a product of other components—ideological commitments and preconceptions, societal posture and cultural style—as well as a leadership's belief in its mission, and mass support, spontaneous or induced, in pursuit of such a mission).

These various inputs together ultimately shape perception of power, but their impact is not necessarily direct. The final power (or "capability") image they project is enhanced or diminished by certain highly visible "dynamic factors" (some of which occasionally may be manipulated deliberately through "disinformation" and other methods). These factors include: the demonstrated determination and capacity of a leadership to exploit the physical might at its disposal for the attainment of its political goals (or its inability to do so, an outcome that is determined largely by the intensity of prevailing constraints—domestic, bureaucratic, ethical and other); its visible fixity of purpose; its performance in seizing and maintaining the initiative (a seemingly tactical question which, in fact, reflects the basic Weltanschauung of a regime); and, finally, prevailing trends (i.e., whether the might of a state seems to be waxing or waning).

To sum up: it is the basic physical and psychological power "inputs," as modified by the various "dynamic factors" that, in the end, project power, i.e., create a perception of power—a perception which molds the policy decisions of the main adversaries, their respective allies and clients, and third parties. This perception, therefore, *is* a form of political reality and, whether objectively warranted or not, it is equivalent to power.

This equation[7] is complex enough, but the individual items of which it is composed, even when viewed in isolation, are not necessarily quantifiable and comparable since they have to be evaluated in contexts that, more often than not, are asymmetrical. To take one example: strategic nuclear "parity," even assuming that it existed, would not imply a *balance* between the United States and the Soviet Union. Given its unilateral advantages in terms of geography, theatre forces, political momentum, initiative and other non-nuclear factors, the Soviet Union, in fact, would enjoy superiority in the focal areas of probable conflict, even if it "merely" neutralized the credibility of the U.S. strategic forces (i.e. the likelihood of their utilization in any context other than the defense of the continental United States). To express it in a different form: since U.S. nuclear forces were meant to constitute the "equalizer" to make up for the various Soviet advantages, the neutralization of that equalizer leaves the other side ahead. It is surprising just how many analysts have managed to overlook, or forget, this underlying asymmetry.

Nor are "psychological inputs" likely to prove more equivalent, or quantifiable, than weapons systems or economic data. To take the USSR, again, as an example: the Soviet leadership, its own cynicism, factional struggles, and the apathy of the masses notwithstanding, continues to be motivated by residual ideological faith in the dialectic which imbues it with an ongoing sense of "mission." Consequently, there is little diminution of support in Moscow for the view that international affairs inevitably must reflect a fundamental adversary relationship, especially between the USSR and its "main enemy." For the same reason, Soviet leaders have not ceased to feel that it is incumbent upon them to "win"—without having to pay an unacceptable price, of course—since whoever fails eventually to achieve this aim, or stands still over a lengthy period, is relegated irrevocably to the "rubbish dump of history." (The potential destruction or disintegration of the Soviet state itself, or of the Soviet regime, would constitute an unacceptable price. The application of the dialectic does not mean, needless to say, that the USSR is committed necessarily to eschewing any and all political "cease-fire" arrangements. Deals along these lines may be acceptable, provided they cover only some areas and are not intended to last indefinitely. However, a permanent "freezing" of the situation along existing lines is deemed unacceptable, since it would amount to a renunciation of the very concept of "winning" and of the dialectic itself.)

In terms of "psychological inputs" also, therefore, there are fundamental asymmetries and the adversaries of the Soviet Union tend to be at a disadvantage over the short run. The Western elite is steeped in a Weltanschauung which, at one and the same time, is more narrowly practical and more generously optimistic or, perhaps naive, than that of the Soviet leadership. It postulates a neatly rational "cost-benefit" model of human affairs that grades "gain" and "loss" on a rather different scale than the USSR. The contemporary version of the Judeo-Christian ethic does, of course, acknowledge the reality of competition, both between individuals and larger social entities, including states. It assumes, however, that this particular form of "dialectic" is tightly constrained by sophisticated self-interest, causing each party to weigh "rationally" the possible benefits of "winning" as against its potentially high costs in terms of "absolute" values, as the West sees them, such as human life and human welfare, both in the material and in the spiritual sense. Thus, the "reasonable" man, who has been the ultimate ideal of Western society since the Age of the Enlightenment, will tend always to compromise, to seek a deal in which a fair balance may be struck between the various costs and benefits.

It is almost inconceivable to most Western thinkers and statesmen that there may be societies and leaders who do not necessarily follow or even comprehend this model. Hence, the peculiar difficulties encountered in negotiations between representatives of open and closed societies, in which the former usually will assume that the objective is "compromise" while the latter will take for granted that the aim of diplomacy is to achieve "by other means" what, perhaps, cannot be gained by force alone, namely "victory" of one sort or another. In Game Theory terms, the open society is less inclined than its adversary toward zero sum games. As a result of these factors, an essentially "defensive" Western posture is left to confront a relatively dynamic, "offensive" Soviet approach or, more precisely, a less "driven" U.S. leadership must deal with a more highly "charged" Soviet regime. A "sensible" Western leader may be inclined to accept the practical consequences of a given situation where a "correctly thinking" Soviet leader may attempt to change or manipulate the situation itself. It is precisely these disparities that render the mechanistic and essentially symmetrical action-reaction model so inappropriate.

It is fairly clear that there are links between these dissimilar U.S. and Soviet "psychological inputs" and many of the "dynamic factors" which, as postulated in this analysis, enhance or diminish the power image projected by the two global antagonists (an image that, of course, reflects also the various "inputs" mentioned above, both physical and psychological). Such linkage is evident especially with regard to three of these "dynamic factors," namely, the demonstrated determination and capacity of a leadership to exploit the physical might at its disposal for the attainment of its political goals, its visible fixity of purpose, and its performance in seizing and maintaining the initiative. As far as the first and second "factors" are concerned, clearly a Western elite that demonstrates such deep concern about the "costs" of "winning" is, psychologically, more vulnerable to pressure and threats and, consequently, less credible in confrontation situations than a closed society which places (or appears to place) the highest premium on "victory" itself. In a showdown, all other aspects being equal, the latter appears likely to "outstare" the former. Indeed, with these concepts in mind, the Soviet leadership has taken good care to orchestrate its commitment to the aim of "winning" by demonstrating its willingness and ability to use the military might at its disposal in the pursuit of political goals. This has been done both directly, as with the Soviet invasions of Hungary, Czechoslovakia, and, now, Afghanistan, and more obliquely, through surrogates (Cubans, East Germans, and others), or by means of the establishment of a Soviet military presence supportive of a client's military operations (as in Nasser's Egypt during 1970, or, more recently, in Cuba, to substitute for Cuban effectives "exported" overseas). Of course, there are also instances of resort to military power by the United States; however, they cannot be viewed as belonging to the same category of "demonstration of willpower," since, usually, America has been "reacting" merely to perceived intrusions into "its sphere," whereas the USSR, in the cases of Afghanistan and Egypt (for that matter, also Cuba, ninety miles from Miami), as well as through its surrogates in Western Africa, the Horn and South Yemen, has been operating distinctly beyond the Eurasian perimeter of the Warsaw Pact. In Admiral Gorshkov's favorite definition of the Soviet Navy's mission, the USSR has been extending its "prestige and influence." In almost all of the instances mentioned it has been the Soviet Union that has seized and maintained the initiative (in other words, it is "acting," not "reacting").

Not surprisingly, the degree of ability or inability of either leadership to exploit the force at its disposal for the attainment of political goals bears some relationship to the severity of prevailing constraints—domestic, bureaucratic or ethical. With regard to this topic, there have been major disparities always between open and closed societies. The bureaucratic, or factional, conflicts and rivalries of the USSR constitute a rather different (usually lesser) order of constraint qualitatively from the web of limitations on the conduct of U.S. policy imposed by the media, public opinion, a frequently self-assertive legislature, an independent judiciary, and the moral and psychological inhibitions of the executive itself. While neither society can escape its own contemporary ethic, the Soviet Union's current philosophy happens to favor resort to whatever means may be required for "winning," as has been demonstrated, while the present-day United States still has to operate in the lingering aftermath of a period that militated against American utilization of force. These asymmetries, needless to say, are linked organically to the contrasting nature of the two polities. While, on the American side, some profound changes appear to be affecting the constraints described above, both adversaries and friends seem to be acting still under the (possibly mistaken) impression that the "Vietnam syndrome" persists and will continue to circumscribe the actions of the United States. This factor cannot but affect general perceptions of the intensity of power projected respectively by the Soviet Union and the United States.

A further essential ingredient shaping these perceptions pertains to the last of the "dynamic factors" mentioned earlier, i.e. prevailing trends. In this context, it is only of marginal relevance whether or not the Soviet Bloc actually has "overtaken" the West militarily. What seems beyond question, is that the other side at least has achieved strategic nuclear "parity," i.e. it has "caught up," while, quantitatively at any rate, its superiority in theater forces is unchallenged. Here it must be remembered that, in the eye of the observer, power is perceived not statically, like a still photograph, but dynamically, like a moving picture. The onlooker does not view sides A and B in terms of their current positions alone, but rather he plots graphs from their relative standings in the recent past through their present positions, then projects them forward into the future (more or less in linear fashion). The competitor that has caught up with his adversary, therefore, is projected already as being ahead, if not now then tomorrow.

To use a currently fashionable term, the significant issue is who has momentum, a matter of equal importance in primaries and in sports. The latter, of course, always has been viewed as "conflict carried on by other means," as the ancient Greeks understood very well, and it presents, therefore, a perfectly valid analogy for politics and military strength alike. Every fan knows better than to ask merely what the score is; whether it is hockey or baseball, to discover that the sides are tied 3:3 does not mean at all that they enjoy parity at that moment. The real question is which team was leading 3:1 a short while ago and which was trailing in the score. The former has just "blown a lead" and is inevitably demoralized, while its adversaries and their fans enjoy the electrifying impact of "momentum."

Soviet defense literature demonstrates intimate familiarity with such subjective factors—indeed, this is hardly surprising since the authors, military or civilian, have been schooled in the Leninist approach with its particular penchant for the dynamics of history. At the same time, Soviet writers show special awareness of the fact that subjective elements are reinforced immeasurably by visual demonstration. Here, once again, our old standby, Admiral Gorshkov, has given colorful expression to this particular consideration. After pointing to the buildup of sheer military might as an effective way of intimidating potential adversaries, he enters the caveat that this approach may not always produce:

> . . . . intended goals, primarily because the weapons being demonstrated appear before the viewers only as a potential threat. The navy is another matter. Warships appearing directly off the shore represent a real threat of operations whose time and execution are determined by those in command. Whereas such a threat was quite great in the past, today it is much more so, since modern warships are platforms for nuclear-missile weaponry and aircraft whose range can cover the entire territory of a state.

> In many cases, naval demonstrations have made it possible to achieve political goals, without resorting to an armed struggle merely by exerting pressure through one's own potential power and by threatening to initiate military hostilities.

Thus, the navy has always been an instrument of state policy, and an important support for diplomacy in peacetime. This is fostered by the very nature of a navy and the properties inherent in it, namely a constant high degree of combat readiness, mobility, and the ability to concentrate one's own forces in selected areas of the ocean in a short time. Moreover, the neutrality of the waters of the World Ocean makes it possible to carry out the movement and concentration of naval forces without violating the provisions of international law and without presenting the opposing side with formal reasons for protest or other forms of counteraction.[8]

This excerpt, from Gorshkov's now "classical" book, presents us with as trenchant a description of power projection as we can hope to find.

NOTES

1. S. G. Gorshkov, "Navies in War and Peace," *Morskoy Sbornik*, No. 12, 1972.
2. Professor Col. M. P. Skirdo, *People, Army, Military Leader*, Moscow, 1970, pp. 96–150.
3. V. M. Kulish, *Military Power and International Relations*, Mezhdunarodnyye Otnosheniya, Moscow, 1972, pp. 217–229.
4. Professor Col. M. P. Skirdo, *People, Army, Military Leader*, Moscow, 1970, pp. 96–150.
5. V. V. Larionov, "The Transformation of the 'Strategic Sufficiency' Concept," *U.S.A.: Economics, Politics, Ideology*, No. 11, Moscow, 1971.
· 6. A. Trofimenko, "Political Realism and the 'Realistic Deterrence' Strategy," *U.S.A.: Economics, Politics, Ideology*, No. 12, Moscow, 1971.
7. The term "equation" was not intended to be taken literally, of course, even when it was first presented about eight years ago—although the author notes that some have chosen to do so in rather mechanical fashion.
8. S. G. Gorshkov, *Sea Power of the State*, Military Publishing House, Moscow, 1976.

3

The Logistics of Pax Britannica: Lessons for America

Geoffrey Kemp and John Maurer

INTRODUCTION: THE IMPORTANCE OF STRATEGIC ACCESS

The purpose of this chapter is to highlight the role of logistical infrastructure and technological change in the projection of power by imperial political systems. These elements of grand strategy are especially important today as the United States tries to reconcile its military resources with its worldwide political and economic commitments. Because Great Britain needed to provide security for an empire upon which the "sun never set," a comparison of the contemporary problems facing American planners with the experience of the British Empire around the turn of the century sheds light on the logistic constraints in projecting military power. In the first two decades of this century, Britain discovered the burdens of defending its empire growing heavier when confronted by intensified competition from envious rivals longing for their "place in the sun." Technological change in the means of transportation and communication—both decisive factors in the logistics of power projection—further eroded Britain's world position. Faced by this combination of circumstances, Britain's military strength rapidly became inadequate to uphold its imperial stance. As had been Britain's case, the United States will find its world position much more costly to maintain in the last two decades of the century because of the Soviet military buildup and the vast geographic distances that American military forces must overcome for a forward strategy.

It is becoming increasingly clear that while access to Middle East oil will remain a vital interest for the foreseeable future, the logistics of undertaking any military commitment to the Middle East poses severe problems for any major contingency. Former President Carter, in his last State of the Union message, reiterated American concern for the security of the Persian Gulf: "Let our position be absolutely clear: an attempt by any outside force to gain control of the Persian Gulf region will be regarded as an assault on the vital interests of the United States of America. And such an assault will be repelled by any means necessary, including military force." Without the oil of this region, a catastrophic fragmentation of the social and international order of the industrial democracies would occur. James Schlesinger was right in pointing out that Soviet Russia's "control of the oil tap in the Middle East would mean the end of the world as we have known it since 1945." Such a radical transformation of the world's balance of power against the United States cannot be tolerated if America is to remain the leader of the Free World.

Although Washington's concern for the security of this region appears to reflect a new "commitment," the importance of Middle East oil was recognized by American planners in the early days of the postwar era. When Russian troops failed to pull out of Azerbaijan by a previously agreed deadline of March 2, 1946, the Truman administration faced a serious crisis with its recent wartime ally over Iran. Nor should it be forgotten that one of the Kremlin's goals was access to oil rights in northern Iran. Less than a year later, in a study approved by the Joint Chiefs of Staff dated February 10, 1947, American war planners concluded: "In a future major war, the total United States military and civilian requirements cannot be met . . . by all the then current production in the United States and United States controlled foreign sources, *including* that in the Near and Middle East."[1] War plans developed two years later in 1949 for a confrontation between the United States and the Soviet Union stated that the successful conduct of the war called for control of the oil fields of the Middle East by the West. "If the Near and Middle East oil areas are not retained, or retaken in the early phases of the war," this war plan maintained that "the oil position of the Allies would necessitate subsequent actions to retake it."[2]

In the last decade, America's world position has faced the dual threats posed by Soviet Russia's attainment of parity in strategic nuclear weapons (as recognized in SALT I), and by the vulnerability of the industrialized democracies because of their dependence on Middle East oil (made apparent a year later, in the aftermath of the 1973 Yom Kippur War). The conjunction of these two adverse developments makes the protection of the Persian Gulf oil fields a more difficult and expensive proposition than before.

The very dimensions of the problem of protecting Persian Gulf oil fields from attack by the Soviets or their clients—the large area to be defended and the vast distances from the United States to be overcome—present American war planners with a formidable task. From the eastern seaboard of the United States, the Persian Gulf lies approximately seven thousand miles away by air. The distances by sea that must be traversed are much longer. Once deployed into the region, military forces will have to protect and maintain thousands of miles of pipelines, thousands of wells, and the vast collection of installations needed to produce oil. In the words of Army Chief of Staff General Meyer, the capability to defend Persian Gulf oil supplies, "without compromising the decisive theater in Europe, is the most demanding challenge confronting the military in this decade."[3]

Throughout history, other great powers have faced a similar strategic dilemma of finding the military power needed to uphold a policy of defending perceived vital interests that lie at great distances from the centers of political decision-making and the sources of military strength. To be sure, the perception of what constitutes a vital interest has changed from one epoch to the next. Access to grain supplies played a critical part in the grand strategy of the Athenian, Roman, and Byzantine Empires. The treasure *flota* of gold and silver from the New World provided the wealth needed to maintain the sprawling Hapsburg dominions during the sixteenth and seventeenth centuries. During the last century, Britain required access to overseas food supplies and raw materials to feed and employ its population. Total collapse threatened these empires if their vital supplies of grain or gold or raw materials could be interrupted by their rivals. With time, however, some of these interruptions could be overcome by finding new sources of supply, or by technological innovation. A fascinating example of this type of development is the failure of the South's "King Cotton" diplomacy during the Civil War. Britain and France developed new sources of cotton in Egypt and India to help offset a sharp curtailment of supply from the United States produced by the onset of conflict. Though the economic dislocation caused by this shortage was severe, it did not prove serious enough to induce Britain and France to enter the war on the side of the Confederacy to gain access to cotton.

Often, however, there is no foreseeable alternative. In those cases, the problem remains of moving these vital commodities, and providing for their protection at the source and during transit. Yet the amount of military protection that can be given to these arteries of empire is itself dependent upon logistic considerations. Logistic constraints, such as the mode of transportation and communication, define and determine the scope of military operations to a far greater extent than is usually admitted by military historians interested in providing operational descriptions of battles and campaigns. These constraints on strategy can be changed over time by technological developments altering the mode of transportation and communication. While generally not as startling as technological innovations in weapons systems, changes in the means of transportation can have a revolutionary impact on strategy because accepted notions of time and space governing the movement of military forces are transformed. The continuing importance of the Panama Canal in American strategy provides an excellent illustration. Before its completion in 1914, policy-makers and naval planners had to decide whether the battlefleet should be deployed in the Atlantic or the Pacific, or be divided between the two oceans. These questions received special prominence in the aftermath of the Russo-Japanese War, where the division of the battleships of the Russian navy permitted the much smaller Japanese battlefleet to first destroy the Russian fleet in Port Arthur before the arrival of reinforcements of the Baltic Fleet.[4] There can be little doubt that President Theodore Roosevelt had this example in mind when he admonished his successor, William Taft: "Under no circumstances divide the battleship fleet between the Atlantic and the Pacific Oceans prior to the finishing of the Panama Canal."[5] For many years after its completion, the canal's locks placed constraints on the dimensions of ships planned by the Navy. The proposed construction of a new sea-level canal through Panama, capable of permitting passage of aircraft carriers, would permit policy-makers more flexibility in the sensitive area of naval deployments.[6]

Thus, even after the advent of the thermo-nuclear device and the ICBM, this more traditional aspect of grand strategy, namely the ability to deploy military power to secure access to vital commodities, remains important. The irony of the Vietnam War was that the United States had a superb, secure logistical infrastructure in the Far East to support its massive military involvement. Yet today, with the political and economic stakes much higher than they ever were in Vietnam, the United States is woefully unprepared to fight a war of similar magnitude outside of Europe. One reason for this must be geography and the very different logistic base capable of supporting possible American military operations in the Middle East.

PAX BRITANNICA: MARITIME POWER, COAL AND CABLE

History provides many examples of imperial systems whose inhabitants relied heavily on seaborne transportation for their economic livelihood, common defense, and sense of political unity. The expansion or collapse of these empires depended upon maritime power being able to protect their sources of economic strength and their seaborne lines of communication. Of course, since people live on the land and not on the sea, great maritime empires develop, alongside their vital seaborne links, an inland transportation system necessary for their national life. This is well illustrated by the British, who constructed not only a chain of naval bases to support their fleet and merchant marine, but also railroads throughout the Empire and their homeland. Despite this impressive amount of railroad building throughout India, Africa, Canada and the United Kingdom, the British Empire's fate rested on the ability to keep open her sea lanes. This has been stated in classic form by one First Lord of the Admiralty in 1894: "The freedom of sea communications between Great Britain and the outer world is as essential to her existence as the passage of air through the windpipe of any human being is to the preservation of his life."[7] Nor is this assertion exaggerated, since a Royal Commission on Food Supply in 1905 found that Britain imported half its meat supplies and four-fiths of its principal foodstuff, wheat, while the stock of all grains in the United Kingdom would last at best only seventeen weeks.[8] It is not surprising to find that these figures were used by the Admiralty time and again to show the necessity of the Royal Navy being superior to any likely combination of European naval powers, as measured in terms of capital ships, while possessing a large number of cruisers to patrol the Empire's sea lanes around the globe. Admiral Jackie Fisher, when First Sea Lord in 1904, put it most succinctly when he wrote: "The Navy is the 1st, 2nd, 3rd, 4th, 5th . . . *ad infinitum* Line of Defence! If the Navy is not supreme, no Army however large is of the slightest use. It's not *invasion* we have to fear if our Navy is beaten, IT'S STARVATION!"[9]

During the last century, the *Pax Britiannica* rested not only on the strength of the Royal Navy, but on the domination of the world's coal trade by the British Empire. The steamship powered by coal had supplanted the sailing ship as the primary mode of sea transportation during the nineteenth century. The old saying, "Steam is an Englishman," seemed to be borne out because until 1880 Britain produced and exported more coal to fuel these steam engines than the rest of the world combined. Even after the rapid increases in coal production in Germany and the United States that accompanied industrialization in those two countries, Britain still controlled the world's maritime coal trade. Right down to the outbreak of war in 1914, the German port cities on the North Sea coast continued to depend heavily upon British coal as a fuel supply.[10] The unsurpassed quality of the coal from Newcastle, South Wales, the Clyde, and the Mersey for naval steam engines, the commanding position of Britain's merchant marine, and the possession of a chain of coaling stations throughout her Empire, ensured British dominance of the world's maritime coal trade.[11]

Britain used this commanding position to help or hinder the naval movements of other powers. For example, before the outbreak of hostilities with Spain in 1898, Dewey used the British base at Hong Kong as if it were American. Had the British government chosen to, it could have greatly hindered the movement of Dewey's squadron to the Philippines by not permitting him to take advantage of its coaling station.[12] Similarly, the famous voyage of the American battlefleet around the world in the years 1907–1909—the cruise of the Great White Fleet—depended on access to British supplies of coal and bases for a large part of its journey.[13] As late as 1913, when a crisis developed with Japan over laws passed by the California legislature prohibiting aliens from owning land, the United States Navy required British colliers to carry out the advance of the battle fleet across the Pacific envisioned under the Orange Plan.[14] Thus, in this period, any large movement of American warships outside of the Western Hemisphere relied on the availability of British coal.

Perhaps the best example of how Britain's control of the maritime coal trade could hinder the movements of another power's navy occurred during the Russo-Japanese War of 1904–1905. In order to defeat the Japanese Navy in the Far East, Russia attempted to concentrate its scattered naval forces by sending its Baltic Fleet on an 18,000-mile journey to link up with its Pacific Fleet based at Port Arthur. This concentration, however, could only be accomplished if the Baltic Fleet received approximately a half-million tons of coal. Supplying this fleet with coal presented the Tsarist government with a set of logistic and political problems that would prove difficult to solve. Russia lacked the number of colliers needed to move the large amounts of coal required and did not possess any coaling stations on the fleet's route. Only with the aid of another great power, either Germany or Great Britain, could the means be found to supply the Baltic Fleet with coal. Britain was the power best able to help Russia. Before the war, Russia had bought coal for the Baltic Fleet from a British firm because of the inferior quality of Russian coal when compared to "Welsh Cardiff." At the outbreak of war, however, the First Sea Lord, Admiral Fisher, told this British firm that it would not be "expedient" to continue deliveries since Britain and Japan had entered into an alliance in 1902. Whatever slim chance remained of purchasing British coal evaporated after the Dogger Bank Incident almost precipitated war between Russia and Britain. To find the necessary colliers and coal, Russia turned to Germany and signed an agreement with the famous shipping magnate, Albert Ballin, of the Hamburg-American Line. Before long, however, Russia discovered that its dependence on Germany for its coal supplies carried a political as well as a monetary price. When the Baltic Fleet reached German Southwest Africa, the German government stopped shipment of coal until the Kaiser had a chance to suggest to the Tsar the possibility of a comprehensive German-Russian security pact. Less than halfway to its destination, and far removed from its base at Kronstadt, the Russian Baltic Fleet was stranded off the coast of Africa! Tsar Nicholas was caught in an embarrassing dilemma: if he did not give a satisfactory reply to the Kaiser's suggestion, the Russian fleet would not find the necessary coal supplies to move. The Kaiser knew he had placed the Tsar in a difficult position, and seemed to relish using the supply of coal as a diplomatic weapon. Wilhelm smugly wrote to Chancellor Bülow: "Aber wie der Chinese sagt, in pigeon English: 'if no have got coal, how can do?' " Only by giving the German government assurances of a Russian alliance in case of a war between Great Britain and Germany did the Russian fleet resume receiving its vital coal supplies.[15]

This humiliating episode continues as an irritation in Russian minds, as Admiral Gorshkov's *Sea Power of the State* makes clear. Gorshkov maintains that the Tsarist government "completely failed" to understand the components of sea power Russia needs, given its peculiar geographic circumstances:

> The most important of these was the potential need for inter-theatre manoeuvre by the forces because of the separation of the sea theatres. It was necessary to take into account the absence of possessions and sea routes between the separate theatres equipped with base sites, which was largely the result of the neglect by Czarism of securing for Russia a whole number of islands and overseas territories discovered by Russian seafarers. We should recall, in passing, that the main cause of the loss of these territories was the ingrained misunderstanding of the importance for Russia of sea power.[16]

The inability to concentrate its scattered squadrons resulted in the destruction of Russia's naval power, first at Port Arthur and later at the Battle of Tsushima.

Britain possessed another great advantage over her rivals during the nineteenth century—the domination of the world's telegraph cable communications links outside the continent of Europe. Invented in 1837 by Samuel Morse, this device rapidly began to expand into an international communications system. Those with strategic and commercial interests in London readily appreciated the significance of this development: in time of crisis or war, warning and instructions could be swiftly transmitted throughout the far-flung Empire. The Treasury received startling proof of the efficiency of telegraphic communication in 1857, when the rapid transmission of news about the defeat of the great mutiny halted the movement of troops in Canada destined for India and thereby saved over 50,000 pounds.[17] Cable links could make imperial defense a more co-ordinated and less expensive undertaking.

Yet cable presented military planners with a new set of problems concerned with its influence on strategy. One of the most basic questions that had to be answered was how to protect cable communications from interruptions. A cable running on *land* through the territory of another country could well be cut at those moments when secure communication would be deemed most vital. One solution to this problem was the development of a network of submarine cables that would pass only through the territory of the British Empire. This "Red Line" cable system gave Britain an important advantage over the other Great Powers in diplomatic disputes and military operations outside of Europe.

During the Fashoda Crisis in 1898, Britain used its communication advantage to good effect in its diplomatic dispute with France over the disposition of the Sudan. When French and British expeditions collided at Fashoda, the French commander Colonel Marchand had no means of receiving immediate instructions from Paris, whereas Kitchener remained in telegraphic communication with London. Marchand's inability to communicate with his government led to his withdrawal, and subsequently, to the creation of a French cable link across the Mediterranean. Marchand's retreat from Fashoda weakened France's claim to have a say on the Sudan. On his arrival in Cairo, Marchand was ordered to return to Fashoda by a furious French Foreign Minister, Theophile Delcasse.[18]

Britain's domination of the world's oceans, by means of a comprehensive system of coaling stations and cable lines, as well as the striking power of her battlefleet, permitted her to send overseas expeditionary forces capable of expanding and defending the *Pax Britannica*. In the words of Sir Edward Grey: "The British Army is a projectile to be fired by the Navy." Like the United States in the era of Vietnam, Britain was the only great power at the turn of the century that possessed the capability to deploy and maintain an army numbering over a quarter of a million men at a distance of over 6,000 miles from Europe in South Africa, fighting a grisly protracted war against the Boers. Britain's imperial policy and its diplomatic stance of "splendid isolation" depended on coal and cable.

DECLINE OF THE PAX BRITANNICA: RAILROADS, THE MIDDLE EAST, AND OIL

Britain's defense of her empire rested primarily upon the ability of the Royal Navy to shield it against military expeditions from rival Great Powers. During the nineteenth century, however, the introduction and construction of railroads heightened the overland threat to the Empire's frontiers. Without the use of a railway, the supply of a large invading army (especially in sparsely populated or undeveloped areas) is a difficult proposition; thus, British forces, scattered in garrisons throughout the Empire, provided adequate security against most threats posed by potential intruders, prior to the widespread development of railroads. As the tempo of railroad construction outside Europe increased, military access to the territory of Britain's empire became easier from a logistic standpoint. In 1899, the Permanent Under-Secretary at the India Office stated his fears of this development to Lord Curzon:

> I will confess to you that there are two Powers, and two only, of whom I am afraid, *viz.* the United States and Russia, for the simple reason that they . . . (in the case of Russia) must soon have better military access to an important part of our dominions, than we have ourselves. It is to be regretted that Canada and India are not islands, but we must recognize the fact, and modify our diplomacy accordingly.[19]

By itself, naval power could not prevent the overrunning of these areas: their defense would require a strengthening of their garrisons, or a diplomacy that carefully avoided crises that threatened war. In the case of defending Canada against the United States, Britain chose the course of diplomacy: as one recent historian points out, "the appeasement of the United States at the end of the nineteenth century was the natural, if belated, conclusion of a policy which Great Britain had long since adopted in the interest of her security."[20]

Russia's construction of railways in Central Asia and Siberia posed a much more serious danger to Britain's position in India, Persia and the Far East. The famous geopolitical writer Halford Mackinder compared the power projection capabilities of Britain and Russia at the turn of the century:

> It was an unprecedented thing in the year 1900 that Britain could maintain a quarter of a million men in her war with the Boers at a distance of six thousand miles over the ocean; but it was as remarkable a feat for Russia to place an

army of more than a quarter of a million men against the Japanese in Manchuria in 1904 at a distance of four thousand miles by rail.[21]

The development of Russia's railway system in the Caucasus and Central Asia had clear strategic implications for Britain, including the need to have an army on India's Northwest Frontier large enough to defeat the military power of a continental European state. In the words of a secret War Office *Survey of the Military Resources of the Russian Empire*, Russian railway construction laid on the British "the military burdens and anxieties of a continental state."[22]

Already in 1885, during the Penjdeh Crisis, Britain and Russia were on the verge of war because of the steady Russian advance in Central Asia toward Afghanistan. In 1885, in a fascinating example of multi-crisis, Britain faced the strategic dilemma of confronting the Russians over Afghanistan while the bulk of its army was engaged in the futile rescue attempt of General Gordon in Khartoum. It was no coincidence that the Russians decided, on March 30, 1885, to destroy the Afghan detachment at the Penjdeh oasis, while Wolseley's army, campaigning up the Nile, faced the Moslem army commanded by the fanatical Muhammad Ahmad, who had proclaimed himself the Mahdi. Even the conciliatory Gladstone threatened war against the Russians, asking Parliament for a supplement of 11 million pounds, "of which six million and a half were to meet the case for preparations rendered necessary by the incident of Penjdeh." Only by recalling Wolseley's army could troops be found in case war with Russia occurred. Queen Victoria complained bitterly that Gladstone's policies had brought Britain to this difficult state of affairs: "Mr. Gladstone had alienated all other countries from us, by his very changeable and unreliable policy— unintentionally, no doubt."[23]

The tension between Russia and Britain in this "arc of crisis" remained until the 1907 entente. On many occasions British policy-makers saw a sinister design behind Russian activity in Iran and Afghanistan. In a memorandum written on the defenses on the Northwest Frontier, Lord Kitchener argued: "There can be no doubt whatever regarding the ultimate aims of Russia. That she intends to establish herself in Afghanistan sooner or later is generally established." The War Office endorsed Kitchener's assessment, and added that the threat to India improved Russia's position worldwide in relation to Britain:

> The purpose underlying Russia's patient and methodical advance and her vast expenditure upon unremunerative

railway construction is obvious; without necessarily intend-
ing to conquer and absorb our Indian Empire, she aims at
eventually making her frontier and that of India coterminous,
or at least, bringing it so near that she may be in a position
to strike effectively if Great Britain should . . . venture to
thwart her policy elsewhere.[24]

Russia's railway construction posed a long-term threat that would
prove expensive for Britain to meet and it provided leverage for the
Tsarist government's foreign policy.

Other British officials, like the Viceroy of India Lord Curzon,
believed Russia also harbored intentions of advancing through
Persia to seize a warm water port on the Persian Gulf. The social
and political turmoil within Persia throughout this period seemed to
offer Russian policy-makers a good chance for success. Curzon
predicted that economic and social modernization and the growth of
European influence in Persia would result in a Moslem revival
directed against foreigners, particularly the British, and that Russia
would seize upon the resulting chaos to intervene in support of a
faction controlled by the Tsarist government.[25] Britain's position in
the entire region would thus be seriously undermined by the creation
of a Russian satellite state extending to the Persian Gulf.

In May 1903, this possibility seemed likely enough that the
British foreign secretary Lord Lansdowne warned the Russians, in
the House of Lords, that any attempt to establish a fortified port on
the Persian Gulf would be "a very grave menace to British interests"
and would be resisted by all means available to Britain.[26] To many
British military planners, any attempt to resist Russian expansion
would be futile. Lord Kitchener warned, "we have promised more
than we are able to perform. Guarantees and pledges given
diplomatically must to be effective be founded on military means to
make them good . . . We are in the position of a firm which has
written cheques against a non-existent balance."[27] With its armed
forces raised by volunteer recruitment, Britain found it increasingly
difficult to find the forces necessary to guard the *Pax Britannica*
against the European Great Powers, whose large conscripted armies
could now be brought by railroads into play in the "Great Game" of
empire.

In addition to the added burden caused by the growth of
railroads, technological change tended to undermine the logistic
infrastructure of coal and cable that aided Britain in maintaining its
supremacy at sea. Oil came to be seen as a more efficient fuel for
steam ships—expecially warships. Simultaneously, the development
of wireless as a means of communication made other powers no

longer as dependent on the British underwater cable system. In this new age based on oil and radio waves, Britain's competitive advantage over her rivals in the ability to project military power diminished by degrees and has never been recovered.

Of the two technological developments just mentioned, the more serious challenge to British superiority arose from the growing importance of oil to fuel the military machine. Oil possesses many advantages over coal as a means of fuel for warships. It has a higher thermal efficiency in proportion to weight, which means that for any given weight of fuel and machinery a ship using oil could develop a higher speed and/or range of operation over a ship using coal. Large warships powered by oil increased their range of operation by 40 percent over those powered by coal without having to increase the ship's fuel capacity.[28] Oil also permitted a ship to refuel at sea, a task extremely difficult to do with coal. Oil thus greatly improved the operational and strategic capability of a fleet to remain on station without having to return to base or the shelter of a calm sea under the protection of land to take on coal. Another important advantage of oil was that it did not exhaust the crew during the refueling process, whereas coaling was long, hard, dirty work. One American officer noted that "coaling causes more desertions from the Navy than any other feature of the service."[29] Oil proved easier to use in service than coal. Furnaces fired by oil required less than half the number of stokers needed to tend and clean an engine room using coal. Furthermore, once on board, the coal still had to be shoveled by "black gangs" from the bunkers to the boilers, and as a ship used up its coal more men were required to move coal from the remote and inconvenient bunkers to bunkers nearer the furnaces. A battleship might thereby employ nearly a hundred men just to shovel coal from one bunker to another. On the other hand, oil could be stored in spare places of the hull of ship where it would be impossible to bring coal.[30]

Because of its advantages in warships, the British built destroyers burning oil (the thirty-three-knot Tribal class) as early as 1908. In the next two years' ship-building program, however, the Admiralty ordered the construction of twenty-seven-knot coal burning destroyer flotillas (the Acasta and Acheron classes) because Britain did not possess a domestic source of oil. When he became First Lord of the Admiralty in 1911, Churchill thought the Admiralty's decision to build destroyers fueled by coal, that could manage a top speed six knots slower than oil-fired destroyers, a great mistake. "Building slow destroyers," he scowled, "one might as well breed slow race horses."[31] Beginning with the 1912 building program, Churchill therefore decided to force the issue of shifting to

oil fuel for the fleet by ordering a class of five fast battleships fueled
by oil—the Queen Elizabeth class. In his memoirs, *The World
Crisis*, Churchill called this decision to shift to oil fuel for
battleships the "fateful plunge. . . . Then, for the first time, the
supreme ships of the Navy, on which our life depended, were fed by
oil. The decision to drive the smaller craft by oil followed naturally
upon this. The camel once swallowed, the gnats went down easily
enough."[32]

Yet Churchill's decision provoked a controversy in Britain,
despite the similar decision by the United States Navy, in the
Nevada class of two battleships authorized in 1911, to fuel its
captial ships with oil instead of coal. For, unlike the United States,
Great Britain did not possess any native supplies of oil. This meant
immense expenditures for tankers and the acquisition of a large
reserve of oil. Churchill estimated that at least ten million pounds
would have to be spent to create the logistic infrastructure necessary
for ships driven by oil.[33] Given this project's costs, it is not
surprising that Churchill ran into opposition from some of the other
ministers in the Liberal cabinet, most notably the Chancellor of the
Exchequer, Lloyd George.[34] Despite the formidable political
opposition within his own party to increased naval expenditures,
Churchill believed no more time could be lost since a "year gained
over a rival might make the difference."[35]

To help solve the problems posed by reliance on oil fuel for the
Royal Navy, Churchill turned to Lord Fisher, who earlier as First
Sea Lord had been the main force behind the decision to build the
first all big-gun battleship—the *Dreadnought*. Churchill wanted
Fisher to chair a Royal Commission on Fuel and Engines that would
show the importance of oil fuel in modern war and how supplies of it
could be found for the Royal Navy. On June 11, 1912, Churchill
wrote to Fisher explaining the task of the commission:

> This liquid fuel problem has got to be solved, and the
> natural, inherent, unavoidable difficulties are such that
> they require the drive and enthusiasm of a big man. I want
> you for this, viz. to crack the nut. . . . You have got to find
> the oil: to show how it can be stored cheaply: how it can be
> purchased regularly and cheaply in peace; and with
> absolute certainty in war. Then by all means develop its
> application in the best possible way to existing and
> prospective ships.[36]

Fisher, who called himself an "Oil Maniac," pushed the work of the
Commission, which issued its first report on November 27, 1912.
This first report, classified "Secret," stressed the important

advantages of oil fuel in warships. It also addressed the critical
problem of storing oil, since no commercially viable source of supply
existed in the British Isles. The report concluded by stating:

> The rate of progress in the provision of storage must, of
> course, be proportionate to the increase in number and
> power of the oil-using vessels in the Fleet, and we hold the
> decided opinion that the stock of oil-fuel should never be
> allowed to fall below at least four years' current peace
> consumption. Every acceleration in the accumulation of
> this reserve will directly increase the security of the nation
> against war risks, price combinations and fluctuations of
> supplies.[37]

This stockpile would enable the Royal Navy to continue its
operations in the face of a major dislocation of supply.

Stockpiling oil was not the only problem facing the Commission,
however. There remained the important consideration of finding a
source for this oil that Britain could bring under its control. Most of
the world's production of oil, and the bulk of British investment in
oil, was in the territory and control of another Great Power, either
Russia or the United States. During a time of crisis or war, Britain
could not be caught in the embarrassing position of being dependent
on the good will of another major power for fuel for her fleet, as had
happened to Russia during the Russo-Japanese War. The Commission thus began to look for other areas capable of providing the
Royal Navy with the oil it needed. During the course of its hearings,
the Commission heard pleas from oil companies operating in
Newfoundland, Egypt, Nigeria, and the Scottish shale oil interests
for financial support from the British government in return for
meeting the Navy's oil requirements.[38] The Commission also
received an offer from Royal Dutch Shell to supply the Royal Navy
with oil, and in return the British government would provide Shell
with diplomatic support around the world against its primary rival,
Standard Oil of the United States.[39]

However, a small company operating in Persia, the Anglo-
Persian Oil Company (APOC), managed to convince the British
government that it rather than Shell should receive the government's
support. APOC argued that the world's oil industry was falling
under the domination of two "monopolistic" companies—Standard
Oil and Shell; APOC predicted that without support from the British
government, it would be swallowed by one of these two firms.
Neither of these firms, APOC argued, could be depended upon in a
crisis because they could be controlled by powerful rivals of Britain:
Standard Oil by the United States; and Shell, with 60 percent of its

shares controlled by the Dutch government, could be vulnerable to
pressure from the Netherlands' neighbor, Germany.[40] Faced by this
bleak prospect, the British government decided to purchase a
controlling share of APOC for 2,200,000 pounds.

In his memoirs, Churchill would write that the decision to shift
to oil fuel for the Royal Navy "involved our national safety as much
as a battle at sea. It was as anxious and as harassing as any hazard in
war. It *was* war in a certain sense raging under a surface of unbroken
peace. . . . The oil decision was vital . . . [it] touched our existence."[41]
Later historians would agree with Churchill's verdict, and compare
his actions to Disraeli's purchase of a controlling interest in the Suez
Canal.[42]

While Churchill had found a source of oil for the British
Empire, the outbreak of war in August 1914 prevented the
implementation of the program recommended by the Royal
Commission calling for a four years' peace consumption in reserve
in Britain. Even if war had not occurred, however, the cost of
stockpiling such a large fuel reserve would have been prohibitive.
Churchill, mindful of his critics within the cabinet concerning naval
expenditures, felt that four-and-a-half months consumption, rather
than four years, would be sufficient.[43] This failure to stockpile large
quantities of oil within Britain did not greatly affect the military
strategy of the early stages of the war.

The demands of war in the twentieth century did entail large
quantities of oil, not only for the movements of the fleet, but also to
support the rapidly increasing number of motorized vehicles and
aircraft with the armies in the field. A few statistics will illustrate
this phenomenal growth during the war: In 1914, Britain possessed
63 aircraft, while in 1918, with the creation of R.A.F. she had no
less than 22,000. Meanwhile, General Haig had at his disposal over
1500 tanks on the Western Front. In addition to these figures there
were the aircraft and tanks of the French and American armies.[44]
The great superiority possessed by the Allies on the Western Front
in aircraft, tanks, and motor vehicles in itself largely explains the
German defeat in 1918. At the time, it was said the Allies won the
war on a "flood of oil."[45] None of the General Staffs in 1914 could
have predicted these vast demands for oil of 1918.

Yet the Germans came close to winning the war, after they
resumed their campaign of unrestricted submarine warfare, by
sinking tankers and thus stopping this "flood." The dilemma faced
by the Royal Navy in 1917 clearly shows how vulnerable and
dependent the British Empire had become in a world where oil fueled
the military machine. At the beginning of the submarine campaign,
the stocks of oil fuel on hand stood at 5.1 months' consumption;

three months later in May 1917, this had been reduced to 2.9 months. Some naval bases had been reduced to as little as six days' supply. This fuel problem resulted in orders restricting the movements of the battle fleet, and limiting destroyers to twenty-knots cruising speed, in order to conserve oil. In this dire situation, the Admiralty had to send what one historian has called urgent and humiliating pleas to the United States asking that more tonnage be made available for American oil. Despite its control of APOC, the shortage of tankers forced Britain to draw about 80 percent of its oil supplies from North America. The Admiralty Director of Stores noted in September 1917 that "without the aid of oil from America our modern oil-burning fleet cannot keep the sea." This fear of having to depend on another power for their supplies of oil continued to haunt British policy-makers from the submarine crisis of 1917 to the Suez Crisis and until today.[46]

Britain managed to overcome this oil crisis by the introduction of the convoy system to protect trade during the summer of 1917, and by the novel expedient of using the ballast tanks of cargo steamers and liners as fuel carrying "double bottoms." The War Cabinet ordered this measure in June 1917, and by November, the 443 ships that had been fitted out had brought to Britain approximately 250,000 tons of oil, or the equivalent of the total capacity of fifteen tankers. These measures enabled the Allies to barely meet their oil needs. The situation had seemed so critical at times that the shipping controller had suggested to the War Cabinet in August 1917 that the Royal Navy should stop building ships fueled by oil and revert to coal.[47] Britain's victory had rested on an American "flood of oil."

In the immediate post-war period, the Admiralty wanted to make Britain independent of the United States for its oil supplies. While the war was still being fought, the Admiralty began producing a series of position papers concerning the oil needs of the Empire. These papers called for exclusive British control of the Persian and Mesopotamian oil fields, and a system of pipelines from these fields to the Mediterranean Sea. The opinions of these papers were subsequently reflected in the war aims put forward by Britain.[48] The Admiralty's decision to become independent of American oil added to the Anglo-American naval rivalry over the building of battleships before the Washington Conference. In early 1920, the First Lord of the Admiralty Walter Long delivered a speech declaring that "if we secure the supplies of oil now available in the world we can do what we like." But if Britain did not take this opportunity to gain control over the oil fields of the Persian Gulf, the "others will take it, and with it the key to all future success."[49] After the Washington

Conference eased the tensions of naval rivalry between Britain and the United States, the Admiralty still wanted to create a worldwide oil reserve for the fleet. The Treasury, guided by the precepts of the notorious "Ten Year Rule," blocked this ambitious Admiralty scheme throughout the 1920s and 1930s. Because of the great cost involved, Britain's political leadership recoiled from proposals for making the Empire independent of American-controlled oil supplies. Britain no longer dominated the world's oceans as it had during the earlier period when warships had been propelled by coal.

CONCLUSIONS: THE CONTEMPORARY AMERICAN DILEMMA

Although any comprehensive evaluation of the decline of the *Pax Britannica* would have to include many factors not touched upon in this chapter, there can be no doubt that the changing relationship between logistics, infrastructure and technology played an important role. An intriguing question that comes to mind is the extent to which there may be parallels between the earlier British experience and contemporary problems that face the United States. In the 1880s and 1890s, Britain's capability to project power was envied by the other Great Powers. Britain demonstrated its awesome military power in 1899 when it began to wage war against the Boers in South Africa. Because of its wealth and control of logistic infrastructure, Britain was able to mount a costly, protracted and increasingly unpopular war thousands of miles from its home base. Although Britain eventually triumphed militarily, the war shattered the domestic consensus in favor of empire and highlighted the precarious nature of "splendid isolation" as a national strategy. The war showed the necessity for Britain to pursue actively new cooperative relations with emerging powers, like Japan and the United States, and seek friendlier relations with long-time rivals, like France and Russia, to maintain its deteriorating strategic position. Germany's direct challenge in Europe and the Near East only served further to increase the costs of defending Britain's imperial stance.

In a similar vein, the economic and military power of the United States in the 1960s could be brought to bear thousands of miles from its home base in a protracted struggle against a determined and well-equipped enemy in South East Asia. Its primary adversary, the Soviet Union, was unable to challenge directly American military power in that region because it lacked the logistic and military resources to project power over great distances. After having fought this unpopular and devisive war, and having failed to obtain the objectives for which it had battled in South East Asia, the United States emerged shaken and uncertain about its role in world politics. In addition to the destruction of a domestic consensus on foreign and military affairs, the United States faced a new, more ominous world stage where the Soviet Union was rapidly becoming a military equal through a formidable arms build up; at the same time, dependency on foreign oil eroded the former American self-sufficiency. In one decade, Vietnam and dependency on foreign oil drastically changed the basic underpinnings of American supremacy, just as the Boer War and the importance of naval oil eroded British power in the first decade of this century. The United States is now engaged in a struggle with an aspiring global power moved by a vision of achieving ascendancy over America and its allies, just as Britain's world position was threatened by the dangerous efforts of Wilhelmine Germany to gain for itself a "place in the sun."

Finally, to relate the central theme of this chapter to the current "arc of crisis" in the Middle East, Africa and Asia, the capacity of the United States and the Soviet Union to challenge each other's interests will be determined by a combination of political will, dependable friends and allies, and the capability to project military power. The relative balance in capabilities to project military power will, in the last resort, depend upon logistics and infrastructure as much as firepower and tactics. For this reason, talk of extending Western military responsibilities to include the Middle East and Indian Ocean littoral will remain incomplete unless a more serious effort is made to establish the logistics, support and infrastructure required to sustain limited military operations against Soviet forces. It is not enough to focus on the military order of battle to be deployed—the Army and Marine ground combat units, the carrier groups, and air squadrons—if the logistic infrastructure is inadequate to ensure the initial movement and timely arrival into the region, and the later support needed to sustain intensive combat operations. The destruction of the considerable British military forces sent to Singapore in 1941 and early 1942 should serve as a warning of the fate that could befall American forces hastily deployed to the Middle East without firm logistic support.

Before 1914, the farsighted policies of Churchill and Fisher were designed to maintain Britain's world position in an era when the traditional props of that position were becoming increasingly irrelevant. They understood immediately that Britain's future was bound up with Middle East oil. Although many of the circumstances that American leaders face today are different, the dynamics of the two positions are quite similar. The United States today is finding it more costly to maintain a global posture (inherited from the post–

World War II period of overwhelming strength) in an era of scarcity of critical resources, economic sluggishness, and increased military competition from adversaries.

If the industrial democracies and their friends are to avoid defeat in the Middle East, American policy-makers must take a more global and functional perspective on the underpinnings of American military power. This requires immediate action to bolster the strength of friends and allies in the region who have strong military potential, to secure access to facilities in forward-based countries in the Persian Gulf region, and to build up a much larger stockpile of materiel and the means to deploy it into the area. While this program will be costly, it must be weighed against the far greater costs to be incurred if the United States does not take the lead in protecting friendly states in this vital region from encroachment by the Soviet Union. Without a policy that molds together diplomatic and logistic considerations, and relates the strategic problems in the Middle East to other critical theaters like Europe and East Asia, the United States cannot expect successfully to project military power into the region in defense of its interests.

NOTES

1.   David A. Rosenberg, "The U.S. Navy and the Problem of Oil in a Future War: The Outline of a Strategic Dilemma, 1945–50," *Naval War College Review* 29, 1 (Summer 1976): 53. Emphasis added.

Also see Bruce R. Kuniholm, *The Origins of the Cold War in the Near East* (Princeton, 1980), passim.

2.   Anthony Cave Brown, ed., *Dropshot: The American Plan for World War III Against Russia in 1957* (New York: Dial Press, 1978), p. 156.

3.   Drew Middleton, "U.S. Will Vary Makeup of Rapid Deployment Unit," *The New York Times*, 20 March 1980, p. A14.

4.   Admiral Gorshkov excoriates the Tsarist government for permitting the Russian Fleets to be defeated separately by the Japanese. Had the Port Arthur and Baltic Fleets been united, it would "have radically changed the situation in Russia's favor in the theater of operations." *Sea Power of the State* (Annapolis, MD: Naval Institute Press, 1979), p. 112.

5.   Roosevelt to Taft, 3 March 1909, Elting E. Morison, ed., *The Letters of Theodore Roosevelt* (Cambridge, MA: Harvard University Press, 1954), Vol. VI, p. 1543.

6.   Henry Scott Stokes, "Japan is Hoping to Build a New Canal in Panama," *The New York Times*, 26 March 1980, p. A8.

7.   Arthur J. Marder, *The Anatomy of British Sea Power* (New York: A.A. Knopf, 1940), p. 84. The words of Lord George Hamilton.

8.   *Ibid.*, p. 85.

9.   *Ibid.*, p. 65.

10.   W. G. Jensen, "The Importance of Energy in the First and

Second World Wars," *The Historical Journal* XI, 3 (1968): 542.

11. Bernard Brodie, *Sea Power in the Machine Age* (Princeton: Princeton University Press, 1941), p. 116.

12. *Ibid.*, p. 115.

13. John D. Alden, *The American Steel Navy* (Annapolis, MD: Naval Institute Press, 1971), pp. 129–130.

14. William Reynolds Braisted, *The United States Navy in the Pacific, 1909–1922* (Austin, TX: University of Texas Press, 1971), pp. 129–130.

15. See Lamar J. R. Cecil, "Coal for the Fleet That Had to Die," *The American Historical Review* 69, 4 (1964).

16. S. G. Gorshkov, *Sea Power of the State*, pp. 91–92.

17. Paul M. Kennedy, "Imperial Cable Communications and Strategy, 1870–1914," *English Historical Review* 86, 141 (1971): 730. On the importance of cable communications, see Arthur Hezlet, *The Electron and Sea Power* (London: Windmill Press, R75), pp. 1–82.

18. Kennedy, "Imperial Cable Communications," p. 728, note 1.

19. Kennedy, *The Rise and Fall of British Naval Mastery* (New York: Scribner, 1976), p. 211.

20. Kenneth Bourne, *Britain and the Balance of Power in North America, 1815–1908* (London: Longman's Green Ltd., 1967), p. 410. Also Samuel F. Wells, "British Strategic Withdrawal from the Western Hemisphere, 1904–1906," *Canadian Historical Review* 49, 4 (December 1968): 335–56.

21. H. J. Mackinder, *Democratic Ideals and Reality* (New York: Norton 1962), p. 115.

22. Beryl J. Williams, "The Strategic Background to the Anglo-Russian Entente of August 1907," *The Historical Journal* 9, 3 (1966): 365.

23. William L. Langer, *European Alliances and Alignments, 1871–1890* (New York: Random House, 1966), p. 317.

24. Williams, "Anglo–Russian Entente," p. 365.

25. George N. Curzon, *Persia and the Persian Question* (New York: Barnes & Noble, 1966), vol. II, p. 629.

26. Williams, "Anglo–Russian Entente," p. 362.

27. *Ibid.*, p. 366.

28. Winston S. Churchill, *The World Crisis* (New York: Scribner, 1923), vol. I, p. 133.

29. Alden, *American Steel Navy*, p. 224.

30. Churchill, *World Crisis*, p. 134.

31. *Ibid.*, p. 142.

32. *Ibid.*, p. 136.

33. *Ibid.*, p. 137.

34. Arthur J. Marder, *From the Dreadnought to Scapa Flow* (New York: Oxford University Press, 1961), vol. I, p. 269.

35. Churchill, *World Crisis*, p. 137.

36. *Ibid.*, pp. 137–138.

37. Ruddock F. Mackay, *Fisher of Kilverstone* (London: Oxford University Press, 1973), p. 439.

38. C. Gareth Jones, "The British Government and the Oil Companies 1912–1924: The Search for an Oil Policy," *The Historical Journal* 20, 3 (1977): 648. Also see Marion Kent, *Oil and Empire: British Policy and Mesopotamian Oil* (New York: Harper and Row, 1976).

39. Jones, "British Government and the Oil Companies," p. 649.
40. *Ibid.*, p. 652.
41. Churchill, *World Crisis*, p. 31.
42. Marder, *Dreadnought to Scapa Flow*, p. 271.
43. *Ibid.*
44. W. G. Jensen, "The Importance of Energy in the First and Second World Wars," *The Historical Journal* XI, 3 (1968): 543.
45. *Ibid.*
46. Jones, "British Government and the Oil Companies," p. 661.
47. *Ibid.*, p. 664.
48. See V. H. Rothwell, "Mesopotamia in British War Aims, 1914–1918," *The Historical Journal* XIII, 2 (1970): 289–291. Also, Kent, *Oil and Empire*, pp. 125–126.
49. Stephen Roskill, *Naval Policy Between the Wars* (New York: William Collins Sons Ltd. 1968) vol. I, pp. 219–220.

4

Mobilizing Economic Strength
for Military Power

Fred Charles Iklé

In the present context, the term "power projection" has come to mean the application of military power in areas that are distant from the nation's heartland and distant, also, from the principal members of the Alliance. What are the purposes of such "power projection"?

A thoughtful answer to this question will tell us a great deal about our subject. The purposes for which a nation or an alliance will exert itself in a war are likely to be fluid. War aims are frequently vague and usually comprise multiple or even conflicting objectives. Nonetheless, the exercise of "power projection" must be understood as a means to other ends.

Someone who looks at the world with the bias of an American defense analyst might think the main purpose of "power projection" is to protect and to restore the integrity of some smaller nation allied with the United States, or to ward off localized aggression against American interests and assets. The historic cases of South Korea and South Vietnam or the hypothetical cases of Saudi Arabia or Pakistan come to mind. In such contingencies, if the application of our military power is to succeed, it must have a lasting effect. The enduring protection of the territorial integrity of our ally or friend is the criterion of success. We succeeded in Korea; we failed in Vietnam.

To prevail with an enduring effect, we must outlast the enemy's effort, both in political perseverance and in long-term logistics. We could not have succeeded in the Korean War if, after ninety days, we had run out of ammunition, helicopters and tanks (unless, of course, the North Koreans had surrendered after eighty days).

In the 1980s we must be deeply concerned about the inadequacy of our long-term logistics supply for such "power projections." In the Korean War this was not an issue. In the war in

Vietnam, the North Vietnamese achieved their final victory because we denied continued logistics support to South Vietnam. But that cessation of logistics support was the result of a political decision in Washington. In a future armed conflict, a continued supply of arms and ammunition may be denied to our forces, or to our allies—not by a vote of Congress but by an inadequate production base in the United States. The CIA estimates that Soviet military investment over the last decade exceeded ours by 55 percent. And during the coming years, if we assume a continuation of present U.S. and Soviet spending levels, Soviet military investment will exceed ours by 80 percent.[1] Thus, both the existing arsenals and the active production base of the Soviet Union will substantially exceed ours.

This continuing discrepancy has fundamental implications for our "power projection" in the 1980s. In a conflict where the Soviet Union would not back our enemy, our long-term logistics supply problem, of course, would be trivial. But if our forces, or our allies, would have to fight an enemy who would be receiving unstinting logistics aid from the Soviets and who would be capable of absorbing such aid, we might well lack the basic capability to sustain prolonged resistance.

In most wars during this century in which the United States was involved (Vietnam is the exception), our side ultimately prevailed because we were able to overtake the enemy's war production and to supply our forces far more lavishly. In a future conventional war, the tables might be turned: the "arsenal of democracy" would lag far behind the "arsenal for totalitarianism."

Are we studying the strategies and military tactics that would permit us to adapt to such a situation? For our military experts, this new challenge should mean an intellectual revolution, since our military thinking in the past never had to face such a problem. Our forces might have been outgunned temporarily or in a localized battle, but never in this century were they confronted by an enemy who could marshal superior fire power, superior numbers of aircraft, tanks and other armaments, on a sustained basis, month after month, the first year of the war, the second year, and perhaps beyond.

The American military tradition would be ill-suited for such a contest. It would be handicapped, on the one hand, by its emphasis on massing firepower, providing generous logistics for the troops, and stressing large-scale mobility, and, on the other hand, by its neglect of such tactics as fortifications, improvised supplies, and deception. It is high time that our military experts pay attention to the tactics for "poor man's" warfare.

But there are, of course, more fundamental implications of the fact that in the 1980s, our enemies might marshal for a local war a longterm logistic support superior to ours. As long as this situation obtains, we ought to recognize that our "power projection" would have to serve different purposes. If it is no longer possible to prevail in the local theatre of conflict so as to protect—in an enduring fashion—the contested territory, our war aims traditionally associated with "power projection" are put into question.

Given such a situation, the historic significance of a U.S. effort to intervene militarily could develop in one of two ways. On the one hand, it might all end in a local military defeat, causing severe repercussions for our alliances and for the geopolitical order. The Communist conquest of Indochina comes to mind. But the outcome of the war in Indochina is only an approximate example because our failures there did not stem from the inability of the United States to provide sufficient logistic support. It is one thing to lose a local war for lack of interest or lack of will; it is another thing to lose for lack of sustaining power.

On the other hand, the historic significance of such a U.S. effort to intervene militarily in a distant theatre could develop in a different direction. It could become the initial phase of a protracted global military confrontation. With such a dynamic, our "power projection" might help us to slow down, rather than to prevent, the loss of territory, so as to gain time for a recovery of our overall military strength. The objective would no longer be to obtain a quick settlement, but to effect a favorable shift in the *global* balance of forces by delaying the geopolitical advances of the enemy camp. If this, indeed, became the right way to look at a specific armed conflict, it would entail fundamental implications for the strategy and tactics with which we ought to respond to the war.

The key criterion for success would not be the enduring retention of the contested territory, but improvements in the overall worldwide array of forces and in the capability to generate additional military assets. In the local conflict, the relative rates of attrition might be more important than the territorial outcome of the campaigns. It might almost be said that it would have become our objective to inflict on our enemy a Pyrrhic victory.

This approach to "power projection" in the 1980s is not a strategy of resignation or despair. It seeks to make the best of a difficult situation—the deteriorated military balance and shortages of war reserves. It seeks to exploit the more fundamental assets of the United States.

The United States has substantial assets for a competition in mobilizing economic strength for military power. Compared with the Soviet Union, we have a larger Gross National Product, a greater ability for technological innovation, and a population of almost the same size which has proven its dedication and perseverance. The question is how this potential could be transformed into military assets. We have done it successfully in the past—in 1942–43 and in 1951–53. However, on those occasions the United States required several years for the full increase in arms production. Moreover, today the United States is less well prepared for industrial mobilization so that an even longer "warm-up time" would be required.

High priority should be given to a program that would improve the United States's capability massively to expand defense production in a short period of time. By way of a brief summary, the necessary preparations can be broken down as follows:

First, the industrial mobilization process would have to be started by far-reaching legislative and executive decisions. Broad support by Congress and the public would, of course, be essential. But the concrete decisions would require weeks and months to work out unless prepared in advance. Existing standby legislation and the Defense Production Act are not sufficient.

Second, an administrative structure would be needed to manage the industrial mobilization. In World War II this structure was developed gradually between 1939 and Pearl Harbor Day.

Third, raw materials would have to be available. The existing strategic stockpile for minerals and other nonfuel materials represents an important asset. But its composition should be updated. A plan for the acquisition of important materials and the disposal of the unneeded ores has been worked out, but Congress has not yet approved the necessary funding and authority for disposal.

Fourth, various elements in the production process might be stockpiled or earmarked: plants, machine tools, and components involving long-lead times. In contrast to the administrative preparations, this type of preparation can become costly.

Fifth, since research and development take a long time and are difficult to speed up, they have to be largely completed before the start of any mobilization. It would be desirable to have prototypes of weapons systems developed that would be particularly suitable for quick mass production or particularly important in a mobilization period.

Sixth, to the extent possible, the appropriate military strategy should be worked out beforehand. It would, of course, have to be adjusted if and when the emergency arises. The strategy would govern how the expanded arms production is to be allocated and what are to be the priorities for different weapons systems.

During periods of industrial mobilization in past wars—World

War I, World War II, and the Korean War—the territory of the
United States was essentially immune from enemy attack. Today,
the Soviet Union has, of course, the capability to attack and destroy
the industrial resources of the United States. The argument is
sometimes made that in light of this vulnerability, a strategy that
emphasizes industrial mobilization makes no sense. This argument
assumes that the Soviet Union would not let the United States
mobilize its military strength while remaining a sanctuary. Implicitly
or explicitly, this argument postulates that the Soviet Union, in such
a contingency, would launch a nuclear attack on the United States.
This reasoning is faulty in that it attributes the risk of Soviet nuclear
attack to the American effort of industrial mobilization, instead of to
the weakness of the American nuclear deterrent.

As long as the United States has an adequate nuclear deterrent,
a Soviet nuclear attack should be no more probable during a period
of mobilization than before. While the mobilization effort might add
an element of "provocation," it would also be accompanied by a
greater level of preparedness and alert measures for the strategic
forces. It seems likely that the latter would outweigh the former.

It follows that during a mobilization period, our strategic
deterrent would increase sharply in importance. This suggests that
improvements in strategic forces ought to take precedence over
improvements in conventional forces to implement a mobilization
strategy. That is to say, if the United States is forced to rely
increasingly on a strategy of industrial mobilization to compensate
for the lack of ready forces for "power projection," our strategic
forces must be the bulwark that protects our mobilization assets
during a conventional war. This conclusion contradicts the more
traditional wisdom that we must first strengthen our conventional
forces.

Difficult questions are raised by the military strategy appropriate to the conduct of a conventional war in which the United States
would first have to build up its military strength. The strategy would
have to provide for the recovery of the lost territory so that the status
quo, at least, could be restored. A more ambitious goal would be to
change the military balance in a more permanent way so as to
achieve a solid improvement in our security.

The last two major, localized wars in which the United States
was involved provide a paradoxical contrast in the trade-off between
local and global objectives. During the Korean War, the United
States paid a great deal of attention to the *global* confrontation.
Indeed, the war in Korea was regarded as a possible prelude to a
global war. The massive American effort in industrial mobilization
after the summer of 1950 was devoted in large part to the

strengthening of worldwide U.S. capabilities (especially strategic forces) and to improving the mobilization base for a further expansion of arms production. By contrast, during the war in Vietnam, we neglected our strategic forces and we drew down our conventional forces in Europe. At the end of the Korean War, having focussed on the global military confrontation, we achieved our objective in the local conflict and emerged substantially stronger in our worldwide military posture. At the end of the war in Vietnam, having neglected the global military balance, we suffered both a local defeat and a decline in our global security. Thus, this limited historic experience, at least, would suggest that a strategy that backs up "power projection" with industrial mobilization may accomplish more than an exclusive concentration on the military needs of the local conflict.

NOTE

1.   CIA, National Foreign Assessment Center. *Soviet and U.S. Defense Activities, 1970–74: A Dollar Cost Comparison*, January 1980.

5

The Role of Analysis in Assessing the Maritime and Naval Dimensions of Power Projection

R. James Woolsey

One of the most difficult aspects of dealing with power projection for naval forces is breaking through the traditional intellectual framework for discussing the issue. This chapter, then, will discuss power projection itself only incidentally. First and foremost, it will deal with the difficulties which result from the intellectual framework within which decision-making about this and related naval force structure issues has been practiced for the last twenty years.

In these two decades, the intellectual furniture that most persons have brought to decision-making about defense, and particularly about naval forces, has been—with only small variations in design—of the style made popular in the office of the Secretary of Defense in the early 1960s. This mind-set is quantitative and programmatic in its focus, and rooted in the disciplines of economics and the techniques of professional business schools. Its features are a concentration on objectives, criteria, and options, a commitment to quantify as much as possible, and a determination to focus on changes at the margin. This intellectual framework has generally gone under a number of different titles, but will be called here by the name it originally took in defense—systems analysis—with the understanding this term refers not to any particular office, but rather to an approach, an attitude, a frame of mind.

Systems analysis spread throughout the federal government in the 1960s, and it has heavily influenced the defense debate from outside the Department of Defense as well as from within. For example, the approach is a common one in the Office of Management and Budget and in many parts of the Congress. Indeed, it has come to be a major tool of domestic-policy analysis as well. In light of this, it is time to ask whether it deserves the allegiance paid to it or whether using it as a tool may not entail certain blind spots.

There have been a number of sophisticated academic critiques of systems analysis as a decision-making process. One of the most seminal was Graham Allison's work on the Cuban missile crisis, *The Essence of Decision*. John Steinbruner, now at Brookings, has written incisively on this subject as well.[1] But such critiques have not yet filtered through to create any wide-ranging dissatisfaction with the systems analysis approach toward military decision-making—particularly decisionmaking about force structure—within the U.S. Government.

What follows is an attempt to begin to look at how the habit of viewing naval forces through systems analysts' eyes for the last twenty years has affected our planning for those forces.

"But surely you would agree," it is often said, "that the systems analysis revolution brought rationality to the obsolete system of planning military force structure that reigned in the 1950s—namely, dividing the defense budget into three roughly equal parts and then letting the generals and admirals do what they wanted with it according to their hunches and biases dressed up as military judgment." The answer to that thrust, it would seem, is both yes and no. More precisely, first yes and then later no.

At first the analytical revolution was useful in the way that almost any intellectual framework would have been useful which required one to touch systematically all the bases of military capability. For example, early in its reign systems analysis forced tough and detailed assessments of the match, or, more precisely, the mismatch, between force structure and logistics. It had a major role in encouraging the purchase of more sealift and airlift for Army divisions that otherwise would never have been able to get to war on time. It has helped recently to focus similar attention on missing links in our logistics, and has made other contributions as well.

But such analytical methods themselves have introduced rigidities into the decision-making process over the years that at least delay, and in some cases make more difficult, the solutions to the complex problem of planning naval forces.

What is the nature of some of these iatrigenic—that is, physician-caused—diseases that infect naval forces planning?

Rigidities have been introduced, first of all, because planning military forces has become to an important degree a process that depends on concocting elaborate scenarios for specific geographic areas. Such scenarios must be created in order to test alternative force structure packages in campaign analyses or with other analytical tools in complex computer simulations. This requires boxing in the scenarios with innumerable assumptions. Naval forces have been particularly favored by such attention because they have the misfortune to seem to model quite well—better than, say, infantry combat. It is possible to get quite far into such an enterprise, arguing and haggling about the assumptions, before one realizes that the interesting question is not "Why don't we construct this scenario slightly differently?" but rather "Why are we doing this at all?". Detailed presentations of quantitative evidence by lawyers in regulatory hearings are a similar phenomenon. One must begin to suspect that in such enterprises, it is the interests of those who manage the process that are being served—the lawyers in one case, the systems analysts and their increasingly sophisticated computer simulations in the other—not illumination of the subject.

In any case, as a by-product of these endless exercises, systems analysis has fostered the idea that we can predict the scene and nature of future conflicts, even if we don't plan to be the side to start them, and that we should not proceed with weapons programs until there is agreement about such scenarios. Often, in the case of the Navy, this point is made most petulantly by analysts: "If the damned Navy would just decide where and what kind of war it wants to fight, we could make some progress." But the problem is that the demand for specific scenarios is a big part of the problem. This does not mean that such scenarios should not be used at all in force planning, but their role today is far too great. Their primary relevance is for operational planning—that is, planning how to deploy and use existing forces—not as tools for designing the forces themselves.

As an example, consider the debate about the Navy's new *Aegis* cruisers (CG47s). They will be the key to coping with battle management on and above the surface of the ocean for some time to come, particularly in light of the ever-improving generations of cruise missiles that are going to be deployed at sea. Clearly the Aegis radar will be no panacea, and radars will have to be supplemented by other sensors, but arguments about the scenarios in which Aegis might be used have been at least one factor in the delay in getting it to sea. It has not been the only factor: Aegis was delayed two to three years by disagreements between the House and the Senate in the early 1970s over whether it should be placed on ships propelled by gas turbines or by nuclear power. Some analysts have said that deploying Aegis in numbers should be delayed until our understanding of the scenarios in which it would used is clearer—that if the Navy would just stop trying to design forces to sail up close to the Soviet Union, within range of Soviet land-based aircraft, and conduct offensive strikes early in a war, there would be little need for such elaborate and expensive new systems.

The problem is that several of our allies—Norway, Turkey, Japan, and others—have the misfortune to be situated rather close to the Soviet Union, and it would be in neither their interests nor ours to design forces on the assumption that these allies are to be behind enemy lines.

A second problem is that, while we have been discussing scenarios, the Soviet leaders have been building Backfire bombers, assigning many of them to naval aviation, and bringing much more of the world's oceans within range of their land-based air. These areas include (using realistic mission profiles for the Backfire) the Atlantic down to the Azores, the Mediterranean, the northern half of the Indian Ocean, and the Pacific from just past Pearl Harbor on to the northwest. Aegis is clearly going to be needed in those areas to cope with cruise missiles that might be launched by Backfires during wartime. But detailed analysis continues to proceed, some of it attempting to show how we might be able to avoid sending naval forces into many of *these* regions in wartime as well. And so on.

The point is that we need to spend our time not on continual haggling about appropriate scenarios, but on making weapons platforms themselves relatively insensitive to technological change. As the next generation of Soviet anti-ship systems follows the Backfire, we would like to be able to cope with it, if possible, without redesigning the whole Navy. The truth is that we do not know where or when our naval forces will have to fight, and the lead time for weapons design and production far exceeds our ability to forecast those scenarios. The carrier *Midway* is homeported in Japan, having had her keel laid some thirty-six years ago in the midst of a war with Japan. That is quite a change in scenario. One big reason why *Midway* and other aircraft carriers have been such successful and long-lived instruments of naval warfare derives from the fact that it is relatively easy to modernize them and to change their mission—e.g., from antisubmarine warfare to projection and back again—merely by changing the aircraft assigned to them. *Midway* is on perhaps her sixth or seventh generation of aircraft.

Instead of clinging to a fascination with forecasting scenarios as the basis for planning naval forces, we should change the way we design and produce weapons so that other naval forces can be as successful as the carriers in adapting to new and necessarily unanticipated situations.

Today, designing a weapon system such as Aegis, then designing a ship around it, and then constructing both, can take one to two decades. If a more modular method of constructing weapons and sensors could be devised, the process of modernization might begin to be brought into line with the necessarily uncertain view of the future.

The most difficult part of such a change involves ship electronics. Microprocessing, very large-scale integration, and other wonders that have been wrought by our electronics industry are beginning to make it possible to design the electronics for ships in a very different way than is done today. Rather than designing a ship's information system around a central computer, it is becoming possible to do distributed processing of signals and information, making each sensor and weapon far more independent than it is now and far more capable of being changed without the enormously expensive redesigning of the software for the entire ship. Such a revolution in electronics can readily be followed by a revolution in weapon and sensor construction methods, so that each weapon or sensor could be fitted into one or two sizes of standard modules for quick installation on ships, much the way pods are changed on aircraft today.

Thus, we would have to pretend no longer that we are farsighted—that we are going to be able today to make the decision whether ships for the twenty-first century should be designed primarily for power projection or sea control, for example. If a destroyer or cruiser could pull beside a tender and be loaded with modules containing eight-inch guns and land-attack cruise missiles, when such prove to be necessary for the mission, or with antiair warfare or antisubmarine warfare systems for another mission, we would be able to solve many of the problems of force planning after we know what we are trying to do rather than, as now, when we necessarily don't understand what we're trying to do.

The electronics revolution should also make it possible to divorce sensors from launchers to a much greater degree than is now the case, adding further short-run flexibility to our ability to design forces.

For example, if a submarine or a surface ship were designed to be able to carry and launch vertically any of several types of missiles—antiair, conventional land-attack, nuclear land-attack, and so on—and data links existed to one or more types of aircraft or remotely-piloted vehicles (RPV's) carrying various sensors for targeting such weapons, we would not have to decide today whether we were designing forces for power projection or sea control. A destroyer launching conventional land-attack cruise missiles on data provided by, say, its own V/STOL aircraft or RPV's would be functioning as a tool of power projection. The same destroyer, launching a surface-to-air missile against an enemy aircraft detected by an Air Force AWACS aircraft would be functioning in a different role. Did we buy the destroyer for protection or antiair warfare? Who cares? The objective, after all, is to destroy the enemy, not to guess the scenario ahead of time. But systems analysis has led us to concentrate our force planning on a hopeless task—predicting future wars—rather than a useful one: designing forces to be relatively insensitive to the nature and location of future wars.

A second major problem which systems analysis has helped to create is to divert attention from the primary task—destroying the enemy—to secondary matters.

This is in part a problem of language. Recently-retired Vice Admiral James B. Stockdale, former naval aviator, POW, Medal of Honor winner, and man of letters, once wrote:

> War is a unique human enterprise that cannot be managed on the margin. Clausewitz wrote: "War is a special profession, however general its relation may be and even if all the male population of a country capable of bearing arms were able to practice it, war would still continue to be different and separate from any other activity which occupies the life of man." Contrast this with a paragraph from a study done in 1974 entitled *U.S. Tactical Air Power:* "Waging war is no different in principle from any other resource transformation process and should be just as eligible for the improvements in proficiency that have accrued elsewhere from technological substitution." This is simply not true. There are men who in battle can realize proficiency that would be labeled "impossible" by any systems analyst, men who can make $2+2=5$ time after time on the basis of their personal courage, leadership, strength, loyalty and comradeship. When the chips are down, and you're facing real uncertainty instead of that on a projected Profit and Loss sheet, you need something more than rationalist stuffing. The first step is to acknowledge that fighting men resent being manipulated by carrot and stick enticements; they find no solace in being part of some systematic resource transformation process when they're told to go in harm's way. In short, you can't program men to their deaths; they have to be led . . . .[2]

Admiral Stockdale was talking about fighting a war, not so much planning for one, but the point is rather similar. War is about destruction—ruthless, devastating, horrible destruction. We fail to understand it when we don't talk about it that way—concentrating on what we are trying to destroy—and when we discuss it instead entirely in the language of economics, management, and analysis.

Analysis has helped to build up, though, categories for planning naval and other military forces which do not really focus our

R. James Woolsey   61

attention on destruction of the enemy. Of the common categories frequently used to assess naval forces—power projection, sea control, presence, etc.—only power projection is a relatively precise concept, focused on the destruction of a certain specific type of enemy targets—targets ashore. The other concepts, "sea control" and "presence," are not really particularly useful categories for analyzing naval forces. Rather, they are sort of intellectual moraines—lines of stone that have been laid down by the national security debate glacier as it has moved through Washington, which appear to have some purpose but are in fact only random deposits showing the glacier's past progress.

"Sea control" was a concept created, originally, for a useful purpose. It was an intellectual device for calling attention to the Soviet submarine threat and for saying, indirectly, that the Navy should stop spending all of its resources on carrier aviation and power projection—that it should also begin to focus on dealing with the Soviet submarine and other threats on the high seas. But "sea control" is not sufficiently precise to provide any particularly useful guidance in designing naval forces. Even less so is the notion of "presence." As a description of what one does with what one has, "presence" may be a useful notion—deploying naval forces where the enemy can see them can have some foreign policy utility. But as a criterion for force design and force planning, "presence" is a very unsatisfactory notion. It all too readily leads analysts into the idea that a ship's fighting capability does not much matter, as long as it can be seen. One has great difficulty imagining any of the giants of naval history and strategy — Drake, Nelson, Mahan, Nimitz — requesting ships from their governments so that they might go and "be present" somewhere.

Systems analysis, in the third place, has concentrated attention on marginal change. In one sense, focusing on the margin merely means ignoring sunk costs—as such, it is the first rule of most successful businessmen and all successful poker players. But too often the analytical approach has led many to concentrate their time and effort on merely deciding how many fewer of these or how many more of those should be purchased each year. This produces a certain instinct for the capillaries—not the most useful instinct to cultivate if one is seeking to win real, rather than bureaucratic, battles. Contrast the marginal approach with the attitude toward warfare expressed by the ancient Chinese strategist and thinker Sun Tzu. Sun Tzu once wrote that there are four ways to defeat an enemy: the least desirable, because it is the most difficult, is to destroy the bodies of his people and soldiers; next, somewhat easier, is to destroy his logistics; third, easier still, is to destroy his alliances, but best and easiest of all is to destroy his strategy. One way to think of this latter course, destroying an enemy's strategy, is that one is seeking, figuratively, to destroy the mind of the enemy's commander. One looks, then, for ways to make a large part of the enemy's investment in forces worthless by ingenious combinations of technology and tactics—much the way Napoleon used light-weight, horse-drawn artillery as a major element in shattering eighteenth century concepts of warfare. Sun Tzu and Napoleon did not have an instinct for the capillaries.

Finally, analysis has helped to create a major problem in diverting attention from the terribly important role of *synthesis* in naval force planning.

Real warfare has quite frequently been far richer and more varied than the artificial analytical categories into which we attempt to stuff it. What type of operation, for example, was Guadalcanal? Was it projection? In a way—but the Marines initially walked ashore unopposed and much of the land fighting was their resistance to a *Japanese* effort at power projection. Was it sea control? Partly. There were several ship-to-ship naval engagements interspersed throughout the fighting ashore. By late October of 1942 four of the five carriers with which we had begun the war in the Pacific had either been sunk or seriously damaged and were out of action. Only *Enterprise* remained, and many of the carrier aviators flew against Japanese targets from Henderson Field on Guadalcanal itself. What would be the nature of a modern Guadalcanal-like battle in the North Atlantic in which NATO was attempting to defend Iceland from Soviet attack? How would forces designed for projection, anti-air warfare, antisubmarine warfare, and other tasks work?

The clearest answer is that they would work together or they would not work at all. And the force structure and force design implications of that need to work together are even more demanding today than they were at the time of Guadalcanal. When a Soviet submarine launches a cruise missile, an antisubmarine warfare problem becomes within a split second, an antiair warfare problem. Modern naval warfare may well be conducted simultaneously in four radically different environments—in the air, on the surface of the sea, beneath the sea, and on nearby land. And all of these mediums and the weapons and sensors designed to operate in them affect one another. Who is pulling all of this together—the systems analysts? Clearly at some stage analysis of some sort must be done. But if the analysts and the offices which they represent dominate the force structure and force design debate, there will be far too little emphasis on intelligence, command, control, communications, electronic warfare, and the many other aspects of modern naval warfare that are difficult to separate into discrete boxes—and far too little emphasis on designing forces to supplement one another in unexpected ways to deal with the exigencies of battle. Program-by-program analysis, as currently practiced, has had almost nothing to say about designing forces to work together in a modern Guadalcanal, so that platforms may be used in unexpected ways—for example, equipping attack submarines with conventional warhead cruise missiles so that they may augment carriers by attacking land targets in a projection role. Program-by-program analysis has had almost nothing to say about the importance of being able to substitute one sensor for another—for example, equipping platforms with infrared sensors to augment radar in case radars are jammed or otherwise made useless. Indeed, the mood of certainty that such analysis projects and the compartmentation it fosters indirectly discourage such flexibility.

These are not details. Thinking about these kinds of problems is a central and much neglected aspect of planning naval forces. But where is the *synthesis* being done to balance the analysis? Where is the centripetal, to balance the centrifugal, force?

In sum, systems analysis has made some contributions, but it has too often diverted attention from making naval forces more readily modernizable; emphasizing what needs to be destroyed; generating strategic breakthroughs; and synthesizing our ability to fight on, under, over, and near the sea.

Some of the individuals who have been its priests have made valuable contributions to the defense debate, but as an intellectual framework for planning naval forces for projection and other naval missions, it has overstayed its welcome.

NOTES

1. John Steinbruner, *Cybernetics and National Security* (Princeton, New Jersey: Princeton University Press, 1974).

2. Adm. James B. Stockdale, "Taking Stock," in *Naval War College Review*, February 1979, p. 2.

6

Historical Continuities in Naval Power Projection

Michael Vlahos

This assessment is an attempt to define a set of analytic indicators of the power potential and power projection of modern maritime states. Navies have always possessed the potential to influence the strategic balance on land. Through the centuries, navies have been utilized to achieve state objectives in conflicts against hostile states or state-coalitions.

Maritime power projection is the use of naval forces to achieve decision in war, and exert decisive suasion in crisis-peace. Military pressure, in peace and in war, can be as efficiently—and as decisively—applied by sea as by land. This use of force is not confined to combined operations—the empolyment of maritime means to move military forces to a crisis-area or to *schwerpunkt*. "Pure" maritime power projection, in contrast to the straightforward sea-movement of military force, is force focused directly or indirectly "against the shore" by the basic instrument of naval power, the armed ship (called, in its evolutionary heyday, the Capital Ship.)

This historical assessment concentrates on the power potential and power projection of maritime systems; specifically, the classic maritime system of the last century, the British Empire. For the United States, the British system has served both as the unstated structural and emotional model of a global maritime system. British strategic usage of the Capital Ship from 1815 to 1941 in power deployment and in power projection, in peace and in war, remains the basic historical image guiding contemporary American strategy at sea. For this reason this chapter is, in a sense, a "structural history"; it attempts to describe both continuity and change in the evolution of national naval strategies. It does not attempt to chronicle the acts of "decision-makers" and "managers," or to unravel the bureaucratic wrangling behind the act. It is, by contrast, a demonstration of strategic objectives, and a measurement of results, revealed through geographic force deployments: the "where" of ship deployment describes both the perceived operations limits and the goals of national naval strategy.

In the assessment that follows, through the salient crises faced by the British Empire—from the final exile of Bonaparte to the destruction of Force Z—an attempt has been made to "measure" maritime power potential and power projection. Naval readiness and deployment and surge performance, as well as the perceived strategic balance, are included. The Capital Ship, whether sailing liner, or ironclad, or dreadnought battleship, is the key indicator in this set of situation charts.

Both the United States and the Japanese Empire are offered, toward the end, for continuity and for control. Japan, the archetypal regional maritime system, is the control. The United States, evolving in this century from a hemispheric to a transoceanic maritime system, is the link of continuity.

How like Great Britain at the height of her power is America today? To confront clearly our own notions of the role of maritime power projection, we must face the real experience, and not merely the mythology, of our role-model.

METHOD OF ANALYSIS

Maritime power potential and power projection can be divided into four essential components: (1) Naval readiness; (2) The strategic balance at sea; (3) Naval spheres of control; (4) Strategic mobility. Each of these components is further distilled into a raw index of maritime power potential / projection, according to the readiness and usage of the Capital Ship Order of Battle (OB), at each crisis or contingency situation-chart:

1. Naval readiness:
   a. Active / reserve ratio
   b. Total effective Capital Ship strength
2. The strategic balance at sea:
   a. TE/OB vs. estimated effective OB, primary potential enemy
   b. TE/OB vs. estimated OB, potential enemy maritime coalition
3. Naval spheres of control:
   a. Normal spheres of operation / Capital Ship deployment
   b. Out-of-area deployment as a percentage of active battle-strength

      c. Out-of-area deployment as a percentage of TE/OB
    4. Strategic mobility:
      a. Strategic mobility / battleline crisis-surge performance

ACTIVE / RESERVE RATIO

This is a measure of those Capital Ships in current active commission deployed at sea, out of the raw total of all Capital Ships then officially on the Navy List. On a dynamic plane, the strength of the active percentage of raw OB is a measure of the perceived security needs of a maritime state-system in the period preceding a crisis. If you will, it is a sliding scale of the "peace."

TOTAL EFFECTIVE CAPITAL SHIP STRENGTH

This is the true measure of *deployable* maritime power: the actual potential of a state to project itself by sea. Not all of a maritime state's effective OB will ever likely be in full commission. The larger the effective Capital force, as a percentage of the total OB, the more modern is the Battle Fleet, the more sea-worthy, the more ready to fight: the more the common, published, and public Navy List represents the reality of naval power.

TE / OB vs. ESTIMATED EFFECTIVE OB, PRIMARY POTENTIAL ENEMY

The "primary potential enemy" is the foundation for all war-planning and all procurement. The most likely adversary at sea is the yardstick of relative Fleet strength. Once a competitive maritime state-system is determined to be a potential *combat* opponent, over a projected span of five to ten years, then the perceived strategic threat offered by this state, and its navy, can form the basis for long-range building programs. In a strict defensive posture, perceived Capital strength for combat operations may be acceptable on a 60–70 percent level. For offensive operations against another Fleet, superiority on a 150–200 percent level might be the acceptable minimum.

TE / OB vs. ESTIMATED OB, POTENTIAL ENEMY MARITIME COALITION

This is the "worst case," the nightmare scenario of national survival. In the assessment of national intelligence, it must be assumed that the readiness of the coalition Capital Ship OB will reflect a decision for war of the enemy's (s') choosing, and an estimated enemy OB must include *all* known effective units: manned, loaded, and ready for sea.

NORMAL SPHERES OF OPERATION / CAPITAL SHIP DEPLOYMENT

Peacetime operational deployments of a maritime system

reveal two internal strategic perceptions of the nature of their security system:

1. The demarcation of the maritime security perimeter: the staking-out of oceanic zones of control and influence.

2. The strategic pivot of system-security: the Capital Ship point-of-concentration, guarding at once the most vital and the weakest links.

OUT-OF-AREA DEPLOYMENT AS A PERCENTAGE OF
ACTIVE BATTLESTRENGTH

"Out-of-area" is defined here as a deployment zone outside the regional *oikoumene* of which the maritime state is a distinct geographical and cultural member. For Great Britain, out-of-area operations are a function of transoceanic movement of Capital Stength, outside of the littoral waters of the European region. In this context, the Mediterranean, the Baltic, and the Black Seas are considered a part of Great Britain's regional sea-system, not simply the English Channel and the North Sea. For the United States, out-of-area operations are defined as essentially exo-hemispheric, beyond the patrolling arc of Hawaii and Greenland. For Japan, out-of-area operations begin outside the waters of the island chains flung out by the Japanese homeland: the Bonins and the Ryukyus and the Kuriles. In this sense, the Yellow Sea, the East China Sea, and the Sea of Japan encompass a regional sea-system.

OUT-OF-AREA DEPLOYMENT AS A PERCENTAGE OF TE / OB

This is the strongest of a maritime system: the proportion of Capital Units deployed out-of-area, as a percentage of the *total* usable power projection assets at its disposal, underscores the geopolitical margins of national interest and national security. Peacetime out-of-area deployments traditionally describe the dynamics of diplomatic / military presence and patrol-suasion. Only a high, extended, and formalized ex-regional Capital Unit deployment, where out-of-area operations involve a significant proportion of the total effective OB, can describe a truly transregional security system.

STRATEGIC MOBILITY / BATTLELINE CRISIS-SURGE PERFORMANCE

Where out-of-area TE / OB percentages express the security margins of maritime systems, strategic mobility is the baseline of maritime power projection within the critical security sphere of the state system. Whether endo- or ex-regional, the ability of a navy to places its Capital Ship assets at the threatened and decisive point of crisis is the critical element in maritime systems-survival. As a proportion of the Total Effective Capital OB, that slice of the Battleline brought to bear to a crisis theater-of-operations is a real measure of power projection response time. This time-lapse gauges more than fleet efficiency; it is the translation of power potential into power projection.

ASSESSMENT

In attempting to assess the implications for naval power projection twenty situation charts are presented in Table 1. This commentary will focus on five essential factors shaping the employment of maritime power since 1815:

1. The constraints in Naval readiness
2. Capital point of concentration as strategic fulcrum
3. Objective definition through "worst case" coalition planning
4. Power projection through regional containment
5. Capital ship evolution and power projection redefinition

THE CONSTRAINTS IN NAVAL READINESS

Naval readiness is the baseline of maritime power projection. The active/reserve ratio, and the total effective Capital Order of Battle, are its two linear indicators.

A navy's active/reserve ratio is, typically, highest before a war, and lowest after its termination. Two classic examples of this correspondence are the British and American navies immediately after their most legendary, and most intense sea wars. In 1825, a single decade after Waterloo, the Royal Navy had but 6 percent of its battlefleet in full commission, and at sea. Supreme at sea, still basking in the yet unchallenged repose of complete victory, the fleet of his Britannic Majesty, in the aftermath of Napoleon, assumed a posture not unlike that of the United States Navy on the eve of Korea in 1950—in mothballs.

In a period of perceived prewar tension, by contrast, a battlefleet can, if resources are made available over time, be maintained in near-full commission. This condition of peak readiness is, inevitably, also a function of concentration in home ports. Extended sea deployments quickly degrade overall naval readiness. Not surprisingly, the British, American, and Japanese battlefleets, by concentrating in home waters in periods of tension, perceived as "prewar", and lasting no more than ten years, were able to reach rather remarkable readiness levels. Britain, from 1907 to 1914, was able to progress from 80 percent to 99 percent active, with *all* at sea on the brink of war in July 1914. The United States Navy, in the five years preceding Pearl Harbor, was able to keep its Capital Ship strength above the 90 percent mark, although the fleet was divided in the summer of 1941. The Imperial Fleet of Japan, in both 1904 and 1941, was at the peak, with 100 percent of its Capital OB ready for action.

Two structural constraints must be mentioned. One is the relative size of the Capital OB. The larger the battleline, the smaller is the chance of a 100 percent readiness level. The smaller the number of Capital Ships, the more significant is the operational loss of a single unit. The second constraining factor is time. Ships, even the big ships of the battleline, are prey both to normal materiel-depreciation and to encroaching systems-obsolescence. Reconstruction and modernization programs for strategic weapons systems cannot be postponed indefinitely, and typically require from two to four years in dockyard. This explains why both Japan and Italy could not contemplate war before 1940. The old big ships, as well as the new, were just not ready.

As an index of perceived national security / system needs, the active/reserve Capital Ship ratio is an historical mirror of grand strategy at sea. If Great Britain, in the doldrums of the 1820s, could maintain security with but 6 percent of its Capital strength active, then the gradual elevation of that percentage throughout the century marks a slow, but deteriorating maritime position. By the 1860s, the Royal Navy was holding at roughly a 33 percent active level. After the turn of the century, the German security threat created a perceived "prewar" takeoff, with the active percentage rising steadily to nearly 100 percent.

If the active/reserve ratio is a measure of the level of threat or of complacency in national security perception, then the TE/OB mark is the "bottom-line": the measure of naval, and by extension, national "health." Period by period, year by year, the total effective Capital Ship order-of-battle must form the actual basis for calculating the strategic balance at sea. The Navy List is the public image, for consumption and for media show. If the TE/OB is significantly smaller than the total "listed" Capital Ship strength, then a dangerous perceptual disjunction will exist between the trappings and the substance of national maritime power. Ideally, the TE/OB should never fall below 100 percent; any ineffective unit will become a materiel drain on a naval administration, and a perceptual drain on national command authorities. If the TE/OB falls below 70 percent, and this figure leaks out, then all the dynamics are in motion for a classic naval "panic." In three of the periods assessed here, when TE/British Capital Ship strength fell below the 70 percent level—1839, 1858, 1882—were years immediately preceding the major naval panics of the nineteenth century. The fourth period, at the turn-of-the-century, led to the flamboyant, but necessary, scrap-heap of "Jackie" Fisher, which pumped up the TE/OB from 50 percent in 1901 to 75 percent in 1905.

CAPITAL POINT OF CONCENTRATION AS STRATEGIC FULCRUM

That discrete area of Capital Ship concentration in time of peace, the commanding position wherein a navy compasses its strategic sea-assets to form a battlefleet, in its choice may unmask strategy. In motive, its reveals:

1. The most efficient sallying-point for a maritime system's "fire brigade"
2. That sea-space of highest vulnerability, facing the most likely threat, to maritime systems-security
3. The perceived sea-cockpit of national interest

Great Britain's capital point of concentration shifted from crisis to crisis. In the decade following the "Great War" against Napoleon, there was concentration, and no battlefleet. By the 1830s there was at least a battle squadron at sea, hovering near Portugal or on the Tagus. In the first Egyptian Crisis, the cockpit was the Eastern Mediterranean. The Crimean War created a bipolar, flanking concentration on the Russian Baltic and Black Sea littorals. In the second half of the nineteenth century, the Mediterranean held pride of place as the principal station of the British battlefleet, a station employing all of the most modern ironclads. Not until the genesis of the German threat, with a battlefleet nearly as close as DeRuyter's two-deckers of the 1660s, did British Home Waters become again the pivot-point of Capital Ship Concentration.

The British capital point of concentration was easily shifted from crisis to crisis within the European littoral sea-region. Only twice after 1815 did the Royal Navy concentrate a battle squadron outside of the European region: in the North American area, during our civil war, and in the China Seas, in the years immediately preceding the Russo–Japanese War. Even these deployments, although significant, represented but a small proportion of the Navy's TE/OB. British sea power, and its power projection, were essentially regional, much as was that of Japan and the United States before 1941.

OBJECTIVE DEFINITION THROUGH "WORST-CASE"
COALITION PLANNING

British maritime strategy was shaped by adversary-planning. Throughout the nineteenth century, planning focused on scenarios against the primary potential enemy at sea. France remained the emotional adversary of historical memory, alternating for brief periods with Russia. After the Second German Navy Bill, the Wilhelmine Reich quickly attracted the obsessive focus of strategic assessment.

At each crisis-point involving Capital Ship power projection, the Royal Navy could feel secure that it possessed a battlefleet at least the *equal* of its primary potential enemy. Only for a fleeting moment in the late 1850s, during the delicate technological displacement from sail to steam, did early French procurement give the Second Empire a temporary lead in TE/OB, quickly wiped out by a spate of mid-Victorian three-deckers.

The driving historical image in British adversary-planning was the coalition scenario of the wars of the French Revolution and Empire, and more dimly, of the war for America. In these bitter matches, Franco-Hispanic-Dutch squadrons threatened the physical security of the home-islands. The potential, however remote, of such a recrudescence haunted staff-planning in the nineteenth century, and all but destroyed it by the fourth decade of the twentieth century.

Two factors intervened throughout the nineteenth century to spare Britain the agony of a superior, combined enemy fleet in the Channel, à la 1780:

1. Potential maritime coalitions generally involved continental powers whose fleets were too widely separated by strategic geography to unite effectively without warning.
2. With two exceptions, potential coalitions were confined to the European littoral sea-system: a strategic region easily dominated by the Royal Navy, operating essentially on integrated internal sea-lines.

The two exceptions were in 1861 and 1901. Against American and Russian battle squadrons, British ex-regional Capital Ship deployments were made. These amounted to a significant proportion of the available, active Capital Ship strength: 45 percent in 1861, 25 percent in 1901. These squadron movements seriously depleted the Royal Navy in the European region. In 1861–64, in conjunction with major troop movements to Canada and the Caribbean, this deployment seriously limited diplomatic options during the Second Schleswig War. In 1901, the loss of available Capital Ship strength in the European theater, compared to a likely European fleet-coalition of France and Russia, essentially forced Britain to conclude its first fomal alliance since the Napoleonic period: a pact with the feisty junior fleet of Japan. Adversary-planning, like a mirror, reveals the features and the definition of maritime strategy.

POWER PROJECTION THROUGH REGIONAL CONTAINMENT

In the nineteenth and twentieth centuries, Great Britain was a regional, ecumenical power, tied both to European interests and politics and to the vagaries of the continental balance of power. British maritime strategy, was a function of regional responses to "local" adversaries within the geo-cultural community of which it was a member.

Almost as a strategic by-product, Great Britain was able to achieve imperial—and, by extension, world-wide—objectives through this regional containment of hostile, rival powers in the European *oikoumene*. Throughout the nineteenth, and the first four decades of the twentieth centuries, the "surge" capability of the British battlefield was constrained, not by lack of resources or of bases, but by an acute awareness of the strategic balance at sea *in Europe.*

Even so, regional containment provided Britain with world-wide benefits. Britain snared a global maritime empire through default—or, more precisely, through preemption—and not through deployment. *Never,* from 1815 to 1941, did the Royal Navy deploy more than 19 percent of its TE/OB outside of the traditional European operating area. Only twice, in 1861 and in 1901, did these out-of-area Capital Units steam as command squadrons. In late 1941, the Navy dispatched Force Z—17 percent of the remaining TE/OB—to Singapore. This was the first wartime deployment of British Capital Ships outside the European area since Nelson chased Villeneuve to the West Indies in 1805.

The United States Navy, by contrast, revealed from 1907 to 1914 a much higher surge-potential than the entire historical experience of the Royal Navy from 1815 to 1941. The World Cruise, and three tours of Northern Europe and the Mediterranean by the massed Atlantic Fleet, each involved more than 50 percent of the American TE/OB. This was a precedent placed by the United States Navy in peace, to be bettered only by Pacific performance in the Second World War, where more than twenty Capital Ships in company—carriers and fast battleships—steamed at will off the coasts of Japan.

The United States, in hemispheric detachment, was forced to uphold world-wide interests through a transoceanic projection of maritime power. From the early years of this century, a trans-Pacific offensive, involving the full TE/OB, became the "Basic War Plan—Orange." Britain, planning for local containment of European adversaries, never fully realized the structural basis of system-security: what the British preferred to call "Imperial Defense." The relative quiescence of American sea power throughout the nineteenth century shielded Britain from the recognition of a potential ex-regional maritime threat to system-security. Only during the American Civil War was the Royal Navy forced to draw down its regional Capital OB to reinforce "British North America." The linkage between ex-regional deployment and a loss of diplomatic suasion in the European Community was not recognized. In 1901, the linkage was rather more explicit. The stationing of a modest battle squadron in China forced Britain to choose between a Far Eastern, or a local, European containment of a potential Franco–Russian coalition. Alliance with Japan achieved both objectives.

The full implications of ex-regional maritime threats to the British sea-system were still not fully understood. Jellicoe's warning of 1919, and his recommendations for a permanent Capital Squadron deployment "East of Suez", were discarded with condescension.

Japan was the first real maritime threat to British system-security outside of the European region. Faced with an ironic reversal of the 1901 dilemma, Britain had essentially two strategic choices. A biregional battlefleet could be developed, with a "fast wing" of superior Capital Ships, capable of rapid deployment from European to Malayan crisis-area. The main fleet could then have maintained the established strategy of regional containment in European seas, with a detachable surge-force to serve as an ex-regional strategic deterrent. As an alternative, Britain could admit that maritime theater-supremacy was the limit of the British security-sphere; that the Royal Navy was, after all, the fleet of a powerful, but essentially regional, state.

The "Geddes Ax" and the Washington, Five-Power Pact robbed the Royal Navy of all chance to enforce the first choice. Historical mythology, and historical pride, would not permit the latter.

Over the course of a century and more of naval supremacy, Britain had created a set of precise images of the nature and of the origin of its globe-spanning empire. The most ingrained, and the most ineradicable, was the myth of the British Navy as a truly global force. In the mid-1930s, with resurgent German and Italian Fleets germinating, yet again, the potential for a hostile maritime coalition in the European sea-theater, the concept of "Main Fleet to Singapore" could not be discarded. Frantic attempts were made to appease the Germans and the Italians, to keep their new battleships on the sidelines if war were to flare in the Far East. There were other warning signs. The Royal Navy's most recent experience with major, extended ex-regional deployment—of *several* battle squadrons—was in 1780–1782. Admiralty staff planners confessed that

the odyssey to Singapore would consume at least *four months*.
"Main Fleet to Singapore" was a case of historical mythology
shaping reality in the pursuit of imperial strategy. Mythology won
out over experience. Today, in mocking testament to its failure, the
Prince of Wales and *Repulse* rest on the muddy floor of the South
China Sea. Thus, British ex-regional power projection, for a century
untried, remained unrealized.

CAPITAL SHIP EVOLUTION AND POWER PROJECTION REDEFINITION

The traditional usage of maritime power projection was
confined to the limit of classic Captial Ship firepower, in the form of
coastal interdiction. As blockade and, in special circumstances,
coastal bombardment, battleship power projection could, and did,
exert "strategic" suasion. In actions directed against the military
assets and national resources of a hostile state, the battleship could
be used as a strategic instrument in squadron concentration, and
often as a significant proportion of the Capital TE/OB. The
blockading of the French Atlantic battle squadrons at Brest, from
1803 to 1805, consumed an average of 62 percent of the Royal
Navy's dangerously stretched TE/OB. The bombardments of St.
Jean d'Arc, Sebastopol, Bomarsund, and Alexandria, and blizzard-
forcing of the Dardanelles in 1878, each employed *at least 50
percent* of the active, precrisis Capital OB. Fisher's blockade plans
against the Wilhelmine Reich in 1907, and the actual Dreadnought
noose drawn around the North Sea in 1914, demanded 84–100
percent not merely of the active OB, but of the TE/OB.

With the trasition of Capital Ship platform from battleship to
aircraft carrier during the Second World War, the same pattern of
Capital concentration was employed by the United States Navy in
power projection missions against the Japanese homeland. Unlike
the battleship, the aircraft carrier offered, in the immediate postwar
period, a weapons-technology of high development potential: the
manned aircraft. By 1950, the aircraft carrier was able to strike deep
within the geographic "heartland" of a hostile continental state. The
ability of carrier battle groups to influence ground operations on a
continental landmass was decisively proven during the Korean war.

This historical displacement of maritime power projection from
coastal to continental interdiction—in significant usage—has been
confined to the Carrier Task Force operations of the United States
Navy. The geostrategic position of the Western Hemisphere created
for the United States a kind of environmental determinism which
encouraged the development of a doctrine of transoceanic power
projection. After its Pacific victory, the American Navy recognized in the carrier task force the instrument, not only to exert,

but to maintain a global, maritime projection of power.

Unlike the perfect peripheral placement of the British Isles, situated so as to reach both flanks of the European littoral sea-system and close the world ocean to continental powers by drawing the noose of a regional sack, the United States was forced to bridge both oceanic margins. In order to contain the maritime assets of the contemporary potential enemy, the United States Navy must deploy its current Capital Ships—in multi-carrier battle-groups—along the sea-margins of Eurasia, several oceanic theaters removed from our own home waters.

Never has so much of a maritime state's Capital Ship assets been so routinely and consistently deployed out-of-area. Today, American ex-regional Capital Ship operations account for 39 percent of our active battlestrength, and nearly a third of our entire TE/OB. With 77 percent of our big ships in commission, we are operating our battlefleet at war-readiness levels, and the carriers— as recent breakdowns have signalled warnings again and again—are simply getting worn out.

CONCLUSION

The implications of this analysis are clear: the United States of America is the first global maritime system. By deployment, and through continuous operations, both in diplomatic and in combatant sea scapes, our navy has sustained a performance unequalled by historical myth or reality. By all of the key indicators of naval power projection, this nation not only routinely maintains a transoceanic system of maritime security. It has become quite clear that both this nation and the entire Western Alliance are dependent on global maritime security. Our clutch of carrier Capital Ships helps insure the survival of the West. The conclusion of this investigation, therefore, is also clear. Never has so vast a maritime system been so forcefully nor so consistently sustained. Yet never has such a system long endured with so few capital units in its defense.

TABLE 1.
STATE SYSTEM: British Empire

DATE: 1825–1829

POLITICAL / MILITARY CRISIS / CONTINGENCY:

Portuguese Succession /
Greek War of Independence

ACTIVE / RESERVE RATIO (% ACTIVE, IN COMMISSION, AND AT SEA):

6%   6 Active, 91 Reserve

TOTAL EFFECTIVE CAPITAL SHIP STRENGTH (FROM OB TOTAL ABOVE):

69%   67 Effective Capital Ships

TE / OB vs. ESTIMATED EFFECTIVE OB, PRIMARY POTENTIAL ENEMY:

139%   67 Britain / 48 France

TE / OB vs. ESTIMATED OB, POTENTIAL ENEMY MARITIME COALITION:

113%   67 Britain / 48 France, 11 United States = 59

NORMAL SPHERES OF OPERATION / CAPITAL SHIP DEPLOYMENT:

Mediterranean (1)   Halifax (1)   Lisbon (1)
Particular Service (1) South America (1)   Home Waters (1)

OUT-OF-AREA DEPLOYMENT AS A PERCENTAGE OF ACTIVE BATTLESTRENGTH:

33%

OUT-OF-AREA DEPLOYMENT AS A PERCENTAGE OF TE / OB:

4%

STRATEGIC MOBILITY / BATTLELINE CRISIS-SURGE PERFORMANCE:

(No signficant out-of-area surge during this period.)

STATE SYSTEM: British Empire

DATE: 1832–1836

POLITICAL / MILITARY CRISIS / CONTINGENCY:

Belgian War of Independence /
Carlist Uprising

ACTIVE / RESERVE RATIO (% ACTIVE, IN COMMISSION, AND AT SEA):

11%   9 Active, 74 Reserve

TOTAL EFFECTIVE CAPITAL SHIP STRENGTH (FROM OB TOTAL ABOVE):

70%   58 Effective Capital Ships

TE / OB vs. ESTIMATED EFFECTIVE OB, PRIMARY POTENTIAL ENEMY:

123%   58 Britain / 47 France

TE / OB vs. ESTIMATED OB, POTENTIAL ENEMY MARITIME COALITION:

56%　　58 Britain / 47 France, 45 Russia,
　　　　11 United States = 103

NORMAL SPHERES OF OPERATION / CAPITAL SHIP DEPLOYMENT:

Particular Service (4)　　East Indies (1)　　　　Lisbon (4)

OUT-OF-AREA DEPLOYMENT AS A PERCENTAGE OF
ACTIVE BATTLESTRENGTH:

11%

OUT-OF-AREA DEPLOYMENT AS A PERCENTAGE OF TE / OB:

1.7%

STRATEGIC MOBILITY / BATTLELINE CRISIS-SURGE PERFORMANCE:

(No significant out-of-area surge during this period.)

STATE SYSTEM:　British Empire

DATE:　1839–1842

POLITICAL / MILITARY CRISIS / CONTINGENCY:

Egyptian Crisis /
First China War

ACTIVE / RESERVE RATIO (% ACTIVE, IN COMMISSION, AND AT SEA):

24%　　21 Active, 66 Reserve

TOTAL EFFECTIVE CAPITAL SHIP STRENGTH (FROM OB TOTAL
ABOVE):

57%　　50 Effective Capital Ships

TE / OB vs. ESTIMATED EFFECTIVE OB, PRIMARY POTENTIAL ENEMY:

106%　　50 Britain / 47 France

TE / OB vs. ESTIMATED OB, POTENTIAL ENEMY MARITIME COALITION:

49%　　50 Britain / 47 France, 45 Russia,
　　　　10 United States = 102

NORMAL SPHERES OF OPERATION / CAPITAL SHIP DEPLOYMENT:

Mediterranean (17)　　China (3)　　　　Jamaica (1)

OUT-OF-AREA DEPLOYMENT AS A PERCENTAGE OF ACTIVE
BATTLESTRENGTH:

19%

OUT-OF-AREA DEPLOYMENT AS A PERCENTAGE OF TE / OB:

8%

STRATEGIC MOBILITY / BATTLELINE CRISIS-SURGE PERFORMANCE:

1840:   Mediterranean (10)→(17)
        121% of Deployed, Pre-Crisis OB
        34% TE / OB

STATE SYSTEM: British Empire

DATE: 1853–1856

POLITICAL / MILITARY CRISIS / CONTINGENCY:

Crimean War

ACTIVE / RESERVE RATIO (% ACTIVE, IN COMMISSION, AND AT SEA):

20%   14 Active, 57 Reserve

TOTAL EFFECTIVE CAPITAL SHIP STRENGTH (FROM OB TOTAL ABOVE):

73%   52 Effective Capital Ships

TE / OB vs. ESTIMATED EFFECTIVE OB, PRIMARY POTENTIAL ENEMY:

123%   52 British / 42 Russian

TE / OB vs. ESTIMATED OB, POTENTIAL ENEMY MARITIME COALITION:

Same

NORMAL SPHERES OF OPERATION / CAPITAL SHIP DEPLOYMENT:

Home Waters (6)   North America (1)   Mediterranean (7)

OUT-OF-AREA DEPLOYMENT AS A PERCENTAGE OF ACTIVE BATTLESTRENGTH:

7%

OUT-OF-AREA DEPLOYMENT AS A PERCENTAGE OF TE / OB:

2%

STRATEGIC MOBILITY / BATTLELINE CRISIS-SURGE PERFORMANCE:

1854:   Home→Baltic (16)   1854:   192% of Deployed,
        Mediterranean→   Pre-Crisis OB 52% TE / OB
        Black Sea (11)

1855:   Home→Baltic (16)   1855:   214% of Deployed,
        Mediterranean→   Pre-Crisis OB 158% TE / OB
        Black Sea (14)

STATE SYSTEM: British Empire

DATE: 1858–1859

POLITICAL / MILITARY CRISIS / CONTINGENCY:

Franco–Austrian War /
Indian Mutiny

ACTIVE / RESERVE RATIO (% ACTIVE, IN COMMISSION, AND AT SEA):

24%   16 Active, 52 Reserve

TOTAL EFFECTIVE CAPITAL SHIP STRENGTH (FROM OB TOTAL ABOVE):

49%   35 Effective Capital Ships

TE / OB vs. ESTIMATED EFFECTIVE OB, PRIMARY POTENTIAL ENEMY:

106%–92% 35 Britain / 33–38 France

TE / OB vs. ESTIMATED OB, POTENTIAL ENEMY MARITIME COALITION:

69%   35 Britain / 38 France, 7 Russian, 6 United
           States = 51

NORMAL SPHERES OF OPERATION / CAPITAL SHIP DEPLOYMENT:

Channel (5)   East Indies (1)   Mediterranean (4)

OUT-OF-AREA DEPLOYMENT AS A PERCENTAGE OF ACTIVE BATTLESTRENGTH:

6%

OUT-OF-AREA DEPLOYMENT AS A PERCENTAGE OF TE / OB:

3%

STRATEGIC MOBILITY / BATTLELINE CRISIS-SURGE PERFORMANCE:

1859:   Mediterranean (4) →(10)
        63% of Deployed, Pre-Crisis OB
        29% TE / OB

STATE SYSTEM: British Empire

DATE: 1861–1865

POLITICAL / MILITARY CRISIS / CONTINGENCY:

American Civil War /
Second Schleswig War

ACTIVE / RESERVE RATIO (% ACTIVE, IN COMMISSION, AND AT SEA):

33%   22 Active, 44 Reserve

TOTAL EFFECTIVE CAPITAL SHIP STRENGTH (FROM OB TOTAL ABOVE):

100%   66 Effective Capital Ships

TE / OB vs. ESTIMATED EFFECTIVE OB, PRIMARY POTENTIAL ENEMY:

1320%–215% 1861: 66 Britain / 5 United States
           1864: 69 Britain / 32 United States

TE / OB vs. ESTIMATED OB, POTENTIAL ENEMY MARITIME COALITION:

550%   1861: 66 Britain / 5 United States, 7 Russian

NORMAL SPHERES OF OPERATION / CAPITAL SHIP DEPLOYMENT:

North America (2)   Mediterranean (14)   Channel (6)

OUT-OF-AREA DEPLOYMENT AS A PERCENTAGE OF ACTIVE
BATTLESTRENGTH:

9% → 45%

OUT-OF-AREA DEPLOYMENT AS A PERCENTAGE OF TE / OB:

3% → 15%

STRATEGIC MOBILITY / BATTLELINE CRISIS-SURGE PERFORMANCE:

1861:   Mediterranean → North America (5)
        Channel → North America (3)
        45% of Deployed, Pre-Crisis OB
        15% TE / OB

STATE SYSTEM: British Empire

DATE: 1870–1871

POLITICAL / MILITARY CRISIS / CONTINGENCY:

Franco-Prussian War /
Alabama Claims

ACTIVE / RESERVE RATIO (% ACTIVE, IN COMMISSION, AND AT SEA):

43%   15 Active, 20 Reserve

TOTAL EFFECTIVE CAPITAL SHIP STRENGTH (FROM OB TOTAL
ABOVE):

100%   35 Effective Capital Ships

TW / OB vs. ESTIMATED EFFECTIVE OB, PRIMARY POTENTIAL ENEMY:

120%   35 Britain / 29 France

TE / OB vs. ESTIMATED OB, POTENTIAL ENEMY MARITIME COALITION:

66%   France / United States
74%   Russia / United States
       35 Britain / 29 France, 23 Russia,
       24 United States = 76

NORMAL SPHERES OF OPERATION / CAPITAL SHIP DEPLOYMENT:

Channel (6)   East Indies (2)
Mediterranean (5)   North America (2)

OUT-OF-AREA DEPLOYMENT AS A PERCENTAGE OF ACTIVE
BATTLESTRENGTH:

27%

OUT-OF-AREA DEPLOYMENT AS A PERCENTAGE OF TE / OB:

11%

STRATEGIC MOBILITY / BATTLELINE CRISIS-SURGE PERFORMANCE:

(No significant out-of-area surge during this period.)

STATE SYSTEM: British Empire

DATE: 1878

POLITICAL / MILITARY CRISIS / CONTINGENCY:

Russo–Turkish War

ACTIVE / RESERVE RATIO (% ACTIVE, IN COMMISSION, AND AT SEA):

32 %   19 Active, 40 Reserve

TOTAL EFFECTIVE CAPITAL SHIP STRENGTH (FROM OB TOTAL
ABOVE):

71%   42 Effective Capital Ships

TE / OB vs. ESTIMATED EFFECTIVE OB, PRIMARY POTENTIAL ENEMY:

221%   42 Britain / 19 Russia

TE / OB vs. ESTIMATED OB, POTENTIAL ENEMY MARITIME COALITION:

69%   42 Britain / 19 Russia, 42 France = 61

NORMAL SPHERES OF OPERATION / CAPITAL SHIP DEPLOYMENT:

Channel (3)   East Indies & Pacific (3)
Mediterranean (10)   North America (1)

OUT-OF-AREA DEPLOYMENT AS A PERCENTAGE OF ACTIVE
BATTLESTRENGTH:

24%

OUT-OF-AREA DEPLOYMENT AS A PERCENTAGE OF TE / OB:

10%

STRATEGIC MOBILITY / BATTLELINE CRISIS-SURGE PERFORMANCE:

Channel (3) → Baltic (12)
Mediterranean (10) → Dardanelles (9)
     100% of Deployed, Pre-Crisis OB
     50% TE / OB

STATE SYSTEM: British Empire

DATE: 1882–1885

POLITICAL / MILITARY CRISIS / CONTINGENCY:

Occupation of Egypt /
Russian War Scare

ACTIVE / RESERVE RATIO (% ACTIVE, IN COMMISSION, AND AT SEA):

33%   18 Active, 36 Reserve

TOTAL EFFECTIVE CAPITAL SHIP STRENGTH (FROM OB TOTAL ABOVE):

46%   25 Effective Capital Ships

TE / OB vs. ESTIMATED EFFECTIVE OB, PRIMARY POTENTIAL ENEMY:

112%   25–28 Britain / 22–25 France

TE / OB vs. ESTIMATED OB, POTENTIAL ENEMY MARITIME COALITION:

69–62% 25–28 Britain / 22–25 France, 14–20 Russia = 36–45

NORMAL SPHERES OF OPERATION / CAPITAL SHIP DEPLOYMENT:

Mediterranean (9)   China and Pacific (3)
Channel (5)   North America (1)

OUT-OF-AREA DEPLOYMENT AS A PERCENTAGE OF ACTIVE BATTLESTRENGTH:

22%

OUT-OF-AREA DEPLOYMENT AS A PERCENTAGE OF TE / OB:

16%

STRATEGIC MOBILITY / BATTLELINE CRISIS-SURGE PERFORMANCE:

1882: Mediterranean (9) → (14)   77% of Deployed, Pre-Crisis OB
                                   56% TE / OB
1885: Channel (5) → Baltic (13)   72% of Deployed, Pre-Crisis OB
                                   46% TE / OB

STATE SYSTEM: British Empire

DATE: 1893–1896

POLITICAL / MILITARY CRISIS / CONTINGENCY:

Franco–Russian Alliance /
Venezuelan Dispute /
Kruger Telegram

ACTIVE / RESERVE RATIO (% ACTIVE, IN COMMISSION, AND AT SEA):

30%   19 Active, 44 Reserve

TOTAL EFFECTIVE CAPITAL SHIP STRENGTH (FROM OB TOTAL ABOVE):

73%   46 Effective Capital Ships

TE / OB vs. ESTIMATED EFFECTIVE OB, PRIMARY POTENTIAL ENEMY:

121%   46 Britain / 38 France

TE / OB vs. ESTIMATED OB, POTENTIAL ENEMY MARITIME COALITION:

81%   46 Britain / 38 France, 19 Russia = 57

NORMAL SPHERES OF OPERATION / CAPITAL SHIP DEPLOYMENT:

Channel (5)   China–Pacific (2)   Mediterranean (12)

OUT-OF-AREA DEPLOYMENT AS A PERCENTAGE OF ACTIVE BATTLESTRENGTH:

11%

OUT-OF-AREA DEPLOYMENT AS A PERCENTAGE OF TE / OB:

4%

STRATEGIC MOBILITY / BATTLELINE CRISIS-SURGE PERFORMANCE:

2 BB's January–October, 1896, "Flying Squadron":
10% of Deployed, Pre-Crisis OB

STATE SYSTEM: British Empire

DATE: 1898–1901

POLITICAL / MILITARY CRISIS / CONTINGENCY:

Fashoda Crisis /
Anglo–Boer War

ACTIVE / RESERVE RATIO (% ACTIVE, IN COMMISSION, AND AT SEA):

34%   22 Active, 40 Reserve

TOTAL EFFECTIVE CAPITAL SHIP STRENGTH (FROM OB TOTAL ABOVE):

50%   32 Effective Capital Ships

TE / OB vs. ESTIMATED EFFECTIVE OB, PRIMARY POTENTIAL ENEMY:

145%   32 Britain / 22 France

TE / OB vs. ESTIMATED OB, POTENTIAL ENEMY MARITIME COALITION:

89%   France / Russia
64%   France / Russia / Germany
          32 Britain / 22 France, 18 Russia, 10 Germany

NORMAL SPHERES OF OPERATION / CAPITAL SHIP DEPLOYMENT:

Channel (8)   China (3)
Mediterranean (10)   North America (1)

OUT-OF-AREA DEPLOYMENT AS A PERCENTAGE OF ACTIVE BATTLESTRENGTH:

17% → 25%

OUT-OF-AREA DEPLOYMENT AS A PERCENTAGE OF TE / OB:

13% → 19%

STRATEGIC MOBILITY / BATTLELINE CRISIS-SURGE PERFORMANCE:

1901:   China (3) → (6)
         25% of Deployed, Pre-Crisis OB
         19% TE / OB

STATE SYSTEM: British Empire

DATE: 1904–1905

POLITICAL / MILITARY CRISIS / CONTINGENCY:

Russo–Japanese War

ACTIVE / RESERVE RATIO (% ACTIVE, IN COMMISSION, AND AT SEA):

56%   34 Active, 27 Reserve

TOTAL EFFECTIVE CAPITAL SHIP STRENGTH (FROM OB TOTAL ABOVE):

75%   46 Effective Capital Ships

TE / OB vs. ESTIMATED EFFECTIVE OB, PRIMARY POTENTIAL ENEMY:

216%   46 Britain, 6 Japan / 24 Russia

TE / OB vs. ESTIMATED OB, POTENTIAL ENEMY MARITIME COALITION:

68%   46 Britain, 6 Japan / 24 Russia, 20 Germany,
         30 France = 52/74

NORMAL SPHERES OF OPERATION / CAPITAL SHIP DEPLOYMENT:

Home Waters (17)   China (5)   Mediterranean (12)

OUT-OF-AREA DEPLOYMENT AS A PERCENTAGE OF ACTIVE BATTLESTRENGTH:

15%

OUT-OF-AREA DEPLOYMENT AS A PERCENTAGE OF TE / OB:

11%

STRATEGIC MOBILITY / BATTLELINE CRISIS-SURGE PERFORMANCE:

(No significant out-of-area surge during this period.)

STATE SYSTEM: British Empire

DATE: 1906–1907

POLITICAL / MILITARY CRISIS / CONTINGENCY:

First Moroccan Crisis (Panther)

ACTIVE / RESERVE RATIO (% ACTIVE, IN COMMISSION, AND AT SEA):

80%   45 Active, 11 Reserve

TOTAL EFFECTIVE CAPITAL SHIP STRENGTH (FROM OB TOTAL ABOVE):

100%   56 Effective Capital Ships

TE / OB vs. ESTIMATED EFFECTIVE OB, PRIMARY POTENTIAL ENEMY:

254%   56 Britain / 22 Germany

TE / OB vs. ESTIMATED OB, POTENTIAL ENEMY MARITIME COALITION:

Same

NORMAL SPHERES OF OPERATION / CAPITAL SHIP DEPLOYMENT:

Home Waters (39)   Mediterranean (6)

OUT-OF-AREA DEPLOYMENT AS A PERCENTAGE OF ACTIVE BATTLESTRENGTH:

0%

OUT-OF-AREA DEPLOYMENT AS A PERCENTAGE OF TE / OB:

0%

STRATEGIC MOBILITY / BATTLELINE CRISIS-SURGE PERFORMANCE:

1907 (Plan):   Baltic (45)   100% TE / OB
                North Sea (11)

STATE SYSTEM: British Empire

DATE: 1914

POLITICAL / MILITARY CRISIS / CONTINGENCY:

Balkan Crisis (Sarajevo)

ACTIVE / RESERVE RATIO (% ACTIVE, IN COMMISSION, AND AT SEA):

99%   76 Active, 1 Reserve

TOTAL EFFECTIVE CAPITAL SHIP STRENGTH (FROM OB TOTAL ABOVE):

100%   77 Effective Capital Ships

TE / OB vs. ESTIMATED EFFECTIVE OB, PRIMARY POTENTIAL ENEMY:

192%   77 Britain / 40 Germany

TE / OB vs. ESTIMATED OB, POTENTIAL ENEMY MARITIME COALITION:

Same

NORMAL SPHERES OF OPERATION / CAPITAL SHIP DEPLOYMENT:

Home Waters (65)   China (4)   Mediterranean (7)

OUT-OF-AREA DEPLOYMENT AS A PERCENTAGE OF ACTIVE
BATTLESTRENGTH:

5%

OUT-OF-AREA DEPLOYMENT AS A PERCENTAGE OF TE / OB:

5%

STRATEGIC MOBILITY / BATTLELINE CRISIS-SURGE PERFORMANCE:

Channel / North Sea, July–August 1914 (65)
    84% TE / OB

STATE SYSTEM: British Empire

DATE: 1935–1936

POLITICAL / MILITARY CRISIS / CONTINGENCY:

Abyssinian Crisis

ACTIVE / RESERVE RATIO (% ACTIVE, IN COMMISSION, AND AT SEA):

53%   8 Active, 7 Reserve

TOTAL EFFECTIVE CAPITAL SHIP STRENGTH (FROM OB TOTAL
ABOVE):

100%   15 Effective Capital Ships

TE / OB vs. ESTIMATED EFFECTIVE OB, PRIMARY POTENTIAL ENEMY:

167%   15 Britain / 9 Japan

TE / OB vs. ESTIMATED OB, POTENTIAL ENEMY MARITIME COALITION:

136%   15 Britain / 9 Japan, 2 Italy = 11

NORMAL SPHERES OF OPERATION / CAPITAL SHIP DEPLOYMENT:

Atlantic (4)   Mediterranean (4)

OUT-OF-AREA DEPLOYMENT AS A PERCENTAGE OF ACTIVE
BATTLESTRENGTH:

0%

OUT-OF-AREA DEPLOYMENT AS A PERCENTAGE OF TE / OB:

0%

STRATEGIC MOBILITY / BATTLELINE CRISIS-SURGE PERFORMANCE:

(15) → Singapore   100% TE / OB (In four months)
(Admiralty Ops. Plan)

STATE SYSTEM: Japanese Empire

DATE: 1904–1905

POLITICAL / MILITARY CRISIS / CONTINGENCY:

Russian War

ACTIVE / RESERVE RATIO (% ACTIVE, IN COMMISSION, AND AT SEA):

100%   12 Active (Includes armored cruisers)

TOTAL EFFECTIVE CAPITAL SHIP STRENGTH (FROM OB TOTAL ABOVE):

100%   12 Effective Capital Ships

TE / OB vs. ESTIMATED EFFECTIVE OB, PRIMARY POTENTIAL ENEMY (IN THEATER):

109%   12 Japan / 11 Russia (Includes armored cruisers)

TE / OB vs. ESTIMATED OB, POTENTIAL ENEMY TOTAL AVAILABLE OB:

48%   12 Japan / 25 Russia

NORMAL SPHERES OF OPERATION / CAPITAL SHIP DEPLOYMENT:

Home Waters (12)

OUT-OF-AREA DEPLOYMENT AS A PERCENTAGE OF ACTIVE BATTLESTRENGTH:

0%

OUT-OF-AREA DEPLOYMENT AS A PERCENTAGE OF TE / OB:

0%

STRATEGIC MOBILITY / BATTLELINE CRISIS-SURGE PERFORMANCE:

(Japanese battleline in home waters throughout period.)

STATE SYSTEM: Japanese Empire

DATE: 1941

POLITICAL / MILITARY CRISIS / CONTINGENCY:

Indo–China Occupation
(South) to Decision for War

ACTIVE / RESERVE RATIO (% ACTIVE, IN COMMISSION, AND AT SEA):

100%   10 Active

TOTAL EFFECTIVE CAPITAL SHIP STRENGTH (FROM OB TOTAL ABOVE):

100%   10 Effective Capital Ships

TE / OB vs. ESTIMATED EFFECTIVE OB, POTENTIAL IN-THEATER MARITIME COALITION:

91%   10 Japan / 9 United States, 2 Britain = 11

TE / OB vs. TOTAL POTENTIAL MARITIME COALITION OB:

35%   10 Japan / 17 United States, 12 Britain = 29

NORMAL SPHERES OF OPERATION / CAPITAL SHIP DEPLOYMENT:

North Western Pacific (10)

OUT-OF-AREA DEPLOYMENT AS A PERCENTAGE OF ACTIVE BATTLESTRENGTH:

0%

OUT-OF-AREA DEPLOYMENT AS A PERCENTAGE OF TE / OB:

0%

STRATEGIC MOBILITY / BATTLELINE CRISIS-SURGE PERFORMANCE:

Potential to South / Central Pacific (10)
100% TE / OB

STATE SYSTEM: United States of America

DATE: 1907–1909

POLITICAL / MILITARY CRISIS / CONTINGENCY:

Fleet World Cruise

ACTIVE / RESERVE RATIO (% ACTIVE, IN COMMISSION, AND AT SEA):

74%   23 Active, 8 Reserve

TOTAL EFFECTIVE CAPITAL SHIP STRENGTH (FROM OB TOTAL ABOVE):

100%   31 Effective Capital Ships

TE / OB vs. ESTIMATED EFFECTIVE OB, PRIMARY POTENTIAL ENEMY:

110%   31 United States / 28 Germany

TE / OB vs. ESTIMATED OB, POTENTIAL ENEMY MARITIME COALITION:

72%   31 United States / 28 Germany

NORMAL SPHERES OF OPERATION / CAPITAL SHIP DEPLOYMENT:

Atlantic (19)   China (4)

OUT-OF-AREA DEPLOYMENT AS A PERCENTAGE OF ACTIVE BATTLESTRENGTH:

17%

OUT-OF-AREA DEPLOYMENT AS A PERCENTAGE OF TE / OB:

12%

STRATEGIC MOBILITY / BATTLELINE CRISIS-SURGE PERFORMANCE:

World Cruise (16)
 69% of Deployed, Pre-Contingency OB
 51% TE / OB

STATE SYSTEM: United States of America

DATE: 1937

POLITICAL / MILITARY CRISIS / CONTINGENCY:

Sino–Japanese War

ACTIVE / RESERVE RATIO (% ACTIVE, IN COMMISSION, AND AT SEA):

93%   14 Active, 1 Reserve

TOTAL EFFECTIVE CAPITAL SHIP STRENGTH (FROM OB TOTAL ABOVE):

100%   15 Effective Capital Ships

TE / OB vs. ESTIMATED EFFECTIVE OB, PRIMARY POTENTIAL ENEMY:

166%   15 United States / 9 Japan

TE / OB vs. ESTIMATED OB, POTENTIAL ENEMY MARITIME COALITION:

Same

NORMAL SPHERES OF OPERATION / CAPITAL SHIP DEPLOYMENT:

Pacific Coast (15)

OUT-OF-AREA DEPLOYMENT AS A PERCENTAGE OF ACTIVE BATTLESTRENGTH:

0%

OUT-OF-AREA DEPLOYMENT AS A PERCENTAGE OF TE / OB:

0%

STRATEGIC MOBILITY / BATTLELINE CRISIS-SURGE PERFORMANCE:

(Orange Plan) Trans-Pacific (15)   100% TE / OB

STATE SYSTEM: United States of America

DATE: 1980

POLITICAL / MILITARY CRISIS / CONTINGENCY:

Iran Crisis

ACTIVE / RESERVE RATIO (% ACTIVE, IN COMMISSION, AND AT SEA):

77%   13 Active, 4 Reserve

TOTAL EFFECTIVE CAPITAL SHIP STRENGTH (FROM OB TOTAL ABOVE):

100%   17 Effective Capital Ships

TE / OB vs. ESTIMATED EFFECTIVE OB, PRIMARY POTENTIAL ENEMY:

(Soviet fleets confined to regional sea control, sub-capital OB.)

TE / OB vs. ESTIMATED OB, POTENTIAL ENEMY MARITIME COALITION:

(Soviet fleet without significant maritime partner.)

NORMAL SPHERES OF OPERATION / CAPITAL SHIP DEPLOYMENT:

Pacific (6)   Atlantic (7)

OUT-OF-AREA DEPLOYMENT AS A PERCENTAGE OF ACTIVE BATTLESTRENGTH:

39%

OUT-OF-AREA DEPLOYMENT AS A PERCENTAGE OF TE / OB:

29%

STRATEGIC MOBILITY / BATTLELINE CRISIS-SURGE PERFORMANCE:

Iran, March 1980 (3)
    23% Deployed, Pre-Crisis OB
    18% TE / OB

Selected Bibliography

Bartlett, C. J. *Great Britain and Sea Power, 1815 – 1853.* Oxford, 1963.
Baxter, James Phinney. *The Introduction of the Ironclad Warship.* Cambridge, Mass.: Harvard University Press, 1933.
Bennett, Frank M. *The Steam Navy of the United States.* Pittsburgh: Warren and Company, 1896.
Bourne, Kenneth. "British Preparations for War with the North, 1861 – 1862." *The English Historical Review,* Vol. 76 (October, 1961), 600–632.
Brassey, Sir Thomas. *The British Navy: Its Strength, Resources, and Administration.* 5 vols. London: Longmans, Green, 1882–83.
Brassy (Lord), *The Naval Annual,* 1886 Portsmouth: J. Griffin and Co., 1886 (annual editions through 1979).
Clowes, Sir William Laird. *The Royal Navy: A History from the Earliest Times to the Death of Queen Victoria.* 7 vols. London: Sampson, Low, Marston and Company, 1901–1903.
Colburn's United Service Magazine and Naval and Military Journal. London: Hurst and Blackett, 1829–1874 (After 1874, became *Journal of the Royal United Service Institution*).
Cooper, James Fenimore. *History of the Navy of the United States.* Philadelphia: Lee and Blanchard, 1840.

Crawfurd, H. W. *The Russian Fleet in the Baltic in 1836.* London: James Ridgway, 1837.

Department of Intelligence, Naval War College. *Fleet Organization: Blue, Red, and Orange.* (Confidential). June, 1936. Record Group II, Naval War College Naval Historical Collection.

Dewar, Captain A. C. and Bonner Smith, D., eds. *Russian War, 1854, Baltic and Black Sea: Official Correspondence.* The Navy Records Society, London, 1943.

Douglas, General Sir Howard. *On Naval Warfare with Steam.* London: John Murray, 1860.

Eardly-Wilmot, Captain S. *The Life of Vice-Admiral Edmund, Lord Lyons.* London: 1898.

Earp, G. Butler. *The History of the Baltic Campaign of 1854, from Documents Furnished by Vice-Admiral Sir Charles Napier, K.C.B.* London: Richard Bentley, 1857.

Great Britain, Admiralty. *The Navy List.* London: John Murray. Published quarterly.

Great Britain. Parliament. Parliamentary Papers:
  Accounts and Papers.
    1889 (90), I.
  Accounts and Papers.
    1893 (465), XIV.
  Estimate for Naval and Military Operations, 1861, XXXIX. 377.
  Fleets. Great Britain and Foreign Countries.
    127–205 1912, ses. 1911 (142).
    527–619 1913, ses. 1912 (127).
    113–188 1914, ses. 1913 (537).
  By Command:
    Germany. Naval Law Amendment Bill. ses. 1912.
    (CD. 6117), 668–75.
  Naval Expenditure (Principal Naval Powers).
    267–75 1910, ses. 1909 (251).
    265–73 1911, ses. 1910 (269).
    300–308 1912, ses. 1911 (265).
    274–81 1913, ses. 1912–13 (300).
    470–19 1914, ses. 1913 (274).
  Ships in Commission: 1842.   1842 (425) XXVII. 345.

Halpern, Paul G. *The Mediterranean Naval Situation, 1908 – 1914.* Cambridge, Mass.: Harvard University Press, 1971.

Hamilton, C. I. "Sir James Graham, The Baltic Campaign and War Planning at the Admiralty in 1854." *The Historical Journal,* Vol. 19, I (1976), 89–112.

Hamilton, Sir Richard Vesey, ed. "Letters and Papers of Admiral of the Fleet, Sir Thomas Byam Martin." *The Navy Records Society,* London: 1901.

Herwig, Holger H. *The Politics of Frustration: The United States In German Naval Planning, 1889 – 1941.* Boston: Little, Brown, 1976.

Jane, Fred T. *All the World's Fighting Ships: 1898.* London: Sampson, Low, Marston and Co., 1898 (annual editions through 1979).

Jane, Fred T. *The Imperial Russian Navy, Its Past, Present, and Future.* London: W. Thacker, 1904.

Kemp, Lieut.-Commander P. K., ed. "The Papers of Admiral Sir John Fisher." Vol. II, *The Navy Records Society.* London: Spottiswoode,

Ballantyne and Company, 1964.

King, J. W. *The Warships and Navies of the World.* Boston: A. Williams, 1880.

Lockroy, Edouard. *La Defense Navale.* Paris: Berger–Levrault, 1900.

Marder, Arthur J. *The Anatomy of British Sea Power, A History of British Naval Policy in the Pre-Dreadnought Era, 1880 – 1905.* New York: Alfred A. Knopf, 1940.

Marder, Arthur J. *Fear God and Dread Nought: The Correspondence of Admiral of the Fleet, Lord Fisher of Kilverstone.* 3 vols. Cambridge, Mass.: Harvard University Press, 1952–9.

Ministere de la Marine et des Colonies. *Repertoire Alphabetique de Batimens de Tout Rang, Armes pour l'Etat de 1800 a 1828 compris, et des officiers, qui dans cet Intervalle, en ont eu le commandement.* Paris: De l'Imprimperie Royale, Juillet, 1830.

	Repertoire Alphabetique. . .
1ᵉʳ supplement	du 1ᵉʳ Janvier 1829 au
	31 Decembre 1834
	Repertoire Alphabetique. . .
2ᵉ supplement	du 1ᵉʳ Janvier 1835 au
	31 Decembre 1844
	Repertoire Alphabetique. . .
Paris: Imprimerie	du 1ᵉʳ Janvier 1845 au
Imperiale, 1859	31 Decembre 1854
	Repertoire Alphabetique. . .
Paris: Imprimerie	du 1ᵉʳ Janvier 1855 au
Nationale, 1868	31 December 1868
	Repertoire Alphabetique. . .
	du 1ᵉʳ Janvier 1896 au
	31 December 1878

Napier, Vice-Admiral Sir Charles. *The War in Syria.* London, 1842.

Parkes, Dr. Oscar. *British Battleships, Warrior to Vanguard: A History of Design, Construction, and Armament.* London: Seeley Service, 1956.

Patterson, A. Temple, ed. "The Jellicoe Papers." Vol. I, *The Navy Records Society.* London: Spottiswoode, Ballantyne and Company, 1966.

Ronciere, Chevalier de la, and Clerc–Rampal, G. *Histoire de la Marine Francaise.* Paris: Librarie Larousse, 1934.

Ropp, Theodore. "The Development of a Modern Navy: French Naval Policy 1871 – 1904." Ph.D dissertation, Harvard, 1937.

Tronde, O. *Batailles Navales de la France.* Paris: Challamel Aine, 1868.

Tupinier, Le Baron Jean Marguerite. *Rapport sur le Materiel de la Marine.* Paris: Imprimerie Royale, 1837.

United States Navy Department. *The Navy List.* Washington, D.C.: Government Printing Office.

Very, Lieutenant Edward W. *Navies of the World.* New York: John Wiley, 1880.

Woods, Robert H. and Rush, Lieut.–Commander Richard, U.S.N. *Official Records of the Union and Confederate Navies during the War of the Rebellion.* Washington: Government Printing Office, 1894.

7

The Employment of Sea Power as an Instrument of National Policy

Alvin J. Cottrell

A prognosis of the world situation for the 1980s and 1990s argues in general for the future primacy of maritime policy in U.S. strategy. In particular, it demands that U.S. maritime strategy be prepared to meet successfully an era of continued competition with the Soviet Union beyond the traditional locales of superpower competition. In all of the regions surrounding the Eurasian heartland, Moscow and Washington will compete to ensure that inevitable political changes have a positive impact on their national interests. From the American perspective, that change must represent an orderly, stable transition that does not jeopardize America's increasingly fragile structure of interests and those of its allies, not only in terms of political interests, but commercial, financial and security interests as well. A national strategy aimed at such stable, orderly change will require effective policy instruments that can be flexibly applied in regions where the issues of power and political influence still hang in the balance. If these instruments are not deployed successfully to prevent instability, then they must be capable of responding to restore order.

Central to such a strategy is the ability to project naval force overseas and maintain sea control, not only enroute but in the area that is the ultimate objective. These two concepts of naval strategy are inextricably related, although the debate over U.S. naval requirements has tended to treat them as though they were discrete and, more important, mutually exclusive. Quite clearly, to be able to project force, one must maintain control of the sea. Less obvious but equally true is the fact that to maintain adequate control of the sea, the United States must be capable of projecting sufficient force at great distances from its shores. As suggested, a fundamental problem in fashioning and deploying U.S. naval forces stems from the foregoing categorization of missions and functions. Deriving from budgetary imperatives rather than from those of strategic planning, the terms "power projection" and "sea control" have been seized upon by those unfamiliar with the basic principles of sea power. By assuming a "shooting war" in Europe, for example, such people now postulate that carrier battle groups—which they also see as useful only in high-threat area operations against the USSR—would play no significant role and, therefore, need not be retained as a component of American sea power.

This point of approach is flawed in several respects. To begin with, it ignores that fact that most warships have multimission capabilties. That is to say, they can be used in power projection, sea control, presence, or other modes. Further, it overlooks the fact that the two categories themselves are not neatly separable. To project sea power into a given region, one must ensure local control of the sea along the naval forces' transit route as well as in the operating areas in the vicinity of the objective. Similarly, in protecting transit routes for either naval or merchant convoys, it may be necessary to project carrier and amphibious landing power to seize or neutralize discrete positions ashore from which an adversary could continuously menace those convoys.

Finally, the foregoing categorizations have made difficult a proper understanding of naval presence, its utility and employment. It is the successful naval presence—encompassing the potential to control discrete portions of the oceans as well as to project power ashore, along with the clearly perceived national will to employ force, if necessary—which accomplishes the prime missions of presence forces: deterrence and promotion of regional stability.

Increasingly, the military balance at sea is influenced by developments on land. A capability to project power which would then have an impact on land-based developments could well make the difference in the American ability to maintain sea control in a region such as the Persian Gulf or Western Pacific.

Successful application of sea power is a function of the numbers of naval ships, their weapons capabilities and—often overlooked—overseas installations. These factors are closely interrelated, and the problems now facing U.S. planners reflect this interrelationship. U.S. naval capabilities have declined in numbers by half. From a decade ago, the number of U.S. naval forces has been reduced from about a thousand to under five hundred. Given such reductions, the United States will be increasingly less able to project naval forces without access to an overseas basing infrastructure in or near the littoral of Eurasia. The United States could have handled naval force projection from bases or facilities on the coasts of the United

States with recourse to only a few scattered facilites abroad, if it had built a navy suited to this purpose. Such a force does not now exist, however, it is highly unlikely to emerge in the future, given the current limitations in the naval shipbuilding budget. Thus, the once high hopes of projecting force from an afloat navy, without a significant basing structure, have been dashed.

Greatly complicating the problem is the fact that from 1953 to the present the United States has seen its overseas air and naval bases decline from 150 to about 30. It now enjoys roughly equal access to overseas naval and air facilities as the Soviet Union. The loss of such facilities has seriously detracted from the credibility of projected U.S. military power as it is perceived by regional actors. Nowhere is this more obvious than in the current U.S. effort to deploy a permanent maritime force to the Indian Ocean – Persian Gulf region.

When Britain withdrew its forces from the Indian Ocean region on November 30, 1971, the United States decided not to replace British forces with a large scale permanent naval force of its own. Instead, the United States sought to rely on its small Middle East Force (one command ship and two destroyers) located at the former British facilities on Bahrain. The result was that the United States occasionally exercised forces in the Indian Ocean which would then disappear. Even the hard-fought successful battle to establish a modest naval and air facility at Diego Garcia failed to be perceived by regional states as evidence of real U.S. staying power because of the heavy Congressional opposition. The perception of a United States militarily committed in the region was further weakened by President Carter's efforts to negotiate a naval arms limitation agreement with the Soviet Union. The agreement would have placed restrictions on naval operations and the naval presence of both superpowers.

The consequence of these trends is that some kind of U.S. presence has become necessary, not only for logistical reasons, but also for purposes of American credibility. Without the requisite numbers of naval units, that presence must take the form of facilities. And without a basing structure, the regional leaders will view present U.S. efforts to deploy forces in the area as a transitory move to be ended if and when the crisis simmers down. The crisis in the Indian Ocean – Persian Gulf area, which began with the fall of the monarchy in Iran and has been further heightened by the Soviet invasion of Afghanistan, demonstrates the failure on the part of the American leadership to understand the use of naval power for undergirding stability.

In international crisis management, as in local law enforcement, clearly anticipatory and preventive capabilities are more effective than a hurried and haphazard assembly of *reactive* forces once the crisis is raging and threatening to spread beyond control. There is little doubt that the current U.S. naval projection in the Indian Ocean is hastily reactive, haphazard in terms of form and function and questionable in durability. The United States has deployed more than twenty vessels to the area and is attempting by such a massive reaction to do what it was unwilling to try only two years ago when a relatively modest carrier task force of eight to ten ships might have helped to discourage regional antimonarchists from moving to upset the established order in Iran. Moreover, the naval force has been drawn in part from U.S. carrier forces in the Seventh Fleet in the Pacific, where they have helped to carry out the important function of supporting East Asian stability. These forces cannot be spared for very long without provoking doubts among regional leaders in Japan, Korea, the Philippines, and even the People's Republic of China, about their own futures and orientations against the background of ever more tenuous linkages to U.S. military power.

Similarly, subsequent withdrawal of a nuclear-powered carrier battle group from the Mediterranean for use in the Indian Ocean produced similar political effects in NATO Europe. Parenthetically, one is compelled to note that the nonstop, high-speed transit of this battle group from the Eastern Mediterranean to the Indian Ocean offered dramatic testimony to the value of nuclear propulsion insofar as warships are concerned. The problem, of course, is one of securing access to vital oil resources, which, in turn, involves at least four security problems: (1) security and stability of the oil-producing countries; (2) security of oil fields and facilities; (3) security of the oil loading terminals in the Gulf, and (4) protection of the sea lines of communication (SLOCs).

The goal in deploying naval forces should in the first instance be the security of the oil-producing countries. If not enough effort is applied to this concern, the United States will increasingly face the possiblity of dealing with all the remaining aspects of oil security indicated above, including SLOC protection. Deterioration of the geopolitical situation in this area will exacerbate potential dangers to the security of oil wells, terminals, and SLOCs because, as the political situation changes, the chances increase that hostile forces along the sea lane littoral will be able to harass the sea lines. Also, if access to oil is lost, protection of the SLOC obviously becomes unnecessary.

This is now the potential situation along the 600 miles of the Iranian shore of the Gulf from Abadan to Hormuz. The problem of SLOC protection has changed radically in the Persian Gulf since

February of 1979 when the Shah was overthrown. Before that time, Iraq was the only potentially hostile regime on the waterway— although occupying barely enough of the littoral to qualify as a Persian Gulf state. The demise of the Iranian military forces, however, catapulted Iraq into the position of the principal military state of the Gulf, giving her much more influence on the littoral than it would have had if Iran's miltary posture had not been so drastically weakened.

The focal point of U.S. interests in the Gulf is obviously Saudi Arabia because of Western dependence on its present oil production and its great oil reserves. The destruction of the Iranian kingship has increased the threat to the Saudi monarchy. The question now is whether a permanent large-scale U.S. naval presence can deflect, dilute, or deter the threat to the Saudi kingship. Indeed, the shift in the geopolitical environment of the region has been such that a permanent U.S. naval presence will be required simply to offset the political–military changes on the area's land mass. While Saudi Arabia is the key to U.S. interests, there can be no doubt that its protection is impossible, except in a broader regional security context. In other words, the credibility of the United States as far as the Saudis are concerned must be established on the basis of a regional military presence and not just as a function of bilateral relationships with Saudi Arabia.

One can only wonder at the reasoning of those in the Carter Administration who opposed modest efforts to undergird stability in the region prior to the Iranian revolution. This position was ostensibly based in part on the assumption that naval forces do not have much political influence. The administration later seemed to believe, however, that a double dose of the remedy is a cure to check the threat of spreading instability. Surely, if naval forces can help to impede the spread of political instability—as the Carter Administration indicated by its massive deployment of naval forces to the Indian Ocean—these same forces could have been credited with some political value in maintaining stability.

In an effort to find a solution to its predicament, the Carter Administration was engaged in a quest for the requisite means to sustain a military role in the region. Its efforts included not only the current deployment of U.S. naval vessels and Marine components into the area, but longer-range plans for the creation of a Rapid Deployment Force, and a much-publicized search for the needed structure of air and naval facilities to support meaningful and flexible U.S. military capabilities in future contingencies. Such efforts have been enhanced with even greater effort in the Reagan Administration.

The nagging question that still hovers over these efforts—which are being conducted in an atmosphere of near-frenzy—is whether they are not already too late. The question is a function of the rapid tide of events and forces in the region, as well as of the delicate interaction of factors that go into the acquisition of military facilities abroad and/or rights of access to such facilities.

As far as timing is concerned, the current U.S. naval deployment in the region already underscores the penalties of past U.S. procrastination. The large-scale escalation of the U.S. naval presence in the Indian Ocean was made necessary by the failure to stage a more measured build-up of U.S. power in the years following Great Britain's withdrawal from the region—particularly after 1973, when the expansion of Soviet power, the tremors of regional instability, and the threats to vital U.S. interests were clear handwriting on the wall. The naval force now in the area is necessary to demonstrate U.S. resolve, to effect a certain shift in the "geopolitical momentum" in the region, and to serve as a backdrop for U.S. efforts to carve out an infrastructure of supporting bases and facilities.

Looking to the future and the broader aggregation of naval and air power—and supporting facilities on land—that the United States will have to assemble in the Indian Ocean, it may not at some future point in time need as large a force as twenty-five vessels if the situation stabilizes. Something along the lines of the Sixth Fleet Task Force 60.2, which operates in the Mediterranean with one carrier and nine other vessels, may well prove adequate to the mission. But such a force will be adequate only if the United States is able to reverse the unfavorable perceptions of its military credibility which were spawned by the Carter Administration, and there are signs that these perceptions are being slowly reversed at the present time, especially in Saudi Arabia, which is a country crucially important to the success of our policy. One must recognize, however, that the U.S. commitment to the Persian Gulf—Indian Ocean area will be less acceptable to the leaders of littoral states if it appears to be only a token force and does not represent any substantial change in the U.S. commitment. The United States should do something to escalate unambiguously its symbolic commitment. This could be done perhaps be designating the force as a "fleet," even if only half as many ships are deployed as are normally committed to a fleet. At the present time, however, this force of thirty ships, including two aircraft carriers, is indeed a fleet by any standards.

The credibility of the naval presence in the Indian Ocean would be enhanced significantly if the United States were to "homeport" an aircraft carrier in one of the littoral states. The homeport is needed primarily for reasons of logistics and recreation, but at the same time will serve as evidence that the United States is firmly committed to retaining a presence in the area. U.S. facilities in other countries rather automatically commit the United States to countering external aggression against host countries. However, there is the argument that such facilities often invite aggression by local dissidents. Regional perceptions are a function not simply of the negative fear of aggression, or of positive belief in the ability and willingness of the "guest power" not only to help against aggression, but also of the need to give that measure of extra protection against the heightened risks incurred by the base privileges themselves. The host country, in short, looks for what may be called a "preferred" insurance policy. In examining possibilities for homeports, while quite distant, Prime Minister Malcolm Fraser has offered Cockburn Sound on Australia's West Coast near the city of Perth.

In the first five years after World War II, the United States, relying on the significant infrastructure it had begun to build during the war, encountered no great obstacles to overseas base rights and military access privileges. Within the past decade, the global logistics structure of the United States has dangerously crumbled because of the shifting balance of power and the diminished credibility of the United States as an agent of local security insurance. Consequently, the problems for the United States are global in scope. In the Indian Ocean–Persian Gulf region, where it is seeking not only the retention of old military footholds but the creation of new ones, the United States faces an uphill climb. The political terrain has not been altogether favorable, given the new regional fears that have been spawned by revolutionary turmoil and Soviet expansion, but the United States under the Carter Administration and continuing under President Reagan has been successful in negotiating some of the needed infrastructure.

The Pacific basin will continue to place great demands on the U.S. naval capability. The United States must continue through the projection of maritime forces to undergird political security in the Pacific, but this mission is jeopardized by demands elsewhere and insufficient naval capabilities to meet those needs. For example, as already noted, the American naval presence in the Pacific is now being weakened by the sudden need to divert ships, particularly carriers, from the Pacific to counter politcal instability and conflict in the northwestern Indian Ocean. Furthermore, under the so-called swing strategy Pacific naval forces are to be swung to the North Atlantic in case of a NATO war on the assumption that a NATO war will be confined to the North Atlantic region. Such an assumption is questionable at best and foolhardy at worst. The United States must realize now that a NATO war will be global in scope, and that the Soviets will have to be confronted on a worldwide basis. A NATO war will have to be dealt with, for the most part, by the forces already deployed. Estimates are that it would require forty days to swing carriers from the Pacific around South America—they could not transit the Panama Canal. If, as some contend, a NATO Central Front war is not likely to last that long, carriers so diverted would contribute nothing in either theater.

It is reasonable to argue that only by putting substantial pressure on the Soviet Union in the Pacific theater could initial conventional NATO force deficiencies in Central Europe be compensated for until those forces were resupplied. The pressure that could be applied initially by the Alliance is largely confined to naval, marine, and air power. To be effective in pinning down equivalent Soviet manpower, however, pressure would have to be applied in the form of substantial land forces that, realistically, could only be supplied on a timely basis by the People's Republic of China (PRC) along the Sino–Soviet border.

The need to apply pressure on the Soviet Union in the Pacific theater requires the United States to break away from its so-called swing strategy. Pressure in the Pacific might require the United States either to attempt to contain the Soviets in their key Pacific bases—i.e., Vladivostok and Petropavlovsk—or to attack these bases at the outset. The destruction of these major Soviet bases would insure U.S. control of Pacific SLOCs. The strategy of maintaining pressure on the Soviets in the Pacific involves maintaining sufficient naval power there to provide for an offensive capability against Soviet military bases in the area. That kind of capability, however, would also provide psychological support for Japan and, particularly, other territories within easy range of Soviet naval and air power.

The long Sino–Soviet estrangement is currently responsible for pinning down almost one fourth of Moscow's total military capabilities. It has prompted the observation in some quarters that the PRC can be considered an honorary member of the NATO Alliance in that it contributes as much to the defense of NATO's Central Front by diverting Soviet forces as any other member of the Alliance, except the Federal Republic of Germany and the United States.

It is the PRC's contribution to NATO that in some measure makes possible the declared change of U.S. strategy from what was called a "two and a half" war strategy to one now labeled a "one and a half" war strategy. In essence, the "one and a half" war strategy envisages the United States fighting a major war in the east or the west, but not both simultaneously. Without a very strong U.S. naval presence in the Pacific, however, the PRC's willingness to accept the risks of confrontation with the Soviet Union would be diminished.

The presence of sizeable U.S. naval forces in the Pacific could encourage the Chinese to confront the Soviets along their borders and perhaps deter a NATO war, or, failing that, prevent the Soviets from applying their full capabilities to a war in the North Atlantic area. In any case, the Soviets would have to assess the PRC's probable actions before considering an attack on Europe. Chinese resolve might also depend on whether the PRC could expect to be resupplied by U.S. maritime forces.

One must assume that the Chinese are as concerned as our Pacific allies about U.S. talk of defending Western Europe at the expense of the Pacific powers. Acceptance of such a policy—even if only for strategic logistic planning purposes—could set in motion diplomatic moves by potential friends or allies that could more than compensate the Soviets for any force the Alliance could bring to bear along the Central Front. For example, it might propel the Chinese to consider some form of Soviet-PRC rapprochement. Japan and other U.S. allies might seek other forms of accommodation with Moscow, especially in light of Moscow's growing military capabilities in the region.

For example, the Soviets now boast their first carrier in the Pacific. Although it is no match for the large-deck carriers of the American navy, it nonetheless has the capacity to take tactical aviation to sea in the form of the new *Forger* V/STOL aircraft. The deployment of this carrier and four accompanying warships from European Russia to Soviet Far Eastern naval bases was completed in the summer of 1979. As this force passed up the East Asian coast, it was monitored by the Japanese and Chinese alike.

It is often argued in NATO circles, especially by the European members, that the North Atlantic area must be given priority. This is true only insofar as NATO forces *per se* are concerned. It is not necessarily true for national forces not committed to NATO, particularly those of the United States deployed in Asian waters. It can be argued that the NATO commitment is almost equally fulfilled by maintaining a high level maritime fighting capability in the Western Pacific or the Indian Ocean. NATO forces on Europe's Central Front have been numerically inferior to the Warsaw Pact forces since the inception of the treaty. If redressing this conventional imbalance in Central Europe is not to be achieved in theater—and this seems to be the case—then the regional inferiority of NATO forces must be offset by confronting the Warsaw Pact, and especially the Soviets, with a global strategy. If a concentration of

Warsaw Pact forces is allowed and if they are permitted to choose the regional conflict venue, they will surely gain a decisive advantage. Soviet chances of emerging victorious from a global conflict are much less certain.

It is vital, therefore, for the United States to maintain not only its naval forces in the Pacific, but also its present security arrangements with Japan and the Philippines. It also suggests that to consider the withdrawal of U.S. troops from Korea would be a mistake. To tamper with any part of these arrangements could lead to an adverse security perception on the part of American friends and allies, and damage the possibility of a global option as part of a broadened defense concept for NATO. The tendency to compartmentalize U.S. policy in the Pacific by treating western Pacific problems as country problems, rather than as matters of global strategy, could be disastrous to NATO as well as to the stability of Asia.

Most powerful states have feared the possibility of fighting two wars on two fronts. Germany has been in this position twice in this century, although between August 1939 and June 1941 in World War II Hitler sought to neutralize the eastern front with the Molotov–Ribbentrop Pact, so that it could engage the West. In the postwar world, Soviet–Warsaw Pact forces replaced Germany as the potential antagonist in Europe. Now it is the Soviets who must be concerned about a two-front war against its force in Europe and the Pacific, including the PRC, which will have at least naval and air support from the United States. If the United States decides to relieve them of this strategic dilemma as it plans the defense of the NATO region, it will be removing one of the greatest obstacles to their potential success.

The swing strategy, which made sense in earlier times when the United States Navy had over twenty-four carriers, has little to commend it today when U.S. forces include only twelve carrier groups or half that number. Moving these forces to the Atlantic would concede the Pacific to the Soviets and strengthen their ability to concentrate on the North Atlantic region. We should remember, too, that none of these carriers could transit the Panama Canal and would have to go around South America. If the war's duration were less than forty days, as many analysts believe, these ships would not arrive in time to participate. At the same time, their redeployment would have weakened the security situation for the West throughout the Pacific and Indian Oceans. In short, despite objections to dropping this swing strategy, it can be credibly argued that NATO defense is as crucially related to U.S. maritime policy decisions in the Pacific and Indian Oceans as it is to plans for fighting on the

Central Front and its flanks in the north and south of Europe.

Of vital importance to the United States in implementing a Pacific strategy will be continued access to its present basing facilities—primarily those in Japan, the Philippines, and to a lesser extent, Guam. Of all these facilities, the United States would be most severely limited in adequately projecting force if it were to lose access to the Philippines. It is probably the single most important basing facility the United States has anywhere in the world, especially the Subic Bay naval base. The United States only a year ago emerged relatively unscathed in negotiations with the Philippines over continued access to Subic Bay and Clark Air Force base, but the problem will come up again and there is no substitute for this naval facility in projecting adequate force into that region.

What satisfactory options are available to the United States if it loses access to the Philippine facilities? Clearly, withdrawal to the Marianas or Guam is a poor alternative at best and should be considered only as a last resort. It is often overlooked by proponents of falling back to the Marianas or Guam that it would add significantly to the transit time to the South China Sea and much greater time to the Indian Ocean. For example, locating in Guam would add three days to the journey to Diego Garcia. Subic Bay's natural assets—a well-protected harbor in a tropical climate with a depth in excess of forty-five feet—have made it a coveted prize of major naval powers ever since the Spanish government began constructing a naval facility there in the late nineteenth century.

Guam, in comparison, has a very modest harbor which cannot accommodate warships larger than a cruiser and not even all cruisers could anchor there. Aircraft carriers, which require very large turning radii and draw about thirty-seven feet of water, cannot use Apra Harbor. For this purpose, it would be necessary to consider other areas in the U.S. Trust Territories in the Pacific Islands, such as Malakal Harbor, or Babelthuap in the Palau Islands. These areas are still further removed than Subic Bay from the Indian Ocean / Persian Gulf or the South China Sea. Palau and the Marianas—given the distances involved—are located in a disadvantageous position for support or projection of naval power into the Indian Ocean or the South China Sea.

Such a move would be disastrous given the delicate political— military balance in the Pacific, which rests so heavily on regional perceptions of the credibility of U.S. military capabilities in the area. At the other end of the spectrum, the United States could remold its armed forces in order to make them more self-sufficient and independent of overseas basing structures. This, however, would take a major commitment of resources to acquisition of expanded force levels and the development of new defense technologies—a commitment which domestic attitudes within the United States appear to preclude, at least in the near future.

Decisions regarding the bases, especially those in the Philippines, must be considered against the broader framework of western Pacific regional security. The Philippines bases are intimately related to regional security perceptions, especially of Japan, China and South Korea. Any suggestion that the United States is preparing to withdraw from the Philippines, or even that we would accept conditions on our use of the bases which these nations could perceive as damaging to the U.S. ability to shoulder its security role in the Pacific, could have severe repercussions in these key Asian states. This would also be true if the U.S. Navy were to withdraw to Guam and the Marianas. The latter are too far away to support adequately a U.S. commitment in the Japan–Korea–Taiwan region, and too far away to counter the Soviets in the far north of the area. Furthermore, any reduction—naval or air—in U.S. access and use of the Philippine bases would be likely to make U.S. facilities in Japan more of a hostage to Japanese domestic politics, bringing about increased restrictions on the U.S. ability to operate militarily from Japan. Loss of the Philippine basing complex would encourage neutralism or a "go-it-alone" policy on the part of Japan which could have severe political–military ramifications among Japan's neighbors. Important activities, such as U.S. air surveillance from Japan, the use of Japanese ports by U.S. nuclear submarines, and the homeporting of a U.S. aircraft carrier in Japan, could be terminated. If so, the United States would no longer be able to maintain a one-for-one deployment in the region rather than the traditional three-to-one deployment, i.e., three carriers for each one deployed—one on station, one ready for deployment, and one in reserve. These bases enable the U.S. Navy to advance the operations of the Seventh Fleet by several thousand miles.

There is the additional question of whether a clear modification in U.S. operational access to the Philippine bases would be misinterpreted by North Korea, and enhance the possibility of their attacking South Korea. When complete, American ground force withdrawals—now being held in abeyance—will substantially reduce the credibility of the U.S. deterrent to a North Korean attack. Any perceived deterioration in the U.S. ability to counterattack from key U.S. bases in the area will most likely contribute to a further weakening of U.S. military credibility in the region and could encourage adventurism on the part of North Korea.

Even though the naval facilities are more vital to U.S. projection strategy and military effectiveness in the area, it is likely that the elimination of the U.S. facility at Clark Air Base would be perceived by local states as a significant degradation of the U.S. military commitment. Thus, it would seem prudent not to make any separation in the treatment of Subic Bay and Clark Air Base with respect to relocation. Any diminution in U.S. use of facilities jn the Philippines which made such a selective change in our posture there would be almost certainly perceived as a sign of retrenchment on the part of the United States.

Whatever is done by way of seeking alternatives—and this may possibly be necessary (e.g., relocating to Guam and the Marianas)—to the present U.S. military position in the Philippines would have to be done with extreme care and tact. A convincing argument can be made that, given the present political and military fragility of the Pacific environment, the timing is wrong for any change. Even open suggestions of change in the U.S. military posture would suggest a further retrenchment or lessening of commitment on the part of the United States.

Finally, the United States must think of restructuring its projection strategy to meet the demands of the new global multipolarity. The sizing, composition, and deployment of U.S. naval forces still tend to reflect the World War II balance of political and military power. Many demands on naval forces will arise in areas where the major powers are not directly involved and may be handled by something less than an attack aircraft carrier. For example, in responding to requirements from the government of Kenya in 1976, we dispatched an amphibious carrier with Harrier V/STOL aircraft at Kenya's request to participate in its national independence day celebration. It symbolized to real or potential enemies of the regime at home and in the region that the United States would answer Kenya's call for such support. Kenya has since responded affirmatively to our request for enhanced use of naval and air bases on its soil during the 1979–80 crisis period in the Indian Ocean. Even where there is a need for carrier deployments, however, these should be changed to meet new priorities if possible, without undercutting projection to other areas, such as has been the case in 1979 of withdrawals from the Pacific in order to meet the demands of large scale deployment in the Indian Ocean.

In sum, for purposes of future employment of sea power, the sizing, composition and disposition of U.S. forces should tend to reflect the new global multipolarity. We must have a power projection capability that suits the new shifting world political–military environment, rather than reflecting old habits. Such a line of argument suggests several general conclusions.

First, the United States must seek to prevent or inhibit those

geopolitical shifts on land that are inimical to its maritime—
especially naval—interests. In the Indian Ocean, for example, the
United States still has friends; but only through an active foreign
policy which bolsters those friends and gives them confidence in our
military credibility will the United States be able to retain what
remaining influence it now enjoys in the region. If it fails to do this,
the role of U.S. naval operations in the region will be greatly
diminished.

Second, the United States must realize that to prevent such
shifts effectively, it must utilize instruments on both land and sea.
This realization suggests the need for an infrastructure to support
both land and maritime operations. Infrastructure in this context
means basing facilities. The United States must reverse the present
trends that find its overseas basing structure diminishing while that
of the Soviet Union is increasing.

Finally, the maintenance of stability must be a prime objective
of U.S. foreign policy; and the maintenance of stability requires the
projection of military forces to support diplomatic and economic
initiatives. The projection of naval forces, and particularly superpower naval forces, is necessary to insure equipoise in the forward
littoral regions of the world.

Problems of crisis proportion resulting from a destabilized
situation are always extremely difficult to deal with once instability
develops. Hence, the primary objective of U.S. miltary policy and
strategy must be one of, in the first instance, maintaining and
enhancing political stability, and secondly, that of dealing with the
results of destabilization. Naval forces are the service which is best
suited to this preventive role.

8

The Rapid Deployment Force: U. S. Power Projection and the Persian Gulf

Jeffrey Record

Deterring overt Soviet aggression in the Persian Gulf region and preserving uninterrupted access to Persian Gulf oil are the two principal rationales underlying the Rapid Deployment Force (RDF), formed by the Carter Administration in the wake of the Soviet invasion of Afghanistan in December 1979.

The Reagan Administration has endorsed the RDF and has provided strong budgetary support for almost all of the Carter Administration's RDF-related procurement and research and development programs. To date, however, the present administration has been no more successful than its predecessor in overcoming the three major obstacles confronting the effective application of U.S. military power in the logistically remote Persian Gulf. Those obstacles are: insufficient force, insufficient strategic mobility, and the lack of politically secure military access ashore.

Although the Department of Defense is aware of these problems, few military men or force planners seem to have fully grasped their profound operational and logistical implications. An intervention force has been created that is critically dependent on the presumed goodwill of unstable potential host regimes in the region, whose interest in the Gulf are far from indentical to ours. No attempt, such as expanding force levels, has been made to resolve the dilemma inherent in the Carter Doctrine's imposition of a major new strategic commitment upon forces already severely taxed by pre-Afghanistan obligations. And although a number of desirable new strategic mobility initiatives are now underway, they will not bear meaningful fruit for at least half a decade.

A REVEALING WAR GAME

Evidence of this strategic incomprehension was abundant in a war game conducted in the summer of 1980 by the U.S. Readiness Command, which until mid-1981 was the parent military authority of the RDF. The war game, known as Gallant Knight and conducted largely on computers, postulated a successful U.S. defense of Iran against a full-scale Soviet invasion.

The prospect of a Soviet invasion of Iran has been publicly raised by former Joint Chiefs of Staff Chairman General David C. Jones, and the RDF contingency planners are considering it seriously. The character and planned capabilities of the RDF seem increasingly oriented around a U.S. defense of Iran, on the dubious assumption that an American intervention force capable of defending Iranian oil fields from direct Soviet aggression would be more than able to defeat what are perceived to be "less demanding," non-Soviet threats to Persian Gulf oil. Testifying before a Senate Armed Services Subcommittee shortly after President Reagan's inauguration, Jones stated that the twenty-six Soviet divisions deployed opposite Iran were being rapidly upgraded, and warned of a possible Soviet thrust into that country, still at war with neighboring Iraq. Gallant Knight proposed the commitment of some 325,000 U.S. troops to Iran and the Arabian peninsula in an attempt to block a Soviet invasion through the Transcaucasus. The war game sought to preserve Iran's oil rich Khuzistan province by halting Soviet forces in the rugged terrain of the Zagroz Mountains.

Leaving aside the question of whether the Congress, the nation, or any administration would be willing to shed American blood on behalf of a rabidly anti-American government whose most significant foreign policy act to date has been the taking and torturing of U.S. diplomatic personnel, it is not at all obvious that Iran is militarily defensible against a Soviet attack, at least by the United States.

Strategically, the commitment of substantial U.S. forces to Iran would automatically endanger the defense of Western Europe. Most of the ground combat and tactical air force units earmarked for the rapid deployment mission are also assigned to the no less critical mission of reinforcing NATO.

No military force can be in two places at the same time, and it is difficult to envisage any major shooting war between the United States and the Soviet Union being confined to Iran or the Gulf alone. As noted by Senator William Cohen, chairman of the Senate Armed Services Subcommittee on Sea Power and Force Projection, "In all probability such a conflict would spill over into at least the European theater, raising the grim prospect of a war on two independent fronts against an adversary possessing superior forces on both, and enjoying the advantage of interior lines of communication."[1]

However, even if the United States were not faced with insufficient forces, the U.S. defense of Iran currently postulated by Pentagon force planners seems less the product of real world considerations than of the "world of Disneyland," as one member of the Joint Chiefs has privately remarked.[2]

Against the twenty-six Soviet divisions deployed opposite Iran, the United States cannot count a single ground combat unit stationed anywhere ashore in the greater Gulf region. To mount a defense of Iran, RDF ground and tactical air forces—almost all of which are based in the United States—would have to be flown or shipped to the Gulf. Unfortunately the United States today does not possess sufficient airlift and sealift capabilities to move these forces to the Gulf in time.

It is noteworthy that Gallant Knight was played with lift capabilities—including the controversial proposed CX air transport—not scheduled for service until the late 1980s, and that even with these projected additional capabilities it took some six months to deploy the necessary forces to the Gulf. One wonders what the Russians will be doing during those 180 days.

A defense of Iran also would require prehostilities access not only to Iran but also to the Arabian peninsula. Pentagon planners concede that no major U.S. fighting force in Iran could be logistically sustained without the creation of a support infrastructure on the peninsula. Access to air bases in Turkey is also considered essential for the purpose of mounting an air interdiction campaign against Soviet forces pouring through northwestern Iran. Finally, it is presumed that the U.S. Navy will be able to keep open the critical Strait of Hormuz against anticipated attacks by Backfire bombers, Soviet attack submarines, and Soviet tactical air forces operating out of Afghanistan.

These are heady, indeed mind-boggling, assumptions. No country on the Arabian peninsula has been, to date, willing to permit the United States to station forces on its territory even in peacetime. In a crisis, would the Turks, the Saudis, and the Omanis be prepared to expose their countries to potential Soviet retaliation for the sake of assisting the United States in defending Iran? Would the government of Iran, even in the face of a Soviet invasion, be prepared to invite onto its own soil forces of the "satanic" United States? Could the U.S. Navy keep open any narrow body of water within easy reach of massive land-based Soviet airpower?

The burgeoning focus of RDF contingency planners on a

defense of Iran is a focus not just on something that may be inherently indefensible but on what is, of all threats, perhaps the least likely to materialize. Far more likely and immediate threats face the United States in the Gulf. While the possibility of overt Soviet aggression against Iran cannot be entirely dismissed, one might assume that the failure of 100,000 Soviet troops to pacify fifteen million xenophobic Muslims in Afghanistan would diminish the Kremlin's appetite for taking on forty million more in Iran. More to the point, recent events in the Gulf region have conclusively demonstrated that U.S. interests there are more immediately threatened by indigenous revolutionary upheavals and local wars than by Soviet aggression. Soviet forces did not overthrow the Shah, seize Mecca's Grand Mosque, start the war between Iraq and Iran, bomb Beirut, or assassinate Anwar Sadat. Yet these events have had a far more profoundly adverse effect on America's strategic position in the Gulf than the possibility of a Soviet invasion of Iran.

It defies both logic and common sense to assume, as the Pentagon appears to, that a massive, firepower–oriented, logistically cumbersome, and land-dependent intervention force of the type now being created would also be effective against lesser, more diffuse, and more pressing threats. In this regard, it would seem that little has been learned from America's military engagement in Indochina.

UNCERTAIN ACCESS

Secure military access ashore in the Persian Gulf is essential, certainly in contingencies entailing a prolonged land campaign. To get ashore, intervention forces must have access to ports, airfields, and other reception facilities. To stay ashore, they require continued access to proximate logistical support bases. Neither is available to the RDF in the Gulf region.

With the exception of the tiny atoll of Diego Garcia, some 2,500 miles from the Strait of Hormuz, the United States possesses no military bases in that vast area of the world stretching from Turkey to the Philippines. (In contrast the Soviets have large installations at Cam Ranh, Socotra, and Aden, and longstanding access to the Iraqi bases at Umm Qasr and Al Basrah.) Nor are prospects favorable for the establishment of a "Subic" naval facility or "Clark" air force base in the region.

The political sensitivity of potential host nations to a permanent U.S. miltary presence on their own soil is certainly understandable and is manifest in their refusal to permit the peacetime stationing of any operationally significant U.S. forces on their territory. Such a presence "would validate the criticism of radical Arabs about how the conservative [Gulf] states are toadies of the imperialists," and thus "increase the chances of the internal turmoil that constitutes the main potential threat."[3] Moreover, many Gulf states, including Saudi Arabia, continue to regard Israel as a greater threat to the security of the Arab world than the prospect of an "Afghanistan" on the Arabian peninsula. Israel's annexation of the Golan Heights in December 1981 certainly has done little to shake this view.

To its credit, the Department of Defense does appear cognizant of the political barriers to the establishment of a permanent U.S. military presence ashore in the Gulf region and accordingly has tried to gain right of access to selected facilities in times of crisis. Agreements along these lines have been concluded with Kenya, Somalia, and Oman.

Yet simply having the promise of access to facilities on a contingency basis is no substitute for U.S. controlled and operated bases not subject to the political calculations of host governments. The same internal political considerations that deny the United States a permanent military presence ashore in the region could well deny the United States access to facilities in the event of a crisis, irrespective of the agreements that have been negotiated. It is worth recalling that during the October War of 1973, the United States was denied overflight rights by NATO allies, countries usually regarded as more reliable than non–treaty U.S. "friends" in the Gulf. More instructive were the severe restrictions imposed by Oman on U.S. forces participating in Bright Star II, an RDF exercise conducted in the Middle East in late 1981. Under pressure from Saudi Arabia, Oman reduced the planned Omani portion of the exercise to a twenty-four hour presence ashore by a small U.S. Marine Corps landing party.

The internal political fragility of potential U.S. friends and allies in the Gulf is exacerbated by the questionable capabilities and competence of their military establishments. The present Iraqi–Iranian war has done little to enhance the dismal military reputation of the Arab world—national military forces on the Arabian peninsula are negligible in size, questionable in quality, or both. Enormous defense expenditures by many Gulf states appear to have produced little in the way of technically competent, properly integrated, and well–led military forces. Even the large and experienced armies of Iraq, Iran, and Pakistan have been demoralized by defeat, revolution, or internal division along political and ethnic lines. In short, U.S. intervention forces could expect little effective support on the battlefield even from host nations requesting intervention.

The adverse consequences of local military incompetence

should not be underestimated, although U.S. intervention would, of course, benefit from it in contingencies involving aggression by a regional state. The Guam (Nixon) Doctrine is worth noting at this juncture because the sustained application of major U.S. military power in the Third World is not likely to succeed if unsupported by viable and competent local regimes capable of assuming a significant share of the land battle. This is surely one of the principal geo–strategic lessons of the U.S. intervention in Indochina.

On what grounds can the United States count in the Gulf on the kind of indigenous effort that would be required in the face of direct Soviet aggression or aggression by a Soviet client state? The availability of such support is ultimately a function of the political stability of the regime supplying it; its effectiveness is a product of the size and competence of the regime's military forces. For decades the West enjoyed in the Shah of Iran a powerful and seemingly stable local client committed to the defense of shared interests in the Persian Gulf. Today which potential Western client among the littoral states of the Persian Gulf and Indian Ocean can be regarded as both politically stable and militarily competent? Somalia? Oman? Saudi Arabia? Kuwait? The United Arab Emirates? Pakistan? All of these states, and notably Saudi Arabia, which the Reagan Administration has unregenerately embraced as the linchpin of the U.S. strategic position in the Gulf, are governed by military regimes or semifeudal monarchies whose social and political fragility renders them vulnerable to internal overthrow by Soviet–sponsored leftist groups or the forces of Islamic fundamentalism.

In short, in the Persian Gulf area the United States possesses none of the critical operational and logistical benefits that it enjoys in comparative abundance in Europe, and wherever large U.S. military forces are firmly ensconced ashore and can count on the support of powerful and reliable allies. As emphasized by the RDF's first commander, Lt. General Paul X. Kelley, the United States will have to "start from scratch" in the Gulf—against potential adversaries with large military forces already in place in the region or along its periphery.

> There are sizable U.S. forces in place in Western Europe—with the exception of naval forces in the Indian Ocean, we have none in Southwest Asia.

> There are sizable amounts of prepositioned supplies and equipment in Western Europe for reinforcing units—we have none in Southwest Asia.

> There is an in–place command and control system in Western Europe—we have none in Southwest Asia.

There are extensive host–nation support agreements between the United States and West European countries—we
have none in Southwest Asia.

There is an alliance of military allies in Western Europe—
there is no such alliance in Southwest Asia.[4]

Whatever the nonmilitary problems a U.S. military presence
might entail for both the host nations and the United States, its
operational and logistical benefits are undeniable. The issue is the
political feasibility of even a modest U.S. land presence in the
region, such as cadred combat units and prepositioned stocks of
weapons and ammunition. At present, and for the foreseeable future,
it does not appear to be feasible, notwithstanding the expressed
desires of Secretary of State Alexander Haig and Secretary of
Defense Caspar Weinberger.[5]

INSUFFICIENT FORCE

Even were military access in the Gulf not a problem, the
combat commitment of any sizable U.S. force in the region would
automatically weaken the defense of other critical U.S. interests
elsewhere in the world. The decision to form the RDF only from
existing military units, almost all of which are already earmarked for
NATO and the Far East, has served to widen the gap between U.S.
commitments abroad and U.S. capabilities to defend them that was
substantial even before Afghanistan. The decision makes it virtually
impossible to deal effectively with a significant military challenge
in more than one area at a time.

Although U.S. military planning since 1969 has called for
capabilities adequate to wage a major conflict in Europe and a lesser
conflict elsewhere simultaneously—the so-called one-and-a-half
war strategy—the simple truth is that U.S. force levels, now at the
lowest point since the Korean war, are not sufficient to meet the
demands of more than one sizable conflict at a time. The "half-war"
in Vietnam was waged in no small part by U.S. forces earmarked for
European contingencies. Similarly, the U.S. carrier battle groups
deployed in the Indian Ocean since 1979 have been drawn from
NATO's Southern Flank and the Western Pacific.

Even the originally planned increase in the size of the U.S.
Fleet from the present 440-odd vessels to 600 by the late 1980s is
not apt to be adequate. In any event, it is highly doubtful whether the
U.S. Navy, under the current All-Volunteer Force, is capable of
manning a 600-ship fleet; shortfalls in skilled personnel are so severe
that comparatively new vessels have been retired from active
patrolling. Indeed, the Reagan Administration has apparently

dropped its initial commitment to a 600-ship navy, and now speaks officially only of "15 carrier battle groups" and a "three-ocean fleet."

The strategic risk inherent in reliance on forces committed to both Gulf and non-Gulf contingencies would be profound in circumstances involving a U.S.–Soviet confrontation. By virtue of interior lines of communication, larger forces, and greater proximity to both Europe and the Gulf, the Soviet Union could feint in one area, thus diverting rapidly deployable U.S. forces from the real focus of attack.

Our active status strategic reserves are too few to fight even a modest war in the Middle East without accepting calculated risks that uncover crucial interests elsewhere. Even "best case" forces would probably prove insufficient against the Soviets, whose abilities to project offensive power beyond their frontiers have improved impressively in recent years.[6]

INADEQUATE STRATEGIC MOBILITY

Compounding the problems of uncertain access and insufficient force is an inability to move forces that are available to the Gulf in a timely fashion. This problem derives from the RDF's heavy reliance on units stationed in the United States and the steady decay of U.S. strategic sea and air lift capabilities since the late 1960s.

To its credit the Reagan Administration has firmly endorsed most of the RDF–related strategic mobility enhancement programs initiated by the Carter Administration. Those programs include: (1) development and procurement of a new strategic transport aircraft— the CX; (2) prepositioning afloat in the Indian Ocean, aboard twelve specialized maritime prepositioning ships (MPS), of an entire Marine Corps division's worth of equipment and thirty days' worth of food, fuel, and ammunition; (3) purchase of eight commercially-owned 33 knot SL-7 fast deployment logistics ships; and (4) procurement of twenty-six KC-10 tanker aircraft to supplement the present aging fleet of KC-135s. Additionally, a Near-Term Prepositioned Ship (NTPS) force has already been deployed to the Indian Ocean, consisting of seven ships containing equipment, supplies, fuel, and water sufficient to support a Marine Amphibious Brigade of about 12,000 men, and to sustain several USAF fighter squadrons.

Unfortunately, with the exception of the NTPS force, none of these mobility enhancement programs will be realized for at least several years. Moreover, in a development that could compromise chances for any increased strategic airlift, the Congress in late 1981 deleted all funds for the Air Force's preferred CX design in favor of investment in such off-the-shelf wide-bodied designs as the C-5A and/or modified Boeing 747. The Reagan Administration also severely slashed funding for the KC-10 tanker program, essential to sustaining the rapid deployment to the Gulf of land-based tactical air units. In sum, the strategic lift necessary for the RDF as it is now organized and structured is likely to be a long time in coming, and may not arrive at all in sufficient quantity.

THE RDF MISMATCH

The problems of access, insufficient force, and inadequate strategic mobility might have impelled the Pentagon toward both larger force levels and the creation of an instrument of intervention based primarily on on-station seapower and supplemented by robust amphibious assault and other forcible-entry capabilities. An RDF of this kind could be maintained on the scene, and would be comparatively independent of the political good will of unstable host governments. It also would be able, if necessary, to gain access ashore without invitation. Unfortunately, the problems remain.

TENTATIVE RAPID DEPLOYMENT
JOINT TASK FORCE COMPOSITION, 1981

Unit	NATO Earmarked?	Land–Dependent?*
GROUND FORCES		
Army		
18th Airborne Corps HQ	No	Yes
82nd Airborne Division	Yes	Yes
101st Air Assault Division	Yes	Yes
9th Infantry Division	Yes	Yes
24th Mechanized Division	Yes	Yes
194 Armored Brigade	No	Yes
6th Cavalry (Air Combat) Brigade	Yes	Yes
2 Ranger Infantry Battalions	Yes	Yes
Marine Corps		
1 Marine Amphibious Force	?**	Yes
U. S. AIR FORCE UNITS		
1 Air Force HQ	?	Yes
12 tactical fighter squadrons	Yes	Yes

2 tactical reconnaissance squadrons	Yes	Yes
2 tactical airlift wings	No	Yes
U. S. NAVY FORCES		
3 carrier battle groups	Some***	No
1 surface action group	Some***	No
4 aerial patrol squadrons	Some***	Yes

*   Dependent for commitment ashore on access to secure ports and/or airfields, or dependent for subsequent operations ashore on a shore-based logistical infrastructure.

**   Marine Amphibious Forces are considered available for contingencies worldwide.

***   A significant proportion of U.S. naval vessels currently deployed in the Indian Ocean belong to the U.S. 6th Fleet in the Mediterranean. Maintenance of a naval presence in the Indian Ocean at the expense of NATO-oriented naval forces is likely to continue throughout the decade.

As shown in the table, most of the military units now assigned to the RDF are not only already committed to NATO, but also dependent on friendly ports, airfields, and logistical facilities for entry ashore and subsequent sustainability. Only the carrier battle groups and the notional Marine Amphibious Force are deployed or deployable afloat and logistically supportable from the sea;[7] only the Marines, and the Army's 82nd Airborne Division possess the ability to enter territory controlled by hostile forces. Land-dependent units comprise the remainder of forces earmarked for the RDF, which is organizationally little more than a new headquarters charged with identifying, training, and planning the employment of existing forces suitable for Persian Gulf contingencies.

The presumption that the RDF will enjoy uncontested entry ashore in the Gulf is further apparent in the RDF's strategic mobility programs, and in the absence of any proposed increases in amphibious assault capabilities. None of the proposed new ships and aircraft possess any defensive capabilities; all will be unarmed, and the MPS and SL–7 ships will be manned by civilian crews. As such, they—like the bulk of the forces they will be carrying—will be completely dependent on friendly reception ashore.

Given the operational and logistical obstacles confronting the effective application of U.S. military power in the Persian Gulf region, logic and common sense seem to dictate replacement of the present RDF by a small agile, tactically capable intervention force with forcible entry capabilities that is based and supplied from the sea and supported by expanded sea power. Such an intervention force would stress quality, not size; immediate responsiveness, not delayed arrivals from the United States of air-transported army forces and land-based tactical air units; and logistical self-sufficiency, not dependence on facilities ashore. The present composition and capabilities of the RDF are the product less of impartial military judgment than they are of the bureaucratic desire of each service for at least a fair share of the rapid deployment mission. As such, the present RDF can and should be replaced by a new variant of the Navy–Fleet Marine Force "team" utilizing tried and tested organizational structures and operational doctrines associated with the successful projection of power from sea to shore.

Specifically, the author proposes the transfer of the primary responsibility for the rapid deployment mission to the U.S. Marine Corps and an expansion in forcible-entry capabilities through increases in present levels of amphibious shipping and naval gunfire support.

Considering the peculiar obstacles to and requirements for successful U.S. military intervention in the Persian Gulf, a strong case can be made for transferring the mission to the U.S. Marine Corps. The lack of any real prospect for establishing an operationally significant peacetime U.S. military presence ashore in the Persian Gulf dictates primary reliance on sea power, especially on the kind of sea-based capability to project power ashore long associated with the Marine Corps.

The Marine Corps is the sole U.S. force with amphibious assault capabilities, an essential component of any credible U.S. intervention force in the Persian Gulf. Moreover, unlike the Army, which must rely on another service for tactical air support, the Marine Corps has its own air arm, which is compatible with carriers and other sea-based air platforms and is highly integrated with both carrier-based naval aviation and marine ground forces. In short, in contrast to the Army— the Marine Corps' principal competitor for bureaucratic control of the rapid deployment mission—the Corps is fully compatible with sea power—the necessary foundation of a U.S. military presence in those areas of the world where U.S. forces are not stationed ashore. There is also the Corps' long-standing history of successful expeditionary operations in the Third World and its record, as the nation's recognized "force in readiness," of being the "first to fight."

Essential to any credible U.S. intervention force in the Persian Gulf is a strong U.S. forcible-entry capability. The present level of U.S. amphibious shipping is less than one-half that of the planning requirement specified by the Joint Chiefs of Staff (JCS), and naval gunfire support capabilities have been permitted to dwindle to patently unacceptable levels. Serious consideration should be given to

expanding the level of amphibious shipping from the present 1.15–
Marine Amphibious Force (MAF) lift capability to a minimum 2.33–
MAF lift capability, the JCS planning requirement.[8] A 2.33–MAF
capability would permit the uninterrupted deployment in the Indian
Ocean, or other Third World crisis areas, of a least one full amphibious
assault brigade, compared to the present occasional visits of a
battalion-sized landing force, as well as sufficient redundancy for larger
assault operations.

The Reagan Administration's recall of at least two *Iowa* class
battleships to active duty, and the possibility of recalling two *Salem*
class heavy cruisers, could provide U.S. amphibious assault forces the
kind of fire support they have long been denied. The reactivation and
refurbishment of these vessels would certainly enhance Marine Corps
forcible-entry capabilities against lightly or even moderately defended
beachheads, if not against heavily defended shores. The presence in the
Indian Ocean of such vessels, with their awesome capacity for
destruction, also would contribute to deterrence.

A sea–based RDF admittedly would have limited utility in
contingencies demanding sustained inland combat in and beyond the
reach of amphibious assault forces and carrier-based airpower.
Prosecution of sustained inland combat, however, would be
contingent upon secure coastal military lodgments, which can be
gained only by the ability to project power ashore. Moreover, unlike
forces held in the United States for rapid deployment to the Gulf
region, a sea–based RDF is already there.

Finally, as long as U.S. military forces are denied politically
secure peacetime access ashore in the Gulf region, there appears to be
no alternative to primary reliance on sea power.

NOTES

1. Opening statement of Senator William Cohen before the Hearings
on the RDF of the Senate Armed Services Subcommittee on Sea Power and
Force Projection, 3 March 1981.
2. In a conversation with the author in January 1981.
3. Richard K. Betts, *Suprise and Defense: The Lesson of Sudden
Attacks for U.S. Military Planning*, a draft manuscript scheduled for
publication by the Brookings Institution, p. ix–14.
4. Statement by Lieutenant General P. X. Kelly on Rapid Deployment Force Programs, before the Senate Armed Services Committee on Sea
Power and Force Projection, 9 March, 1981, p. 5.
5. "Weinberger Says U.S. Must Expand Mideast 'Presence,'"
Washington Star, 9 March, 1981; and Don Oberdorfer, "Haig: U.S.
Would Resist a Mideast Shift, Hints GIs May be Stationed in Sinai,"
Washington Post, 19 March 1981.

6. John M. Collins, et al., *Petroleum Imports from the Persian Gulf: Use of Armed Force to Ensure Supplies* (Washington, D.C.: Library of Congress Congressional Research Service, 1980), p. 16.

7. Each of the Corps' three Marine Amphibious Forces consist of a division and an associated air wing. None are formally earmarked for the rapid deployment mission. Currently only a battalion landing team is actually deployed in the Indian Ocean.

8. A Marine Amphibious Force consists of a division, air wing, and associated support units. The present level of amphibious shipping is capable of moving only 1.15 MAFs; even then, however, it would take the Navy some 30–45 days to assemble in one place the shipping necessary for a MAF-sized assault, because the vessels are scattered among naval commands throughout the world.

9

Airlifting the Marine Corps: Mismatch or Wave of the Future

Dov S. Zakheim*

At first glance, airlift and the Marine Corps appear to be an unlikely combination. As its name implies, the Marine Corps has traditionally been associated with operations launched from sea-based platforms. As a result of the island-hopping campaigns of World War II and the 1947 National Security Act, the amphibious mission has become virtually synonymous with Marine operations.[1]

A prime characteristic of these operations is their logistical independence. Indeed, one Marine general has gone so far as to deem this characteristic essential to the nature of the kinds of "expeditionary" operations that currently are most closely associated with the Rapid Deployment Force.[2] Amphibious shipping, with its capacity to carry Marines, their equipment, and support, underwrites this independence. It is an independence which airlift, with more limited load-carrying capacity and potential dependence upon the good will of other states for staging and overflight rights, simply cannot provide.

Airlift traditionally has been associated with the Army–Air Force team. The Military Airlift Command (MAC) controls all "common user" airlift assets, that is, the strategic airlift fleet of 70 C-5s and 234 C-141s[3] and the tactical airlift fleet of 474 C-130, 64 C-123, and 48 C-7 aircraft. (All C-7s and C-123s and a portion of the C-130 fleet are in the reserve forces.) Every Army division is a

* Views represented herein are entirely those of the author. The Congressional Budget Office, where he is employed, bears no responsibility for the contents of this chapter or the opinions of the author.

The author is indebted to David S. C. Chu, Edward A. Swoboda, and Nancy Swope for their helpful comments on drafts of this chapter.

potential user of airlift. Airlift is most critical, however, to the 82nd Airborne and 101st Air Assault Divisions, which long have served as part of the U.S. rapid-response projection forces,[4] as well as to those Army divisions that have been earmarked for speedy deployment to Europe in the event of a buildup to a NATO–Warsaw Pact conflict. Rapid deployment, whether to Europe or elsewhere, also defines airlift requirements for tactical Air Force units. Their operations are dependent upon the support equipment that MAC must transport to the designated combat theater.[5]

The image of a Marine Corps Airlift Command is further reinforced by the Corps' possession of its own integral airlift assets. The Corps operates its own force of KC-130s, which are primarily tactical transports but could be used to carry relatively small payloads (up to fifteen tons) for distances up to 3,000 nautical miles. As the "K" in its designation implies, however, the KC-130 is configured as a tanker and, for the most part, would be unlikely to be used either as a tactical or a long-range transport.[6]

In addition, the Marines have made a major commitment to battlefield air mobility, in the form of the helicopter elements of their division / wing structure. No Marine division can match the helicopter complement of the U.S. Army's 101st Airmobile Division, which, at least theoretically, is totally helicopter mobile.[7] Nevertheless, air wings associated with Marine divisions do have a larger helicopter complement than all other Army divisions and, unlike those divisions, include both medium- and heavy-lift helicopters capable of moving several tons of equipment in addition to personnel for combat radii of up to 100 nautical miles.

Logistical independence and maritime orientation notwithstanding, Marines often were dependent upon airlift resources during the Vietnam conflict, both for major intratheater moves and for movement into and out of Vietnam. Perhaps more important, in terms of planning for the future, the Corps has become more closely identified with airlift in the past few years within the context of its potential employment in a NATO–Warsaw Pact war, particularly with respect to operations on NATO's Northern Flank.

AIRLIFTING MARINES FOR DEFENSIVE OPERATIONS: THE NORTHERN FLANK

A Marine deployment to Iceland, northern Norway, or Denmark, to defend one or more allied-controlled land masses that stand astride the Soviet fleet's (and Soviet Naval Aviation's) critical pathways to the Atlantic, has long been an important wartime option for alliance planners. In the past, however, the option, particularly with respect to Norway and Denmark, was more frequently viewed in amphibious terms. More recently, the redefinition and compression of expected warning time available to the Nordic allies has placed a greater premium on rapid reinforcement of NATO's Northern Flank and has resulted in proposals for the airlifting of Marines to that region.

Proposals to airlift Marines to Scandinavia in a crisis are the product of political as well as military calculations. Iceland, Norway, and Denmark have all shown a marked reluctance to entertain foreign troops on their soil. Iceland permits only a limited U.S. presence on its territory; Norway and Denmark forbid the basing of any foreign troops on their territory. An airlift of Marines during a crisis would ensure speedy reinforcement of all three states at a time when additional foreign troops would be critical. It would afford NATO an additional crisis-management tool, an eleventh-hour means of deterring a Pact attack by asserting, in the starkest military terms, NATO's determination to defend its territory.

Because of the nature of force balances in the Baltic and the Kola–Finnmark regions around North Cape, the level of NATO reinforcement required to defend Denmark and Norway would be significantly greater than that required for Iceland. In order to facilitate the rapid movement of troops and equipment to these regions, the United States and Norway have agreed that Marine equipment be "prestocked" in central Norway.[8] Similarly, it has been suggested that Marine equipment be prestocked in Denmark. In both cases, remaining essential equipment, together with Marine troops, could then be airlifted into the region during a crisis, permitting an extremely rapid force disposition with all equipment in place. Prestocking provides the Scandinavians a political benefit that goes beyond the deterrent effect that rapid reinforcement yields. It embodies a reassurance to Norway, Denmark, and, to some extent, Sweden and Finland of the U.S. commitment to defend against aggression in the north without upsetting what those states perceive as a delicate "Nordic balance."

Proposals for Marine Corps reinforcement of the Northern Flank highlight the importance of prestocking as a critical, and possibly permanent, conceptual and practical link between airlift and the Marine Corps. Nevertheless, as envisaged in the context of NATO strategy, prestocking facilitates fundamentally defensive operations, namely, protection of Danish, Norwegian, and Icelandic territory against Warsaw Pact aggression. It is therefore noteworthy that even before prestocking was adopted either as U.S. Marine Corps or NATO policy for northern Europe, it had already become a component of a proposal that could involve the use of Marines for projection operations—the Administration's plan for a Rapid Deployment Force. For the first time, Marine intervention for *offensive* operations may be as closely dependent upon airlift as upon sealift.

How significant is this linkage, especially when applied to projection operations, to the future of the Marine Corps? Does it represent a change in the Corps' strategy, its tactics, or its organization? These questions cannot be answered without first reviewing both the Carter Administration's unfinished Rapid Deployment Force concept and the premises that underlay it.

THE RAPID DEPLOYMENT FORCE

The Rapid Deployment Force (RDF) does not embody a new concept. For many years, the Marine Corps and the Army airborne divisions constituted a rapid deployment force in practice, if not in name. Thirteen years ago, the Johnson Administration put forward a plan for fast logistics ships (FDL) and C-5A cargo aircraft, to add substance to the premise that U.S. land force units could indeed deploy "rapidly" overseas in response to crises outside Europe.[9] The current rationale for the RDF is not much different from that which General Harold K. Johnson, Army Chief of Staff, presented before the House Armed Services Committee when testifying in justification of the FDL program:

> There are . . . a range of possible methods for achieving a rapid response capability. They run all the way from very large forces permanently stationed overseas to a large central reserve capable of rapid deployment. The JCS and the Department of Defense have for several years believed that the best strategy lies in a combination of measures involving some forward deployments together with a central reserve, all of which is mobile, and some of which is capable of very rapid deployment. . . . If a large force is to be rapidly deployed from the central reserve, some heavy equipment must be prepositioned. . . . Land prepositioning is, however, relatively inflexible. In conjunction with aircraft it enables rapid response only to a contingency which develops near the point of prepositioning. . . . We need to take the step in sealift comparable to that which the C-5A represents in airlift. It is for this purpose that the FDL is being designed . . . . In short, to achieve the objectives of rapid deployment, we must have the flexibility that comes from multiple means.[10]

The "original" Rapid Deployment Force never came into being. While the C-5 program was approved, the FDL plan ultimately was killed. Indeed, the C-5 was soon afterward advertised as geared primarily to the support of U.S. forces in a NATO, rather than a non-NATO, conflict.

The RDF plan includes the two key elements of its predecessor: a new class of transport aircraft (labled the CX) and a new class of cargo ships (termed maritime prepositioning ships—MPS) aboard which equipment will be prepositioned overseas. A decision upon a specific aircraft type has yet to be made.

The U.S. Air Force has recommended that the CX be significantly smaller than the C-5, so that it would be less demanding upon taxi and parking capabilities of mid-sized airports. The Air Force's "Draft Request for Proposal" reportedly states that the CX should have a payload of 130,000 pounds, sufficient to carry either one XM-1 main battle tank for 2,400 nautical miles or two XM-2 armored fighting vehicles, weighing roughly 100,000 pounds, for about 2,800 nautical miles. Both systems could otherwise be carried only by the C-5 (and are therefore labeled "outsize" equipment). The CX also reportedly will have the ability to operate at "austere" airfields with runways as short as 3,000 feet. It is estimated that up to 1900 CX aircraft are planned, at a total program cost of apporximately $8 billion.[11] Three contractors are known to be preparing bids on the CX; the plane is unlikely to enter the airlift force before late 1985.[12]

The MPS proposal actually incorporates three elements. Initially, the Carter Administration implemented a short-term "quick fix" to permit equipment for a brigade to be prestocked by 1981. For the longer term, plans call for a total of 12 ships, eight new maritime prepositioning ships designed to have an independent unloading capability, and four "roll-on/roll-off" ships, already constructed, which will be modified to match MPS characteristics. These ships will permit heavy equipment for a division to be prepositioned overseas by the end of the 1980s. The first maritime propositioning ship was requested in the fiscal year 1981 budget.

Despite the obvious similarities with the Johnson Administration program, the RDF plan differs from its predecessor in a number of critical respects. These involve the concept of a "force" specifically dedicated for quick-response missions, the elements of that force, and the importance of new overseas military facilities to its operation.

To begin with, President Carter created a new Rapid Deployment Joint Task Force, a unified command led by a Marine three-star general. In the past, "rapid-deployment" forces were organized under the Strike Command or its successor, the Readiness Command, which will continue to function despite the creation of the new task force.

The appointment of the first Marine ever to serve as a unified commander points to another major difference between earlier and current formulations of the U.S. rapid deployment concept.[13] The 1967–1968 plan focused primarily on the Army, whose heavy equipment would either be prestocked aboard FDLs or lifted on C-5s, C-141s, and smaller transports. The current RDF proposal accords a critical role to the Marine Corps, not only as an amphibious element within the force's multidivisional structure, but also as the beneficiary of equipment aboard the prepositioning ships. Like designated Army divisions (of which the most obvious candidate is the 82nd Airborne), Marine forces would be flown directly to crisis locales, where they would "marry up" with equipment deposited on shore by the ships.

Finally, development of Diego Garcia as a home port for the MPS, and as a possible staging base for airlifted forces and naval task forces, involves a major change in the regional focus of the RDF. In the late 1960s, the Johnson Administration, even when thinking beyond Vietnam, focused heavily on East Asia, primarily Korea. The RDF is fundamentally a Middle East strike force, with Diego Garcia the nearest U.S.-operated facility and with the development of facilities in Egypt, Oman and Somalia as additional "host"-operated locales for Middle East operations.

The RDF certainly does not imply total Marine Corps reliance upon prestocking and airlift for in-theater sustainability when operating in the Middle East. Indeed, one of the first operational manifestations of the Carter Administration's desire to move combat forces more quickly to the scene of a Middle East crisis was the deployment of a Marine Amphibious Unit (MAU) to the Indian Ocean for an indefinite period. Furthermore, the Department of Defense has indicated that two additional sea-based Marine elements, the MAU that normally operates in the Mediterranean and a Marine Amphibious Brigade (MAB) deploying from the Pacific, would be critical components of a rapid U.S. response to Indian Ocean developments in the foreseeable future. Nevertheless, the RDF concepts calls for a significantly larger force of Marines— initially a brigade and ultimately at least a division—to arrive in the Middle East by air rather than by sea.[14] Thus, airlift, rather than amphibious lift, will be the prime source of Marine mobility for those operations that more and more are becoming synonymous with the long-standing Department of Defense concept of the "half-war."

It might be argued that airlift and amphibious lift complement each other. To the delight of those who wish to increase the levels of both types of lift resources, it would appear that such is the case. Airlift provides rapid mobility; amphibious lift, sustainability. Airlift implies dependence upon a land-based logistics chain and a benign and hospitable environment at the point of disembarkation, but offers a flexible means of landing near the combat zone. Amphibious lift embodies logistical independence and is geared to forcible entry, but is of little value for combat in regions remote from the shore.

Nevertheless, the primacy of airlift for Marine operations that previously were inextricably linked to amphibious assault invites a reevaluation of its benefits and, therefore, of the possible opportunity cost of emphasizing airlift in its place. Such a reevaluation goes to the heart of the amphibious mission, particularly its value to rapid-response operations such as those aniticipated in the Middle East.

A NECESSARY EXCURSION—PROSPECTS FOR THE MARINE'S AMPHIBIOUS MISSION

It has become extremely fashionable to assert that the opposed amphibious assault operation no longer is a viable tactic. Even unsophisticated military establishments currently can employ precision-guided munitions (PGMs) against assaulting forces. In this view, slow-moving amphibious formations present such easy targets for entrenched defenders that they will be unable to mount assaults with the careful timing that is critical to their success. In addition, it is argued, there is little cause to assume a need for large-scale assaults, such as those mounted in the Pacific campaigns of World War II. Small-scale landings are the most that can be expected of Marine amphibious forces. Major landings from the sea would in future be relegated to administrative operations—that is, unopposed landings in friendly (or at least neutral) environments. Thus, the argument concludes, the Marines must shift the locus of their procurement, training, and force structure from one that is geared to amphibious operations to some other mission.[15]

The Corps could certainly gear more of its operations to air transport, as the Rapid Deployment Force concept implies. Indeed, as has recently been suggested, the Marines could assume the tasks of the Army's 82nd Airborne Division, which in turn would be disbanded. At the same time, less emphasis might be placed on amphibious operations, and planning for sealift would envisage primarily administrative landings.[16] Certainly the Rapid Deployment Force concept anticipates administrative landings, by sea as well as by air. Is amphibious assault—of the opposed variety—truly passé, however? Should all rapid movement be assumed to be administrative, as seems to be the case with both the air and sea mobility aspects of the RDF? A closer look reveals that both judgments may be premature.

Amphibious assault is a means to achieve tactical surprise. It enables an attacker to choose his location for combat, forcing the defender either to spread his formations thinly over a wide area in anticipation of an attack or to risk being outflanked, and possibly encircled, by forces spearheaded by sea-based assault units. The Pacific campaigns certainly do not provide a good paradigm for amphibious assaults in the latter part of this century. But the landing at Inchon may do so. Inchon, it will be recalled, was considered too teacherous a landing site for amphibious units and was thinly defended by the North Koreans. The landing itself did not involve a division-sized assault. Instead, two brigades came ashore to conduct the most critical, and successful, flanking operation of the Korean War.

To be sure, Inchon represented strategic as well as tactical surprise. Strategic surprise may be more than any amphibious force can hope for, given the speed with which states with advanced intelligence-gathering mechanisms are ready and willing to pass current "real-time" information to their less sophisticated allies. Tactical surprise is another matter, however. Ship-to-shore movements can take place in hours, rather than days, particularly if supported by helicopters and/or highspeed landing craft (such as those the Soviets possess and the United States is developing). The speed with which forces can be landed ashore can still severely tax the command, control, and communications (C^3) capabilities of most states. Without the benefits of C^3, defenders will have difficulty coping with amphibious assaults; PGMs are of little use if their owners do not know where to point them.

Moreover, administrative lift—whether airlift or sealift—may require preceding amphibious assault. The friendly third country forces that are expected to control aerial maritime ports of disembarkation may not be available when required. They may be defending other important objectives, or may be unequal to the task of defending ports and airfields. Thus, even if air and sea transports arrive unscathed at their off-loading berths, they may be subject to attack upon arrival. Only airborne or amphibious operations can ensure that a protected area will be established within which *follow-on* administrative lift, whether airborne or seaborne, can take place. Given the great distances that must be covered when operating in the Persian Gulf/Arabian Sea/Indian Ocean region, and the length of coastlines adjacent to potentially important objective areas for U.S.

forces, amphibious assault may promise greater flexibility and tactical surprise, and therefore greater success, than paratroop operations.

It is significant that the Soviet Union currently is improving its capability to conduct opposed amphibious assaults. Despite their success, recent Soviet overseas projection operations, which involved the use of airlift and sealift as well as naval support and surrogate forces, implicitly required both the benign neglect of the United States and the absence of opposition at landing sites.[17] The Soviets evidently are not satisfied with their ability to employ administrative landing techniques to move their forces overseas. They are developing new systems that will provide them with the airborne firepower support and long-range sustainability they currently lack. In particular, their new aircraft carriers and amphibious ships will significantly enhance their capability to mount opposed assaults. Although the Soviets reportedly stock equipment in the Persian Gulf and elsewhere,[18] they are making a major investment in logistical independence. Clearly, the Soviets do not view opposed assault, especially amphibious assault, as passé.

Amphibious assault is far from an outmoded tactic. It could be critical to the success of rapid deployment operations when initial administrative operations were infeasible. Should airlift, linked with administrative sealift, therefore be the predominant mode of transport for the Marines operating with the RDF? Perhaps not.

MARINES AND AIRLIFT: ACCOMMODATION OR MARRIAGE?

Airlift must play an important role in any rapid deployment scheme. Only airlift can move troops and their equipment over thousands of miles in a matter of days. In the absence of airlift, land forces could respond quickly to crises in remote locales only if they, or at least their equipment, were stationed in the regions where crises were anticipated. Indeed, a combination of these approaches constitutes current U.S. strategy for the deployment of Army forces in Europe, while forward Army deployment, for the time being, constitutes a key element of the U.S. deterrent force in Korea. Outside Korea and Europe, however, the Army simply cannot expect to operate as a rapid-response force unless airlift is made available to it.

There is one final alternative for land forces that are required to respond quickly to overseas contingencies. Instead of being forward deployed on land, they could be forward deployed at sea. In other words, they could be amphibious forces. Whereas this approach is not practical for the Army, which does not conduct amphibious training, it constitutes a long-standing role of the Marine Corps.

It may indeed be shortsighted to designate air transport for troops and some or all of their equipment as the primary mode of transit for the Marine Corps as long as the Corps is expected to constitute part of the RDF.[19] Reliance upon airlift in conjunction with administrative sealift robs the Corps of its unique ability to achieve tactical surprise ashore from a base at sea. This ability could well be critical to the success of a quick-response military operation: as a forward-deployed amphibious force, Marine units constitute an important hedge against the possibility that today's "host nation," meticulously supporting prepositioned equipment and maintaining reception facilities, could be transformed into tomorrow's "threat." In the Middle East and the Horn of Africa, where shifting alliances are not uncommon, this possibility is far from remote. Moreover, by supplementing a possible Navy "presence" with a separate sea-based land force "presence," forward-deployed amphibious forces add substance to a deterrent against hostile activities whose effectiveness can only be measured when it fails.

Without doubt, maintenance of an amphibious capability in conjunction with the RDF can only be achieved at a budgetary price, and not a minimal one either. The cost of the first of a new class of amphibious dock landing ships (LSD-41) designed to carry the Marines' most modern fast landing craft (the 40+ knot air-cushioned landing craft, or LCAC) exceeds $340 million (fiscal year 1981 dollars). Acquisition of a multipurpose amphibious ship, which could carry planes, troops, and equipment, may require funding on the scale of approximately $900 million. Expenditures far in excess of these amounts will be necessary if the Marines are to maintain a credible at-sea Indian Ocean posture while not reducing their commitments elsewhere. (Indeed, the LSD-41 was requested by the Carter Administration as part of a program to modernize the current amphibious lift force, not to augment its current levels.) Procurement of a force of ships sufficiently large to support a Marine Amphibious Brigade in the Indian Ocean could amount to nearly $9 billion.[20]

Moreover, as noted earlier, the new airlift program will not be inexpensive. Indeed, the estimated $6–8 billion program cost for the CX may prove far too low. Assuming a unit cost of no more than $49 million, and a requirement for the CX force to lift a mechanized Army division to the Persian Gulf within 21 days, the program cost for this mission alone could be closer to $20 billion.[21]

Is it more cost-effective to procure shipping to support the deployment of a Marine Amphibious Brigade (with 12,000 troops, at most 70 tanks, and a squadron of attack aircraft and helicopters) within five steaming days of the Persian Gulf? Or should we expend over twice the cost of shipping for a MAB to procure sufficient airlift to move the 40,000 troops, 306 tanks, 490 armored personnel carriers, and other equipment that comprise the combat and support elements of a mechanized division to the Gulf within 21 days? The answer depends upon the measure of effectiveness that might be applied. Measured as the rate of firepower relative to time, the MAB probably dominates. Measured in terms of aggregate firepower deployed, however, the division/airlift option is to be preferred. But which is the appropriate measure? Unfortunately, we have no way of determining the point at which a given level of force might be critical in determining the outcome of a crisis that might lead to hostilities, particularly when we cannot be sure exactly who will become involved in such hostilities.

Perhaps the most that can be said is that too much reliance should not be placed upon one or another mode of deployment. If airlift and amphibious lift are truly complementary, they must be treated as such. In that case, the allocation of funds to the Rapid Deployment Force should be reorganized so as to provide an augmented capability to mount opposed landings either in addition to, or as a partial substitute for, the increase in administrative lift capacity (whether by air or by sea) that is currently planned. On the other hand, a major amphibious lift capability may be viewed as irrelevant to the RDF, either because optimism leads to the belief that facilities will always be available or because pessimism leads to the conclusion that we should procure as much force as possible for the mobility dollars that we spend.[22] It might then be best to pull the Marines out of the RDF altogether (with the exception of such contributions as their afloat battalions in the Mediterranean and Pacific might make), and apply them to other tasks where Army forces cannot as easily substitute for their unique capabilities.

Appendix

CX and Amphibious Lift: Some Comparative Costs

CX REQUIREMENTS AND COSTS

The calculations in this chapter estimate the number of CX aircraft required to move the outsize and oversize cargo associated with an Army mechanized infantry division to the Persian Gulf in twenty-one days.[23] The actual CX requirement could be considerably greater, however. Current Military Airlift Command assets, including civilian reserve units, are likely to be fully occupied for the better part of a month, moving only a part of the Rapid Deployment Force, namely the 82d Airborne and 101st Air Assault Divisions, to the Persian Gulf.[24] They might not be sufficient, therefore, to move the other forces that would have to be airlifted. These include support for any Air Force tactical fighter wings that might be part of the RDF, and bulk cargo associated with the airborne, air assault, and mechanized infantry divisions. Nonetheless, the following analysis assumes that MAC assets, supplemented by civilian reserve units, would be sufficient to move these additional RDF elements within the postulated 28-day period. In so doing, it probably understates CX requirements.

The following assumptions also apply:

○ Total outsize and oversize tonnage associated with a mechanized division equals 81,291 short tons.[25]

○ The maximum CX allowable cabin load for a mechanized division is 36 short tons.[26]

○ The longest distance that the CX would have to fly unrefueled (critical leg) is 3,200 miles.[27]

○ Total distance traveled is 6,800 nautical miles.[28]

○ The "block speed" of the CX (that is, the average of its take-off, landing, and cruising speeds) is equal to that of the C-141, or 403 nautical miles per hour.[29]

○ The utilization rate, or average daily use of the entire CX fleet, is 12.5 hours.[30]

○ The "productivity factor" applied to major MAC strategic transports to allow for empty or otherwise nonproductive return flights has been applied to the CX; this common factor is 0.445.[31]

○ The CX will cost no less than $49 million to procure.[32]

○ An additional 20 percent of the unit equipage (UE) aircraft required to carry the mechanized division would be needed to allow for pipeline aircraft (that is, to cover for those in overhaul), as well as for attrition aircraft.[33]

Given these assumptions, determination of the cost of a CX force that can lift a mechanized infantry division to the Persian Gulf is a three-step process. First, it is necessary to establish the tonnage that the CX force would be required to lift daily within a 21-day period. This is found simply by dividing the total tonnage to be lifted (81,291) by 21, for a resulting requirement of 3,871 tons daily.

The next step is to determine the number of CX required to carry 3,871 tons daily. This number can be found by applying standard equations for daily airlift requirement, which are expressed as

$$N_i = \frac{D_i \times L_{ij}}{U_i \times S_i \times R_i \times P_{ij}}$$

where

N_i is the number of aircraft, i, required
D_i is the total distance aircraft, i, travels
L_{ij} is the daily lift requirement
U_i is the utilization rate of aircraft, i
S_i is the block speed for aircraft, i
R_i is the productivity factor for aircraft, i
P_{ij} is the payload (allowable cabin load) for aircraft, i, given
cargo of force, j

and

i   is the CX
j   is the Mechanized division
$D_i = 6,800$
$L_{ij} = 3,871$
$U_i = 12.5$
$S_i = 403$
$R_i = 0.445$
$P_{ij} = 36$

The resulting number of CX aircraft required equals 326 planes.

Finally, the third step is to apply the factor to account for pipeline and attrition aircraft. This factor, set at 20 percent, results in a requirement for 326 x 1.20, or 391, aircraft.

Assuming a $49 million unit cost for the CX, $19.2 billion would have to be expended to procure enough CX aircraft to lift a mechanized division to the Persian Gulf in three weeks.

AMPHIBIOUS SHIPS

A Marine Amphibious Brigade constitutes a Marine brigade and one-third of an air wing. In rough terms, the number of ships required to support a MAB will be three times the number required to support the battalion/wing detachments that constitute a Marine Amphibious Unit (MAU).[34]

Four to six ships normally furnish lift for a MAU.[35] These ships include helicopter platforms, tank and dock landing ships, cargo ships, and a command ship. The four-ship figure applies when a large, general purpose, air-capable amphibious ship (LHA) is included in the amphibious task group. The LHA combines the capabilities of three other ships—a cargo ship, a dock landing ship, and a helicopter carrier. To the LHA must be added another dock landing ship (LSD), which is designed to carry air-cushioned landing craft (LCAC) and other units, a tank landing ship (LST), and an amphibious command ship (LCC). Thus, twelve ships are required to support three battalions.

Of course, if a brigade is to be on station at all times, additional ships are required as backup units. Normally, the ratio of total forces to forward-deployed units approximates 3:1.[36] Amphibious ships could be homeported in Diego Garcia, however. The ratio could then decline to a 1.2:1.[37] This ratio must be applied to each ship type, so that four ships of each type actually would be required (that is, 3 ships x 1.2 = 3.6 ships, rounded to four).

Costing Amphibious Ships: Allowing for Real Cost Growth. Costing the ship types listed above is an extremely hazardous exercise. Apart from the LHA, none has been funded for over ten years, and the last LHA was funded in fiscal year 1971. Estimating the costs of follow-on ships of types currently in the fleet requires not merely an adjustment for inflation, but also an allowance for real cost growth. Cost growth results from several factors, such as increases in the size of a ship and improvements in its electronics and armament. Thus, for example, a follow-on ship of the new LSD-41 class, which represents a variant of the LSD-40 that was procured in fiscal year 1967, will cost $322 million, four times as much in real terms as the earlier ships. It will be a somewhat larger ship, however, and carry a close-in air defense system that is more modern and complex than the two guns which provide the older LSD with AAW protection.

The LSD-41 is the only new amphibious ship in the Administration's current program. Other ships may or may not reflect similar cost growth patterns. Recent estimates that a new LHA might cost roughly $900 million to procure reflect a real cost increase of 150 percent.[38] This figure probably accounts for recent shipbuilding claims settlements for the LHA program that increase the unit price of each ship in the current class. The lower level of real cost growth for the LHA may, however, be peculiar to that ship because, of the four classes under consideration in this section, only the LHA is currently under construction. A follow-on ship might therefore involve fewer design and system modifications.

This chapter makes the following assumptions about amphibious ship costs:

○ LHA costs in fiscal year 1981 dollars represent a 150

percent increase over the fiscal year 1971 dollar cost of the most recently acquired LHA.
o LSD, LPD, and LCC costs reflect a 400 percent real increase over the most recently acquired ships of those classes.

Following are the historic then-year costs, the inflated costs, and estimated current costs (including cost growth, rounded to the nearest $10 million) of the ships in question, in millions of dollars.

Ship	Historic Cost (FY Program)	Inflated FY 1981 Cost	Estimated Cost
LHA	302 (1971)	598	900
LSD	32 (1967)	82	330
LST	25 (1966)	66	260
LCC	70 (1966)	185	740

Applying the factors outlined above, the cost of four ships of each type totals $8.92 billion.

CONCLUDING OBSERVATIONS

The preceding addresses comparative investment costs only. It does not fully account for all life-cycle costs, which include manpower, operations and maintenance, and procurement associated with overhauls and mid-life conversion. Two factors deserve particular note. Employment of the CX could generate a requirement for acquiring additional KC-10 tanker aircraft for the Air Force at a cost of approximately $50 million each. The CX will not be able to transport an XM-1 tank to the Persian Gulf without aerial refueling. On the other hand, Marine Corps end strength might have to be increased if the Marine rotation base cannot support an additional afloat brigade. The preceding analysis merely seeks to illustrate both the magnitude of costs associated with either option and the policy choice implicit in any decision between two very different projection capabilities geared to rapid-response operations.

NOTES

1. The National Security Act of 1947 (P.L. 80–253 [61 Stat. 495] as amended through September 30, 1973) specifies that the "Marine Corps shall be organized, trained and equipped . . . for service with the fleet in the seizure and defense of advanced naval bases and for the conduct of such land operations as may be essential to the prosecution of a naval campaign. . . . The Marine Corps shall develop, in coordination with the Army and the Air Force, those phases of amphibious operations that pertain to the tactics, technique and equipment used by landing forces."

2. Maj. Gen. B. E. Trainor, "Intervention—What, How and Who?"
(paper presented to Congressional Research Service/Congressional Budget
Office Marine Corps Workshop, January 8–9, 1980; processed), p. 3.
Marine forces may, of course, require U.S. Navy protection. They need not
depend on foreign assistance, however.
3. The numbers cited in the text reflect unit equipment (now termed
Primary Aircraft Authorization, or PAA) aircraft. The airlift fleet actually
includes more aircraft (for example, 77 C-5s), with the increment to PAA
serving as pipeline and attrition aircraft.
4. See Dov S. Zakheim, *U.S. Projection Forces: Requirements,
Scenarios, and Options*, Congressional Budget Office, Budget Issue Paper
for Fiscal Year 1979 (April 1978), pp. 9–11.
5. The Navy also relies upon MAC for certain support elements,
though to a lesser degree than the Army and Air Force; and, like the Marine
Corps, it has some organic airlift replenishment capability (C-1 and C-2
force).
6. The KC-130 is the only tanker outside the Strategic Air
Command structure.
7. Readiness rates of less than 100 percent render it extremely
unlikely that sufficient helicopters would be available to move the entire
101st Division simultaneously.
8. "Norway Approves U.S. Pact," *Washington Post*, 14 January,
1981, p. A18. "Prestocking" is a concept that is virtually identical to
"prepositioning," the term associated with the NATO POMCUS program
for the Central Region.
9. "Statement of Secretary of Defense Robert S. McNamara before
the House Committee on Appropriations on the Fiscal Year 1967–1968
Defense Program and the 1967 Defense Budget" (1966; processed), pp.
128–30. An even earlier variant of this plan, which McNamara later
described as "only interim adjustments," involved acceleration of C-141
development and reactivation of 15 troop transport ships. (See McNamara,
p. 125.)
10. Statement of General Harold K. Johnson, Chief of Staff, U.S.
Army, *Military Posture and H.R. 9240*, Hearings before the House
Committee on Armed Services, 90:1 (March and April 1967), p. 580.
11. For reported proposals for CX characteristics, numbers and costs
see "Air Force Expects CX Mission Element Need Statement Soon,"
Aerospace Daily, 4 March 1980, p. 9.
12. Benjamin F. Schemmer, "Brown Directs C-X 10C by September
1985," *Armed Forces Journal International* (March 1980): 30–31; and
"USAF's CX Group Now Sees Plane Roughly Half the Size of a C-5A,"
Armed Forces Journal International (February 1980): 18, 20, 71;
"Difficulty on CX Funding," *Flight International* CXVIII, 1 Nov. 1980,
p. 1677.
13. The Joint Chiefs of Staff reportedly reached a "gentlemen's
agreement" whereby a Marine General would alternate with an Army
General as RDF Commander. *Washington Post*, 3 June 1981, p. 1.
14. John K. Cooley, "U.S. Reaction Time to Persian Gulf Is Limited
By Its Air, Sealift Capacity," *Christian Science Monitor*, 4 February
1980, p. 3; U.S. Department of Defense, *Annual Report, Fiscal Year 1981*,
p. 211.
15. A widely discussed critique of the amphibious mission appears in
Martin Binkin and Jeffrey Record, *Where Does the Marine Corps Go From*

Here? (Washington, D.C.: The Brookings Institution, 1976), pp. 30–41.

16. Ibid., pp. 78–79.

17. See Stephen S. Kaplan, *Mailed Fist, Velvet Glove: Soviet Armed Forces As A Political Instrument* (Washington, D.C.: The Brookings Institution, 1979; processed), especially pp. 14–63 ff.

18. See Drew Middleton, "Soviets Said to Build Arms Caches in Libya, Syria, Persian Gulf Area," *New York Times*, 14 March 1980, p. 11.

19. As previously noted, airlift is critical to the Army's RDF role; and, if the Army is assigned virtually the entire RDF mission, airlift must predominate.

20. At least twelve ships might have to be procured to support a brigade in the Indian Ocean. Factors centering on this figure are discussed in the section entitled "CX and Amphious Lift: Some Comparative Costs."

21. This figure excludes research and development costs, as well as the procurement cost of additional tankers that may be required to support a CX deployment (see section entitled "CX and Amphibious Lift: Some Comparative Costs").

22. One must, of course, be struck by the fact that the pessimism regarding force level requirements does not extend to the availability of reception facilities.

23. There are three categories of cargo, defined by the relationship of their volume to current airlift assets. Bulk cargo can be lifted by all MAC aircraft and commercial carriers. Oversize cargo cannot be lifted by narrow-body commercial carriers. Outsize cargo can be lifted only by C-5s.

24. John J. Hamre, *U.S. Airlift Forces: Enhancement Alternatives for NATO and Non-NATO Contingencies*, Congressional Budget Office, Background Paper (April 1979), p. 57; and Zakheim, *U.S. Projection Forces*, p. 82.

25. U.S. Air Force information, cited in Hamre, *U.S. Airlift Forces*, p. 74.

26. The mechanized division is a heavy division. Its cargo includes many items with greater density than those associated with lighter divisions. The expression of average density or allowable cabin load associated with the CX was derived as a function of total allowable cabin load of sixty-five tons. Source for CX factors: "Air Force Expects CX Mission Element Need Statement Soon," p. 9; source AMST factors: Air Force Regulation 76–2 update for generic AMST performance.

27. This distance is roughly that between Dover Airforce Base and either Israel or Cairo, Egypt. This estimate derives from the postulated CX ability to lift 65 tons (the weight of an XM-1 tank) for 2,400 nautical miles and 50 tons (two XM-2 equivalents) for 2,800 nautical miles. (See "Air Force Expects CX Mission Element Need Statement," p. 9.) This estimate, which is consistent with the 36-ton maximum allowable cabin load for mechanized division cargo, probably is too high, however, since cargo aircraft lift capacity tends to decline in non-linear fashion as a function of distance. In any event aerial refueling certainly would be required to transport an XM-1 tank to the Persian Gulf, unless the CX made at least one additional landing between Lajes and Israel or Egypt.

28. This is roughly the distance between the U.S. East Coast and the Persian Gulf region, assuming a route across the Atlantic Ocean and Mediterranean Sea.

29. An approximation of block speed is:

Average Leg Distance

$$\frac{\text{Average Leg Distance}}{\text{Cruise Speed}} + 25 \text{ minutes}$$

The C-141, with a cruise speed of 425 knots, has a "block speed" of 403 knots for a 3,200 nautical mile distance.

30. U.S. Air Force programmed rates, cited in Hamre, *U.S. Airlift Forces*, pp. 70–72.

31. U.S. Air Force Regulation 76–2, cited in Hamre, op.cit.

32. The $45 million represents the lower end of the $45–$55 million program unit cost range estimated for the CX, inflated to fiscal year 1981 dollars. See 'Air Force Expects Mission Element Need Statement Soon," p. 9. Program unit cost includes research and development costs.

33. This factor is probably somewhat low: If, for example, it is assumed that 10 percent of unit equipment aircraft are required for the CX pipeline, only 0.67 percent would be allowed for annual attrition over a 15-year period.

34. Given the capacity of current amphibious shipping, the number of ships required to support a MAB would probably exceed that for three MAUs. On the other hand, were larger, more modern amphibious ships than those currently in the fleet acquired for the MAB, the number of these newer ships would approximate the requirement for supporting three MAUs with current amphibious forces.

35. See Binkin and Record, *Where Does the Marine Corps Go From Here?*, pp. 25–26. Binkin and Record list three to five ships per MAU, but do not include a command ship (LCC).

36 This statement is based on the assumption that the rough calculation of three units to support one on permanent deployment applies to amphibious ships as well as to aircraft carriers, for which the calculation is most frequently employed. For a detailed description of carrier deployment cycles, see Dov S. Zakheim and Andrew Hamilton, *U.S. Naval Forces: The Peacetime Presence Mission*, Congressional Budget Office, Background Paper (December 1978), pp. 75–80.

37. Ibid., p. 79.

38. See Ibid., p. 63.

10

A Clear and Present Danger:
Soviet Airborne Forces in the 1980s

C. Kenneth Allard

The decade of the 1980s began with the Western World, in some disarray, contemplating the implications of the Soviet Union's intervention in Afghanistan. The most obvious fact of that invasion is that for the first time since World War II, regular Soviet tactical formations have been deployed and committed to combat outside a bloc country. Apart from the general questions of Russian intent raised by this action, the West must ponder the implications of the Soviet Union's capability to deploy large numbers of its forces across distances and within time spans previously thought unattainable. The military correspondent of *The New York Times*, Drew Middleton, put the point succinctly:

> The primary lesson for the United States and its allies in the Soviet Union's swift airborne movement into Afghanistan is that the Russians have the ability to move significant numbers of troops in a relatively short time into situations they consider critical to their policies.[1]

Coming at a time when the Iranian hostage crisis had provided an object lesson in the realities of geopolitics and the limitations of U.S. power projection, the Soviet capability must be seen as a counterpoint which is both worrisome and enviable.

The truth of the matter is that there is little about the expansion of Soviet airborne capabilities which is very sudden; its progress has been incremental, without the dramatic appeal which attends the launching of an aircraft carrier or the testing of a new strategic missile. Not surprisingly, most students of Soviet military affairs concerned with the question of power projection have concentrated their attention elsewhere. The expansion of Soviet naval capabilities under Admiral Gorshkov has monopolized most of this attention, and a substantial body of literature has now emerged which centers on the coercive properties of "Soviet naval diplomacy."[2] Airlift capabilities have generally been treated almost as an afterthought in this literature, usually under the category of "other interventionary forces."[3]

These "other forces" have received some attention from defense analysts concerned with "worst-case" theorizing about the character of high-intensity warfare involving the Warsaw Pact and NATO, analyses which reflect the conventional missions of the airborne troops which would presumably be a part of any attack by the Group of Soviet Forces, Germany. Most, if not all, of these scenarios have used airborne interdiction as a reference point for the initiation of general hostilities, even when the escalation stops short of an unlimited nuclear exchange.[4] Classical military theory acknowledges both airlift and sealift as standard methods of power projection, while also admitting a third category—the stockpiling or prepositioning of military supplies.[5] The Russian variation of that practice has been the shipment of large stocks of weapons and other equipment to client states and to surrogates fighting in countries like Angola and Ethiopia. The greater part of the gross tonnage involved in these arms "transfers" has been moved by sea, usually in ships of the Soviet merchant marine. Only recently, therefore, has there been any notable recognition of the growing Soviet capability for sustained heavy airlift operations in support of their adventures in the Third World.[6]

With the invasion of Afghanistan, the combination of this new airlift capability together with the strategic use of the Soviet airborne forces—the *Vozdushno-Desantnyye Voyska* or VDV—can be seen as a qualitatively new dimension in the means available to Soviet leaders to underwrite their foreign policy objectives. The modernization of these forces over the last decade has reflected the primacy of their conventional wartime missions; however, modernization has also equipped them to perform as a highly capable intervention force at considerable distance from Russian or Warsaw Pact territory, should Soviet interests require them to do so. This chapter thus seeks to examine the Soviet airborne potential in its two most important aspects: airborne troops and the transport air force. Those capabilities will be examined from the perspectives of historical development and current operational possibilities, with particular reference to the Afghanistan experience. Finally, the airborne potential will be discussed in terms of its implications for the nature and extent of the "strategic reach" of the Soviet Union in the 1980s, and the question of preemptive power projection.

SOVIET AIRBORNE TROOPS

The Red Army was quick to embrace the "revolutionary" concept of airborne warfare, conducting some of history's first airborne operations in Soviet Central Asia against resisting Islamic tribesmen.[7] Soviet interest continued into the 1930s, profiting from a companion interest by the Germans and the sponsorship of Marshal Tukhachevskiy. The British, meanwhile, viewed the entire idea skeptically:

> We doubt whether such tactics could be practiced in a civilized army. They are probably only possible in a country like Russia where the people can be driven like cattle and imbued with fanatical ideas.[8]

The gains of the prewar era were quickly wiped out, however, with the opening guns of Operation Barbarossa when the Germans, in addition to their other early successes, managed to destroy virtually all the Red Army's transport aircraft.[9] Airborne operations were, as a result, extremely limited in scope for the rest of the war, being confined to *desant* (assault) tactics in support of conventional ground attacks.[10] Although postwar Soviet airborne forces were reorganized into three corps (100,000 men) and placed in a separate directorate under the Ministry of Defense, they still continued to be limited in effectiveness by inadequate air transport capabilities. They were, however, entirely capable of mounting the battalion-sized tactical *desants* called for by Soviet military doctrine, principally to achieve surprise and shock effect in attacks against rear-area enemy targets. But in no sense were they much more than that, and they were certainly incapable of a major power projection mission.

These limitations did not, however, prevent Nikita Khrushchev from engaging in some rhetorical hyperbole in the aftermath of the Suez Crisis in 1956. His *ex post facto* intimations that large numbers of Soviet airborne "volunteers" stood ready for deployment to the Middle East in support of the Arab cause made for some interesting speculation. Most Western military experts at the time were not impressed by any obvious Russian capability for airborne force projection, but the crisis marked the first time that a potential power projection mission for the Soviet airborne forces received public attention.[11]

The year 1956 also marked the maiden flight of the Antonov-12 transport plane, similar to the U.S. C-130 Hercules, and it entered service three years later. Its payload of 20,000 kg and range of 3600 kilometers gave the Soviet transport air force (VTA) for the first time a respectable mid-range cargo aircraft, one which quickly became the premier machine for transporting paratroops. The 1960s also marked a decade of significant development in the field of airborne equipment, much of it made specifically for these forces, including tactical transport vehicles, light artillery, mortars and self-propelled antitank guns such as the ASU-57.[12]

These new capabilities were much in evidence when Soviet airborne forces spearheaded the invasion of Czechoslovakia in 1968. Under the cover of MiG-17 jet fighters, Soviet air transports landed at the Prague airport in the first minutes of the operation. Linking up with KGB (Soviet secret police) forces already in place, the airborne troops quickly fanned out from the airport to seize key objectives within the Czech capital: government buildings, communications centers and power plants. At the same time, other airborne troops were landed in a series of coordinated assaults which allowed the Soviet forces to establish control over two other major airfields in the area. Thus, they were able to begin a massive airlift of supplies and equipment through these airheads, a link which became ever more critical as the logistic and communications services of the regular Soviet ground forces fell into some disarray. Indeed, the efficiency of the airlift was credited with having staved off a logistical debacle as the ground forces quickly overreached the follow-on capabilities of their organic supply trains. Despite the fact that their landings in Czech territories were unopposed and therefore carried out under optimal conditions, the airborne forces were nevertheless credited by most observers with a performance which was well executed and conspicuously successful.[13]

By 1973, it was obvious that the evolution of the Soviet airborne forces had given a new credibility to the previously nascent ability of the USSR for power projection. During the Yom Kippur War, in October of that year, both the Soviet airlift capability, in assisting the rapid resupply of Egypt and Syria, and the apparent alert of its airborne forces for an interventionist role loomed large in Western calculations, eventually triggering a worldwide alert of U.S. military forces. That response reflected the new reality which backed up Brezhnev's note to President Nixon on 24 October, declaring the USSR's unilateral intention to move troops to the Middle East to bring about a cease-fire.[14] The fact that the confrontation of the superpowers over this issue eventually resulted in a virtual imposition of a cease-fire on their respective friends without the necessity for actual intervention should in no way diminish our appreciation of the new force possessed by the Kremlin. As Graham Turbiville observes, "the seven Soviet airborne divisions served the USSR well by remaining on alert in the

Soviet Union. The threat of their use was probably as effective a means of promoting Soviet aims as their actual movement to Egypt or Syria."[15]

EQUIPMENT, ORGANIZATION AND EMPLOYMENT

The year 1973 was also a banner year for the Soviet airborne forces because it marked the fielding of a new fighting vehicle, the *Boevaia Mashina Desantnaya* (BMD), which represented an entirely new dimension in combat capability and was specifically designed for the airborne mission. Although armored vehicles such as the ASU-57 had long been a part of the airborne inventory, the BMD was responsible for a quantum jump in the tactical firepower and mobility of the Soviet airborne division. Since it was equipped with the Sagger antitank missile launcher and a 73 mm main gun (comparable to the U.S. Sherman tank with its 76 mm gun), the BMD could engage armored targets at ranges of up to 3000 meters. With three mounted machine guns and a crew of six paratroopers able to engage targets through firing ports while still "buttoned up" and on the move, the BMD could also be thought of as a true infantry fighting vehicle—and an effective one at that. Mobility was achieved by an efficient power plant which could propel the vehicle to speeds of at least forty mph overland and six mph in water, since it was also fully amphibious.[16] Its ability to produce shock on the battlefield—a requirement for any fighting vehicle—was a function both of its speed and its armament, and of the fact that, weighing just under nine tons combat-loaded, it could easily be airlifted in significant quantities by both tactical and strategic transports.[17] The entire divisional complement of 107 BMDs, for example, could be airlifted in just twenty-seven sorties of the AN-22 fleet.[18]

In an important sense, the BMD represents an answer to the classic problem of airborne employment: the limited mobility of the airborne infantry, once landed, and their vulnerability to larger, better-armed reaction forces. With the BMD, Soviet paratroopers can land and deploy in remote, more secure locations and then proceed rapidly to their final objectives in more heavily defended areas. Their ability to engage opposing armored forces and all but the most heavily fortified positions means that the paratroopers would have reasonable prospects for success against any but a thoroughly aroused and determined opponent in most power projection scenarios. The BMD will not, of course, be quite so effective should such an opponent be capable of organizing coherent anti-armor defenses, particularly if those defenses are built around modern tanks. Impressive as it may be, the BMD is still a light armored vehicle and as such is not likely to do well in head-to-head engagement against, say, the Chieftain, the Leopard or M-60 series tanks. Fortunately for the Soviets, sophisticated arrangements for combatting armored threats are not a characteristic feature of many of the areas in which the airborne forces might conceivably be employed in a power projection mission.

Since the introduction of the BMD, the Soviets have made a number of adjustments in the airborne division and in its combat support arrangements. A BMD regiment replaced one of the three traditional parachute regiments in each operational airborne division. Supply and service activities were consolidated into a single battalion, as were the previously separate functions of motor maintenance and transport. The revised organizational pattern of the division and its key equipment holdings are shown in Table 1. Of particular note here should be the familiar triangular pattern of Soviet tactical formations (three combat regiments of three battalions each, etc.), plus the comprehensive nature of the combat support given the division commander. While the combat support units may

TABLE 1
SOVIET AIRBORNE DIVISION WITH BMD REGIMENT

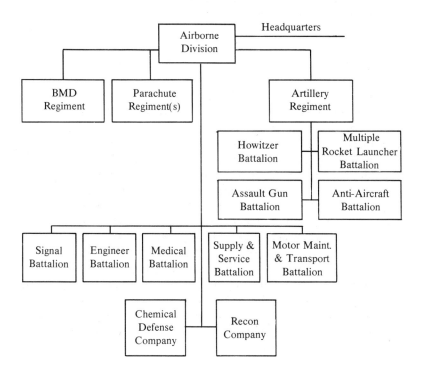

MANPOWER TOTALS:	OFFICERS	MEN	TOTAL
Airborne Division	800	7673	8473
BMD Regiment	140	1451	1591
Parachute Regiment	171	1873	2008

KEY EQUIPMENT

Artillery		Anti-Aircraft	
122 mm Howitzer	18	ZSU 23-2 (Towed A/A System)	36
120 mm Mortar	18	SA-4 SAM (Poss. deploy. only)	36
Mult.-Rocket Launcher	18	SA-7 Grail	36*

Anti-Tank		Other	
ASU 57/85 Assault Gun	30	BMDs	107
85 mm Field Gun	18	AKS-74 Assault Rif. (5.45 mm)	Ind.
Sagger ATGM	27	AT-4 Spigot ATGM**	Unk.
		AGS-17 Grenade Laun. (38 mm)**	Unk.

*   Some sources indicate that the Soviets may be proliferating the SA-7 —a manpacked, heat-seeking missile—throughout the airborne divisions, possibly increasing the total inventory to about 200.

** Indicates a new weapon system possibly present in the airborne inventory.

SOURCES:
Handbook on Soviet Ground Forces (U.S. Army)
Soviet Army Operations (U.S. Army)
Soviet BMD Equipped Forces (Dye)

not always be deployed *in toto*, their existence within the divisional structure allows considerable flexibility in "tailoring" support requirements to specific missions. Probably the most striking feature of the division is the extent to which it embodies the concept of all-around defense and comprehensive firepower. From the equipment list, it will be seen that antitank and antiaircraft defenses have proliferated as much within airborne forces as they have within other elements of the Soviet ground forces, while also incorporating impressive gains in cross-country mobility. The eighteen artillery tubes and heavy mortars are similarly supplemented by a corresponding number of truck-mounted, multiple rocket launchers of the BM-21 series, the latest installment of the famous Katyusha (Stalin's Organ) launchers of World War II. This impressive weapon is capable of delivering forty 122 mm rockets in salvos at ranges of up to 15,000 meters.[19] The paratroopers were also among the first Soviet forces to be equipped with the new AKS-74 assault rifle, a weapon which has attracted some interest in the West with its combat baptism in Afghanistan.

Given the powerful armaments of the eight operational airborne divisions, what is their basic mission?[20] One clue, from Soviet sources, can be found by examining their potential use in conventional wartime situations. The Soviet Dictionary of Basic Military Terms states that "an airborne division is intended to carry out missions deep in the enemy's rear, in coordination with ground troops, and also with the air force and the navy."[21] Much the same thought is expressed in Sokolovskiy's definitive work, *Military Strategy*, where the Marshal adds the following:

> Moreover it should be expected that the role of airborne troops in operations of a future war and their importance among Ground Troops will increase considerably. This can be explained by the changing nature and increased number of tasks to be performed. In the last war, airborne troops were used chiefly in support of ground troops in defeating enemy groupings, while they now must also perform independently such missions as capture and retention or destruction of nuclear missile, air force and naval bases, and other objectives deep within the theaters of military operations.[22]

There is no reason to doubt Sokolovskiy, not only because the theme is consistent throughout Soviet military literature, but also because there are sound tactical principles behind the concept. Although Western writers have tended to question the validity of the airborne role under conditions of modern, high-intensity, linear warfare, the Soviets have shown remarkable consistency in employing large-scale airborne assaults in conjunction with major military exercises.[23] In addition to the strategic airborne assault mentioned by Sokolovskiy, military analysts recognize three other types of *desant* operations common to Soviet tactical practice.[24] Special-purpose units are also trained and organized for these missions: the *reidoviki* ("raiders") for long-range commando operations and the *vysotniki* ("high altitude parachutists") for intelligence, reconnaissance and sabotage operations.[25] All of these functions suggest that the Soviets remain convinced that unconventional shock warfare has its place on the modern battlefield. Also the pattern of deployment of the eight airborne divisions shown in Table 2 suggests both the primacy of the NATO threat—as seen from Moscow—and the fact that airborne employment would also be a logical Soviet tactic in other theaters of operation as well.

The nature of the wartime mission also equips the airborne units well for employment in more limited scenarios. Their equipment is highly mobile and, as noted above, it is capable of projecting a high volume of firepower. Airborne training, even when taken in conjunction with regular ground forces, stresses independent, protracted operations, more often than not under varying terrain and climatic conditions. An important part of the organizational routine is directed toward insuring that an unusually high degree of political motivation remains a characteristic feature of all airborne units. The paratroops themselves are also shown a degree of individual attention which is rare in the Soviet military:

> Recruits are handpicked upon enlistment. They undergo rigorous training in specialized schools for airborne troops. The ideal graduate is a tough, politically-minded soldier who can function as an accomplished commando fighter. . . . Their special training and highly specialized assignments make each division [of paratroops] into a typical commando unit or . . . the backbone of a larger, 'softer' force.[29]

TABLE 2
PROBABLE DEPLOYMENT OF SOVIET
AIRBORNE DIVISIONS

Division Designation	Location	District	Probable Primary Mission Target
76th Guards Airborne Division	Pskov	Leningrad	Finland, Norway, Sweden (NATO north flank)
31st Guards Airborne Division	Kaunas	Baltic	Denmark, Northern Germany
103rd Guards Airborne Division	Vitebsk	Carpathian	NATO Central Army Group
106th Guards Airborne Division	Tula	Moscow	Strategic reserve; special missions
102nd Guards Airborne Division	Kishinev	Odessa	Southern NATO, Turkey, Middle East
104th Guards Airborne Division	Kirovabad	Transcaucasus	Middle East, Persian Gulf
Unknown division (98th Guards?)	Fergana	Turkestan	Persian Gulf, or possible training division
Unknown division (99th Guards?)	Belogorsk	Far East	People's Republic of China

SOURCE:
German Magazine *QUICK*, "Der Geheime Aufmarsch der Russen" (The Secret Build-Up By The Russians), No. 5, 22–29 January 1976, p. 28–33.

NOTES:
(1)   Mission targeting is primarily suggested by location of the division in
relation to known or expected threats. Additional contingency missions worldwide are also, according to Soviet sources, a feature of all airborne divisions.
(2)   Given the paucity of open-source material on Soviet airborne deployments
and the reluctance of the Soviets themselves to clarify such matters in a reliable
fashion, some on the divisional locations cited here (particularly the one listed
at Belogorsk) may not be completely accurate.

The utility of such units in political conflicts of varying degrees
must seem worthwhile to the Soviet leaders, for the attention
lavished on the airborne contingents seems unusual, even when
allowances are made for their important wartime missions. Recent
events in Afghanistan have suggested that this enthusiasm may not
be without some justification; but before examing that situation we
must analyze the forces available to support airborne power
projection.

SOVIET AIRLIFT: TRANSPORTS AND CAPABILITIES

If this study has been at some pains to describe the development
of combat power associated with airborne troops, it is because those
forces represent a kind of end-product of this branch of power
projection. Of no less importance, however, are the parallel
developments in Soviet airlift capabilities, since military transport is
in a sense the arm that swings the fist. The Soviet leaders have
maintained for some time the largest standing airborne force in the
world; but it has not been a credible force for power projection until
quite recently, when the addition of powerful transport aircraft
began to enable greater numbers of troops to be transported to more
distant objectives. The Soviet Air Force is responsible for all airlift
activities under a special branch known as *Voyenno-Transportnaya
Aviatsiya* (VTA), or Military Transport Aviation. Its performance
and equipment show that a considerable amount of attention is paid
by Soviet planners to the creation of a balanced system of air
transport, fully capable of operating at both tactical and strategic
ranges.

The evolution of the long-range transport aircraft in the VTA
inventory is shown in Table 3. The AN-12 started the decade as the
workhorse of the fleet and remains so to this day, despite the steady
retirement of the older models first brought into service in 1959. It is
a four-engine aircraft with a highly reliable service record, having
been initially developed for service with the airborne troops, both as
a cargo carrier and as a jump platform. The Antonov series
continued in 1965 with the development of the AN-22, a huge
turboprop aircraft which, until the American C-5A Galaxy came

into service, boasted the largest payload of any aircraft in the world.[27] In a recent study, Peter Borgart suggests that technical problems halted the production run of this aircraft in 1974, giving added impetus to the developments of the Il'yushin-76, the first Soviet jet transport.[28] The latter half of the decade showed the IL-76 continuing its production run and assuming an ever more prominent place in the inventory. Two of its most notable features include an ability for short take-offs and landings from primitive airstrips,[29] as well as large rear doors that apparently permit in-flight drops of troops and equipment.[30]

TABLE 3
DEVELOPMENT OF TRANSPORT AIRCRAFT BY YEAR

	AN-12	AN-22	IL-76
1970	730	10	—
1971	730	10	—
1972	730	20	—
1973	730	20	—
1974	680	50	—
1975	670	50	10
1976	630	50	40
1977	600	50	80
1978	600	50	80
1979	600	50	100***

Aggregate Tonnage 1970: 16940
Aggregate Tonnage 1979: 22000 (approx. 30% increase)
SOURCES:
  Military Balance 1978–79 and 1979–80
  International Defense Review 6/79 and 8/79 (Borgart)
  Handbook on Soviet Ground Forces (U.S. Army)
  American and Soviet Military Trends (Collins)
  Soviet Armed Forces Annual Review 1979 (Jones)

*** This figure is not held by all sources. *Military Balance 79–80* gives it as 50, while Borgart lists the total at 100. Collins, however, lists the total for 1977 as 80, while Jones puts the 78–79 total at the same figure. The trend and Borgart's more exact figures in other categories support the higher figure used here.

The two most critical features of the transports are range and lift capacity. Figures for these and a number of other critical airlift components are presented in Table 4, in order to show the true capabilites of the VTA inventory to project airborne units and their most critical equipment. The most basic criterion is that of range, and all three of the strategic transports can operate fully loaded to an unrefueled range of at least 200 miles. (There has been some confusion as to the range of the AN-12, unusual for an aircraft of its vintage, but the most authoritative sources support the 2000-mile radius.)[31] The two more recently developed planes, the AN-22 and IL-76, are capable of even greater performance, at ranges as great as 3000 miles.

TABLE 4
LIFT CAPACITY BY TRANSPORT TYPE

	AN-12	AN-22	IL-76
Range at max payload (miles)	2236	3100	3100
Cruising speed (mph)	360	395	430
Lift capability (tons)	22	88	44
BMD lift per plane	2	4	3
Max. troops per plane	100	200	150
Max. paratroops per plane	65	150	120
Planes in-service VTA (from Table 2)	600	50	100
VTA availability @ 80%	480	40	80
Planes in-service Aeroflot	150	36	25
Aeroflot availability @ 50%	75	18	12
Total Aircraft available by type (Aeroflot + VTA)	675	58	100
Aggregate Lift Capability by Lift Category (Exclusive Totals)	1350 BMD 67,500 troops 43,875 paras. 14,800 tons	232 BMD 11,600 troops 8,700 paras. 5,104 tons	300 BMD 15,000 troops 12,000 paras. 4,400 tons
Probable use pattern by aircraft type	Multipurpose Cargo & troops	Airlanded heavy lift	Primary airborne platform in 80s

SOURCES:
   All the World's Aircraft (Jane's)
   American & Soviet Military Trends (Collins)
   The Soviet War Machine (Bonds)
   International Defense Review 6/79 & 8/79 (Borgart)
   BMD-Equipped Soviet Forces (Dye)
NOTE:
   Borgart and Jane's both discuss the development of the follow-on transport to the AN-22, a super heavy-lift transport known as the AN-

40. Borgart suggests that, although its range will be held constant, its capabilities will be approximately half again as large as those of the AN-22. Applying that formula (AN-22 capability x 1.5) to the above lift data, the AN-40 capacities are: Range: 3100 miles; Cruising speed: 525 mph; Max lift: 120 tons; No. BMD: 6; No. Troops: 300; No. Paratroops: 225.

Although the range statistics are impressive, they need to be compared with the relevant lift data. For that reason Table 4 lists the number of BMDs that each aircraft can carry, as well as the total number of paratroops or combat-loaded soldiers that could be carried in each sortie (i.e., one plane flying a single mission). The total number of available transports is then shown by type based on in-service holdings of both the VTA and Aeroflot, the Soviet airline, which could be called upon. An availability rate of 80 percent is posited for VTA assets, a figure which, though arbitrary, is not unreasonable for a generated mission posture. A lower availability rate of 50 percent is used to estimate the number of aircraft which could be supplied by Aeroflot on short notice without disrupting critical services or necessitating major airframe modifications. The total number of aircraft of each type is then derived and multiplied by the four critical categories of lift: equipment tonnage, number of BMDs, number of troops and number of paratroopers. The results are set forth as mutually exclusive aggregates of each category to show the possible combinations available to lift planners (100 BMDs versus x amount of troops and so on).

The wide range of such choices in mission planning is one of the many imponderables encountered in any analytical effort which seeks to compare present Soviet air transport capabilities with the airborne force structure to obtain a more precise idea of their true "strategic reach." Equally vexing are the questions of mission, tactical situation, and combat support forces—to say nothing of the logistics needed in any force projection operation. It is also difficult to know how the Soviets may attempt to compensate in other categories for the extra weight brought about by the addition of the BMD. A Soviet airborne commander, faced with the problem, might reasonably pare down the number of assault guns carried on a particular mission, or else do without several batteries of surface-to-air missiles in the absence of an active air threat. Not surprisingly, estimates of airborne force projection potential tend to vary rather widely in Western sources, while Soviet articles on the subject have, if anything, accentuated the confusion still further. A 1970 article in *Red Star*, for example, described the airdrop of one airborne division during the "Dvina" maneuvers in March of that year: "In the course of 22 minutes, nearly 8,000 paratroopers with full equipment—both light and heavy—were landed in the enemy's rear area."[32]

Fascinating though such assertions are, they tell us little about how an airborne force is likely to be configured and supported in any scenario involving less than total war, particularly if such a scenario were to involve a power projection mission beyond the borders of the Soviet Union. However, it is possible to make some reasonable estimates of how such a force might be organized and transported, using such data as are available from public sources. These data are necessarily crude, inexact and very much at the "macro" level, but they are helpful in gaining an appreciation of just how many airborne troops can be projected by the USSR in a given situation as well as the dimensions of what it would take to support them. With these limitations in mind, we now turn to these data.

MATCHING POWER TO PROJECTION

Several assumptions govern the treatment of this theoretical scenario for force projection. First, there are a variety of sound tactical reasons behind the idea that landing at an airport is more efficient than the faster but more troublesome method of dropping men and equipment by parachute. For these reasons, we will assume that the initial airborne assault force would be air-dropped with the mission of seizing airfields and landing facilities to allow the rest of the force to be air-landed. Second, Soviet tactical doctrine has historically stressed the idea that combat forces must be capable of operating to the greatest extent possible independent of logistical constraints. With this idea in mind, we assume that the airborne force would be tailored around the divisional assault elements: the parachute and BMD regiments, with only a skeleton force along to furnish essential services such as signal, air defense and artillery. Third, we assume that the priority of supply would be directed toward providing essential divisional equipment as well as critical supply items: ammunition, fuel and food to the forces on the ground. Fourth, although the three major Soviet long-range transports are multi-purpose aircraft, the division of labor suggested by Table 4 will be adhered to, with the AN-22 primarily used for transporting bulk equipment, the AN-12 for bulk supplies and the IL-76 for general requirements.

In Table 5, we see how the assault elements of three airborne divisions could be transported by the aircraft available from the strategic transport inventory. For clarity, these capabilities are shown by type of aircraft, although it is of course doubtful that a Soviet planner would organize the force along these lines. The contingent transported by the IL-76 fleet would, in accordance with our initial assumption, be air-dropped, while the rest of the force would be air-landed.

Table 5 shows that even the projection of a force this large would not seriously strain the combined resources of Aeroflot and the VTA, which could handle the mission *in a single sortie of the aircraft involved.* While additional airborne divisions could theoretically be added to the force projected here, it is doubtful that the Soviet high command would wish to commit more than three divisions to a single operation, probably preferring to rely instead on regular Soviet ground forces for additional reinforcements if necessary. The hours shown for each aircraft to fly to a 2000-mile range are shown for each category of transport, a figure based on the range limitation of the AN-12.

TABLE 5
PROJECTION FORCE CAPABILITIES BY
TRANSPORT TYPE

Aircraft Type: Ilyushin-76
Total Available: 100

Force	Equipment	Men	Aircraft Required
BMD Regiment	105 BMD	1591	45
Parachute Regiment	Supplies; light weapons	2008	17
Parachute Regiment	Supplies; light weapons	2008	17
			79

Summary: Force projected equals one divisional assault force air-dropped. Total aircraft remaining: 21; Hours to 2000-mile range: 5.

Aircraft Type: Antonov-22
Total Available: 58

Force	Equipment	Men	Aircraft Required
BMD Regiment	104 BMD	1591	34
Parachute Regiment	Supplies, weapons	2008	8
			42

Summary: Force projected is two-thirds division assault force air-landed. Total aircraft remaining: 16; Hours to 2000-mile range: 5.

Aircraft Type: Antonov-12
Total Available: 675

Force	Equipment	Men	Aircraft Required
BMD Regiment	106 BMD	1591	75
Parachute Regiment	Weapons	2008	20
Parachute Regiment	Weapons	2008	20
Parachute Regiment	Weapons	2008	20
			135

Summary: Force projected is a reinforced airborne division, with the extra regiment bringing the total on the ground to three full divisions, or one airborne corps.
Total aircraft remaining: 540; Hours to 200-mile range: 6.

NOTES:
1. Hours to max range calculated for the 200 mile radius of the scenario.
2. Figures listed show only a *single sortie* of the VTA aircraft committed to the operation in order to illustrate the number of forces which could be projected in a single stroke.

In Table 6 the additional lift requirements necessitated by the major items of airborne divisional equipment are plotted against aircraft capabilities. While the tonnage capacities of each transport might allow them to carry more than the aggregate tonnage shown in some system categories, there are important load constraints for some of the major systems, based on density and critical length or bulk dimensions: where these constraints exist, they have been noted on the chart and calculated into the figure shown for required sorties. The selection of transport aircraft emphasizes again the heavy equipment role of the AN-22 and its importance in allowing the airborne division to enjoy comprehensive fire support once landed. It should be noted that the figures shown on this chart reflect the equipment density and airlift required for the equipment of a single division.

The critical question of logistical support is addressed next in Table 7, for the three most critical categories of supply: ammunition, fuel and food. The absence of any comprehensive information on the logistics of the Soviet airborne division forces a reliance on some indirect, but not unreasonable, estimates for all three categories. As stated in the "basis for estimate" section of Table 7, U.S. Army logistical tables are used for a baseline figure, with differential estimates then made for items peculiar to the Soviet inventory, such as the BMD. The probable aircraft choice here emphasizes the cargo-carrying role of the AN-12 which, while more constrained in gross tonnage capacity, offers important advantages for operating from shorter, more primitive airstrips—and thus allows logistical planners some flexibility in planning airfield use to facilitate distribution. While the ammunition and fuel totals may seem somewhat inflated for a force which may or may not be directly engaged in high-intensity combat operations, Soviet practice emphasizes logistical austerity in other areas to allow a correspondingly greater degree of freedom to the commander in planning maneuver and fire support; therefore a similar predilection is assumed here.

TABLE 6
LIFT REQUIREMENTS OF AIRBORNE
DIVISIONAL EQUIPMENT

System	No. / Division	Weight / System	Total / Division	Load Constraints	Sorties Required	Probable Choice
ASU-57	30	3.3 tons	99 tons	2: AN-12; 3: IL-76; 4: AN-22;	AN-12: 15 IL-76: 10 AN-22: 8	AN-22: 8
85mm gun	18	1.9 tons	34.2 tons	Tonnage	AN-12: 2 IL-76: 1 AN-22: 1	AN-12: 2
SAGGER AT-3	27	24.2 lbs.	0.3 tons	Tonnage	Single sortie	AN-12: 1
ZSU-23-2	36	1.04 tons	37.44 tons	Tonnage	AN-12: 2 IL-76: 1 AN-22: 1	IL-76: 1
SA-4 GANEF	36	12.0 tons (approx.)	432.0 tons	AN-22: 2 only	AN-22: 18	AN-22: 18
SA-7 GRAIL	36	22 lbs.	0.4 tons	Tonnage	Single sortie	AN-12: 1
122mm. how.	18	6.49 tons	117.0 tons	Tonnage	AN-12: 6 IL-76: 3 AN-22: 2	IL-76: 3
120mm mortar	18	300 lbs. (approx.)	2.7 tons	Tonnage	Single sortie	AN-12: 1
BM-21 MRL	18	11.3 tons	203.4 tons	AN-12: 1 IL-76: 3 AN-22: 4	AN-12: 18 IL-76: 6 AN-22: 4	IL-76: 6

Total Tonnage / Division: 926.44 tons
Total Sorties By A/C Type: AN-12:   5
                             IL-76: 10
                             AN-22: 26

SOURCES:
All The World's Aircraft (Jane's)
Soviet War Machine (Bonds)
International Defense Review (Borgart)

NOTES:
1.   Load constraint figures show maximum number of systems which can be loaded by aircraft type, based on cubic feet/density or gross tonnage. The column "Sorties Required" shows numbers required for *each* aircraft category to transport the total divisional system. The probable choice selection shows the most likely type of aircraft to be given the mission, together with the required number of sorties.
2.   The SA-4 antiaircraft missile system is air-transportable and has sometimes been photographed in conjunction with airborne exercises, but there is no solid evidence to place any major SAM system in the *regular* equipment table of the airborne division. However, given Soviet emphasis on comprehensive air defense and the analytical necessity to allow for contingency planning built around the necessity to secure the air space above the landing zones, the SA-4 is cited as a lift requirement here. Obviously, its elimination from the force loading in the absence of an air defense threat would make Soviet lift requirements even lighter.

TABLE 7
PRINCIPAL LOGISTIC LIFT REQUIREMENTS
OF A SOVIET AIRBORNE DIVISION / WEEK

Category of Supply	Basis of Estimate	Sorties Required by A/C Type
Ammunition	Figures obtained from the U.S. Army's principal logistics manual FM 101-10-1 suggest gross ammunition consumption rates for an airborne division under varying combat conditions. For seven days combat under these varying conditions an average figure of 419 short tons (STON) is obtained as a daily rate and multiplied by seven to achieve the rate for a week (2933 STON). To allow for the dissimilarity of the Soviet BMD, which is not matched by any comparable vehicle in the U.S. inventory, an allowance of 30 lbs/round is made, multiplied by the 107 BMDs in the division, times 210 (basic load times seven) = 337 STON. TOTAL AMMUNITION REQUIRED: 3270 STON	*AN-12: 149 IL-76: 75 AN-22: 38

*   Indicates probable choice of aircraft

Category of Supply	Basis of Estimate	Sorties Required by A/C Type
Fuel: Petroleum, Oil and Lubricants (POL)	Estimate is based on consumption figure of 75 gals/day for each of division's principal combat vehicles:	

	No. / Division	Gals. / Week	Total Gallons
BMD	107	75 (7)	56,175
SA-4	36	75 (7)	18,900
			75,075

	Basis of Estimate	Sorties Required by A/C Type
	Allowing an additional 24925 gals. for trucks, jeeps and other vehicles, TOTAL POL REQUIRED: 100,000 GALLONS (378,000 LITERS). Estimate also assumes Soviet use of the PDSJ-1 bulk fuel container (200 liters) which would require 1890 canisters. AN-12 capacity is 84 containers / sortie; IL-76 capacity is 168 containers / sortie. (AN-22 does not carry them.)	*AN-12: 23 IL-76: 12
Combat Rations	FM 101-10-1 is again referred to in the absence of any hard data on Soviet combat rations. Assuming, however, that the Soviets can duplicate the U.S. performance of packaging rations to feed four soldiers / day in a case weighing 25 lbs., the following estimate can be made: 5607 men / division (from Table 5) divided by 4 = 1401.75 x 25 = 35043.75 lbs. TOTAL RATIONS REQUIRED: 35043.75 lbs. = 17.52 tons/day or 122.64 tons/week.	AN-12: 6 *IL-76: 3 AN-12: 2

Sortie Totals
AN-12: 172
IL-76: 3

* Indicates probable choice of aircraft

SOURCES:
US Army Field Manual 101-10-1 (Staff Officer's Logistical Guide)
International Defense Review (Borgart)

In Table 8, we are ready to sum up the combined impact of the airlift requirements generated in this scenario. Multiplying the divisional requirements identified in earlier Tables to take account of the force projected in the scenario, we derive a total of 1039 sorties required to transport the force and maintain it for a minimum of one week. For the convenience of the argument, we have also taken the number of transports committed to the original projection mission and used this figure as a constant for the aircraft available to support its logistical requirements—although here again this would probably not be the case in actual combat operations. But even assuming that it were, the number of sorties per aircraft remains surprisingly low, particularly in the case of the IL-76; if the total number of sorties were, say, raised to 1500, the IL-76 fleet could handle it with little difficulty, thus allowing even more flexibility in

TABLE 8
RECAPITULATION OF AIRLIFT REQUIREMENTS

INITIAL ASSAULT FORCE: (From Table 5)

Single sortie by all aircraft		AN-12: 135
		IL-76: 79
		AN-22: 42

DIVISIONAL EQUIPMENT: (From Table 6)

Single Division	AN-12: 5	
(926 STON)	IL-76: 10	
	AN-22: 26	
Three Divisions		AN-12: 15
(2778 STON)		IL-76: 30
		AN-22: 78

DIVISIONAL LOGISTICS: (From Table 7)

Single Division	AN-12: 172	
(3392.64 STON)	IL-76: 3	
(100,000 GALS POL)		
Three Divisions		AN-12: 516
(10,178 STON)		IL-76: 9
(300,000 GALS POL)		

TOTAL SORTIES:	AN-12: 801
	IL-76: 118
	AN-22: 120
	1039
AVAILABLE AIRCRAFT:	AN-12: 135
	IL-76: 79
	AN-22: 42
	256
AVERAGE SORTIES/AIRCRAFT:	AN-12: 5.93
	IL-76: 1.49
	AN-22: 2.86
	3.43

managing the flow of supplies and additional manpower. It is appropriate here to emphasize again that these figures are at best a rough estimate of the relationship between airborne potential and the power to project it, and that there is considerable room for argument concerning the extent to which such a scenario reflects real world conditions. However, the exercise does serve to show that the potential for projecting such a potent strike force is well within the present capabilities of the Soviet armed forces.

The exercise also suggests, however, some important constraints which should be balanced against those capabilities. For one thing, the mounting of over 1000 sorties requires extensive airport facilities on both ends of these flights. If the target area is located at a distance beyond the round trip radius of the transports, then aviation fuel availability on landing or refueling on the return leg become important considerations. Despite Soviet claims that entire divisions can be dropped within minutes, more routine practice suggests that they too fully appreciate the value of air-landing, a practice which is more efficient but greatly extends the time required to off-load supplies and prepare the aircraft for its return flight. Under these conditions, in fact, the size of the airport facility as a whole is critical since sufficient storage and marshalling areas must be immediately at hand if aircraft are not to get "stacked up" with no place to go. In short, the size of the airhead, fuel availability, and the efficiency with which incoming flights can be controlled, landed, unloaded and sent off are factors which determine not only the potential mission but also the size and composition of an airborne force.

The distance to which such a force could be projected is principally limited by the range of the AN-12 to a radius of 2000 miles from the Soviet Union or Warsaw Pact territory, assuming no mid-route refueling. Even so, that limit encompasses the entire Middle East, the Near East, Western Europe and the northeast quadrant of Africa, from Libya to Kenya. With the use of refueling facilities, say in South Yemen, the range is extended still farther, although the operation becomes correspondingly more complex. The range of the aircraft is also sensitive to overflight considerations with their rights of passage over neutral territory, but these have not troubled the USSR unduly in the past. Of more concern is air superiority or at least air neutrality in the area of the landing zones. Any power projection scenario becomes more complicated if it involves the possiblity of combat, particularly if it calls for an airborne movement. The large, lumbering transports are highly vulnerable to interceptor aircraft or, at lower altitudes, to well-directed ground fire. Either possibility would require tactical fighter escorts; not only would these fighters complicate the operational and coordination aspects of the mission, but their more pronounced range limitations might also be an inhibiting factor in more distant intervention scenarios. This is not to say, however, that the problem of providing tactical air cover at extended ranges is an insoluble one for the USSR: in-flight refueling, prepositioning of fuel stocks and aircraft, or even the "borrowing" of regional surrogate air forces would be among the possible options that might be available. Secrecy, deception and surprise—the traditional attendants of airborne tactics—can also play an important role in obviating the need for close air support in power projection missions. The classic example was provided by the Entebbe raid which, though limited in scope, used stealth to effect an unimpeded approach and landing; one of the first priorities of the raiders was then to disable or destroy the MiG fighters of the Ugandan air force parked nearby.

Within the 2000-mile limit the USSR can fully exploit the natural advantages of geography. The transports returning from the mission of emplacing our theoretical airborne corps could be rapidly reloaded with either additional supplies or troop reinforcements. The transports might be augmented as well by other carriers, especially if the target area had access to coastal facilities which could be serviced by the Soviet Navy or Merchant Marine. An excellent example of a comparable scenario was provided as recently as October 1979 when, according to one press report, the AN-22 fleet was used to fly "two brigades" (i.e., regiments) plus artillery and armored vehicles, "from southern Russian landing bases to landing fields in South Yemen and Ethiopia," having followed a circuitous route over the Persian Gulf and around the Arabian peninsula.[33] Although this account is sketchy, there is little doubt that the armored vehicles were BMDs and the troops were part of an airborne division.

While the potency of the airborne threat is most acute within the 2000-mile limit, it exists in a more than theoretical sense at ranges "to the operational radius of modern aircraft," to quote the phrase used by General Margelov, Chief of Soviet Airborne Troops.[34] In the case of the AN-22 and the IL-76, that range extends to over 3000 miles and, as we have seen, those transports together can project up to two divisions in a single sortie. While they could also be used to sustain such a force, it is equally clear that the effort would involve real difficulties, particularly if the AN-12 could not be refueled en route and were thus eliminated from playing a useful role in the operation. This is one reason why the development of the AN-40 transport, the replacement for the AN-22, is a matter of great interest. Peter Borgart explains that the aircraft is still in the design or prototype phase and that its development may be slowed by difficulties in procuring an acceptable jet engine for an aircraft which is thought to be half again as powerful as the AN-22.[35] Should the AN-40 be successfully developed and acquired by the VTA in significant quantities, this aircraft, in combination with the steadily increasing numbers of the IL-76 fleet, would give the USSR a truly intercontinental reach with its airborne forces. For the present, however, its extended regional reach is sufficiently strong to support large-scale airborne operations in a number of areas of interest to the Soviet Union. One of those areas is Afghanistan.

MATCHING POWER TO PROJECTION: SOVIET AIRBORNE FORCES IN AFGHANISTAN, 1979

While the USSR has an undeniable ability to place large numbers of airborne forces in distant places, the experience of the Soviet airborne troops sent to Afghanistan in late December 1979 suggests that significant results can often be obtained with a much smaller force. A brief treatment of their role in this situation is therefore instructive, and will demonstrate the fact that this topic is of more than theoretical interest.

The background of the Soviet decision to intervene in Afghanistan is now sufficiently well understood to support the contention that the final planning for the operation probably began following General Pavlovskiy's (Commander-in-Chief, Soviet Ground Forces) second visit to that country in mid-October. Following subsequent meetings in early December a force of 50,000 troops was assembled on the northern Afghan border.[36] On 8–9 December, "an airborne regiment of 1500–1800 troops" was flown into Bargram airbase north of Kabul; the move excited wide speculation in press reports since this was the first overt sign of Soviet intentions to enter the fighting directly.[37] On 20 December, the unit headed north to the guerilla-controlled area of the Salang Pass in order to secure the "highway between Kabul and the Soviet border, the eventual invasion route for overland forces."[38] The same press report described the force as "a special unit of Soviet troops with unusually heavy armament of tanks and artillery;"[39] but the size and equipment configuration leave little doubt that the unit—the first Russian combat force to enter Afghanistan—was simply a BMD regiment. In that regard it certainly was a "special unit"—but hardly unique.

On 24 December, an airlift began "averaging one flight every ten minutes of daylight, from dawn on the 24th of December to nightfall on December 26th," eventually bringing in 5000 airborne troops.[40] That figure closely approximates the total assault forces for an airborne division deployed with its organic BMD regiment (5190); the number of BMDs subsequently seen in Kabul would also tend to confirm the divisional strength figure. The division apparently had most of 27 December to consolidate its positions in the city; meanwhile, President Amin had an afternoon courtesy call from a Soviet government minister, accompanied by the Soviet ambassador.[41] At about seven o'clock that evening, however, the Soviet paratroopers simultaneously struck at the telecommunications center, key government buildings and the presidential palace. The force which surrounded Amin's palace was "spearheaded by light tanks [i.e., BMDs] that had been airlifted in [and] was composed of no more than two or three battalions."[42] Most probably this was the division's BMD regiment which, together with the other two parachute regiments, did a creditable job of executing its requirements with speed and precision. By the next morning Kabul was calm and the airlift began again. Soviet motorized rifle and armored forces had crossed the border during the night and were now on their way to assigned positions within Afghanistan.

Admittedly, the Soviet leaders enjoyed great advantages from their contiguous border with the target country, the most significant of which was the ability to mass large quantities of troops just across the line. In the event, they had to travel less than 200 miles overland to reach Kabul, and they clearly benefited from the BMD regiment prepositioned to cover the most critical part of their advance. The airborne units, however, had the most demanding part of the mission and performed well. To be sure, political control and deception made possible the unopposed landing of the airborne division in Kabul and facilitated its movement to key targets. However, it should be remembered that the paratroopers were, for the most part, in combat for the first time. They had also been transported from four embarkation areas in western Russia (Vitebsk, Smolensk, Pochinok and Seshcha), a distance of some 2300 miles to Kabul.[43] There they were required quickly to orient themselves, and to carry out a sophisticated military operation with clockwork timing. The paratroopers' training has obviously had the intended effect and must, in Soviet eyes, fully justify the time and money spent on their development.

The VTA also comes in for a certain amount of credit for their part in the operation, although the closeness of the Soviet border did make their task easier, allowing them to employ the full range of tactical and strategic transports; complete control of the airfields in Kabul also permitted maximum efficiency in use of the air corridors. With these advantages, it is hard to avoid the conclusion that most commercial airlines would have done as well. However, the Soviets have had some difficulty handling large logistical movements in the past, particularly when they had to be moved by air. Their experience in large-scale movement and logistical support operation cannot but be for the best in terms of developing experience in the administrative side of large airlift operations.

COMPARATIVE ADVANTAGES: AIRBORNE VERSUS OTHER METHODS

The example of the airborne intervention in Afghanistan leads directly to the question of the relative merits of this form of power projection over the others which are available to the Soviet leadership. There are, of course, few absolutes to be discovered since the "choice of weapons" in any intervention scenario is dependent not only on the intent to intervene (discussed below) but also on the relative stakes involved, the local political and military situation and the possiblity for superpower confrontation. A great deal similarly depends on geography: a Soviet decision to intervene in Sri Lanka would, for example, be strongly affected by the numbers of Soviet ships which could support such an operation, as well as the extent to which those ships could be threatened by the U.S. Navy. Soviet power projection has also been characterized in recent years by a renewed commitment to an old tactic, the use of surrogates to further Moscow's objectives in the Third World; the use of these proxies has allowed the development of new client states while permitting the USSR to escape the onus and direct costs of "personal" involvement. Indeed, these methods were so successful that, until the Afghanistan invasion, it was a part of the conventional wisdom that the Soviets would never intervene in a situation directly unless it threatened a new apocalypse.

If we are now witnessing a growing ability and willingness on the part of the USSR to project its power abroad in more direct ways, it is important to be precise about what advantages would accrue to an airborne intervention, especially since the disadvantages of political and military risk seem so obvious to Western minds. Four basic factors seem most likely to affect such a decision:

1. Speed: Airborne intervention is the most rapid means of power projection available to the Soviet leadership, a concept which is of importance for two reasons. First, the rapidity of an airborne deployment allows a wider "decision gate" in responding to events: final decisions can be postponed even while the forces are alerted for a potential movement. A naval deployment involves a much earlier commitment if the ships are not already on station, even though it too can later be amended or cancelled. Second, the speed of the airborne deployment allows greater flexibility in responding to a rapidly unfolding situation: the airborne force can reach objectives in hours whereas naval forces may take days or even weeks— assuming that the target is within range of a naval force at all.

2. *Surprise and Deception:* The Soviet penchant for these qualities, as the Russians themselves put it, "is well known," particularly when it comes to intervention scenarios. The most notorious example of this feature in modern times was the concerted effort by Brezhnev and Kosygin in August, 1968 to reassure the Czech leadership of their honorable, pacific intentions—almost up to the very moment of the invasion. Airborne movements offer important advantages for both strategic deception and tactical surprise, a fact much commented upon in the aftermath of the Afghanistan invasion, since it now appears that U.S. intelligence may have been mistaken on the extent of the Soviet build-up and the role of the initial airborne units committed.[44] One newspaper went so far as to quote a recent article by a Soviet army major, which was printed in *Red Star:*

> It must be said how important it is to conceal one's true intentions, manpower, equipment and combat resources from the enemy. Frequently, in order to achieve this and lead the enemy into a mistake, something more is required than cunning, even on a very large scale.[45]

An airborne movement can embody these principles: it can originate in remote airfields, travel by routes and altitudes that minimize radar detection and observation, and even create diversions or indirections en route that tend to conceal its true objective until the final approach. Most of all, the speed of the movement is an aid in surprise, if only because it becomes difficult for opposing intelligence systems to collect the information and process it in time for a decisionmaker to have anything but an historical interest in the matter. Naval movements, by contrast, are much slower and more difficult to conceal, since freedom of the seas and existing conventions allow ships of opposing navies to shadow each other closely while in international waters.

3. *Political Warfare:* All Soviet armed forces theoretically exist in order to defend the "Socialist motherland" and to advance the revolutionary cause world-wide. The airborne forces, because of their unique position and capabilities, represent an important political asset in themselves, one which can, moreover, go hand-in-glove with the *sub rosa* arts of political warfare practiced by the KGB. One British authority calls the close cooperation between the airborne forces and the KGB "characteristic," citing the tightly

coordinated pattern of their activities in the opening hours of the Czech invasion.[46] Subsequent histories of the Afghanistan intervention will undoubtedly provide further evidence on this point. The basic organizational mission of the paratroops—long-distance raids, sabotage and seizure of key facilities—is easily adapted to "peacetime" use in delivering either a *coup de main* or a *coup d'état*: the imperative in either case is to achieve quick, decisive results with a small, elite force. The organizational processes of airborne recruitment, training and daily activities reinforce this objective, as well as insuring the instant availability of these forces for either conventional or political warfare.

4. Bureaucratic Perceptions: The airborne forces enjoy a relative advantage in political warfare of a quite different sort—the bureaucratic process of influence-building in the upper echelons of the Ministry of Defense and the Politburo. In any bureaucracy there is an inevitable competition for funds, personnel and equipment, and therefore for the missions which will reasonably support such allocations.[47] This precept is doubly true if the bureaucracies happen to be military, and the attention lavished on the airborne forces is ample testimony of their success in these struggles. In part, this is due to the recognition that these forces have a valid peacetime mission in projecting Soviet power; one does suspect, however, that some jealously guarded prerogatives are at stake as well. The Soviet Navy has enjoyed substantial and continuing support in building its own power projection forces in the last fifteen years. Despite Admiral Gorshkov's success, the Soviet Union remains essentially a land power, both by tradition and bureaucratic preference. Thus, the development of the airborne forces might be seen even as a hedge erected by the Ground Forces against the Navy's total expropriation of the power projection mission. Bureaucratic favor of this sort does not always equate, of course, with an automatic preference by the political leadership to choose the airborn forces over any other form of intervention, especially since a multitude of other factors will always be involved in such a decision. However, the visibility of these forces, the presence of their advocates in high councils of state, and their unmatched record as a tool for strategic intervention strongly suggest that their employment will inevitably be a "live option" in future scenarios.

The four relative advantages summarized here are not intended to suggest, however, that the other methods of strategic intervention fade into insignificance by comparison. Bruce Porter has observed that varying types of strategic intervention strategies—arms shipments, use of proxies, enhanced teams of "advisors," KGB manipulation, etc.—are strongly affected by both the local level of conflict and by Soviet perceptions and objectives.[48] The Soviet Navy has similarly been able to play a greater role in support of Kremlin statecraft over the last ten years, and every trend points to its continued expansion in the future. Indeed, should the Soviets deploy more carrier-centered battle groups and greater numbers of amphibious assault and cargo ships of the *Ivan Rogov* and *Ropucha* classes, they will be capable of supporting a wide range of intervention strategies throughout areas of the Third World previously beyond their effective reach. Naval forces of this kind are also inherently capable of performing joint operations in which carrier-based air cover and over-the-beach logistical support can play decisive roles in complementing an airborne assault. It is just such an integration of these varied combat arms which has been a hallmark of U.S. military doctrine and a consistent feature of such operations as the 1965 incursion into the Dominican Republic. Current Soviet practice suggests that they have been fully attentive to the lessons of both the theory and practice of joint operations, and that they are intent upon ending U.S. domination of this form of power projection.

THE LARGER PERSPECTIVE:
PREEMPTIVE POWER PROJECTION

The discussion thus far has centered on the capabilities of Soviet airborne forces. The more difficult problem, of course, is not capability but intent: for this part of the question we must turn to the larger dimensions of Soviet foreign policy objectives to determine the most likely situations which would stimulate a direct Soviet involvement—with the attendant possibility of airborne employment. As the earlier discussion suggests, the commitment of these forces has not been taken lightly, nor opted for in every conceivable instance where their use might have been of some advantage. The airborne forces, moreover, have never been employed by themselves but, true to established Soviet tactical doctrine, have always been part of a much larger intervention by elements of the regular ground forces. In both Czechoslovakia and Afghanistan, that intervention was clearly a major foreign policy initiative—an intent—which merely utilized the military arm (the capability) as the executor of "policy by other means."

Even with the great strides made in the general development of Soviet military power over the last decade, there is little reason to believe that these priorities will be reversed or that the tail will come to wag the dog. However, it is another question entirely if relative power asymmetries in the American–Soviet military force projection equation will induce a greater Russian willingness to engage in bolder adventures on the basis of a greater competitive edge. If one considers the area of the Eurasian land mass and its adjacent territories, nowhere are these asymmetries—or "windows of opportunity"—greater than in the area of the Persian Gulf–Indian Ocean. Nowhere else are Western interests so critically engaged but so poorly defended, and in few other areas are the geopolitical trends running so clearly in Moscow's favor. The Soviet leaders have denied vigorously that their actions in Afghanistan are a prelude to further moves against the oilfields, or that they are part of a larger, grand strategic design to establish hegemony over the region. While not accepting these assertions at face value, many Western observers remain skeptical that the Soviets would deliberately follow a course of action which would almost certainly bring about a direct confrontation with the United States and its attendant possibilities for nuclear war.

Probably the most interesting facet of the problem has been the extent to which other Soviet actions in the region have been treated so casually over the past several years. While there is little reason to believe that the April 1978 coup in Afghanistan was anything other than a spur-of-the-moment opportunity for the Russians, the USSR has been considerably more manipulative in its actions elsewhere in the area. Their involvement in the Horn of Africa, which from a strategic standpoint has far more importance for the Indian Ocean–Persian Gulf area than it does for Africa as a whole, was relatively low-key, indirect and conducted largely through the use of surrogate forces; more significant, however, were the vast amounts of Soviet equipment brought into Ethiopia and the presence, widely reported in the West, of senior Soviet officers who were in virtual command of field operations. Edward Luttwak has recently written of Soviet efforts to build an armored force manned by Cubans stationed in South Yemen, and has speculated that the only conceivable use for such a force would be in a Soviet-sponsored move against the Sultanate of Muscat-Oman, which effectively controls the southern access to the Strait of Hormuz.[49] Adding some urgency to his thesis of Soviet involvement on the Arabian peninsula was the attack mounted on the Grand Mosque in Mecca in November 1979, which nearly succeeded in its apparent objective of assassinating the Saudi royal family. Since the attack, evidence has mounted of the involvement of Cuban and Russian "advisors" in training and equipping the terrorist group for this mission.

While these actions are not conclusive proof of a Soviet "master plan" for the Arabian peninsula, they certainly suggest that this is an area in which the USSR appears to be seeking direct influence by indirect means. If this is true, and to the extent that this strategy of indirection continues to work, the Soviet leaders are unlikely to venture into a more direct involvement: after all, why tamper with success? There is, however, reason to suspect that the ante has gone up in the region. For one thing, the raid on the Grand Mosque appears to have had a considerable psychological impact upon many of the regimes in the area, however much they may be trying to display an attitude of business-as-usual. There is consequently a likelihood of increased attention by these countries to the capabilities of their indigenous security forces. More importantly, there is a question of involvement in the region by Western military forces, most notably those of the United States, in response to the potential loss of either oil-rich sheikdoms or strategically situated entities such as Muscat-Oman. In the aftermath of the Afghanistan invasion, Carter Administration spokesmen such as Clark Clifford went so far as to raise the specter of potential nuclear conflict in the region, and the creation of an effective Rapid Deployment Force targeted on Southwest Asia quickly became an urgent military priority.

While these measures were taken with the idea of deterring the Soviet Union from any wider involvement in the area and in particular from threatening Western oil supplies, the situation as it now stands poses an interesting problem for Soviet foreign policy. The Persian Gulf presents the USSR with important opportunities for national aggrandizement intertwined with what is still a relevant consideration for the Soviet leadership: support for wars of national liberation. While the USSR can exploit internal unrest in a number of countries in the region through manipulation and subversion by the KGB and irregular forces, there is a question as to just how far these methods can take it given the recent changes in the regional environment. For example, if Edward Luttwak's putative Cuban–Yemeni armored force were to launch a decisive struggle to bring down the Sultan and seize control of the land area overlooking the Strait of Hormuz, how can the USSR be sure that this action will not precipitate U.S. intervention? If such an intervention does take place—and a conventional Leninist analysis would certainly suggest that it might—is there any way to halt a potential U.S.–Soviet confrontation leading to a nuclear exchange?

One way of precluding either eventuality would be for the Soviets to follow a strategy of preemptive power projection, a concept which calls to mind Nathan Bedford Forrest's old axiom about "getting there firstest with the mostest." In this case, however, the idea of "firstest" is the more important concept, since the objective is to force the other power either to retreat entirely or else risk a face-to-face tactical engagement that carries the inherent risk of nuclear escalation. The key requirement in such a strategy is to project a credible combat force into a disputed area with sufficient speed and surprise so as to present the opposing superpower with a *fait accompli*. In an important respect, the strategic aims of this form of power projection are not simply limited to military seizure of a key city or geographic feature. Even more important are the paralytic effects of a swiftly executed, preemptive deployment upon the decision-making apparatus of the opposing superpower, which, when confronted by such a modern-day version of Scylla and Charybdis, is left with no alternative but to seek its own survival. An analogous situation is common enough in chess, in which the queen's bishop can make a long, diagonal strike to seize an exposed piece and place the opposing king in check; the king must then be moved from danger, even if it means sacrificing a valuable but lesser piece.[50]

One of the more agreeable features of such a strategy, from a Soviet point of view, is that it can be combined with a variety of facesaving measures, which, however transparent to the rest of the world, provide an important ideological cloak of legitimacy. In Afghanistan, for example, the Soviets have repeatedly claimed that they were invited in by the legitimate government to oppose an externally-driven threat. Much the same kind of scenario can easily be envisioned in other countries: Soviet-inspired internal uprisings result in the formation of a "provisional revolutionary government" which, prior to consolidating power or even while still engaged in combatting local security forces, broadcast an appeal for Soviet assistance. Under the cover of such a request, Soviet airborne forces would be the most logical ones to be employed. Their transports are capable of reaching any country in the region within a matter of hours, their combat potential renders them capable of providing a decisive edge in most tactical situations, and their political motivation and training makes them highly suitable for such a role. Most important, however, is the fact that the speed of such an airborne employment would present the Western world with a *fait accompli*: Soviet forces would be in place and it would now be our turn to cross a border. Under these circumstances, it is difficult to see any other response but a troubled acquiescence by the West.

Such a scenario is not at all far-fetched in almost every conservative Arab regime in the Middle East; in Iran, the only surprising thing is that such an eventuality has not already occurred. Each of the required elements would seem to be present: internal strife, a strong domestic communist party, a pronounced capability for clandestine action by the local Soviet embassy, and the proximity of regular Russian ground forces which could invade the country from three separate directions. Thanks to the Shah, Iran also has a number of modern airport facilities—more than most other countries in the region—which would be entirely capable of supporting a multidivision force. The most likely staging areas within the Soviet Union for such a move are on both sides of the Caspian Sea, and their effectiveness is enhanced by the significant numbers of forward air bases and landing fields located throughout the Caucasus region. These facilities would enable a Soviet force to enjoy the same type of unconstrained logistical and tactical support accorded the troops in Afghanistan.

Elsewhere in the region, the Soviet advantage is not so preponderant, but it nevertheless remains significant. A Soviet airborne force landing in Riyadh, for example, could not count on a rapid link-up with regular ground forces unless rights of passage were obtained from Iraq, or unless some other way were found to offset the fact that no direct overland links exist which could be readily exploited by regular Soviet tactical formations. There are also significant constraints on the numbers of runways in the region which could accommodate the major Soviet transports, and in particular the AN-22 with the 6500 feet of runway space it requires for take-off.[51] Howver, these drawbacks could be alleviated to some degree by innovations which would hardly over-tax Soviet capabilities. The absence of a ground link-up might be offset by either the expansion of an airhead or by the presence of an indigenous force which was sufficiently strong to turn the airborne augmentation into a decisive advantage. The constraints on runway space are harder to overcome, but not unduly so. Air-dropping, though not the preferred way to go, is a constant feature of Soviet tactical exercises and can be handled on a large scale with some efficiency. In the areas of the region which are contiguous to the sea, there is also a possibility for logistic and limited tactical support by the Soviet Navy.

The potential use of the Soviet airborne forces as an element of preemptive power projection thus represents a remarkably flexible strategic asset should Soviet foreign policy turn out to be as expansionist in fact as it now appears to be in the minds of many Western analysts. Strictly speaking, these forces have been developed around a valid conventional mission and without many of the more obvious earmarks which would have signalled a dedicated intent to commit them as an intervention force in limited warfare scenarios. The fact remains, however, that the airborne forces currently represent a highly capable intervention force, even though their equipment and transports do not incorporate many of the high technologies that many seem to equate with strategic potency. The efficiency and care which has marked their development now means that the Soviet leadership can, with high confidence, project large numbers of Soviet airborne forces to any point within two thousand miles of Russian or Warsaw Pact territory, should an unfolding situation require such a response. For the West, this Soviet capability looms as an unhappy fact of life for the current decade; it contrasts with the relative power disadvantages with which the United States must now contend, particularly in the area of the Persian Gulf. Just how great this power differential is at the present moment was recently underscored by a Congressional study of comparable U.S. airborne capabilities; the study concluded that it would take more than eleven days for the single U.S. airborne division to reach the area of the persian Gulf.[52] The contrast with the demonstrated strength of the Soviet airborne forces—with its strategic reach measured in hourse—is a chilling one, reminding us againt that these forces do indeed present a clear and present danger.

NOTES

1. Drew Middleton, "Soviet Display of Flexibility," *New York Times*, 28 December 1979, p. 1.
2. To borrow the title of the latest book in this field, *Soviet Naval Diplomacy*, ed. Bradford Dismukes & James M. McConnell (New York: Pergamon Press, 1979).
3. For example: Ibid., Appendix B, "Other Interventionary Forces—Military Transport Aviation and Airborne Troops."
4. Perhaps the most topical example of the genre is Genral Sir John Hackett's book, with its somewhat lurid title, *The Third World War: August 1985* (New York: Macmillan, 1978).
5. A theoretical, if non-technical treatment of these categories is contained in Richard B. Rainey, "Mobility: Airlift, Sealift and Pre-positioning," RAND Corporation Study, February, 1966.
6. For example: the difference listed for airlift and sealift tonnage to Egypt and Syria during the Yom Kippur War in Dismukes & McConnell, *Soviet Naval Diplomacy*, Table 5.8, pp. 208–9. However, William Schneider, Jr. states that Soviet airlift was "decisive" not only in Egypt–Syria in 1973, but also in Angola, Ethiopia, and Afghanistan. "Soviet Military Airlift: Key to Rapid Power Projection," *Air Force Magazine* (Annual Soviet Aerospace Almanac) 63, No. 3 (March 1980), p. 86.
7. This section draws heavily from Roger A. Beaumont's discussion of the history of airborne warfare in Chapter Five of his book, *Military Elites* (New York: Bobbs, Merrill & Co., 1974).
8. Ibid., p. 80, citing "Parachute Tactics," *The Aeroplane*, 6 November 1935, p. 550.
9. Ibid., p. 81. See also John Erickson, *The Road to Stalingrad* (New York: Harper & Row, 1975), especially Chapter 4.
10. See Peter Vigor's lively account of World War II *desants* in "The Forward Reach of the Soviet Armed Forces: Seaborne & Airborne Landings," *Soviet Military Power & Performance*, ed. John Erickson and

E. V. Feuchtwanger (Hamden, CT: Archon Books, 1980).

11. See Graham H. Turbiville's comments in this regard, "Soviet Airborne Troops," *Soviet Naval Influence*, ed. Michael MccGwire and John McDonnell (New York: Praeger, 1977).

12. Ibid., p. 280.

13. Leo Heiman, "Soviet Invasion Weaknesses," *Military Review* LXIX, No. 8, August 1969, pp. 38–45. See also Philip A. Karber, "Czechoslovakia: A Scenario of the Future?" *Military Review* LXIX, No. 2 (February 1969), pp. 11–21.

14. Stephen S. Roberts, "Superpower Naval Confrontation," in Dismukes & McConnell, *Soviet Naval Diplomacy*.

15. Graham H. Turbiville, "Soviet Airborne Troops," p. 288.

16. Ray Bonds, ed., *The Soviet War Machine* (London: Salamander Books, 1976), p. 183. (Hereafter referred to as *SWM*)

17. The author wishes here to acknowldge his debt to the best of these discussions, a research paper by LTC Joseph Dye, "Soviet BMD-Equipped Forces," completed in April, 1978 under the auspices of the U.S. Army's Institute for Advanced Slavic Studies, Garmisch, West Germany.

18. Ibid., p. 26.

19. Bonds, *SWM*, p. 194.

20. This number is subject to some doubt. Most academic publications list the total number of airborne divisions at seven but the authoritative *Military Balance 1978–79* (London: International Institute for Strategic Studies, 1979) lists the total at eight. In *Soviet Army Operations*, the U.S. Army Intelligence and Threat Analysis Center states that the eighth division is a training command (Arlington Hall Station Virginia: U.S. Army Intelligence and Threat Analysis Center Report #IAG 13-U-78, April 1978, p. 45.

21. *Dictionary of Basic Military Terms* (Moscow: Voyenizdat, 1965), reprinted under U.S. Air Force auspices and published by the Superintendent of Documents (Washington: U.S. Government Printing Office, n.d.), p. 45.

22. V. D. Sokolovskiy (Marshal of the Soviet Union), *Soviet Military Strategy*, 3d. ed., ed. Harriet F. Scott (London: MacDonald's & Jane's, 1975), p. 250.

23. According to Graham H. Turbiville, these landings have become "commonplace" since the early 1970s. See Turbiville, "Soviet Airborne Troops," p. 286.

24. *Soviet Army Operations*, pp. 3–7.

25. Dye, "Soviet BMD Equipped Forces," p. 7.

26. Amnon Sella, "Patterns of Soviet Involvement in a Local War," *Royal United Services Institute for Defense Studies*, June 1979, pp. 54–55.

27. Peter Borgart, "The Soviet Transport Air Force," *International Defense Review* XII (July 1979), p. 945. I am greatly indebted to this account for the wealth of technical detail it contains on existing and planned VTA transport aircraft.

28. Ibid.

29. Ibid.

30. Bonds, *SWM*, p. 90.

31. John M. Collins, *American and Soviet Military Trends* (Washington: Georgetown University Center for Strategic and International Studies, 1978) lists the range of the AN-12 as 400 nautical miles (p. 304)

while Bruce Porter lists the range at 750 miles, "The Technology of Intervention: Advances in Soviet Military Capabilities" (Unpublished Ph.D. dissertation, Harvard University, 1979), p. 106. Both figures are refuted by Peter Borgart, "Soviet Transport Air Force," who lists the range at 3600 km. Bonds, *SWM*, also lists the 3600 km range or 2236 miles (p. 87). The U.S. Army *Handbook on Soviet Ground Forces* (Washington, D.C.: U.S. Government Printing Office, 1975) gives the figure as 2100 miles (pp. 6–98). I have selected the only estimate to emerge twice, not for that reason alone, but also because the 2000-mile figure is similar to the range of comparable U.S. aircraft like the C-130 Hercules.

32.   *Red Star*, 12 March 1970. Cited in *Review of the Soviet Ground Forces, Defense Intelligence Report RSGF 2-77*, October 1977, Defense Intelligence Agency, Washington, D.C., p. 68.

33.   "Russia's Secret Airflift," *Newsweek*, 26 November 1979, p. 33.

34.   Y. Alekseev and E. Tserkover, "The Wings of the Guards" (Interview with General Margelov) Nedelya #19 (April 30–May 6, 1967), pp. 4–5. Cited by Graham H. Turbiville, "Soviet Airborne Troops," p. 287.

35.   Peter Borgart, "Soviet Transport Air Force," pp. 948–9. Based on this projection of the AN-40's potential (AN-22 x 1.5) its basic operational characteristics are estimated in Figure III.

36.   *Christian Science Monitor*, 14 January 1980, p. 10.

37.   William Beecher, "A Buildup By Soviets At Afghan Border," *Boston Sunday Globe*, 23 December 1979, p. 1.

38.   Don Oberdorfer, "Soviet Invasion Propels Afghanistan Into Center of World's Attention," *Boston Globe*, 3 January 1980, p. 10.

39.   Ibid.

40.   Ibid.

41.   Ibid.

42.   *Washington Post*, 7 January 1980, p. 16.

43.   Cover story, *Newsweek*, 7 January 1980, and *New York Times*, 27 December 1979, p. 1.

44.   "US Intelligence Failure," *Newsweek*, 14 January 1980, p. 22.

45.   Soviet Army Major M. A. Ziyeminsh writing in *Red Star* (n.d.); quoted by *Christian Science Monitor*, 4 January 1980, p. 1.

46.   Brigadier Maurice A. J. Tugwell (British Army), "Day of the Paratroops," *Military Review*, March 1977, p. 51.

47.   The classic account of the "bureaucratic politics model" is, of course, contained in Graham Allison, *Essence of Decision* (Boston: Little, Brown & Co., 1971). More topical analyses are found in Timothy J. Colton, *Commissars, Commanders & Civilian Authority: The Structure of Soviet Military Politics* (Cambridge: Harvard Univ. Press, 1979) and Edward L. Warner, *The Military in Contemporary Soviet Politics* (London: Praeger, 1977).

48.   Bruce Porter, "Intervention Advances in Soviet Military" (cited in note 31).

49.   Edward N. Luttwak, "Cubans in Arabia?" *Commentary* 68, No. 6 (Dec. 1979), pp. 62–66.

50.   Writing in a more theoretical vein some years ago, Thomas C. Schelling raised a similar point in describing as a "pre-emptive maneuver" the 1958 landing of U.S. Marines in Lebanon as a signal of the seriousness of American intentions. "It is harder to retreat than not to land in the first place; the landing helped put the next step up to the Russians." By

voluntarily surrendering this initiative, the U.S. effectively "coupled capabilities to objectives." Thomas C. Schelling, *Arms and Influence* (New Haven: Yale University Press, 1977), p. 49.

51. I am indebted to David McGarvey of the RAND Corporation for pointing out that the scarcity of airfields in the Persian Gulf area could actually be an advantage to the Soviets, since they have sufficient forces to seize all of the important airfields in the area contiguous to the Gulf. The West might then well have to resort to a hard-fought "stepping stone" strategy in which the Soviets would hold an overwhelming advantage.

52. U.S. Congress, Congressional Budget Office, *U.S. Airlift Forces: Enhancement Alternatives for NATO and Non-NATO Contingencies* (Washington, D.C.: Government Printing Office, 1979), p. 23, Figure 1. The CBO study, however, was highly approximate and did not purport to show anything more than an aggregate of total transit time. Lead elements of a U.S. airborne force—perhaps up to a full brigade in strength—could reportedly be in the Middle East in 36–48 hours.

11

Global Power Projection—The U.S. Approach

Barry M. Blechman

In considering the projection of military power, it is helpful to analyze the purposes and modes of such activity. Military power can be used to defend the nation's interests in many different ways. To start with, military power can be used either directly or indirectly. Military forces are employed directly to secure certain specified objectives through their own innate capabilities by destroying or seizing a target. The April 1980 attempt to rescue the American hostages in Tehran, for example, was a direct application of military power. The hostages would or would not have been released as the direct result of the efforts of the rescue team itself.

Military power also can be used indirectly, to cause others to take actions which accomplish our objectives. It has been suggested in the press, for example, that an effective way to secure release of the hostages would have been to institute a naval blockade of Iran. That would constitute an indirect use of military power, as the purposes of the blockade would be to persuade Iranian authorities that the price of holding the hostages was too high, and that therefore *they* should take actions necessary to secure the hostages' release.

Military forces also can be employed more or less actively in pursuit of national objectives. The mere existence of military forces, or decisions to acquire new types or additional quantities of military forces, are passive activities that influence national security in both direct and indirect ways. Directly, such decisions (or the absence of such decisions) contribute to (or diminish) the preparedness of American military forces to carry out whatever tasks they are assigned. Indirectly, along with other policies, such decisions—which are projected verbally—signal American resolve, commitment, and determination to allocate the resources necessary to defend the nation's interests to decision-makers around the globe.

As shown in Table 1, military forces—on an increasing scale of activism—also can be transferred to others (through sales or grants), shared with others (through port visits and similar phenomena), and used demonstratively to indicate or buttress threats, warnings, commitments, and so forth. At the high end of the scale, military forces can be employed to commit violence to obtain certain ends. Even in these cases, however, the use of military power can have either direct or indirect purposes. The atomic bombs dropped on Japan in 1945, for example, were not used directly to end the war, but to persuade Japanese decision-makers, particularly the Emperor, to take steps to terminate the conflict.

In thinking about the projection of American military power, we most often think of direct and active uses of force. The most

TABLE 1

Potential Roles of Military Power

extensive military involvements of the United States since 1945, in fact, were direct and violent uses of military power. In both Korea from 1950 to 1953 and Southeast Asia from 1965 to 1972, the United States employed its military forces directly to combat and defeat the armed forces of other nations.

Paradoxically, the more common examples of the projection of American military power involve less active, more indirect uses of military power. In these incidents, physical changes are made in the disposition of American military forces with the purpose of indirectly influencing the outcome of specific situations abroad. Examples are legion, including, among several hundred others, the airlift to Berlin in 1948, the landing of Marines in Lebanon in 1958, the placement of NATO forces on alert in the aftermath of the Soviet invasion of Czechoslovakia in 1968, and the visit of an American destroyer to Mogadiscio at the time of the Somali–Ethiopian conflict in 1978.

These incidents vary greatly in terms of the size and type of forces involved, the political situations at which they are directed, and the effectiveness of American military forces when used in these roles. What the incidents have in common, however, is that in each, U.S. policymakers sought to project American military power into a situation in an indirect or political way; to make clear to foreign decision-makers that American military capabilities, and therefore American interests, were a factor which would have to be considered.

These demonstrative uses of American armed forces have been analyzed in a study published by the Brookings Institution.[1] The purposes of the study were to describe patterns in the occurrence and character of such incidents, and to begin to get at the question of effectiveness—to shed light on when the demonstrative use of the armed forces is, and when it is not, an effective instrument of American foreign policy. Some findings of this study are summarized below.

STYLES AND PATTERNS IN AMERICAN DEMONSTRATIVE USES OF MILITARY POWER

A great many more incidents involving demonstrative uses of military power have taken place than is typically realized: some 215 occurred between 1945 and 1976. If the study had been extended to 1980, one would probably have found that the total had risen to about 250.

The annual frequency of incidents varied sharply over time, as is shown in Table 2.[2] For the first few years following the Second

World War, the number of incidents each year was fairly low. The frequency of incidents then rose somewhat during the later 1940s, dropped during the Korean War, began to rise again in the mid-1950s, and then increased sharply until 1965, when it fell precipitously. Annual frequencies remained at low levels through the mid-1970s. Again, if the study had been extended to the present, we would no doubt have found a new upward trend in the annual frequency of incidents in which American decision-makers made demonstrative use of military power.

How does one account for this variation in frequency over time? The study examined several factors that have been hypothesized to explain such variations in the historic pattern of American military operations, and found that only three were statistically significant in explaining the variation. Table 2 also shows how closely the actual frequency fits a curve based solely on these three predictive factors.

TABLE 2

Frequency of Incidents

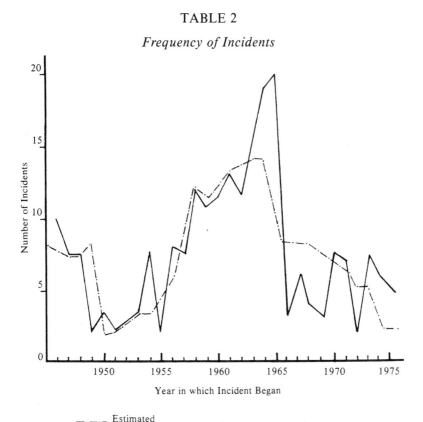

Year in which Incident Began

_ . _ . _ Estimated

_____ Actual

The first predictive factor is whether the United States was then or had been involved in either the Korean or Southeast Asian Wars for three years prior to the year being studied. The reasons are apparent: when the nation is involved in a major way in a military conflict, decision-makers are reluctant to commit additional resources to new situations, which, even if they posed only minimal demands initially, could involve dangers of escalation, of placing greater demands on the military force posture. Furthermore, in the three-year periods subsequent to these conflicts, there obviously has been a psychological reaction which acted as a deterrent to possible American proclivities to project military power abroad.

The second predictive factor is the amount of conflict within the internal system. There are several indices available which seek to measure international tension, and they all yielded similar results. The more conflict in the international system, the more opportunities presented for the use of military power, the more often the United States was likely to become involved. The same, of course, would hold true for the Soviet Union.

The third predictive factor is more interesting; it is the national sense of confidence about the future. In addition to polling data, we employed an index commonly used by economists—a discounted version of the Standard and Poor's Market Index—to measure this phenomenon. The Standard and Poor's Index was adjusted to compensate both for inflation and real economic growth. The resultant measure, or incremental changes in the resultant measure, indicate changes in the nation's sense of the future. When the nation is confident of the future, after controlling for real growth and inflation, investors are more likely to be willing to invest in the stock market. On the other hand, when people are pessimistic about the future, the discounted Standard and Poor's index is likely to decline. We found a strong relationship, almost as strong as the first two factors, between this sense of confidence and the propensity of decision-makers to project military power abroad. The more optimistic the nation, the more likely it is to become involved militarily overseas.

The study also found a large number of factors which were unimportant. For example, the President's popularity did not correlate with the frequency of these incidents in any significant way, no matter how changes in the poll data were led or lagged to account for differences between popular and elite opinion. We tested several variations of theories that Presidents turn to adventures abroad when they get into trouble at home; there was no meaningful relationship between these variables.

Table 3[3] shows the distribution of incidents by region. Very few

incidents occurred anywhere in the Southern Hemisphere throughout the postwar period, and that includes Latin America south of the
Caribbean littoral nations, Africa south of the Sahara, and South
Asia. These large areas accounted for a very low number of
incidents between 1945 and 1976, something less than 10 percent of
the total, and that was fairly consistent over time. In the more recent
period, however—the period since 1975—it is clear that the United
States has begun to become involved more frequently in sub-
Saharan Africa and Southwest Asia; that represents a very distinct

TABLE 3

Distribution of Incidents by Region and Time Period

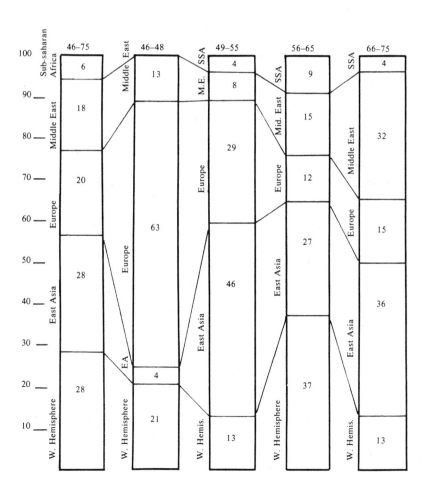

change in the pattern of American behavior from the immediately preceding years.

In the early post–World War II period, most of the incidents took place in Europe. These were largely of two types: (a) drawing the line in Central Europe—demonstrating to the Soviets how far they could or could not go in consolidating their power in Eastern Europe; and (2) cementing ties with nations in Southern Europe— the Sixth Fleet or other naval forces were used frequently in connection with domestic conflicts in Italy and to improve relations with Spain and other countries in the region. However, an increasing share of the incidents have taken place in the Middle East. More of the Middle Eastern incidents concerned conflicts among Arab nations than conflicts between Israel and the Arab nations—not an obvious finding.

Finally, in the late 1950s and early- to mid-1960s, the period of sharp increase and even sharper decline in the frequency of incidents, the Caribbean accounted for a large share of the incidents. These were associated both with the rise of Fidel Castro to power in Cuba and, subsequently, with U.S. actions to stem insurgencies inspired and supported by the new revolutionary Cuban government.

Table 4[4] describes the types of forces that were involved in the incidents. Not shown on the figure is the question of the size of the forces that were employed. Most of the incidents were relatively minor; that is, they involved relatively small forces—for example, a couple of destroyers. In a surprising number, some eighty of the incidents, however, what was defined as major forces were involved. A major force was taken to mean at least two carrier task groups, and/or more than a battalion of ground forces, and/or at least one wing of Air Force tactical aircraft.

In the type of force employed, there is obviously a strong bias toward the use of the Navy. The Navy was involved in nearly one-half of the incidents for essentially three reasons: First, naval forces are simply much easier to move in terms of logistics; they carry their goods and services with them, so to speak. Second, the use of naval forces provides greater political flexibility; moving a ship closer to a region of conflict is less of a commitment than moving ground forces or ground-based air power into the region, because the naval force can be withdrawn as easily as it is moved toward the conflict, which has its advantages. (It also has its disadvantages, which are discussed below.) Third, until recently, the U.S. Navy was the only service which had a sense of itself in such missions. The historic purpose of the Navy has always included a strong element of diplomatic or foreign policy activity. Throughout American history, naval officers have often been the only representatives of the

American government in different regions, and this tradition of the naval diplomat has persisted in the Service and in the Service's sense of itself and its utility.

TABLE 4

Distribution of Incidents by Type of Force Involved

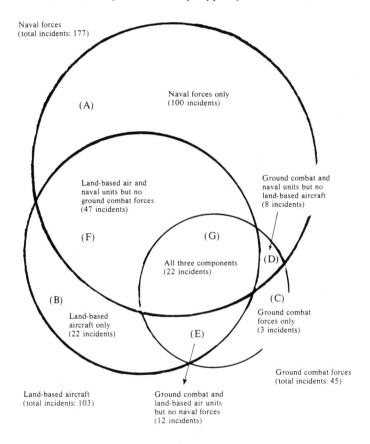

Naval forces
(total incidents: 177)

(A)   Naval forces only
       (100 incidents)

Land-based air and   Ground combat and
naval units but no   naval units but no
ground combat forces   land-based aircraft
(47 incidents)   (8 incidents)

(F)   (G)   (D)

       All three components
       (22 incidents)

(B)   (C)
Land-based   Ground combat
aircraft only   forces only
(22 incidents)   (E)   (3 incidents)

                             Ground combat forces
                             (total incidents: 45)

Land-based aircraft   Ground combat and
(total incidents: 103) land-based air units
                       but no naval forces
                       (12 incidents)

A surprising number of incidents included a nuclear dimension; these are listed in Table 5.[5] Some nineteen incidents—nearly 10 percent of the total—involved, among other factors, changes in the disposition of U.S. strategic nuclear forces. That is a much larger number than most observers would have predicted and indicates that, for whatever reasons, American decision-makers, or at least American military decision-makers, saw a need or potential utility for strategic nuclear forces in a variety of situations. In retrospect, some of the incidents listed in Table 5 appear frivolous. In early post–World War II days, the United States tended to deploy nuclear-configured aircraft rather more readily than it does at present. This is not to say that the aircraft had weapons aboard. In all probability, in most incidents they did not. But aircraft known to be configured for nuclear missions were used rather generously in, let us say, very strange incidents. Others of the incidents, of course, were more serious.

An important question is whether signals may have been given by the movement of strategic forces even when such signals might not have been intended. For example, the list in Table 5 includes several incidents in the Mediterranean in the 1950s. These were cases when the Sixth Fleet carriers were employed in Middle Eastern crises at the time when these carriers played central roles in American planning for nuclear war with the Soviet Union. In all likelihood, for most people involved in the decision (although the memoirs of former SAC commanders provide a different perspective) the thought of threatening strategic war was never contemplated. Yet, to the Soviets and to other actors in the situation, the key factor may have been that the United States was making important changes in the disposition of its strategic forces in connection with what otherwise might have appeared to be a fairly local and not significant situation.

TABLE 5

Incidents in Which Strategic Nuclear Forces Were Involved

Incident	*Date*
U.S. aircraft shot down by Yugoslavia	November 1946
Inauguration of president in Uruguay	February 1947
Security of Berlin	January 1948
Security of Berlin	April 1948
Security of Berlin	June 1948
Korean War: Security of Europe	July 1950
Security of Japan/South Korea	August 1953
Guatemala accepts Soviet bloc support	May 1954
China–Taiwan conflict: Tachen Islands	August 1954
Suez crisis	October 1956
Political crisis in Lebanon	July 1958
Political crisis in Jordan	July 1958
China–Taiwan conflict: Quemoy and Matsu	July 1958
Security of Berlin	May 1959
Security of Berlin	June 1961

Incident	Date
Soviet emplacement of missiles in Cuba	October 1962
Withdrawal of U.S. missiles from Turkey	April 1963
Pueblo seized by North Korea	January 1968
Arab–Israeli War	October 1973

What do military forces do in such incidents? Sometimes they have engaged in passive activities, such as port visits or establishing a patrol. Very rarely have they been involved in anything active, whether a blockade or the use of firepower. Most often, all they did was to establish a presence. This is shown in Table 6.[6] The establishment of a presence serves several purposes for whatever might occur in the future—a direct use of military power. Second,

TABLE 6

Activities of U.S. Armed Forces when in Political Roles

	Number of Incidents	
Type of Activity	*Naval Forces*	*Other Forces Alone*
Providing a U.S. presence	68	1
Visit	44	0
Patrol/reconnaissance/surveillance	35	9
Exercise/demonstration	29	1
Movement of military equipment or forces to a target	22	8
Movement of a target's military forces or equipment	13	8
Evacuation	18	1
Use of firepower	14	4
Emplacing ground forces or occupying territory	10	8
Interposition	6	1
Escort of a target's forces	5	2
Demonstrating transit rights	4	3
Blockade	3	0
Other	4	0

though, the establishment of a military presence also signals to the people involved in the crisis (the foreign decision-makers either involved or potentially involved) that American capabilities are significant and that there is at least a good risk that the United States is willing to commit sizable military forces to obtain its objectives in the situation—an indirect use of military power.

THE EFFECTIVENESS OF
DEMONSTRATIVE USES OF MILITARY POWER

In each of the incidents discussed previously, American decision-makers typically sought to influence the perceptions and behavior of actors in several different target nations. In many cases, they had multiple objectives in mind for each of these actors. When was the demonstrative use of military power effective in securing these objectives? Under what conditions was the projection of military power into political situations most likely to achieve the operational goals of U.S. decision-makers? These are questions of utility. It should be noted at the outset, however, that utility is not synonymous with wisdom. A judgment about the effectiveness of demonstrative uses of military power to secure operational goals does not, for example, say anything about the sensibility of having adopted those goals to begin with. Nor does such a judgment take account of possible negative consequences of the demonstrative military action which did not figure into the original perceptive framework of U.S. decision-makers.

The Brookings study mentioned previously used a dual methodology to evaluate the utility of demonstrative uses of military power. On the one hand, an aggregate quantitative analysis was made of a representative sample of all 215 incidents. On the other, eight sets of detailed case studies of individual incidents were prepared by regional experts.

On the basis of these analyses, it was discovered that the demonstrative use of military power was often an effective means of achieving foreign policy objectives. It was also found, however, that this utility declined over time; that is, the portion of U.S. objectives likely to have been obtained declined as time passed after the incident itself. Four factors seem to have been most important in determining the effectiveness of demonstrative uses of force.

First, the nature of the objective itself is a critical factor. It is more difficult to cause an actor to change behavior than to persuade an actor to continue some previously established behavior. This is true whether the objective is coercive in character (i.e., to compel a real change or to deter a threatened change), or supportive in character (i.e., to persuade an ally to continue some action or to induce a new action).

Second, demonstrative uses of military power are more likely to be effective when specific operational objectives fit closely with previously established patterns of U.S. policy. When the objective deviated from historic expressions of American interests, demonstrative uses of power were less likely to succeed; it seems to be difficult credibly to articulate new commitments through discrete, and probably short-lived incidents. But when the new demonstration of American military strength served mainly to remind observers of historic American interests—as previously expressed in treaty commitments, statements by high-ranking U.S. officials, prior uses of military power in similar situations, or continuing force deployments—the demonstration was more likely to achieve its purposes.

Soviet activity is a third determinant of relative effectiveness. The United States is most likely to be effective when the Soviet Union is completely uninvolved in a situation. When the Soviets become involved diplomatically, achievement of U.S. objectives is somewhat less likely. When the Soviets are willing to become involved with their own military forces, U.S. objectives are again somewhat more difficult to attain. This is not to say that the United States was generally unsuccessful in these latter cases, only that the relative degree of success was less. Further, utility was found not to be related to relative U.S. and Soviet strategic capabilities. With other factors controlled, the effectiveness of U.S. conventional military power in demonstrative roles did not decline as U.S. strategic superiority was eroded through the late 1960s and 1970s.

Finally, effectiveness is related to the degree of political commitment manifested by the character of the military itself—what Thomas Schelling calls the "idiom of action." All else being equal, the more firm the commitment expressed by the demonstrative action, the more likely was the action to be successful. For example, the insertion of a U.S. military presence on the ground—either ground-combat forces or land-based tactical air forces—was more likely to lead to the achievement of U.S. objectives than was the movement of naval forces alone. Precisely for the same reasons that decision-makers prefer the Navy in these roles—the greater flexibility which naval forces provide—the use of the Navy represents a less political commitment and thus less effectively signals U.S. resolve and seriousness. Similarly, when the U.S. military forces involved in the situation actually did something, rather than simply establish a presence, they were more likely to succeed. Actual engagement in operations of one sort or another seemed to establish a firmer commitment than preparations without specific purpose. Thirdly, when nuclear forces were involved in the situation, the success rate also was likely to be greater. A willingness to implicate strategic nuclear forces served to signal that U.S. decision-makers took the situation very seriously indeed. It should be noted, of course, that the precise reason for success—the apparent willingness to run the risks of nuclear war—should contain enthusiasm for use of this means of signalling determination.

In conclusion, it should be noted that while demonstrative uses of the armed forces are often effective ways of achieving near-term foreign policy objectives, in an overwhelming portion of the incidents, relative suçcess eroded sharply over time. It seems that demonstrative uses of military forces serve mainly to delay unwanted developments abroad. These operations seem to provide a respite—a means of postponing adverse developments so that there is enough time to formulate and implement new policies which may be sustained over the long term—policies that make use of many levers of power and which reflect the realities of the domestic and international situation. Characterizing the utility of demonstrative uses of force in this way does not in any sense denigrate their importance. Even short-term success in foreign policy can be critical and most welcome.

NOTES

1.   Barry M. Blechman and Stephen S. Kaplan, *Force without War: U.S. Armed Forces as a Political Instrument* (Brookings Institution, 1978). Mr. Kaplan has written a second study examining the style and utility of Soviet demonstrative uses of military power: *Diplomacy of Power: Soviet Armed Forces as a Political Instrument* (Brookings Institution, 1981).

2.   Barry M. Blechman and Stephen S. Kaplan, *Force without War*, p. 31.

3.   Ibid., p. 33.

4.   Ibid., p. 40.

5.   Ibid., p. 48.

6.   Ibid., p. 54.

12

U.S. Power Projection in the Northern Flank

Kenneth A. Myers

INTRODUCTION

As part of its postwar, forward based military strategy, the United States has engaged in the peacetime deployment of forces abroad to protect national security interests. Those forces stationed on European soil have been assigned primarily a defensive mission. On the other hand, U.S. projection forces have been designed to permit the United States to project its power beyond those geographical areas where American forces are stationed. Just as Congress is requested each year to fund U.S. forces on European soil, so each year the Secretary of Defense requests funding for the operation and modernization of U.S. projection forces. The latter projection forces include two divisions of the U.S. Army XVIII Corps (the 82nd Airborne and the 101st Airmobile Divisions), the three active Marine divisions and air wings along with their amphibious lift, and parts of the seabased Navy (aircraft carriers and their supporting units) and Air Force tactical air forces.

U.S. projection forces are noteworthy for two common characteristics:[1] they are configured for long-distance, forcible insertion into enemy-occupied territory against armed opposition; and they provide or support a rapid and flexible response to Presidential directives for contingency operations, wherein both Marine amphibious formations and carrier task forces in particular can mobilize off a potentially hostile shore without necessarily becoming committed to hostilities.

Department of Defense (DOD) plans its projection forces in light of the demands of the "one-and-a-half-war" strategy—i.e., the capacity to wage simultaneously a major conflict centered in Europe and a less demanding military contingency elsewhere—rather than setting projection force requirements on the basis of the demands of the non-NATO contingencies. Thus, the size and structure of the projection forces derive from the way defense planners estimate they might be used both in Europe and elsewhere. As Dov Zakheim has noted, the assumption that DOD makes "about the relationship of the minor contingency to the major, about the role of the allies, and the involvement of the Soviet Union—all imply a requirement for large numbers of highly capable contingency forces."[2] Thus, the notion that a minor contingency "might occur concurrently with a major worldwide conflict, coupled with an assumption that it would be difficult to shift forces between the conflicts, results in planning for forces in addition to those required for the major conflict."[3]

The requirements for projection forces in a NATO–Warsaw Pact war sets the baseline for overall projection force levels to which requirements for a half war might be added. While the primary combat theater in a European conflict would likely be NATO's central region, with armored warfare likely to dominate the conflict there, projection force units would appear to be most appropriately suited for combat on NATO's Northern Flank, which could well be the scene of NATO–Warsaw Pact operations that extend beyond the Central Region and where the terrain in the areas of Schleswig-Holstein/Jutland and Norway should facilitate the operations of units such as the Army airborne and airmobile divisions and the Marine ground forces. Thus, it is important to examine the suitability of various projection forces for the different European combat environments and to focus on the demands of combat in the Northern Flank sector of a Warsaw Pact–NATO conflict as the key measure of its projection force requirements.

POWER PROJECTION AND THE NORTHERN FLANK

U.S. projection force requirements along the Northern Flank are a function of both the size of attacking Warsaw Pact forces— effectively Soviet forces—and the contributions of the European allies. The Northern Flank is strategically important because it comprises both an overland route that would enable Soviet forces to bypass stronger Allied defenses in central Europe and a sea line to the Atlantic which, if used, would enable Soviet naval units to threaten the resupply of NATO forces in both northern and central Europe. NATO's concern for the defense of the Northern Flank in the event of a major European war has grown of late primarily as a result of increasing Soviet projection capabilities coupled with a decline in Allied (primarily American and British) maritime forces.

In dealing with the issue of power projection in the Northern Flank region, the problems of definition are paramount. In some respects, one may say that the very idea of the Nordic Balance is anathema to the build-up of forces sized to project power into the area: that is, efforts to keep the northern area one of low tensions, a dead area, a vacuum, are designed to prevent or deflect efforts by outside powers to project power into the region. Here, of course, one is referring to power projection in a peacetime environment as well as a crisis period. Indeed, in the North, too narrow and technical—rather too "military"—a definition of power projection misses the point; in the North, power projection must be seen in a more subtle, more political peacetime context. This chapter first examines the issue of power projection in a peacetime and wartime environment from the standpoint of the U.S. Navy and its sea-control mission. Next, it considers the power projection capabilities of the Marines to reinforce a military presence or allies in a crisis or war, and then covers some of the problems associated with the prestocking and prepositioning, other problems that could occur should the Marines be called upon to play a major role in a rapid deployment force oriented primarily toward the Third World. Lastly, power projection in the context of the peculiar politico-military, regional setting that exists along the Nordic front will be mentioned.

SEA CONTROL AND/OR POWER PROJECTION

Apart from its contribution to the strategic nuclear deterrent, the U.S. Navy has three broad missions: sea control, power projection, and peacetime presence.[4] As defined in a recent Congressional Budget Office Issue paper, "these missions actually involve four distinct types of operations: (1) offensive operations against sea and land targets in high-threat areas; (2) defensive operations near the sea lanes to protect transiting forces; (3) offensive operations against land targets in medium- and low-threat areas (Third World, etc.); and (4) presence operations.[5]

In analyzing the Navy's missions in the North Atlantic and Northern Flank regions, concern would be directed primarily to the first two types of operations. Each operation generates a different set of requirements for naval forces. Offensive operations in high-threat areas call for limited numbers of sophisticated escorts to support the fleet's carriers. Defensive operations to protect the sea lanes, on the other hand, may call for a larger number of ships if many convoys require protection. Individual ships need not be so highly capable, however, since they would face only those Soviet units that both had the range to reach the sea lanes and had survived attacks by land-based defensive forces operating as barriers along transit routes from the Soviet Union.

Today, the U.S. Navy not only confronts a Soviet fleet with growing capabilities to threaten U.S. and Western fleets worldwide, but also may be called upon to project power ashore against indigenous forces in Third World areas. There exists a choice between procuring a limited number of expensive, high quality (high-mix) warships which could provide the greatest capabilities in major confrontations with the Soviet Union (such as along the Northern Flank), and procuring larger numbers of less costly, somewhat less capable, and often more specialized (low-mix) units, which would enhance U.S. capabilities for presence and projection operations worldwide.[6]

To date, highest priority is attached by the U.S. Navy to the sea control mission in a worldwide NATO war with the Warsaw Pact. This requires not only defensive operations to defend the immediate vicinity of convoys but also offensive naval attacks on Soviet forces near Soviet territory or bases.[7] A lesser priority has been assigned to requirements associated with Third World contingencies.

Thus, the primary role of the Navy in the North is that of defense of the sea lanes. That task can be performed in two ways: by sealing off the Greenland–Iceland–United Kingdom Gap (GIUK gap) from Soviet attack submarines, and by keeping the sea lanes open through a combination of barriers, area defense, and convoy/escort protection; *and/or* by striking at the source of the danger in and around Kola before the Soviet Navy makes an effort to break out into the Atlantic. Each of these tasks requires different posture emphasis on the part of the Navy in the area—i.e., protection of the sea lanes in and around the GIUK gap requires an emphasis on quantity, less capable individual units, etc. In contrast, the latter approach would require engagement of the enemy in and around Kola which in turn would require the kind of offensive thrust that can only be provided by carrier task forces. The issue, then, is one of whether the Navy should add forces on the margin of its current capabilities primarily with a view to enhance its offensive strike capability against Soviet forces and bases in the context of a Warsaw Pact–NATO conflict, or should it procure forces with a view both to increase its ability to conduct defensive sea-lane protection operations and to conduct a larger number of simultaneous presence and projection missions in situations that fall short of general war. To a great extent, perceptions of mission priorities and choices among ship building strategies that reflect those priorities depend upon critical assumptions regarding (a) Soviet maritime capabilities, priorities and intentions, and (b) the degree of Allied contributions to U.S. naval efforts, particularly sea-lane protection.

Although recent Soviet developments, notably introduction of

Kiev-class aircraft carriers and vertical/short take-off and landing (V/STOL) sea-based aircraft, have intensified analytical disagreements about their roles and missions, the point is that Soviet naval capabilities have improved across-the-board in the past two decades. Not only does the Soviet navy pose a serious threat to NATO's sea lanes, but it has also improved its ability to sustain projection operations at great distances from the Soviet Union. U.S. Navy force planning has tended to emphasize the implications of the first of these capabilities. On the other hand, a number of more recent developments—the Kiev-class carriers, the Backfire bomber, large amphibious ships, and more capable replenishment ships—suggest an additional emphasis on potential Third World intervention and presence operations.

More importantly, Soviet naval procurement and deployment patterns tend to support the view that the primary emphasis is being given to protection of their SSBN fleet in and around the Kola peninsula.

NATO's ability to counter the growing impression of Soviet domination of the vital sea and air spaces of the Norwegian and North Seas must be based upon a careful analysis of the capabilities of the Soviet Northern Fleet and apparent objectives of Russian naval planners. The Soviet Union faces a serious problem regarding the security of its nuclear-powered ballistic missile submarines (SSBNs). Not only are these submarines relatively noisy and thus subject to detection and destruction by Western antisubmarine warfare forces; but, while over 70 percent of those nuclear-powered ballistic missile submarines are assigned to the Northern Fleet, less than 20 percent are routinely kept on station. While the DELTA-class SSBNs can fire their missiles targeted on the U.S. from the vicinity of the Kola base, the range limitations of the missiles on the YANKEE-class SSBNs, which comprise the major portion of the current SLBM force, require the YANKEEs to transit into the Central Atlantic before firing on U.S. targets and thus to cross the ASW barriers that NATO is erecting in forward defense of its transatlantic sea lines of communication.

The Soviet Union appears to have decided to keep many if not most of its nuclear-powered ballistic missile submarines in the north in order to provide them with a significant amount of direct protection and to allocate a significant proportion of their naval general purpose forces to that protection task. The priority accorded to this SSBN protection task has appeared to come at the expense of resources for other general purpose tasks such as the interdiction of NATO's sea lines of communication.[8] Moreover, the priority accorded to the SSBN protection task helps to explain recent Soviet activities on and around the Kola Peninsula.

Recent analyses of trends in the overall Soviet naval force structure would seem to indicate that while quantitative stability has prevailed, it has been the Northern Fleet that has benefitted from the qualitative upgrading of unit capabilities and the shift of the capabilities of the force as a whole. The Northern Fleet has been the major beneficiary of the increase in size of the SSBN force. While the number of major surface combatants available for operations in the north (the Northern and Baltic Fleets) has not changed substantially, it has been the Northern Fleet that has acquired the newly constructed units. Although the general-purpose submarine component has experienced fleet-wide numerical decline, the newly constructed systems for the nonstrategic portion of the submarine arm tend to be distributed to the Northern Fleet in preference to the Baltic Fleet. As Robert Weinland has written:

> These individual changes have produced one very important overall change in the general purpose submarine force, which, in turn, has altered the Soviet Navy's capabilities in certain warfare areas. The submarine force is becoming less a general purpose and more a special purpose force. This is a combined function of the decreasing size of the force and the increasing specialization of the new units it is acquiring. These new units tend to be optimized for special tasks. When coupled with the more demanding character of immediate priority defensive tasks—ASW in defense of the strategic deterrent, ASW and anti-carrier warfare in defense of the homeland—these changes in the size and the character of the Soviet submarine force have resulted in a reduction of the Navy's capability to undertake offensive tasks, like interdicting the sea lines of communication across the Atlantic. And whether that decrease will be balanced by the increase in the air threat to those sea lines of communication represented by the acquisition of BACKFIRE remains to be seen.[9]

But whether analysts emphasize a Soviet priority on the SSBN protection task, or point to the elevation, in Soviet thinking, of the sea lane interdiction task to second place in the order of naval operational priorities, the practical results for NATO are the same—i.e., to retain control of the vital areas of the Norwegian and North Seas as well as the North Atlantic.

SLOC PROTECTION

U.S. naval superiority is crucial for the sea-control task. The antisubmarine mission of the Navy to protect convoys along the SLOCs can be divided into two components: area ASW and convoy defense. Currently, there is an emphasis on convoy defense, with reliance on guided-missile frigates. Yet, on the one hand, the frigates lack the antimissile potential to contribute effectively in a battle group; and on the other, the more expensive cruiser/destroyer fleet for the battle group faces technological and material obsolescence.[10] While U.S. convoy protection against submarines may be in comparatively better shape than other naval warfare tasks, it may be of little use since it assumes a global conventional war persisting beyond one month. More realistically, the major threat may not be a global conventional war but rather American inability to control or influence critical events around the globe. To the extent that such weaknesses are attributable to a lack of conventional forces, including naval forces, priority ought to be given to procuring capabilities commensurate with the major threat. In short, one can make the case that power projection in the Northern Flank may be optimized by the enhancement of battle group capabilities and nuclear-powered attack submarines in preference to SLOC protection, for the former may be more useful for containing crises, for directly challenging Soviet forces and for reinforcing allies.[11]

U.S. NAVAL REINFORCEMENTS

American capability to reinforce allies is distinct from the SLOC protection task. The Navy is supposed to be sized to ensure the reinforcement of Norway. Credible naval forces operating in the Norwegian Sea not only contribute to deterrence but also serve to demonstrate the West's determination to deny Soviet efforts at peacetime domination of the North Atlantic. Soviet surface forces, aircraft, and submarines would constitute the major threats to Western forces in the struggle for the Norwegian Sea.[12] The construction of antisubmarine and antiair barriers at the GIUK gap is designed to prevent Soviet attacks against the SLOCs. However, Norway lies on the Soviet side of this naval barrier.

Allied naval movement into the Norwegian Sea for purposes of reinforcing Norway would likely encounter a stiff Soviet barrier, primarily submarines, designed to secure the Soviet northern flank, protect Soviet SSBNs and maintain the integrity of a sizeable portion of the Soviet Navy.

Before Allied surface forces were dispatched to the Norwegian Sea, Allied submarines and ASW aircraft would have been sent to counter the Soviet submarine barrier. Recent advances in ship and aircraft ASW prosecution would indicate that Soviet submarines will have a difficult task to challenge credibly naval use of the Norwegian Sea.

More than in the SLOC case, American naval forces must be capable of defeating Soviet missile-carrying aircraft, for Soviet naval aviation is the most serious threat to the reinforcement of the Northern Flank. Badgers and Backfires can be massed to saturate the defenses of a task force. To counter Soviet naval aviation in the North, fixed air bases at blocking points or mobile air bases (carrier battle groups) are required. Both would also constitute prime targets for preemption and thus must be defended. Some strides have been made in antimissile defenses of task forces, with notable advances in rapidity in target solution and launch at several near-simultaneous incoming missiles.[13] New systems and capabilities should make surface ships less vulnerable in the future. The capabilities of the F-14 are seen as formidable as against Badgers and Backfires.

At the same time, the concerns over possible Soviet saturation of shipborne antimissile SAM and gun defenses, utilizing coordinated air raids, is being addressed with the DDG-47 Aegis, with its phased array radar working with inertial-guided SAM-2s. Greater attention is also being paid to land-based air to counter Soviet naval aviation in the North, particularly by analysts concerned with growing carrier vulnerability. However, their enthusiasm for land-based air is tempered by another concern—namely, political factors inhibiting receptivity to American force presence.

Thus, the keys to battle for the Norwegian Sea would be the effectiveness of Soviet bomber coordination, on the one hand, and of allied antimissile systems on the other. Put differently, enhancement of battle group capabilities does not necessarily translate into the need for more carriers. Rather, in the North, the antimissile defense requirement along with the need for a dispersal of naval striking power constitute the most pressing demands.[14] Emphasis on the dispersion of naval striking power is strategically related to power projection against the Soviet Union or any other potential enemy in the North.

MARINE REINFORCEMENT OF THE NORTHERN FLANK

Not only has the Northern Flank become a test scenario to determine whether the Navy can survive in a "high-threat" environment, but the recent attention given to the Rapid Deployment Force and its possible uses in non-European contingencies raises questions about U.S. interests and capabilities to play a role in the regional Nordic balance. Naval superiority at the scene of a crisis in the North is one thing; a capability to effect the outcome on shore along the flank is another crisis-related issue.

U.S. defense planning has emphasized the pre-reinforcement of NATO allies during times of crisis. And indeed, the Marine Corps has long been seen as the primary long-distance power projection force of the United States. But the Corps has its share of critics.[15] In addition to a general questioning of the relevance of the amphibious mission to operations in a world of proliferating PGMs (i.e., the growing vulnerability of amphibious ships), critics of the Corps propound two additional arguments of relevance to the issue of power projection in general and in the Northern Flank in particular: one, that the insufficient amphibious lift capability, combined with the distribution of available shipping worldwide, renders the Corps incapable of conducting long-distance, rapid-response projection operations; and two, that the lack of a specific theater orientation for the Corps in Europe (with two of three divisions comprising SACEUR's strategic reserve) leaves the Marines caught between planning and procuring for an armored environment and for a mountainous, wintery environment.

The U.S. efforts to organize a Rapid Deployment Force, in which the Marine Corps would comprise only a portion of the force, has raised important questions about the Corps' missions, relevance, and responsibilities. Marine Corps planners not only have to set their sights on the Persian Gulf–Indian Ocean region, but also contemplate significantly different kinds of warfare capabilities— such as desert warfare requiring more mechanized vehicles. Concurrently, and of equal importance to the Corps' future, the Corps is in demand for the rapid reinforcement of allied forces in Norway and Denmark. The Northern Flank allies have accelerated their demands for the prepositioning of Marine equipment on Danish and Norwegian soil, with the Norwegians emphasizing the reinforcing and supporting role that the Marines could perform in conjunction with Norwegian efforts to blunt possible Soviet attacks along the northern and western corridors, and the Danes stressing Marine support in repelling potential Soviet amphibious attacks against Jutland and the Danish islands. In short, the growing sense of vulnerability to rapid Soviet thrusts designed to preserve the Northern Fleet's access to the North Atlantic has prompted both Northern Flank allies to improve the prospects of timely American reinforcement of the Flank through a combination of prestocked equipment and the use of airlift (commercial in part) for rapidly deploying the ground forces.

The extent of a possible U.S. contribution to each of the two major northern areas would depend primarily upon the level of the Pact forces threatening the Northern Flank and the size and capabilities of allied forces available to meet those threats. The nature of available forces in these areas suggests that, in the event of conflict, Pact forces consisting of East German, Soviet, and Polish units could achieve well over a two-to-one manpower advantage over German and Danish forces in the Schleswig-Holstein/Jutland area, while Soviet forces on the Kola peninsula might outnumber their Norwegian counterparts by an even larger margin.

The balance in air and maritime forces is somewhat more favorable to NATO. German and Danish antiship fighter/bomber and interceptor squadrons, as well as mining capabilities, appear sufficient to pose severe obstacles to Pact attempts to achieve air superiority, provide close air support, and conduct naval operations and amphibious landings in the Schleswig-Holstein/Jutland theater. Similar difficulties would face Soviet forces in Norway. The Norwegians can quickly deploy their interceptor, fighter, and attack aircraft to the North. They maintain both strong coastal artillery defenses and a capable coastal navy with minelaying submarines, Penguin missile-armed patrol boats, and a small number of other warships.

Given the capabilities of the allies most affected by Pact incursions into Schleswig-Holstein/Jutland and Norway, it would appear that the major shortcoming that the United States would have to help overcome is that of ground forces. The forces which the allies could field against the Pact forces appear insufficient for the threat they would have to face, even when the nature of terrain in either area is taken into consideration. Part of the demand for additional forces can be filled by other NATO forces, notably British, Dutch, the Canadian brigades and the Allied Mobile Force, but the remaining shortfall would still have to be filled by the U.S. forces.

The combat environment in both the Schleswig-Holstein and Norwegian areas differs from that of central Germany in that it is more conducive to operations by light forces. The speed of a Pact armored advance into Schleswig-Holstein, with its flat area interspersed with waterways, would be limited by the need for substantial engineering and bridge-building efforts, particularly in the Kiel Canal area. For its part, northern Norway is a rugged region, with few good roads and numerous streams. In both cases, Pact armored units are unlikely to match the speed of advance of their counterparts in central Germany. Given these conditions, lighter NATO defenses could exploit geography to halt and possibly reverse a Pact offensive, with the Marines, or the airborne or air-mobile units, providing a significant part of the defense.

Prestocking requires major categories of expenditures such as military construction, procurement of equipment to be housed in overseas depots, and R&D for systems most appropriate to the regions wherein the Corps would be deployed. Prestocking in the Northern Flank countries presents its own set of unique requirements.[16] In Norway, cold-weather equipment and training for the reinforcing brigade would be a priority, while in Denmark the priority of procuring additional armor to prestock the division operating in Jutland would have to balance against the prestocking needs of two brigades charged with providing protection of the Danish islands against Soviet amphibious and airborne assults.

It must be emphasized that a prestocking program for a Marine Corps dedicated to operations in the Northern European theater would represent a major shift away from the Marine's general purpose role, would signal the dedication of part of the Corps to a specific territorial mission and one that would deemphasize the Corps' amphibious orientation. The Corps would see nearly two of its general purpose divisions converted into a force charged primarily with land warfare missions along the Northern Flank. If equipment were prestocked in Norway and/or Denmark, the Corps, assuming it kept its current size, would cease to be a major component of SACEUR's strategic reserve, thereby vitiating any potential contributions to other NATO sectors. In prestocking for the one brigade that would reinforce Norway in a crisis, cold-weather materiel and equipment to facilitate operations in Norway would have to be combined with more extensive training for the designated Marine units in Norway. The prestocks for Denmark— equipment for four brigades to provide defense of both Jutland and the Danish islands—would require substantial military construction to house the heavy equipment to support the mechanized operations in Jutland.[17]

Prestocking would tend to tie the Marine's commitment to Europe, with the equipment that had been stocked and maintained at levels required for combat in northern Europe available to permit the rapid deployment to battle areas of the arriving troops. In short, prestocking would not only tend to give a European coloration to Marine commitment but would also tend to set the intra-European orientation of the Marine Corps. Put somewhat differently, the priorities that the Corps assigns to possible contingencies will be greatly determined by prestocking.

A marine brigade would be reinforcing the Norwegian Cold Weather Brigade in the North, with the latter's 2000 men doubled or tripled upon mobilization. The standing force of 20,000 Soviet infantry on Kola would be limited by problems associated with the relocation of forces and equipment from the western military districts, for assaults across mountain ridges in cold weather require a high and specialized equipment investment per unit of manpower.

On the other hand, it is the equipment aspect combined with flexible task organization and hard training that optimizes the Marines for the reinforcement function in the North. A Marine brigade of 5000 men and with 100 helicopters provides the nucleus for a mobile defense; reliance on lightweight artillery and air, rather than armor, is compatible with the compartmentalized terrain in northern Norway, assuming optimum prestockings at dispersed bases.

In short, a Marine brigade, properly trained and equipped for cold weather, could bring to bear the mobility and the small unit flexibility suitable to the North Norway terrain. Reinforced ground forces in the North on the defensive would not compare unfavorably to Soviet infantry on the attack. Forewarned allied forces would have to cope with Soviet efforts to seize some air bases in the North by amphibious, paradrop, and overland ground attack. Well-defended airfields in the North also constitute some threat to Kola and thus are supportive of NATO naval movements in the Norwegian Sea. Reallocation of forces necessary to support Soviet attacking forces in place in the North would degrade Soviet resources on other fronts. Moreover, the air component of a task-organized Marine brigade, when added to the Norwegian air arm, should prove adequate against Sovier air bombardments designed to knock out allied air by attacking the air bases and related communications and supply.

STRATEGIC POWER PROJECTION TO KOLA

In addition to the two major U.S. naval roles in the direct defense of the Northern Flank—a naval campaign for control of the Norwegian Sea and the battle on land for northern Norway—the Navy can play an offsetting or deterrent role through its capability to credibly threaten the Kola base complex.[18] Indeed, it would likely be the Soviet concern with the defense of Kola, the hub of the Soviet Navy, that would prompt an attack on northern Norway. If, theoretically, the maintenance of some clear warfighting advantages over the Soviet Union enhances deterrence and provides some leverage in controlling crises in the region, then American nuclear attack submarines, together with SSBNs, would seem to confer such an advantage on the U.S. Navy in the North. But while systems that can credibly threaten Kola may contribute to deterrence of Soviet attack, such systems may not necessarily prove useful in the defense of Norway should deterrence fail.

An offensively-capable U.S. Navy in the North can place Soviet naval forces on the defensive, thereby alleviating the tasks of convoy resupply and reinforcement of allies. But, though one may posit that carriers are needed in the Norwegian Sea to defeat Soviet Backfires that could otherwise deny allied surface combatants and resupply ships access to that sea, carriers also possess attack aircraft as well as fighters, and could be targeted against the Kola base complex before and after Kola-based systems search out allied naval forces.

Thus, a second means of projecting power upon the Soviet Union in the North is carrier-based strike aircraft. Despite the concern that naval air might be both too sophisticated and too vulnerable for the crisis-management task, sea-based air might be able to play a significant role in a conflict on the Northern Flank, for Kola (with its significant general purpose force targets) comes within range of allied strike aircraft. The depth of defenses around high-value targets in the Kola, primarily interceptors, would require a maximization of the numbers of U.S. fighters (F-18s supplementing F-14s) as well as the possible use of land-based tactical air units (F-11s and A-6Es) against Soviet fighter bases.[19] While the present inventory of some 5000 Navy/Marine aircraft will decrease sharply over the next two decades, the United States may wish, if only for purpose of deterrence, to keep open the option of projecting power against the Soviets in Kola, and discussions about positioning Marine A-6 aircraft in Norway and the procurement of land-attack cruise missiles would have a definite bearing on developing such a credible option. With regard to the latter, analysts have speculated about the future use of conventionally-armed cruise missiles for defense suppression purposes in Kola, particularly in efforts to neutralize SAMs and for degrading interceptor responses. The ability of battle groups, then, to project firepower to Kola and the Soviet homeland would add significantly to the defensive burdens of the Soviet Union, complicate Soviet force planning, and challenge a consciously-cultivated Soviet view about the nature and extent of her legitimate defense perimeter in the North.

One of the more recently-expressed worries on the part of Northern Flank allies (and neutrals) is that of deterring Soviet attack on northern Norway while U.S. interests and perhaps forces were elsewhere engaged. Discussions of a Rapid Deployment Force dedicated primarily to the Persian Gulf–Indian Ocean areas have contributed to this concern along the Northern Flank. Given Soviet reliance on the element of surprise, prompt political utilization of adequate warning time and rapidity of reinforcement are crucial to countering the advantages which geography and transit distances confer on the Soviets. The Norwegian submarine force, supplemented by U.S. submarines, would assume the key role in defending against the Soviet surface fleet and Soviet submarines as well as the employment of offensive mining.

And finally, the United States can play a role in deterring Soviet coercion directed at allies in a crisis by periodical operational exercises in the Norwegian Sea and northern Norway. Such exercises can help to deter any Soviet inclination to maneuver military force in crisis periods in order to pressure Norway in particular. Such exercises can further support Norwegian actions to deter or deflect Soviet coercion. The Norwegian government has proven itself adept at making the Soviet Union aware that the ban on the stationing of foreign troops in peacetime on Norwegian soil (as well as the prohibition against nuclear weapons) is a unilateral one and subject to rescission by the Norwegian government at any time, an act that would make Soviet gains stemming from coercion in a crisis disproportionate to the long-term costs to the Soviet Union.

THE CORRELATION OF FORCES

Regardless of the indigenous value to the Soviet Union of holding or controlling additional territory or waters in the area of the Norwegian Flank, the rationale for waging a military attack on Norwegian territory must be closely linked to increased East–West tensions and acute superpower rivalry. Even the potential oil and other resources of the region are not in and of themselves of sufficient value to justify the risks involved in commencing military hostilities in the North. The potential for military conflict between the Soviet Union and NATO in the North is therefore not rooted in the bilateral relationship between Moscow and Oslo, or Moscow and Copenhagen, but in the strategic value of Norwegian and Danish territory or the surrounding waters in connection with a likely or emerging East–West conflict.

Put somewhat differently, Soviet interests and policies in the North are an extension of Soviet global policy and its philosophical outlook on contemporary international relations. In Soviet calculations, the correlation of forces is moving in a direction favorable to Moscow, while the West is perceived as locked in the throes of economic chaos and political indecision—without a sense of purpose. In the North, the Soviet Union expects to be treated as *the* superpower with global interests, and the indigenous Nordic countries, as well as the other superpower, are expected to recognize Soviet regional preponderance and to readjust their foreign policy calculations in consonance with the vital Soviet interests in the area. In Soviet rhetoric, a state of low tension in the area can be maintained only if the West recognizes the futility of contesting Soviet vital interests in the North—in short, recognizes the futility of atempting to project power into the North, either in peacetime or wartime.

"WINNING" AND "LOSING" IN THE NORTH

Analysts will differ as to how a war might start in Europe. The escalation or the expansion of a conflict outside Europe might impel combatants or allies to take military action in Europe in order to shift the attention of NATO powers to the European continent. In this way, the outside conflict might be prosecuted more effectively. War could begin in limited armed aggression by the Soviet Union against Norway in a Soviet attempt to improve its strategic position, to augment its military base structure and to create a buffer to protect the Kola peninsula and/or to gain access to airfields and harbors closer to the Norwegian Sea and the North Atlantic. War might begin in straightforward armed aggression along the central European front, with conflict spilling over into the flanks or taking place in concert with the central European front conflict. Whether one posits a "surprise attack" planning scenario, or limited military action begetting a violent and unintended action/reaction process, a not insignificant conflict could well arise more or less unexpectedly and be fought close to the limits of the combatants' capabilities. But whatever the *casus belli*, the North is important to both the Soviet Union and NATO simply because the outcome of a NATO war could be determined there.

The critical issue in the North is control of the key areas of sea and air space in the Norwegian and North Sea; control of these areas could affect both the strategic balance between the superpowers and the balance of forces at the forward edge of the battle area. How crucial control of these areas may be is dependent on questions of escalation, the time required to contain the Soviet advance on the central front, and the tactics employed by the Soviet Union and the United States to fight the war at sea. However, if the Soviet Union is not able to establish and maintain control of those areas, a significant fraction of its strategic deterrent might be lost. On the other side, the ability of NATO to restore the *status quo ante* would be significantly impaired if the Alliance could not establish and maintain control of those same areas—a prerequisite to the timely transference of men and materiel across the Atlantic and to the front. In short, although neither side could "win" a European war by winning in the North, both the Warsaw Pact and NATO might come close to losing a European war by losing in the North.

PSYCHOLOGICAL AND NAVAL BARRIERS

In the past decade, perhaps the most significant change in the Soviet Navy has been the alteration in its use from that of a purely wartime instrument to that of an instrument of major political influence as well. To that extent, Soviet naval power has become an ever more salient feature of the peacetime political environment in the North Atlantic and Nordic areas. Fleet exercises such as Vesna and Okean as well as recent activities in and around Svalbard are designed in great part as vehicles for influencing in peacetime the preparations for war of potential opponents in ways favorable to Soviet ends. Not only has the Soviet Union managed to create the impression of a strong global navy through the judicious use of forces, but by exercising frequently and visibly in the Norwegian Sea–North Atlantic area, the Soviet Union has created the image of the dominant power in that area, with a legitimate defense perimeter that extends to the Greenland–Iceland-UK (GIUK) Gap.[20] Not only are such exercises designed to impart to third countries the impression that the USSR has already established control over the vital sea and air space of the region, but also that the costs to potential opponents of contesting that control north of the GIUK Gap would be disproportionately high to potential gains.

A variety of systems are necessary to provide defense of the sea-lanes to Europe against possible Soviet air, surface, and submarine attacks if Allied and U.S. forces deployed there are to receive timely and sufficient supplies.[21] Equally important, however, for the Alliance is the need to counter as quickly as possible a growing and alarming impression within the littoral states and segments of their population that the Soviet Union has a penchant for exacting the maximum political mileage from military developments; and the appearance of a naval imbalance in the North Atlantic in favor of the Soviet Union, one carefully cultivated by Moscow, does influence the thinking and actions of the littoral states. The Soviet Union has consciously manipulated its forces in the area in an effort to develop a correlation of forces favorable to the Soviet Union in the event of hostilities and to affect the peacetime perceptions of the littoral states of the correlation. Thus, peacetime actions are required to offset the political impact of Soviet military developments and to enhance the confidence with which the littoral states view the balance in the European theater. It is important that the Soviet Union not be allowed to develop an exaggerated estimate of its own capabilities or an unrealistically low opinion of either the capabilities of NATO or its will to use them if necessary.

Such actions may take the form of a selective augmentation of the U.S. naval presence in northern waters, either on a permanent deployment basis or for frequent training exercises. A reconsideration of the role the U.S. Navy can play north of the GIUK Gap must entail a review of carrier visibility and effectiveness in the area both in terms of its survivability and its ability to accomplish positive area control and projection tasks.[22]

While any other major change in Norway's "base and ban" policy, which prohibits the peacetime stationing of foreign troops and nuclear weapons on Norwegian soil, is neither desirable nor feasible for domestic political reasons as well as likely Soviet reactions, improvements in the prestocking of heavy equipment on Norwegian and/or Danish soil for allied reinforcement, along with the enhancement of the Norwegian and Danish defense capabilities, constitutes a promising means of strengthening NATO's warfighting capability on the Northern Flank. Norway has entered into bilateral negotiations with the United States, Canada, and the United Kingdom on enhanced prestocking arrangements. At least on the Norwegian side, the present Norwegian Defense Commission has opined that the prestocking of heavy equipment in Norway in peacetime, to be used by the allied forces if called upon to assist Norway, is consistent with the unilateral stipulations of the "base" policy.

The desire for a visible but not overly threatening presence, coupled with Norwegian concerns about possible Soviet harassment of oil installations and operations on the continental shelf, or even limited attacks, have led some analysts to suggest greater Western allied involvement in further exploration of natural resources on the continental shelf in the North. As Anders Sjaastad has put it:

In order to enhance deterrence and to raise the level of risk inherent in any Soviet threats of harassment and coercion against Norwegian oil installations in the Norwegian and Barents Seas to that level which obtains in the North Sea, it may be wise for Norway to involve its Western allies more directly in the future exploration and possible extraction of natural resources on the continental shelf in the North. This would not necessarily have to take the form of a strong physical presence in these ocean areas on the part of the Western power. Their consumer interests may be just as well served if Norway and its allies design an oil-sharing scheme which commits the Norwegians to guarantee uninterrupted oil deliveries to Western Europe from production wells in the Norwegian and Barents Seas. In addition, foreign capital and expertise could share in the exploration while Norway reserves to itself the ultimate control over the activities, especially in the areas which are politcally and strategically sensitive to the Soviet Union. The security bonus to Norway stemming from such arrangements could be significant.[23]

These kinds of actions are certainly insufficient in and of themselves to address Soviet military and nonmilitary developments in the area. Nor will such actions necessarily be high on the priority lists of political leaders or military specialists on either side of the Atlantic. They are, however, indicative of the need for partial responses to the political shadows being cast by Soviet military developments in the North Atlantic and Nordic areas.

The United States and its European allies have a pivotal role to play in maintaining a constructive politico–military balance in the North. Long-run threats to regional stability can flow not only from Soviet policies but from economic pressures facing the littoral states and from a weakening of NATO's stance. Perhaps the most serious long-run threat to regional security in the North may stem from a gradual erosion of political and military self-confidence of the littoral states which could slowly change perceptions and decrease their margin of maneuver in the political as well as military fields. Ill-conceived attempts or "quick fixes" designed to correct or reduce the asymmetries in the region could accelerate rather than attenuate the erosion of political and military confidence of the countries in the area. One of the major problems is therefore related to the will and capability of the United States and the Alliance in general to compensate for the psychological consequences of local imbalances. Both theater and strategic deterrence in the center of Europe and naval and air power projection in the North have become ever more important. But while U.S. interest and reassurance in the center of Europe can take the form of the physical presence of American troops, this interest and reassurance must take other forms (some dramatic, others more subtle) on the Northern Flank if the psychological effects of Soviet military might are not to further compound at least the appearance of a political and military imbalance in the North. One form is for the U.S. to maximize its ability to project power in the Northern Flank, be it in peacetime or wartime.

NOTES

1. These characteristics are so defined in Congressional Budget Office, *U.S. Projection Forces: Requirements, Scenarios, and Operations*, April 1978.

2. For a discussion of DOD's considerations of the nature of the half-war, see Congressional Budget Office, *U.S. Projection Forces*, p. 3.

3. Ibid., p. 3.

4. "The U.S. Navy embodies a flexible means of deploying U.S. power to distant regions. . . . Different naval forces are used for the actual projection of U.S. power and its support. Carriers and their task forces fall primarily into the former category; escorts for amphibious ships in transit and underway replenishment units usually fall into the latter." *U.S Projection Forces*, p. 14.

5. These operations are so defined in Congressional Budget Office,

Shaping the General Purpose Navy of the Eighties: Issues for Fiscal Years 1981–1985, January 1980, p. xv.

6. Ibid., p. xiii.

7. As noted in the CBO study: "Depending upon the strategy and circumstance, the sea control and projection missions can be quite distinct or inseparable. For example,

> in the event of a requirement to protect convoys transiting to Europe to support NATO in a conflict with the Warsaw Pact, the sea control mission could be interpreted in one of two ways. First, broadly interpreted, it would involve not merely immediate defense of convoys, but also offensive strikes against the Soviet fleet or even Soviet bases.

In this view, power projection would be subsumed as an aspect of sea control, because the emphasis is on limiting the number of attackers before they can attack the sealanes. On the other hand, to the extent that the sea control mission is defined in terms of the immediate defense of convoys and defensive barriers of air and sea forces operating from land bases along likely Soviet routes to the sea, then "offensive operations—power projection—would be an entirely separate mission, undertaken for purposes other than sea-lane defense." See Congressional Budget Office, *Shaping the General Purpose Navy of the Eighties*, pp. 7–8.

8. Robert Weinland, "The State and Future of the Soviet Navy in the North Atlantic," in M. MccGwire and J. McDonnell, eds., *Soviet Naval Influence: Domestic and Foreign Dimensions* (New York: Praeger, 1977), p. 411.

9. Robert Weinland, "War and Peace in the North: Political Implications of the Changing Military Situation in Northern Europe" (paper prepared for presentation at the conference on *The Nordic Balance in Perspective*, Center for Strategic and International Studies, June 1978).

10. For a brief discussion of the antisubmarine mission and U.S. naval capabilities, see Francis West, "A Fleet for the Year 2000: Future Force Structure," *U.S. Naval Institute Proceedings*, May 1980, p. 76.

11. For the rationales for curtailing the U.S. role in convoy defense, see Ibid., p. 76.

12. For a discussion of the major threats to Western forces in a struggle for the Norwegian Sea, and particularly of the Soviet naval aviation threat, see Francis West, "U.S. Naval Forces and the Northern Flank of NATO," *Naval War College Review*, July/August 1979, p. 18.

13. Ibid., p. 19.

14. For a discussion of the relative priorities to be assigned to antimissile defense and carrier augmentation, see West, "A Fleet for the Year 2000," p. 78.

15. For a summary of the criticisms of the Marine Corps, see *The Marine Corps in the 1980's: Prestocking Proposals, Amphibious Missions, and Other Issues*, Congressional Budget Office, May 1980.

16. Ibid., p. vi.

17. For a discussion of the requirements for prestocking in the North as well as the implications for the Corps' general-purpose role of such a "northern orientation," see *The Marine Corps in the 1980's*, p. xi–xii.

18. For a discussion of "deterrence by threats to Kola" see West, "U.S. Naval Forces and the Northern Flank of NATO," *Naval War College Review*, July/August 1979, p. 22.

19.   The implications of the interceptor threat for air force requirements are discussed in West, "U.S. Naval Forces," p. 22.

20.   For a discussion of the political uses to which the Soviet Union
has put her fleet in Northern waters, see Robert Weinland, "The State and
Future of the Soviet Navy in the North Atlantic," in M. MccGwire and J.
McDonnell, eds., *Soviet Naval Influence: Domestic and Foreign Dimensions* (New York: Praeger, 1977).

21.   See, for example, *The U.S. Sea Control Mission: Forces,
Capabilities, and Requirements*, Congressional Budget Office, Background
Paper, June 1977.

22.   For a discussion of the aircraft carrier option as a solution to the
ASW and interceptor problem in the North Atlantic and the Norwegian
Sea, see *The U.S. Sea Control Mission*, pp. 30–33. For a more general
discussion of the future of airpower at sea, see John Lehman, *Aircraft
Carriers: The Real Choices*, The Washington Papers, no. 52, 1978.

23.   Anders Sjaastad, "Norwegian Perceptions of the Changing
Northern Strategic Environment" (paper prepared for presentation at the
conference on *The Nordic Balance in Perspective*, Center for Strategic and
International Studies, June 1978).

13

NATO in the Next Decade: Issues Confronting the Alliance

Zeiner Gundersen

In discussions of current security problems facing the North Atlantic Alliance, it is necessary to consider the question of what the North Atlantic Treaty Organization is and what it is not. The Alliance is in the first instance a political organization of fifteen like-minded sovereign democracies. Unlike the European Community, NATO is in no sense a supranational organization. There is no difference between this organization and its membership. Any other conception, any notion that the Secretary General and his supporting civilian and military staffs can adopt positions, pursue policies or take actions in any way distinct from those agreed upon by the member countries is wrong and gives rise to misapprehension concerning NATO policy or ability to act as an organization separate from or even superior to its member states.

The founding charter, the North Atlantic Treaty, provides for continuous cooperation and consultation in the political, economic and scientific, as well as military fields. NATO is at the same time a military alliance dedicated to promoting the security of its member states. Its effectiveness is based on the provision embodied in its Charter that an armed attack against one or more member states in Europe or North America shall be considered an attack against them all.

It is important to remember that the Alliance was founded in a bipolar situation dominated by the East–West dimension. The issues of today have been rendered enormously complex by the rise of a multipolar world in which the Alliance must deal with Eastern goals and problems, but also with a web of political, economic and social problems arising from the emergence of new power centers, such as the OPEC cartel and other constellations in the world around us. However, as a regional organization dedicated primarily to ensuring Western security through both political and military means,

NATO's primary focus has properly remained East–West relations. In the course of the generation which has passed since the establishment of NATO there has been considerable change in the nature of relations between East and West. There have been crises alternating with periods of relative stability and calm. But certain basic elements have not changed. NATO has preserved the peace in Europe and the North Atlantic region. The existence of the Alliance and its defensive shield have deterred military adventures here because of the risk of unacceptable consequences to an aggressor. But there has been no fundamental change in long-term Soviet policies. The basic relationship between East and West remains a relationship between adversaries. The Soviet approach to East–West relations continues to be competitive and ideological. It is characterized by the unceasing search for targets of opportunity and the exploitation of Western weaknesses. Recent events certainly bear this out.

In the late 1960s, the Alliance formally dedicated itself to the simultaneous pursuit of two related objectives: to lessen tensions and improve East–West relations, and at the same time to maintain an adequate defense posture which would serve as an effective, credible deterrent to political pressures, adventurism and aggression. These two missions remain fully relevant and vitally important to NATO's collective defense.

The Alliance faces formidable challenges in the realm of deterrence and defense. A steady stream of Soviet assertions that Moscow seeks detente, disarmament and peace have not kept the Soviet Union and its allies from a dramatic and alarming military build-up. The Warsaw Pact today commands the most powerful military forces ever seen in peacetime on the continent of Europe. These forces are growing steadily in quality and effectiveness. Soviet military capabilities go far beyond what the most conservative expert could regard as reasonable requirements for the defense of the Soviet Union and Eastern Europe. It is this large gap between what would be reasonable and what in fact is being done which causes such grave concern, leads to questions about the intentions behind Soviet military policy, and compels the West to look to the state of its own defenses.

The military effort undertaken by the Soviet Union is truly remarkable. It represents an enormous drain on what in many ways is still a developing economy which faces rather bleak prospects in the decade ahead. As a percentage of GNP the Soviet leadership devotes to military spending a multiple of what any NATO member country spends on its defense needs. In absolute terms it is the largest military outlay in the world today. For many years Soviet military spending has grown by 4 to 5 percent in real terms, and these percentage comparisons do not begin to tell the whole story. Military pay scales are far higher in the West than in the East. Hence, NATO must spend more than half of its defense budget to pay its armed forces, but of the Soviet "defense ruble," only 15 kopecks are needed to pay the army, navy and air force, leaving 85 percent available for operating costs and investment in research, development, production and deployment of new weapons and equipment.

The Soviets have achieved, except for parts of their navy, parity or superiority in all branches of their military establishment, in nearly all categories of weapons systems. They have attained rough parity with the United States in strategic nuclear weapons.

The Soviet Union must be expected to continue to introduce new and improved systems such as missiles with multiple independently-targetable reentry vehicles (MIRVs), and with greater accuracy. This would be consistent with their doctrine that even a full-scale nuclear war could be fought to some form of successful conclusion.

The increase in conventional offensive ground forces gives the Warsaw Pact a powerful and flexible capability to mass quickly superior forces at points of their choosing. A high level of readiness has been combined with improvements in tactical and strategic mobility, more and improved artillery, tanks and helicopters and enhanced logistic support. In particular the Warsaw Pact is demonstrating a growing capability to use helicopters in support of the land battle, both in the roles of tactical assault and tactical airlift.

Surface-to-air defenses of the Soviet Union and the non-Soviet Warsaw Pact countries are being constantly improved, and the offensive capability of their air forces has increased following the introduction of new modern multirole fighter bombers with increased payload and ranges and the ability to fly at higher speeds and lower altitudes. NATO faces the danger of saturation of its air defense weapons and command and control systems due to the large number of Warsaw Pact aircraft which can be employed simultaneously and the short warning time provided by ground radars.

The capabilities of the Warsaw Pact navies continue to grow through the qualitative improvements being introduced in their wide-ranging modernization programs, particularly in nuclear submarines. A fourth ship of the Kiev class is under construction; the Soviet fleet is developing replenishment and mining techniques; new amphibious units are being introduced along with modern type platforms such as air cushion vehicles, V/STOL aircraft, ASW aircraft and helicopters.

The Soviet fleets, backed by an integrated merchant navy

capable of giving support to naval ships, are becoming increasingly capable of deploying naval power wherever it is needed. They will be sufficiently powerful and flexible to support a variety of Soviet policies. This is of concern to NATO, given its dependence on worldwide supply lines.

The Soviet Union has a considerable capability for electronic and offensive chemical warfare, and Warsaw Pact forces are well prepared to carry out offensive and defensive radio electronic combat. The attention which is paid to chemical warfare in training and exercises implies a preparedness to use such weapons.

In the area of long range theater nuclear weapons the Soviets have achieved a most significant and alarming advantage; they have proceeded to deploy highly accurate and mobile long range systems—the SS-20 missile and the Backfire bomber—weapons which, from deep within the Soviet heartland, can strike and destroy any target in Europe. Since the SALT agreements define land-based strategic weapons as systems capable of striking one superpower from the territory of another, the SS-20 and Backfire bomber have not been included in Strategic Arms Limitation Agreements, except for a numerical limitation on yearly Backfire bomber production. Their range falls just short of that definition. But obviously they cannot be regarded as tactical nuclear weapons; they are a perversion of that concept. They pose such a threat to the credibility of NATO's deterrent that a more effective response must be developed. The military balance between East and West is complicated further by such obvious advantages accruing to the Warsaw Pact as the geographical proximity of the USSR, the depth of terrain available for operations and the benefits of interior lines of communication.

The substantial leads in most areas of sophisticated military technology enjoyed by the West in the past are no longer readily apparent. For example, the Western lead in missile warheads with MIRVs has been heavily eroded, and Soviet armor and antiarmor capabilities have demonstrated the speed with which technological advance can be given practical application. The fundamental research capability of the Soviet Union is generally as advanced as that of the West and its expenditures on military research and development is substantially greater than within the Alliance. Although the general application of the results of this research is still relatively ineffective in the Soviet Union, the military sector does benefit from highly centralized planning and control over all research and development activities and production resources.

The Warsaw Pact nations can be expected to demonstrate greater initiative and flexibility in new equipment designs than hitherto. Expected improvements in the accuracy of weapon delivery techniques promise significant increases in hit probabilities and more precise missile control over long distances. These improvements will come, however, at the price of manifold increases in the cost of weapons systems. As a result, the technology of conventional (and nuclear) warfare is going to continue to undergo a transformation which will likely be moderated only by the availability of funds.

A significant effect of this technology is that warfare could be expected to become even more intense. Consequently, NATO forces must be prepared to deal with very high combat attrition rates for men and equipment. Successful deterrence in this technological environment is particularly expensive since obsolescence is a constant problem requiring rigorous cost–benefit analysis before specific new technologies are applied to the battlefield. As can be seen, the West faces a major challenge. There is cause for deep concern about what intentions may lie behind this tremendous military effort on the part of the USSR.

Territorial defense obviously plays a primary role. Given Russian experience and a tradition going back for centuries, the Soviet leaders may be genuinely convinced of the need to prepare against attack from the West. Russian military doctrine calls for over-insurance and superiority even in the defensive role. The Soviet leaders also perceive a threat on their Far Eastern frontier.

Another major task of the Soviet armed forces clearly is to preserve the territorial gains won in Eastern Europe during and after the Second World War. The USSR considers this in its vital national interest not only for ideological, political and economic reasons, but also because of the obvious military value of Eastern Europe as a glacis to protect the western parts of the Soviet Union.

But all these factors, together with the difficulties in changing an ongoing industrial production pattern, do not justify the present size of Soviet forces or the continuing build-up. Assuming that a sudden massive military assault on Western Europe remains unlikely in view of the risks involved, the ultimate purpose of the Soviet forces may be seen as something other than direct military use. Indeed the Soviet leaders have made clear that they see military strength as a political weapon—as a means of exerting increasingly irresistible political pressure on the West and thus as an instrument of changing the world balance of power in their favor.

What are we doing about it? An adequate defense posture is clearly necessary, not only to deal with the ultimate and, one hopes, unlikely possibility of outright military aggression, but also to cope with political pressures and blackmail. It remains essential that the

Alliance should be seen by its potential adversaries to have both the physical capability and the political will to deter, and if necessary to resist, aggression.

To achieve this purpose it is not necessary to match the other side man for man and weapon for weapon. Quite a few years ago NATO adopted a strategy of flexible response which rests on a triad of conventional, theatre nuclear, and strategic nuclear forces. The underlying concept is to have the means to respond appropriately to any form and level of aggression, and to retain the option to escalate our military response in such a way as to make the ultimate consequences of aggression incalculable and thus unacceptable for the aggressor.

For this strategy to work—to be credible—it is essential that all three elements of the NATO triad remain strong and effective. Despite the numerical superiorities noted earlier, the overall balance has been such to make the risks of aggression unacceptable.

However, this balance is now in danger., The ratio of forces increasingly favors the East. In light of the military policies pursued by the Soviet Union, NATO governments decided to increase annual military spending by 3 percent in real terms. This was deemed to be the minimum effort to prevent a dangerous destabilization.

The Alliance has also adopted a Long Term Defense Program to modernize and improve its military posture in ten selected program areas over the next fifteen years. This major initiative represents a contribution of great importance in the adaptation of the defense posture of the Alliance to the changing needs of the 1980s. It builds on and complements a wide range of improvements already planned or underway in the fields of NATO armaments, logistics, civil emergency, force planning and command, control and communications. The Long Term Defense Program calls not only for greater efforts in a number of areas of special weakness, but also for more vigorous pursuit of the means of obtaining, through greater cooperation and rationalization, the best return from the national resources already made available or planned for the defense of the Alliance. There has also been short term improvements in NATO's capabilities in defense against armor, in holdings of selected war reserve stocks, in readiness of Allied force and in rapid reinforcement of these forces.

Most land forces are now being equipped with a greater number of modern antiarmor weapons and more of these are planned, together with associated vehicles and helicopters. A new generation of battletanks is being or will be introduced into service in a number of NATO countries. There are long term plans for the replacement of ships of all types and of maritime aircraft. New technology equipment and advanced offensive and defensive weapon systems are planned to be used simultaneously with the ship construction program. New aircraft are replacing older types and there are plans to introduce newer generation aircraft and improved weapon systems into service. In a major cooperative effort, a NATO Airborne Early Warning and Control System will be introduced during the coming years. All three services plan for improvements of electronic warfare, command, control and communications capabilities. Measures are being taken to enhance readiness, the availability of reinforcements (including acceleration of movements) and reception arrangements.

In armaments planning, significant efforts in the area of longer-term planning, cooperative development and production, and reduced barriers to trade and technology sharing continue to improve cooperation among nations towards the goal of increased standardization and interoperability of equipment, systems and operational procedures. Nevertheless, despite substantial improvements already initiated or planned, NATO can no longer rely on a solid technological lead and qualitative superiority to compensate for the numerical inferiority of its forces in Europe.

The deployment of long range theatre nuclear forces by the Soviet Union pesents the Alliance with its most serious challenge in many years. While NATO has nuclear weapons deployed on the continent of Europe, most of these are aging, obsolescent, relatively short range systems not capable of striking Soviet territory. In order to respond to the threat posed by the multiple warheads mounted on SS-20 launchers, NATO has relied on the U.S. strategic and forward-based systems and on the British nuclear deterrent. This situation has opened up a serious gap in the range of options on which NATO strategy is based and weakens the credibility and effectiveness of the deterrent.

It is vitally necessary for both political and military reasons that NATO maintain and, where necessary, restore the military balance which is the foundation for any real progress toward detente, arms control and disarmament. There is not the slightest doubt that the Alliance can do this. The Atlantic Community commands vast resources and maintains a lead in technology. What is needed is clear vision and the will and courage to do what is necessary.

In order to redress the dangerous disequilibrium in theatre nuclear forces all NATO members, with the exception of France, agreed on 12 December 1979 to proceed with a modernization program involving deployment in Europe of new U.S.-produced long range theatre nuclear weapons—the Pershing II missile and ground-launched cruise missiles carrying nuclear warheads. Follow-on actions are under consideration to modernize where necessary short and medium range nuclear delivery systems over the long term. As many NATO governments have since emphasized, these INF modernization efforts must be undertaken with a clear understanding of the relationship of these forces to ongoing and anticipated arms control activities. There is a direct linkage between these two issues, but consideration of their relative merits should not be allowed to delay progress in either field. Although emphasis should continue to be given to improvements in conventional forces, and no increase in overall reliance on nuclear systems or departure from existing NATO policy is anticipated, INF modernization decisions must aim to strengthen NATO's deterrent and defense capabilities while making the wisest possible use of Alliance resources and maintaining Allied confidence and cohesion in support of all elements of the NATO triad.

The importance which the Alliance attaches to negotiating arms limitation agreements, while at the same time taking the necessary steps to maintain a credible deterrent, leads to consideration of another element of Allied policy—the pursuit of detente. This word has given rise to much confusion and controversy. While remaining committed to the pursuit of detente policy, NATO was under no illusions (even before the Soviet invasion of Afghanistan) that detente had achieved anything like genuine relaxation of tensions. More normal relations between East and West remain a distant goal, rather than an established fact. The meaning of the word "detente" seems to be interpreted differently in the USSR than in the West.

Genuine detente must be indivisible. It must be applied in good faith to all areas of the world and to all fields of endeavor. We cannot be content with a selective, "a la carte" approach to detente in which the USSR invokes the blessing of detente when it is to its advantage to do so because it offers improved access to Western technology, trade and investment—but ignores the principles of detente in other areas such as the Soviet military policy just described, or the exploitation of instability and change in the Third World.

In a variety of ways NATO is trying to bring about more normal relations, to break down the walls of suspicion and hostility between East and West, to limit and eventually to reduce military forces, which is the only alternative to an ongoing, astronomically expensive and potentially disastrous arms race. But progress is extremely slow because basic assumptions and the approaches to detente are very different in East and West.

While the West seeks more normal relations and greater stability and security at reduced force levels, the Eastern approach appears to be ideologically motivated and quite opportunistic. The record shows that the Soviets use detente as an instrument of policy when it is to their advantage to do so. Their professed commitment to detente has not inhibited the continued pursuit of ideological struggle nor the progressive expansion of Soviet power and influence, whether political, military or economic.

Military aid, intervention by proxy, and direct Soviet military intervention in areas outside the traditional Soviet bloc have been Moscow's principal instruments in the effort to expand Soviet influence while at the same time reducing that of the West and China. Over the past several years the world has seen on the African continent, in Central America and now with particular gravity in Southern Asia, how effectively the Soviet Union can apply pressure and project military power.

But even though the Soviets and their allies exploit the concept of detente for their own purposes, NATO must not abandon its patient, painstaking, long term efforts to stabilize and improve relations. The West cannot justify a simple continuation in the upward spiral of military spending in which each side provokes the other into ever greater efforts and expenditures. NATO needs to be strong—in part, because that is the only basis to achieve real progress towards arms control and disarmament, as an alternative to the arms race. But the NATO governments must also continue to pursue political activities, individually and, wherever appropriate, collectively in their efforts to influence Soviet policies, to promote relaxation of tensions, and to increase stability at lower levels of military forces.

At this point it is useful to mention briefly some of the focal points of NATO's other activities with respect to the East. First, in the field of arms control certain East–West negotiations are in progress. The principal negotiations concern Mutual and Balanced Force Reductions in Central Europe and the ongoing SALT process. In MBFR progress has been disappointingly slow. For a considerable time now the main obstacle to progress has been major disagreement between East and West concerning the actual numbers of Warsaw Pact forces in the reductions area. In December 1979, the Western side presented proposals for an Interim Phase I Agreement calling for modest and balanced reductions in U.S. and Soviet forces and a package of associated measures covering such matters as verification, measures to increase mutual confidence and ways to assure the security of member countries outside the reductions area. Despite the serious aggravation in East–West relations brought about by recent Soviet actions, efforts to achieve progress should continue. It remains certain, however, that the discrepancy over manpower data will have to be resolved in order to reach a final MBFR agreement.

NATO remains deeply committed to the overall SALT process as a means of assuring strategic balance between the United States and the Soviet Union. Despite Soviet assertions that NATO's decision to modernize its theatre nuclear force posture "destroyed the basis for negotiations," such protestations should not be regarded as their last word and negotiations such as those called for in NATO's INF modernization decision should be earnestly pursued.

These efforts at East–West dialogue receive valuable guidance and impetus through NATO's consultation process. NATO has been the principal forum for Western efforts over thirty years to achieve greater cohesion and solidarity and thus greater effectiveness in dealings with the East. Consultation is a process which continues on a day-to-day basis in the many committees and working groups of the Alliance, starting with the North Atlantic Council.

The physical proximity at NATO headquarters in Brussels of the fifteen member-delegations and of the international civilian and military staffs greatly facilitates consultation, and so does the flexible, informal approach which is practiced. The purpose of consultation may vary from a simple exchange of information and views, which itself is of great benefit to member countries, to efforts to harmonize and coordinate Alliance positions on given issues such as arms control negotiations.

With regard to each of the principal East–West fora, the nature and purpose of consultation are somewhat different. The MBFR negotiations in Vienna are bloc-to-bloc negotiations between NATO and the Warsaw Pact; guidance and instructions to the Western negotiators are developed and agreed upon at NATO. The MBFR negotiations are limited to the Central region but the results could influence the flank countries as well.

In SALT and any forthcoming negotiations on theatre nuclear weapons, the Alliance plays a different role. NATO has not participated directly in what have been bilateral arms control negotiations between the two superpowers, and the Alliance called for bilateral talks in theatre force modernization. However, the North Atlantic Council is the forum in which the United States consulted its Allies regularly and frequently in the course of the SALT negotiations. During the negotiation of SALT II this form of consultation was more than a simple transmission of information. In the future the Alliance will be involved even more intensively in the development of U.S. negotiating positions. The negotiations will probably remain bilateral; however, as a follow-up to the Ministerial decisions taken, a Special Consultative Group established by participating countries will report to the Council on all consultations.

In other areas, consultation serves to exchange information, views and concerns frequently involving issues on which it is neither possible nor necessarily appropriate to arrive at fully harmonized positions.

In its collective military plans and operations NATO is bound by the Treaty area—the territory member states and the North Atlantic from the North Pole to the Tropic of Cancer—but the consultative process enables the Alliance to transcend the geographic limitations of a regional organization and thus to render the Alliance more supple and relevant to present-day developments around the world than it would be otherwise.

The adaptability and flexibility of Western thought and organization which have been demonstrated in the evolution of NATO over the last thirty years will certainly continue. But if there have been great changes in the world in these years, certain fundamental factors have not altered, except to intensify their original characteristics. The USSR continues to be a totalitarian state directed by a small, self-perpetuating group of men. The free and open societies of the West are understandably cautious in dealing with such arbitrary power, uninhibited by the voice of public opinion.

The old axiom of strength in unity which was the base on which the Alliance was built still holds true today: the tasks that lie before the Atlantic Alliance continue to require the solidarity and close cooperation which had made NATO the successful instrument for defense which it has been since its inception.

No one can predict how long NATO will still be necessary, but whatever the time-span, it is hard to imagine a better means for dealing with many of the problems facing the West than the Atlantic Alliance, with its demonstrated capacity to meet new situations and opportunities. While new ways and means may be sought to achieve NATO's aims, it would be well to remember that the principles and purposes set out in the treaty remain as valid today as when it was signed more than thirty years ago.

14

Projection of Military Power to Southwest Asia: an Asymmetrical Problem

James G. Roche

INTRODUCTION

The dramatic events of 1979 drew special attention to Southwest Asia. Not only is it one of the more unstable areas of the world, it is also becoming an area of increased superpower competition. This competition is both political and military, especially in the sense that military power is being used to further the political interests of both superpowers. Southwest Asia has been of great and long-standing geopolitical interest to both Russia and the West. For most of recent history, Great Britain played the leading Western role in the area. However, for the last twenty years or so the United States has been involved to varying degrees, culminating in large military sales and aid programs to Iran and Saudi Arabia.

Since there are no hard and fast rules for defining just what Southwest Asia encompasses, for the sake of discussion, we may define the area as extending from Pakistan to the east to Saudi Arabia to the West. Further, we shall avoid trying to specify a line of demarcation between Southwest Asia and the Middle East.

In thinking of the problem which would face either the Soviet Union or the United States in projecting military power to this region, two major asymmetries loom large: one is technical in nature, while the other is more fundamental. The technical asymmetry has to do with the fact that there are major differences in the infrastructures needed for the projection of military power into the region which is available to either side. The fundamental asymmetry has to do with the differences in purpose and style of each side in its approach to power projection in the region. If we in the United States do not fully understand these asymmetries and the implications for policy of each, we may find we have spent billions of dollars preparing to defend against our analyses, rather than against reality.

ASYMMETRY IN INFRASTRUCTURE

In considering the issue of projection of military power, the concept of infrastructure is of such importance that it deserves to be especially highlighted. This chapter will discuss infrastructure in the broadest of terms. To understand the importance of infrastructure in the Southwest Asian region, we should understand recent trends in Soviet power projection capabilities.

Besides maintaining large standing forces opposite the Central Front of Europe, the Soviet Union, for some years, has had rather good "cross-border" power projection capabilities. These have been oriented towards the northern flank of Europe, the Chinese border, and along the southern border of the Soviet Union. Soviet cross-border projection capabilities have gotten much better over the last ten to fifteen years in terms of appropriate forces, lift, command and control, and logistic support. On the other hand, Soviet capabilities to project their military power to regions at great distance from the Soviet Union are still rather embryonic in nature. For example, in the situation where both the United States and the Soviet Union were faced with having to project military power to a point equally distant from each, the United States, today, would have a significant comparative advantage. Unfortunately, however, the United States and the West are faced with the problem that many of the areas of the world vital to the West are relatively close to the Soviet Union.

The USSR has about twenty-three divisions (some in lower states of readiness) and about 300 tactical aircraft stationed in the military districts north of Iran and in, or north of, Afghanistan. And over the last twenty years or so, the Soviets have invested considerable resources in developing the road, rail, and airfield infrastructure on their periphery, especially in the areas north of Iran and Afghanistan. In the case of the Soviet invasion and continuing operations in Afghanistan, the infrastructure within the Soviet Union has been used extensively for the staging of troops, the operations and maintenance of tactical aircraft, and for command and control. It is ironic to note that the Soviets also built infrastructure within Afghanistan. In the 1950s, while the United States was engaged in reclamation projects and some road construction in southeastern Afghanistan, the Soviet Union was building the road network which was later used to invade the country.

Besides the development of infrastructure within the Soviet Union—facing Southwest Asia—the Soviets have also developed infrastructure in the Gulf of Aden area. Initially, they built facilities in Somalia. More recently, the Soviets have developed extensive infrastructure in Ethiopia and South Yemen. This has consisted of airfield improvements, port upgrades, the establishment of naval repair facilities, and the development of command and control organization. There is a fundamental difference between infrastructure in areas such as Afghanistan or Ethiopia or South Yemen and that on the border of Southwest Asia within the Soviet Union. First, an infrastructure within one's own country permits the use of internal lines of communication. And second, both the infrastructure and the internal lines of communication may be considered especially secure since the issue of "sanctuary" may arise, regardless of the degree of defenses present. That is, in time of regional conflict, one must keep in mind the difference between attacking Soviet facilities in, say, South Yemen, and attacking other facilities which are within Soviet borders, although each may be equally useful in supporting Soviet military objectives.

So far, this discussion has treated the concept of infrastructure in a very narrow sense. But there are other aspects of infrastructure which are as important as facilities, roads, etc. For instance, there is political infrastructure. The Tudeh Party in Iran, the "Loyal" Afghans (and there are some) in Afghanistan, and the Marxists in South Yemen all constitute political elements which would be of great utility to the Soviet Union in periods of conflict. This point can be extended. For instance, the ability to use Ethiopian troops as proxies on the Arabian peninsula, or the use of Cubans or East Germans, or the exploitation of the very large Yemeni population within Saudi Arabia must all be considered to be potentially part of the Soviet infrastructure within the Southwest Asian region. Going even further, it is not unreasonable to consider as part of the infrastructure military and support equipment stored in the Soviet Union which is ready for transfer to client forces or proxy forces within the region.

On the other hand, we should not forget that the Soviets have had considerable difficulties in dealing with people in this part of the world. After all, the Soviets were thrown out of Egypt, the Sudan, and Somalia. But they may have learned a great deal from these episodes.

For many years, U.S. investment in infrastructure in the Southwest Asian region was focused primarily in Iran. With the fall of the Shah and the ensuing political hostilities between the United States and Iran, the United States finds itself in a position of having access to few facilities in other countries of the region. As part of our aid agreement, the United States has developed facilities within Saudi Arabia for the use of Saudi forces. But the Saudis have been quite clear about their desire that the U.S. not station its own forces in Saudi Arabia. In time, we may be able to develop appropriate facilities in Oman, and possibly Somalia. Only on the British island of Diego García are we establishing the type of infrastructure to which we have become accustomed (as we are in Subic Bay or were in South Vietnam). But Diego García is a considerable distance from the mainland of Southwest Asia. Unfortunately, the United States faces real problems in gaining access to those ports and bases which we consider appropriate in this part of the world. As in Saudi Arabia, there are political sensitivities in Oman to the presence of U.S. forces. And the Ogaden problem has caused us great difficulty in making arrangements with Somalia. Some of our problems in dealing with the Saudis and the Omanis have had to do with the emergence of Iraq as a major player in the region. Iraq took the position that neither the Soviet Union nor the United States should establish a presence in the area. However, it is interesting to note that Iraq's protestations coincided with U.S. attempts to establish infrastructure in the region, and not with long-term Soviet programs or moves. Given their difficulties with the Soviet Union during the ongoing Iraqi–Iranian conflict, the Iraqis have lowered their voices when protesting against U.S. attempts to gain access to facilities in the region.

One could argue that the United States has had formidable infrastructure in the region for some time. After all, there are major airfields in Turkey, at least one of which is located in Eastern Turkey not far from the border of Iran. Also, most of the extensive military facilities in Israel are compatible with U.S. military ends. Even more to the point, we are financing the construction of major airfields in Israel as part of the agreement following the Israeli–Egyptian Peace Treaty. However, for various political reasons we feel constrained in exploiting these facilities. But increasingly, the United States believes it will be able to gain temporary access to Egypt's infrastructures in times of crisis, and there are reports of efforts being considered to enhance the capabilities of certain facilities in Egypt. As a general rule, the United States faces a situation in the region where either (1) certain "allies" whose facilities would be of great use to us are reluctant to be seen working for us, or (2) we, for various reasons, do not want to be seen working with other "allies." Thus, a number of our infrastructure problems are of our own making.

Finally, there is an issue of infrastructure which is not often discussed. In Southwest Asia there exists an asymmetry in the infrastructure that would support tactical nuclear conflict. Besides having major bomber fields near their southern borders, the Soviets have emplaced their SS-20 medium range nuclear ballistic missiles within the Soviet Union so as to target the Southwest Asian region as well as other regions.

Many of the Soviet bombers, and all of the SS-20 missiles, are not covered by the SALT agreement. On the other hand, the U.S. cruise missile, which potentially would make major contributions to the nuclear balance in the region, would be covered by the as yet unratified SALT II Treaty, at least during the protocol period. And U.S. B-52 bombers, some of which have participated in exercises in the Indian Ocean region, would also be covered by SALT II. Thus, some of one side's major systems relevant to the military situation in the region are constrained, while those of the other are not.

More important, the fact that the Soviet-based theater nuclear systems could be expected to support nuclear conflict in the region raises two difficult questions. First, if the West were trying to contain nuclear conflict to the region, would it consider targeting such infrastructure? Second, if nonproliferation policies fail, and some regional power obtains nuclear weapons and even modest delivery systems, would it feel less constrained to use such weapons against forward bases than against "homeland" bases? There are no easy answers to either of these questions.

ASYMMETRY IN PURPOSE AND STYLE

Up to this point, we have been discussing the projection of military power in terms which suggest invasion and counterinvasion. However, power projection is *not* synonymous with invasion. Indeed the notion of projecting military power involves a spectrum of means ranging from military aid and advisers, through saboteurs or specially trained small combat units, to large scale insertion of military forces. Having recognized that the projection of military power is a broad concept, we need next to recognize that while the Soviet Union may be engaging in the projection of its military power, the United States, its allies, and its regional friends are engaged in a business which is different in style and purpose. While we may refer to our planning and efforts as power projection, in fact we are in the business of counter–power projection; we are in the position of being on the defensive. Stated simply, we want to hold on to something, while the Soviets want to break that hold. And in so doing, they get to choose the *time*, the *place*, and the *means*. Unfortunately, there already are examples of the Soviet leaders employing different means at different times and in different places in the region. For instance, outright invasion was used in Afghanistan; but in Ethiopia the USSR and the Cubans were invited into the country; in the case of North Yemen, it appears the USSR has been stirring up regional conflict; and, in the case of Iran, it may be fomenting internal instability.

The United States, and the West more generally, finds it in its interests to maintain the stability of the region both for geostrategic reasons and in order to maintain access to vitally needed oil. It is in our interest that the Soviet Union keep out of the area. On the other hand, the Soviet leaders have many reasons for wanting to get involved in Southwest Asia. For instance, in time they may need oil for themselves, although this is a subject under much debate; or, even if they don't need the oil for themselves, they fully understand the leverage they will gain through control over this oil; furthermore, the Russians have always had designs on the area for geostrategic reasons (warm water ports, a "southern buffer," and stepping off points for further adventurism).

Being able to develop leverage over Western energy sources would provide the USSR with a level of deterrent comparable to the U.S. nuclear deterrent of the 1950s. That is, the Soviets could threaten Western access to Persian Gulf oil, and the West, today, would have no comparable response. There are many reasons why the Soviets might wish to develop such leverage. They may wish to encourage the Europeans to resist certain American initiatives to enhance the defense capabilities of NATO; or, they may wish to pressure the Japanese not to cooperate in "unacceptable" ways with China; or, in the case of a major problem in Yugoslavia, the Soviet leaders may wish to place Europe in a situation wherein involvement to maintain the independence of Yugoslavia could lead to major interruptions in energy supplies. The basic point is that the Soviets recognize Western vulnerabilities. They also recognize that it is not necessary that they physically occupy oil fields in order to have leverage over Western energy. For instance, they could pressure Arab oil producers in many ways either to sell a proportion of oil production to them or their allies, or not to sell oil to other countries.

Thus, while the asymmetry in infrastructure is of major importance to military planners, the asymmetries in purpose and style of power projection are far more fundamental, and require different kinds of thinking and planning. In fact, thinking about dealing with the asymmetry in infrastructure should only be done after we have understood the full range of implications of the asymmetries in purpose and style of the two "players."

WHAT DO THESE ASYMMETRIES MEAN FOR US?

Thinking of the projection of military power only in terms of invasion or deterring invasion may lead us to invest enormous resources in too limited a set of responses. While we may not recognize that we are investing in only a limited set of responses to a broad set of potential Soviet moves, the Soviets are sure to recognize this, and to develop plans to exploit the vulnerabilities in our posture. We face some very tough choices. Do we try to pay for an insurance policy to deal with the full spectrum of Soviet power projection means? And in doing so, will we recognize we are not particularly good at certain counter–power projection moves (for instance, we have allowed our counterinsurgency capabilities to atrophy)? Or do we pick some particular "catastrophic insurance" policy and give up on other possibilities? Or, should we leave these other possibilities to someone else to take care of? Before we get too far along in making major investments in military capabilities for the area, I believe it is essential that the U.S., and preferably the U.S. and its major European and regional allies, think through the basic elements of a strategy which is designed to counter the full range of expected Soviet power projection moves in the region.

In doing so, the first order of business is to decide just what our goals ought to be. What is it we most want to be able to do? Besides deterring outright Soviet invasion, do we wish to deter Soviet surrogate involvement? Do we wish also to deter regional conflicts? Further, do we wish to maintain the current regimes in the area? Alternatively, do these latter questions all relate to our interest in maintaining access to oil, and denying the Soviets the ability to gain leverage over this oil? We had better decide what it is that we want to protect or preserve, lest we find ourselves in a situation where, having spent billions to prepare to meet the Soviets in the desert or in the highlands, we wake up one morning and find that some Saudi colonel is leading an uprising, and as an opener, he has just sent three of his followers to Ras Tannūrah to shut down all Saudi oil exports for some time. Having decided, even if only in general terms, what it is we want to be able to do in this region, then we will need to think through the kind of portfolio of counter–power projection moves for which we are willing to pay.

It is essential for the West to be able to deter the Soviet leaders from an outright invasion of a friendly oil-producing state. Public discussion has focused almost exclusively on this issue in recent times. This makes sense given the need to program and budget for the forces required to deter such a Soviet move. And it is already obvious that the asymmetries in infrastructure, among other reasons, will cause the development of appropriate military capabilities to be quite expensive indeed.

It would seem critical, however, also to think about other counter–power projection means. I have in mind such things as the following: the protection-in-depth of critical oil system nodes; the development of forces trained and equipped to fight local insurgents; the provision of advisers, C^3, training, and equipment for local forces (including local security forces); and the development of means to impose costs on the Soviets where they are currently involved—i.e., ways to cause them to bleed so as to motivate them not to become involved in other parts of the region.

Thinking along such lines will make it obvious to us that a lot of trade-offs are required. Because of limited resources, we will have to decide how much emphasis should be placed on developing heavy forces as compared to counterinsurgency forces; we will have to make trade-offs between what the United States should be prepared to do and what other Western allies should be prepared to do; and we will have to deal with similar trade-offs between what countries outside the region should be prepared to do and what local forces, including possible regional forces, should be able to do in terms of deterring various Soviet moves in the region. In addition, do we have enough of the right kinds of tailored equipment (e.g., tank transports and/or desert vehicles) to be able to operate effectively in the region? How will we go about integrating our own C^3 and intelligence systems with those of local forces? And do we have the appropriate kinds of tactical doctrines needed to operate effectively in the full range of contingencies which we envision?

CONCLUSIONS

It is not my purpose to suggest that current United States plans are inappropriate. Rather, I am arguing that the problem of countering Soviet power projection moves in the area, as well as dealing with local instability within the region, require that we think through a strategy which is appropriate for the breadth of the problem and affordable. Asymmetries in infrastructure and in the purpose and style of power projection operations require that we be highly selective in our goals, deciding just what it is we wish to be able to do in the region—alone, in concert with our Western allies, and in concert with local forces and our regional allies. Because of the "loss of Iran" and our current lack of infrastructure in the region, time is of the essence. It would seem clear that we are going to have to think, procure, and start deploying some assets *concurrently*. And if we fail to push our thinking beyond the "counterinvasion" mentality, we may all be faced with a situation of having to walk to work within the next couple of years.

15

Problems of Power Projection in East Asia—
Japanese Perspectives on Asian Security

Hisashi Owada

THE NATURE OF THE SECURITY ENVIRONMENT
IN EAST ASIA

Together with Western Europe, East Asia forms an important military front in Eurasia. As "war in Europe could be accompanied by war and threat of war in Asia,"[1] the two regions are closely related in the military perspectives of the West. However, there are two important differences between the West European theater and the East Asia theater from the perspective of military balance. One is the basic character and modality of alignment that prevails in the two regions. On the European scene, the clear demarcation line between the opposing camps has been established, based on the continuous boundaries running through the central part of Europe. The bipolarization of security interests in the form of NATO–Warsaw Pact confrontation has created a situation where increased tension gives rise to the danger of escalation, which could develop into a large-scale military conflict involving the two opposing groups. By contrast, the East Asian scene is characterized by the absence of such a clear demarcation line between the two opposing groups facing each other in confrontation.[2] Several of the countries in this region cannot be categorically classified as allies or adversaries of the United States. These countries are basically friends of the United States, sharing a number of common political, economic and social orientations, and they are anxious to promote their stability and prosperity on the basis of friendly relations with the countries of the free world. Nevertheless, many of them are not in an alliance relationship with the United States or other Western countries, and are thus more susceptible to influences coming from countries with different orientations.

The major characteristic that distinguishes East Asia from Western Europe is the tripolar geopolitical structure of the region created by the interplay of the United States, the Soviet Union and the People's Republic of China. With the aggravation of the Sino–Soviet rift and the emergence of China as a major actor in the East Asian scene in the past few years, an extremely complicated relationship between these players has come to the surface. Although China at present can hardly be described as a major military power, her role as a major actor in the politico-strategic context of East Asia is already apparent.

These characteristics of East Asia in turn have affected the nature of the security problems of this region. On the one hand, the lack of an established line which determines the respective sphere of domination of the two camps makes the entire region highly unstable—the politico—military geography of the region is always susceptible to modification by force without the risk of a large-scale war between the two camps. The fact that two of the three major armed conflicts in the postwar period, i.e., the Korean conflict and the Vietnam conflict (the Middle East conflict is the exception), have been fought in this region testifies to the intrinsic fluidity, and therefore the vulnerability, of the region. The tripolar character of the newly emerging power structure of this region complicates this situation. It certainly cannot be said that this new power structure has been a positive help toward the establishment of stability in the region.

On the other hand, this same fluidity makes the region extremely sensitive and vulnerable to factors which are not strictly military, but which can broadly be described as politico-military. The determining influence in shaping the balance in the region will not necessarily be the kind of military tension and outbreak of armed conflict that one associates with the European front. Very often, it may well be the political impact of an event or of the emergence of a new situation that will bring about a shift in the security balance.

Given this dual vulnerability in the East Asian region, it will be easy to see that the nature and significance of factors which affect the security of this area are not the same as they are in relation to Europe. Thus, for example, a simple comparison of Soviet military strength with that of others in this region through an arithmetic "beancounting" of total numbers of troops, aircraft and ships will in all likelihood be inadequate, almost to the point of being irrelevant, to an assessment of the security balance of the region.

MILITARY POSTURES OF THE UNITED STATES AND THE SOVIET UNION IN EAST ASIA

It is generally recognized that the Soviet Union has since the early 1960s been consistently trying to increase military expenditures and to reinforce its military strength. As a result, Soviet military capabilities are estimated to have grown to such an extent that the United States and her Western allies are obliged to reexamine the adequacy of their defense preparedness. The United States has for more than ten years not been increasing her military expenditure in real terms except for the war cost in Vietnam. Her Western allies have also been less than enthusiastic in their efforts for military buildup due to economic and other difficulties.

Although the motivation of the Soviet military buildup is something about which one can only speculate, the actual military strength of the Soviet Union has been characterized as being "more than what is needed for purely defensive purposes."[3] We shall examine briefly some of the figures in relation to the Soviet military buildup as it affects the region of East Asia.

Up to about 1960, Soviet troops in the region were thought to be deployed particularly with the United States and Japan in mind. With the aggravation of the Sino–Soviet confrontation, however, and especially following the armed clash of 1969 between Soviet and Chinese forces on the Sino–Soviet border, there has emerged a pattern of consistent reinforcement of forces directed toward China: of the total of 1,830,000 men in 168 divisions that comprise the Soviet army, roughly one-fourth, or some 44 divisions with more than 400,000 men, are positioned along the Sino–Soviet border. Of these, 32 divisions consisting of more than 300,000 men are deployed in the Far East, roughly in areas east of Lake Baikal.[4]

The deployment of air forces takes a similar pattern. Some 2,000 aircraft, which are about one-fourth of the total Soviet air strength of 8,800 combat aircraft, are deployed in the Far East. These include about 450 bombers, 1,400 fighters, and 140 patrol planes. The Soviet air power consists of air forces for frontline, long-range, air defense, transport and naval operations purposes, but the largest component is front-line air forces which are positioned mainly along the Sino-Soviet border, presumably with the primary mission of providing air cover support for Soviet ground troops on the Sino–Soviet border. However, the Soviet long-range air forces, which are stationed mainly in hinterland areas, are said to encompass all of China and peripheral regions of Asia within their radii of operations. In addition, the naval air forces, stationed mainly in coastal Siberia, are active in the Japan Sea and the Western Pacific.[5]

The naval forces of the Soviet Union in the region are represented by the Soviet Pacific Fleet, which, with its strength of 770 vessels amounting to 1,380,000 tons, represents roughly one-third of the entire Soviet naval strength of 2,500 vessels amounting to 4,790,000 tons. The Pacific Fleet can operate over sea areas of the Pacific and the Indian Oceans, with major bases in Vladivostok, which is its command headquarters, Petropavlovsk in Kamchatka and Sovetskaya Gavan in the Maritime province. Their main strength is said to be 20 major surface combat vessels equipped with missiles and 125 submarines, as well as about 310 combat aircraft and the marines of two battalions consisting of 4,800 men.[6]

Finally, as for nuclear capability, about 30 percent of the entire Soviet strategic missile force is thought to be deployed for this region, consisting of SLBMs assigned to the Pacific Fleet, and ICBMs deployed along the Trans–Siberian Railway in inland regions. A considerable number of theater nuclear weapons are believed to be deployed.[7]

But more important than this consistent growth in overall numerical strength is the recent emphasis on the qualitative reinforcement of the Soviet military capabilities in the Asian–Pacific region. The result is that the total military strength of the Soviet Union in this region, and particularly its combat readiness, are believed to have been greatly improved. Particularly noteworthy is the introduction of most modern weapons and equipment. Thus, SA-6 and SA-9 surface-to-air missiles appeared in August 1977. SS-20 IRBMs are said to have been deployed in the Trans-Baikal and Siberian Military Districts. T-64/72 tanks are believed to have been already introduced and there is evidence that TU-26 Backfire bombers will be deployed there. On the Pacific, the Krivak-II destroyers appeared in January 1978, and the *Minsk*, a *Kiev*-class aircraft carrier, and the *Petropavlovsk*, a *Kara*-class ASW cruiser, as well as the *Ivan Rogov* amphibious assault ship appeared in June 1979.[8]

Soviet military activity is equally impressive. It is generally presumed that the ground force divisions, together with their associated air support and organic and other nuclear weapons, are primarily meant for possible action against China. But the naval and air activities in the Western Pacific, which could not be so essential against China, have also been intensified, creating the impression that they are in fact intended not only to enhance the training levels of naval and air forces and to collect intelligence in the area, but that they are also more aggressively "aimed at restricting United States capability to maintain sea control and at increasing the Soviet political and psychological influence on Asian nations through the presence of naval and air forces."[9]

Of more direct security concern to Japan is the fact that, since the summer of 1978, the Soviet Union appears to be engaged in the construction of bases and the deployment of ground forces comprising tanks and other major weapons in Kunashiri and Etorofu in the occupied northern territories of Japan.[10]

By contrast, the military posture of the United States in this region of East Asia and the Pacific has been regarded by many Asian nations as declining. During the cold war years, the United States regarded China and the Soviet Union as a "combined threat" and deployed major forces in Asia in an attempt to curb the expansion and advance of their power. However, the development of the Sino–Soviet rift, the rapprochement between the People's Republic of China and the United States, the termination of the Vietnam conflict and other developments have effected a change in the United States posture. The deployment of American military power in the Asian-Pacific regions has reflected a shift from the "2½ war" to the 1½ war" strategy. The present strategy of U.S. forces deployed in East Asia and the Western Pacific seems to be built on the assumption that "the United States no longer plans forces on the basis of a United States–China conflict" and that "China is a strategic counterweight to the Soviet Union ."[11]

Against this background, the level of United States forces stationed in the Western Pacific has decreased from the maximum of about 830,000 troops in 1960 to 136,700 in 1980.[12] Indeed, it seems that since the end of American involvement in the Vietnam war, the United States military forces in Asia have been geared for deterrence rather than war-fighting purposes. However, in the final analysis, this could be a contradiction in terms, inasmuch as force can be credible and therefore effective as deterrence only if it is ready to be engaged in war-fighting.

In an East Asian setting, the missions of forces deployed for the maintenance of security would seem to be not so easy or simple as they would be in a better defined area, such as Western Europe. Given the basic characteristics, described above, of the security environment in East Asia, American military forces in the region must serve complex purposes, in conjunction with the political and economic instruments of United States foreign policy. Some of the major missions would include the following:

1. To maintain integrity of nuclear deterrence through a strategic submarine fleet equipped with SLBMs;
2. To protect United States forward bases against growing Soviet theater nuclear forces;
3. To deter by conventional air, naval and ground forces against renewed conflict in parts of Asia, such as the Korean peninsula or the Indochina peninsula, including the threat to Thailand;

4. To ensure the security of sea lanes across the Pacific and the Indian Ocean;
5. To maintain the credibility of United States security interests in Asia.

The task is multifarious and enormous. The critical question is whether the strength is adequate to the task.

Against the background of what has been briefly described above, especially the intensified quantitative improvements in the naval and air forces of the Soviet Union, the need for reexamining the military balance in East Asia—particularly the present state of military balance in the naval and air power in the Western Pacific—has become urgent.

ASSESSMENT OF MILITARY BALANCE IN EAST ASIA

In order to assess accurately the present military balance in East Asia, including the impact of the Soviet military buildup in the Far East upon the security of the region, it would be necessary to have not merely a static numerical comparison of the comparative military strengths of the Soviet Union and the United States, but an overall assessment of the combined capabilities of each superpower and its allies and friends respectively, as well as other factors which affect the bipolar relationship between the two camps, notably the impact of the People's Republic of China. Moreover, in attempting a comprehensive assessment of the security situation in East Asia, relative factors other than military forces, including economic strength and technological levels, would have to be assessed.

Setting this point aside for the moment, however, if one tries to compare simply the military strength of the Soviet Union and the United States, the following would seem to be among the most relevant points in an appraisal of the situation.

1. On the nuclear capability of the Soviet Union:
   (a) the significance of the new generation Soviet ICBMs, especially the introduction of the MIRV system for ICBMs and improvements in accuracy; and
   (b) the impact of the development of long-range theater nuclear weapons by the Soviet Union through the introduction of the SS-20 and Backfire bomber.
2. On the conventional capability of the Soviet Union:
   (a) the effect of qualitative improvements in Soviet conventional weapons; and

(b) the impact of the increased capabilities of Soviet
naval forces for maritime operations.

On the nuclear side, it is reasonable to assume that with this
growth of the Soviet nuclear strength, the superiority that the United
States had maintained in the nuclear "triad" until the early 1970s
has been adversely affected. However, in SLBM capabilities, the
United States retains an overwhelming superiority over the Soviet
Union, and this is likely to continue for some time. The United
States places greater emphasis than the Soviet Union on SLBMs
which can function as a second strike force and are therefore an
effective deterrent in the nuclear field, as long as no breakthroughs in
antisubmarine warfare are registered. If this basic condition is not
likely to change through the 1980s, the overall deterrent effect
offered by the United States to countries under the American
nuclear umbrella such as Japan will continue to be credible.

The Soviet deployment of the SS-20 and the Backfire bomber in
the Far East has posed a new problem in this connection, to the
extent that they bring onto the scene new long-range theater nuclear
weapons, against which there are no countervailing capabilities
deployed by the United States or by any of its allies in the Western
Pacific.

As far as Japan is concerned, however, the implications of these
weapons can be overstated. Japan has committed herself to the
"three non-nuclear principles"[13] as one of the basic pillars of her
national policy. Although it stems from the horrifying experience of
Hiroshima and Nagasaki during the Second World War, this policy
has been built on the basic strategic premise that Japan can indeed
depend upon the nuclear guarantee of the United States, whatever
the specific characteristics of the nuclear threat coming from the
other side might be.[14] In this setting, the introduction of the SS-20
and the Backfire bomber capable of carrying long-range theater
nuclear warheads should not change this basic premise about the
essential nature of the nuclear threat to Japan from the Soviet
Union, or the basic strategy to deal with it.

If it is true that in Western Europe the deterrence strategy based
on the perceived coupling between strategic nuclear systems and
tactical nuclear weapons has been threatened by the emergence of
the "gray area" concept,[15] the same strategy has hardly even had a
recognized place in strategic thought in the East Asian theater. This
is not without valid reasons. The politico-psychological dilemma of
Europe—of choosing between the desire to maintain independent
national nuclear strike forces and the fear about "decoupling"—has
been almost alien to this region. The geostrategic situation of East

Asia differs fundamentally from that of Western Europe. In the East Asian setting, the Western Pacific figures prominently in the strategic conception of the area, where the predominance of the United States with its superior SLBM capability and forward bases on outlying islands forms an essential component of the strategy. This is in striking contrast with that of Western Europe, where the Atlantic is perceived rather as a gap to be bridged in an emergency, but which separates the European continent from its ultimate protector.

Moreover, this basic characteristic of the problem would not change, even if one were to concede, for the sake of argument, that the difference between the situation in East Asia and that in Western Europe is not as obvious as has been suggested above, and that the emergence of the "gray area" will be as much a real problem in East Asia as it is in Western Europe. An approach which could offer an effective solution to the European case would not necessarily serve as a viable solution to the Asian case. The European situation, where the existence of two nuclear-weapon states offers a number of alternatives, is simply not a meaningful analogy to the Asian situation where Japan could not exercise a nuclear option.

The question of independent national control of nuclear weapons and the issue of coupling between the battlefield and strategic nuclear level, both of which have confronted the United Sates and its European allies, has no counterpart in the U.S. relationship with Japan. Deployment of theater nuclear weapons in Japan would not give Japan access to the control of such weapons, even setting aside the problem of the three non-nuclear principles. The fact would remain that in the final analysis only the United States could make the decision, whether it involved a theater nuclear weapon deployed in Japan or a strategic nuclear weapon in the United States central system. Therefore, the politico-psychological effect of the deployment of U.S. theater nuclear weapons on the credibility of the American strategic nuclear guarantee would be negligible. The doctrine that theater nuclear weapons are different because of their limited nature as deterrents and are therefore effective in avoiding the danger of nuclear escalation would be too fine to be significant in an East Asian setting. In contrast to the European theater, such a highly sophisticated doctrine has not been accepted by both sides in Asia.

A more serious problem would seem to lie with conventional forces. This is particularly true in the areas of command, control, logistics, air defense and sea defense, especially in antisubmarine operations. Whereas the nuclear threat can be countered primarily by the nuclear deterrent capabilities of the United States, and whereas Japan must, and indeed can, rely upon the nuclear umbrella of the United States, the threat posed by the Soviet Union in conventional forces will have to be met at varying levels and by corresponding means by Japan and the United States, either jointly or separately, depending upon the nature and the scale of the threat which the Soviet Union may create to the security of the area.

Thus, the long-range Soviet bombers including Backfires—about one hundred of these bombers are said to be deployed in the Far East—could pose a conventional-weapons threat to surface fleets in the Pacific. This may be more important than their potential use as carriers of theater nuclear weapons which can be effectively countered by the United States strategic nuclear force. The increased strength of submarines in the Pacific—about ninety are said to be in active service in the Pacific Fleet, including some eighty nuclear-powered submarines—could pose a similar threat to the United States Seventh Fleet and the sea lanes of the Pacific. Both the United States military capability taken by itself, and the present level of Japan–United States security cooperation based on the Security Treaty arrangements, could prove to be insufficient from a purely military point of view for coping with the situation created by these threats. Japan's own defense capability, which is geared exclusively for the defense of Japan against an armed attack, is insufficient for maritime defense in waters in the vicinity of Japan and in air defense. The United States with its Seventh Fleet will presumably have primary responsibility for coping with this situation, but the expanded sea areas of operation for the Fleet, including the Indian Ocean, will be simply too large for the Seventh Fleet at its present level of strength to safeguard sea lanes extending to the Indian Ocean in an emergency situation.

This point assumes particular significance when one considers its implications for the problem of power projection in an East Asian setting. As has been indicated earlier, the Western Pacific is essential to our consideration of the problem of security in East Asia, perhaps even to a greater extent than the Atlantic for the security of Europe. The strategic importance of maintaining control of the Western Pacific thus cannot be overestimated—as lines of communication in peacetime, as routes of transportation of strategic goods, as a theater of operational activities in an emergency and as a line of defense at the time of crisis. Since the capacity to project power will have a significant impact upon the security of the region, both directly in its potential military role in an emergency, and indirectly in its political role as a stabilizing factor, the problem posed by the increased military presence of the Soviet Union in the Pacific, especially in the conventional field, if left unattended, could have potentially serious implications for the long-term security environment of the East Asia region.

FACTORS THAT AFFECT PROJECTION OF POWER IN EAST ASIA

In assessing the possibilities for projection of power in the 1980s in the region of East Asia, it seems important to try to depict different forces at work on the scene and to ascertain exactly how they are going to affect the power projection in this area. In this connection, it may be worth stressing that what makes such projection possible and effective in a given situation will not be so much the physical capacity itself for such projection as the military, political, economic and social climate of the area in question.

THE PROBLEM OF UNITED STATES CREDIBILITY

The problem of power projection in this region is related inextricably to the credibility of the United States. The problem of credibility is, of course, intrinsic to any alliance relationship. The question is how credible is the United States in the context of NATO and the Japan–United States security arrangements. But the problem we face in relation to countries in East Asia is a broader one. We are dealing not only with an alliance relationship. What is at stake is the credibility of the U.S. capacity to maintain stability of an area to which the United States has no formal commitment, as contrasted with its bilateral defense treaties with Japan and the Republic of Korea. Under these circumstances, it will be easy to see that the nature of U.S. credibility is much more delicate and fragile, and that it can easily be damaged by some symbolic action. It should be stressed that the capacity of the United States to project power in this region for the maintenance of security and stability will be materially affected by the degree of her credibility in the eyes of the local populace.

There has never been any secret about the principle of "Europe first" in American defense thinking. Nevertheless, until the end of the Vietnam War, East Asia had been experiencing a unique situation, in which the United States was not only physically present, but was willing to resort to the use of military power in order to achieve stability in the Asian–Pacific area. When, therefore, in the aftermath of the Vietnam trauma, the United States indicated that it was going to withdraw from Vietnam, Thailand, and possibly from other areas, Asian suspicion grew. When the Carter Administration announced its official policy of withdrawing ground troops from the Republic of Korea, that suspicion was virtually confirmed.

This may be to some extent, but not totally, a problem of perception held by many Asian leaders. It is undeniable that in the wake of the Vietnam collapse, the United States did show signs of withdrawing from other parts of the Asian–Pacific region. There may be a perfectly rational reason why the United States forces in the Western Pacific could safely be withdrawn without drastically affecting the military balance in the region. The rapprochement between the United States and the People's Republic of China and the termination of the Vietnam War have brought about a new situation. After all, a large proportion of the naval forces deployed in the 1960s were involved in operations against North Vietnam. An aggressive Chinese attitude against Asian countries aligned with the United States is no longer a problem for which an American counterpoise is necessary to the extent that it was a generation ago. Even on the Korean peninsula, the announcement of the troop withdrawal was based on the assumption that the military balance would be safe without U.S. ground forces, an assumption which was reexamined and discarded as evidence became available to contradict it.

Credibility is basically a problem of politics and psychology. What counts is the reality of what happens or what does not happen, rather then the rationale of why it can happen or why it does not have to happen. And there is in fact more to it than that. Given the general diminution of United States capabilities and the consequent need for defining defense priorities, there is a legitimate question of how far the security of a particular region would count in an examination of the overall security interests of the United States. The trauma of the Vietnam War quite clearly did reduce the perceived interest of the United States in waging crusades to make Asia safe for democracy. Even to thinking Americans, the ways in which Asia affects American security could now appear harder to define. The agonizing reappraisal of American interests in the Asian-Pacific Area has cast a delicate shadow over the psychology of the leaders and peoples of this region.

There seem to be two related, but distinct problems in relation to these countries in East Asia. First, as far as U.S. security interests in the region are concerned, it would seem that after the Vietnam trauma, the United States has not completely recovered or succeeded in identifying her own national interests, nor the security interests of the area in relation to such American interests. The United States has not succeeded in redefining her role in Asia in such a manner that her rhetoric about the importance of East Asia is translated into action. This is not a problem unique to East Asia, but after what has happened in South Asia, the need for such redefinition of the U.S. role in the region would seem to be particularly desirable.

Second, the more difficult problem from the viewpoint of policy implementation is the gap between formulated policy and the capacity to implement that policy. What has been happening in recent years in the Third World illustrates this dilemma. In Angola, and a fortiori in Afghanistan, what has been decisive with regard to the inability to act is not so much the effects of the Vietnam trauma upon the American public and the Congress as the fact that the United States simply is not equipped to counter the attempt by the Soviet Union to exploit the various manifestations of instability.

In a sense, this is only part of a larger problem. Whereas the United States continues to be one of the two superpowers in the military sense, she has to rely, in the execution of concrete policies, upon the cooperation of allies who, as regional powers, may have a different perspective and different security interests. This is particularly true when the area in question does not directly involve the vital interests of all the allies, but is rather part of the Third World; such an area, though highly important for the security interests of a superpower with a global perspective, will not command the same degree of interest and therefore attention from other countries in the alliance. This point is central to the whole question of the effectiveness of power projection in East Asia, which in turn depends upon the fulfillment of at least three conditions: first, that the United States will be equipped with sufficient physical capacity to meet its power-projection goals; second, that its allies will be supportive whenever their cooperation is needed; third, that the local government is amenable to such efforts, from both a strategic and a political viewpoint.

THE SOVIET MILITARY BUILDUP IN ASIA

The impact of the Soviet military buildup upon East Asia can be understood in a similar context. The motives behind the Soviet military expansion with specific reference to East Asia and the Western Pacific are hard to identify. But the following elements seem to be relevant:[16]

1. The Soviet desire to be at least on a level of parity with, and if possible superior to, the United States in military power in the Pacific and the Indian Ocean within the context of global power competition and possibly military conflict;
2. Soviet perparation for potential conflict with China.
3. Increasing Soviet desire to influence events in Asia;
4. Soviet concern for the security of the Soviet Union in the Far East.

Whatever may be the dominant Soviet motivation, the important point for our analysis is the impact of the Soviet military buildup in this part of the world upon the security of the region. The effects may well be different for different countries. For the United States and to a large extent for Japan, the immediate question is one of a military nature: danger of increased confrontation, which poses a potential "military" problem for the defense of Japan and for the military balance in the Western Pacific. The problems involved, including examination of possible responses to this challenge, are in essence not very different from the kinds of problems now confronting the NATO countries, given the overall force expansion and improvement effort by the Soviet Union on the European front.

For many countries in East Asia, with the possible exception of the People's Republic of China, the problem can be very different. For them, the impact of the Soviet military buildup is more indirect and political, rather than direct and military. Many countries in this region are not integrated into an alliance system, although their basic orientation is decidedly toward the maintenance of stability based on the status quo and to that extent sympathetic to the policy orientation of the United States. They are hopeful that the strong presence of the United States, sufficient to counterbalance the Soviet ambition to influence events in Asia, will continue to be felt. Given this basic orientation, the Soviet military expansion, especially if allowed to grow without effective counterbalance from the other side, could lead to a political situation where these Asian countries might feel that the tide would be moving in a different direction. In order to take advantage of this fluid situation, certain countries might engage in more active political and paramilitary activities in the region, which could evoke a chain reaction that would only result in extreme instability. In short, because the impact of the Soviet military buildup upon these countries is political, the response required to cope with this aspect of the problem has also to contain a large political element.

THE IMPACT OF CHINA

China occupies an enormously important place in the politico-psychological game being played in East Asia. Although for the United States, China may well be a factor to be weighed primarily in the context of the military balance between the Soviet bloc and the free world, China is casting her shadow upon all the countries of East Asia in a much more complex form.

To one of the most active players of this game, the Soviet Union, the shadow of China with her orientation, political power, and great stature in the region is a serious factor indeed. The new bonds created between Japan and the People's Republic of China by the normalization of relations in 1972, followed by the conclusion of the Treaty of Peace and Friendship in 1978, could be viewed by Moscow as a mere prelude to a more advanced stage of Sino–Japanese cooperation. Worse still, there could be a suspicion that the United States has now joined in this trio as its most active player/conductor with a view to forming an alliance with a common strategy against the Soviet Union. The entire process of Sino–American rapprochement, resulting in the normalization of relations in 1979, and the continuing process of tightening relationships between the United States and China, may confirm the Soviet Union in her suspicion.

Even in this situation, in light of Moscow's global interests and commitments and its still relatively limited military capabilities in the Far East, the Soviet leaders would probably not want to risk a confrontation with the United States, unless this tripartite relationship among the United States, Japan and China reached a degree of cooperation which threatened important Soviet interests.

This could be the case if Sino–Japanese relationships or the Sino–American relationship should assume the character of a true alliance in which cooperation could extend to the military sphere. From this perspective, nothing can be more destabilizing to the East Asian region than the development of cooperation between China on the one hand and Japan and/or the United States on the other in the direction of a military alliance. China might desire such an alliance for her own security reasons. The United States might wish to follow that path in her excessive concern about the global balance with the Soviet Union. It appears nevertheless important to avoid unnecessary and dangerous confrontations with the Soviet Union, and not to overlook options for policies facilitating an accommodation of Russian interests.

This is important for stability from another perspective—i.e., the impact of the shadow of China upon many countries in the region. For these countries, the stability of the area, based essentially on the status quo, is their best guarantee of security. Any new move which can create more than mere ripples in the quiet situation will be viewed with certain apprehension and suspicion. The privately expressed but nonetheless genuine misgivings about the future of the Sino–Japanese Treaty of Peace and Friendship at the time of its conclusion, though perhaps unwarranted, are a reflection of this sentiment. Given this factor, it would be wrong to try to play a power game of three or four major actors in an Asian setting on the narrow calculation of gains and losses in an essentially bipolar strategic balance, because in the process the very stability of the region might very well be affected.

THE PROBLEM OF INTERNAL STABILITY

There is a common recognition that security becomes a purely military problem only in extremis, when international systems fail to function and the survival of a nation is directly and irrevocably challenged by a naked threat of force.[17] The consideration of security issues should naturally include this extreme situation as an ultimate scenario, but there are a number of other scenarios for which we should be prepared before reaching that final stage. In an Asian setting, especially, it is important to bear in mind that what is the most likely scenario for an erosion of the stability of the area will not be the type of scenario relevant to NATO. In the U.S.–European context, the direct military challenge of one side by the other, even if it might be localized, is a likely scenario for which security preparedness should be geared. In the Asian context, by contrast, what is more likely to happen would be the deterioration of security from inside—the erosion of political stability in one or more countries or on a regional level, which in turn would invite outside intervention. This is after all what has happened in Iran, in Afghanistan and in other past conflicts in Asia. Although it would be useful and important to have a deterrence system that could prevent such outside interventions, such a system would not always be feasible and effective, as again recent events in South Asia have demonstrated. Without discounting the desirability of such a deterrence system, it is important to treat the problem of internal stability as part of a broader system of security.

Internal stability is not only important in itself, it is also essential in determining the effectiveness of military policies, which cannot work without domestic support. One does not have to illustrate this point in great detail. Even in the middle of the fierce military struggle, what ultimately decided the fate of South Vietnam was not the military factor but internal political instability. Similarly, what is disconcerting about the Korean situation at present is not so much the state of military preparedness along the demilitarized zone as the effect of potential developments within the Republic of Korea on its internal stability.

SIGNIFICANCE OF JAPAN–UNITED STATES SECURITY COOPERATION

Any treatment of the problem of security in East Asia would be inadequate if it did not include an appraisal of Japan as an important factor. This is essential, first, because the defense relationship between Japan and the United States established by the Security Treaty forms an indispensable element of U.S. strategy in this part of the world. An appraisal of Japan is relevant to East Asian security to the extent that any major change in Japan's policies would have considerable impact upon the long-term security of the area. This section will examine how security arrangements between Japan and the United States are relevant to identifying problems of power projection in this area.

The original Security Treaty between Japan and the United States was signed in 1951, in the midst of the Korean War and at the height of the cold war confrontation. The revised treaty of 1960 is an improved version of the original treaty, but the basic principles of the arrangement remained the same. According to the terms of the 1960 treaty, the United States is granted the use by its land, air and naval forces of facilities and areas in Japan "for the purpose of contributing to the security of Japan and the maintenance of international peace and security in the Far East."[18] Thus the basic principle of the Security Treaty is that the United States has a strong military presence in the Pacific and the Far East, and is pledged to contribute both to the security of Japan herself, going beyond extending the nuclear umbrella, and to the maintenance of peace and security in the Far East in general.

This point is well illustrated by the "National Defense Program Outline" of the Government of Japan, adopted by the National Defense Council and decided by the Cabinet in October 1976.[19] The Outline is an authoritative statement of the official position of the Government of Japan on national defense. It was designed to set fundamental guidelines for Japan's defense posture in the years ahead, including the maintenance and operation of her defense capability. Thus it is basic to the Self-Defense Force of Japan.

The National Defense Program Outline begins by analyzing the basic currents of the international situation and draws the following conclusions:

1. "Under present circumstances, there seems little possibility of a full-scale military clash between East and West or of major conflict possibly leading to such a clash, due to the military balance—including mutual nuclear deterrence—and the various efforts being made to stabilize international relations."

2. "While the possibility of limited military conflict breaking out in Japan's neighborhood cannot be dismissed, this equilibrium between the superpowers

and the existence of the Japan–United States security arrangements seems to play a major role in maintaining international stability and in preventing full-scale aggression against Japan."

Based on these two premises, the Outline defines the roles of Japan and the United States under the Security Treaty respectively as follows:

1. Against nuclear threat, Japan will rely only on the nuclear deterrent capability of the United States.
2. Should indirect aggression occur, Japan will take immediate responsive action in order to settle the situation at an early stage.
3. Should direct aggression occur, Japan will repel such aggression at the earliest possible stage by taking immediate responsive action and trying to conduct an integrated, systematic operation of its defense capability:
   (a) With respect to limited and small-scale aggression, Japan will repel [it] in principle without external assistance.
   (b) With respect to cases where the unassisted repelling of aggression is not feasible, Japan will continue an unyielding resistance, until such time as cooperation from the United States is introduced.[20]

In short, the defense policy of Japan has been built on the premise that there will be no major war involving Japan as long as the United States and the Soviet Union maintain military balance and especially mutual nuclear deterrence, and as long as the Japan–United States security arrangements will be effectively maintained. Japan has assumed a limited self defense role, while leaving a large part of her defense both in conventional and nuclear areas in the hands of the United States.

One question that is currently being asked is whether this premise is still valid. To be more specific, the premise would appear to include such assumptions as follows:

1. The Japan–United States security system will be effectively maintained in the future.
2. The United States and the Soviet Union will not resort to nuclear warfare or to large-scale conflict which could develop into nuclear warfare.
3. Sino–Soviet confrontation will continue even if partial improvements in their relations are made.

4. The United States and China will take steps to adjust their relations in the future.
5. The status quo will be maintained on the Korean peninsula, and no large-scale armed conflict will break out.

These premises form the basis on which the strategy of the present Japan–United States defense framework is constructed. Although it is not intended here to present an assessment of its validity at the present time, it would seem essential that it be subjected to constant scrutiny, inasmuch as it involves factors that are liable to change.

A more important problem to be considered in the present Japan–United States security arrangement is whether the respective roles that Japan and the United States are expected to assume are being satisfactorily performed, and in particular whether the combined strength of Japan and the United States is being effectively used as a deterrent against a threat to the security of Japan. This problem must be examined against the background of new developments in East Asia that have been discussed above and of the growing awareness for the need to maintain United States military power in the region.

From this perspective, the implementation of the Treaty requires a careful and candid reappraisal. It may be useful to depict some of the more salient problems in this respect, with a view to examining whether, under the new conditions now prevailing in the East Asian region, the two partners of the security arrangements may have to readjust their joint and separate roles for achieving the purposes of the Treaty.

DEFENSE CONTRIBUTIONS OF JAPAN

The first and foremost fundamental problem with Japan's defense policy is the growing gap between the Japanese perception of the part to be played by its Self-Defense Forces and the corresponding American perception. As has been discussed earlier, the fundamental defense framework established by the Security Treaty is based on a division of functions between Japan and the United States. Due to the pacifist, antiarmament psychology of postwar Japan, however, this basic framework has operated in such a way that the Self-Defense Forces, which were created with great difficulty, still suffer a great political handicap. In many respects, they have not succeeded in developing themselves into an effective force capable of coping with a large-scale attack against Japan by conventional means.[21] Nevertheless, because of the expanded economic power of Japan and the relative decline of U.S. military power, the United States has been urging Japan to assume a greater part of the role for her own defense against conventional attack.

In the face of a gap between the global responsibilities of the United States and the shortage of resources to extend sufficient defense capabilities to all the areas threatened by the Soviet military buildup, this attitude is not hard to understand. To that extent, the problem that Japan must face is not very different from that confronted by the NATO countries, in the sense that the easing of the U.S. burden in the strictly delimited area of Japan's own defense will make it possible for the United States to extend its contribution to the security of the broader area of East Asia.

At the same time, it is worth pointing out that Japan has not simply been sitting idle leaving the entire burden of its defense to the United States. Despite various constraints, Japan is already making significant military contributions to the alliance which are not adequately appreciated. There is much talk currently about the fact that Japan's defense expenditure has not crossed the one percent threshold in its ratio to her GNP. It seems important, however, to look beyond statistics to understand the reality. Because of Japan's huge GNP, which reached $1.1 trillion in 1979, Japan with her defense expenditure of about $10 billion for 1979 ranked eighth largest in the world behind the Soviet Union, the United States, China, Western Germany, France, Great Britain and Saudi Arabia.[22] It should also be noted that there has been a remarkably rapid growth in the defense spending of Japan in recent years, a fact which is overshadowed in statistics behind the almost equally rapid growth of Japan's GNP. Thus, during the past decade, Japanese defense spending has risen by more than 360 percent in nominal terms, and by more than 200 percent even in real terms. In real terms, the past five years have shown an annual increase ranging between 14.6 percent to 6.6 percent.[23]

There is indeed a tendency in the United States to express wonder about the defense spending of Japan in relation to her GNP. Yet the one percent threshold in itself is not a useful index of the adequacy of defense. The focus should rather be the adequacy of defense capabilities, and especially their overall effectiveness and contribution to joint defense arrangements under the Treaty.

When judged by this criterion, it is fair to say that Japan's performance has been substantial. While the United States Seventh Fleet in the Pacific has been put under great strain by the Indian Ocean crises and has declined in strength, the Japanese Maritime Self-Defense Force already has taken on added importance.[24]

An illustration of this point by some salient figures will be appropriate:[25]

1. Japan has more ASW surface vessels than does the United States Seventh Fleet.
2. Forty-seven destroyers that Japan has in Asian waters are regarded as representing triple the number of comparable United States ships.
3. Highly sophisticated ASW submarines of Japan now number thirteen, with an additional three under construction.
4. Japan's fleet of minesweepers of forty vessels is regarded as the second largest in the world after the Soviet Union, with a reservoir of highly developed mine-warfare skills and technology.
5. Japan is acquiring at least forty-five of the latest P3C ASW aircraft (the comparable figure of deployment by the United States in the entire Western Pacific is said to be twenty-seven).
6. The Air Self-Defense Force possesses about 440 total front line operational aircraft, and 115 F-15 fighters are going to be introduced as a part of the modernization plan. (Comparable figures for the United States in the entire Western Pacific, including those deployed on aircraft carriers are said to be about 430.)

To sum up, while it is recognized that there is in all fairness still considerable room for improvement of Japan's Self-Defense Forces, especially in such areas as ASW and modernization of early warning systems for air defense, the performance of Japan so far in her sustained efforts toward military buildup and the present level of her defense capabilities in the conventional field are not to be taken lightly in comparison with those of other allies, including NATO members.

COORDINATION BETWEEN JAPAN AND UNITED STATES FORCES

The importance of developing and maintaining an effective system of coordination between the United States forces and Japan's Self-Defense Forces under the security arrangements requires no explanation. If the defense of Japan is not to be left exclusively in the hands of Japan or to the United States, it is only natural to expect that there should be an effective system of cooperation between the two countries. The fact is that such efforts have been less successful than they should have been, because of a series of difficulties, both political and technical. Although there have been significant improvements in recent years, more needs to be done.

Perhaps the most significant development in this respect is the understanding reached between Prime Minister Miki and President Ford in 1975 on the need to hold consultations on means of enhancing Japan–United States cooperation, for the effective attainment of the purposes of the Japan–United States Security Treaty and related arrangments.[26] In the past, there had been no such consultative forum for study and discussion of the means of overall Japan–United States cooperation, including its military aspects. For example, what concrete actions would be taken by Japan and the United States in an emergency situation, such as an armed attack against Japan? In what areas and in what manner and form would the cooperation between them take place in such an eventuality? On these and other equally fundamental questions, an authoritative answer has not been easy to find. Following the new understanding, however, the Subcommittee on Defense Cooperation (SDC) was established in 1976, as a subordinate organ of the Security Consultative Committee, the highest organ of the Japan–United States Security framework under the Treaty. The SDC was assigned "the task of conducting studies and consultations on aspects of Japan–United States cooperation, including guidelines on guaranteeing coordinated joint action by the Self-Defense Forces of Japan and the United States Forces in Japan in the event of an emergency, with a view to effectively attaining the purposes of the security treaty and related arrangements."

As a result of the deliberation of the problem in the SDC for over two years, the "Guidelines for the Defense Cooperation between Japan and the United States"[27] were completed and adopted by the Japan–United States Security Consultative Committee. On the Japanese side, the Guidelines were put to the National Defense Council and had the approval of the Cabinet.

The Guidelines reconfirm the established roles of Japan and the United States for the defense of Japan: Japan will maintain defense capability on an appropriate scale within the scope necessary for her self-defense, while the United States will preserve a nuclear deterrent capability and the deployment of combat-ready forces and other units for reinforcing them. The emphasis here is on ensuring the smooth and effective implementation of joint conduct of coordinated operations in an emergency situation. For this purpose, the Self-Defense Forces and the United States Forces in Japan will conduct studies on joint-defense planning and undertake necessary joint exercises and training. There will be a close exchange of intelligence necessary for the defense of Japan. Second, with respect to concrete actions to be taken in response to an armed attack against Japan, the Self-Defense Forces and the United States Forces in Japan will establish in advance a common standard for the readiness stage that will ensure effective cooperation and that each country will conduct such operational preparations as are necessary, in accordance with the coordinated readiness stage selected by agreement of the two governments. Concrete operational plans cover contingencies in the event of an armed attack in which the Self-Defense Forces will undertake defensive operations primarily within the territory of Japan and its surrounding waters and air space, whereas the United States forces will support the operations and conduct further operations to supplement functional areas which exceed the capability of the Self-Defense Forces. The two forces will act through their respective command and control channels, but there will be a close system of cooperation and if necessary a coordination center will be established. Third, with respect to a situation in the Far East outside of Japan which will have an important influence on the security of Japan, the two Governments are expected to conduct studies in advance on the scope and modalities of facilitative assistance to be extended to the United States forces in this context.

Although the Guidelines are not in themselves a formal agreement between the two governments, and their implementation is left to the judgment of the respective parties, it does represent a significant step forward in an area where concrete planning for such cooperation and coordination had long been wanting.

In appraising the present state of military coordination between Japan and the United States, one important consideration is the constraint built into the present Japanese–United States Security Treaty system—i.e., the one concerning "the right of collective self-defense." Although the two parties recognize in the treaty that they have the inherent right of "individual and collective self-defense" as stipulated in Article 51 of the United Nations Charter, the current official view of the Japanese government is that, under the constitutional restrictions imposed by Article 9, Japan is not entitled to exercise this inherent right of collective self-defense. This constraint could make effective cooperative action through joint operation between the Self-Defense Forces and the United States forces extremely difficult to achieve. The possibility of a joint command and control between the two forces, even for the defense of Japan in case of an armed attack upon her, is thus at present excluded. In spite of this constraint, however, in view of the cooperative nature of the framework of the security arrangements between Japan and the United States, it is obviously of cardinal importance to establish a sophisticated system where the two countries' respective forces can produce the maximum aggregate efficiency and effectiveness in meeting group aggression against Japan. It seems that here is one area in which further imaginative and constructive thinking toward promoting the basic objective of joint defense of Japan will be desirable within the strict constitutional constraint of the provisions of Article 9 of the Japanese Constitution.[28]

MAINTENANCE OF PEACE AND SECURITY IN THE FAR EAST

The United States also has a role in the maintenance of international peace and security in the Far East, and from that point of view as well there is need for the Security Treaty to function so as to make most effective use of the U.S. defense capability. Clearly Japan cannot act outside the scope of its own defense, while the United States is granted under the treaty the right to make use of facilities and areas in Japan as long as such use is legitimately "for the purpose of contributing to the maintenance of international peace and security in the Far East."[29] There is a basic restriction placed upon this action by the agreement calling for prior U.S. consultation with the government of Japan if a military combat operation outside of Japan is contemplated.[30]

This point is highly relevant to the consideration of a problem which has come to assume an increased degree of urgency and reality, i.e., to what extent and in what manner Japan can and should cooperate with the United States in the latter's efforts for the maintenance of security in East Asia and beyond? Within the conceptual framework of the Japan-United States Security Treaty, a situation which threatens "the maintenance of international peace and security in the Far East" can arise outside the geographical limits of the Far East. To the extent that such a situation does in fact seriously affect the security of Japan, the United States is entitled to make use of facilities in Japan to meet this situation, provided that it does not involve a case in which the requirement for prior consultation under the treaty comes into play.

In fact, this issue could create a serious political problem in Japan, given the psychological aversion of the people against anything which even marginally runs the risk of involving Japan in an outside conflict. Hence, for example, political controversy arose when, at the height of the Vietnam conflict, the United States sought to make extensive use of bases in Japan.

Of course, it could be argued that when Asian security is seriously threatened, the security of Japan, which cannot be totally separated from the peace and stability of Asia, would also be substantially affected. To that extent, the activities of the United States for the maintenance of peace and security in the region could be said to possess material relevance to the security of Japan itself, justifying the use of areas and facilities in Japan for the performance of such a purpose. For example, it is conceivable that a crisis situation in the Middle East might develop which could seriously affect the source of supply of oil to Japan. In view of Japan's heavy reliance on Middle East oil, the situation would be directly relevant to the security of Japan.

A critical question in such a situation is whether the Japanese people would face the facts, or allow their antimilitary prejudices to cloud their vision. A mature assessment of world reality on the part of the people is essential to an effective response to a crisis of this sort. Efforts to reach such an understanding have been singularly lacking in the past. Naturally each case would have to be assessed in light of its own special circumstances; but as a minimum, it seems crucial that the arrangements under the Security Treaty should be reliable enough to enable the partners of the alliance to plan their strategies in advance of such a contingency with a clear understanding of what they can expect from the arrangements. This point will be of critical importance in enhancing the security threshold of the region, especially as it could prove to be a decisive factor in the planning of a projection of military power in the region.

ROLE OF JAPAN IN THE SECURITY OF EAST ASIA

One final point should be raised, if only briefly, in connection with the appraisal of the contribution of the Japan–United States Security Treaty to the maintenance of peace and security in the Asian–Pacific region. Although the point does not relate directly to a strategic assessment of the Security Treaty as a defense mechanism, the overall significance of the treaty's framework of cooperation for the security of the region can extend far beyond the technical assessment of the military effectiveness of the present arrangements. Equally important is the question of what might be termed the political aspect of security and of how the Japan–United States framework of cooperation can relate to this problem.

It is generally recognized that the security problem is purely military only in extremis.[31] True, what may determine the fate of a nation in case of a total war is the qualitative and quantitative superiority of weaponry, the quality and the quantity of armed forces, and strategy and tactics. But security is a multifaceted concept. Before reaching that ultimate stage, there are usually different escalating stages of crisis situations— different not only in degree but also in kind. Given the basic nature of the security environment in the East Asian region, and given the characteristics of the security problems which can arise, it seems particularly important to give due attention to such nonmilitary aspects of security as internal stability, social resilience, economic prosperity, and political confidence based on credible policies of outside friends.

It is in this broader context that the question of what should be the role of Japan in the maintenance of security in East Asia has to be considered. No one will dispute that the security of Japan is inseparably linked with the security of East Asia. If only on that narrow ground, Japan has a shared interest in, and responsibility for, the maintenance of peace and stability. A critical question is how Japan can contribute most effectively to this objective.

There is growing concern that Japan, which has grown into a major world economic power, has not been playing a more responsible role commensurate with that power. In fact, this argument surfaces in various fields and in different contexts. In defense and security, the argument has often taken the form of a criticism that Japan's contribution in defense has been insufficient; that Japan has had a free ride without sharing the burden, while enjoying unprecedented economic prosperity; that in a word Japan should do much more in defense. While the basic argument that Japan should accept a greater responsibility in the world today can be legitimate, its indiscriminate application to concrete cases can be less than constructive. It is not enough to say that Japan should do more; the really difficult question is what Japan should do and how she should do it. In the final analysis this question would involve the whole issue of what Japan's orientation should be in the present-day world.[32]

Without attempting to deal with this fundamental problem, it may be suggested that, given the basic nature of the security environment of East Asia described above, and given also the legacies of Japan in her recent past with all their implications, the most constructive role that Japan can play in East Asia would lie in promoting those nonmilitary factors that contribute to the peace and stability of the region. In contrast to Western Europe, East Asia is in the process of responding to the new challenges of the changing international environment. In this task of enhancing security in the nonmilitary field, Japan can, and should, play a much more positive and constructive role. The policy statement enunciated by the Prime Minister of Japan in 1977 in the Manila Declaration,[33] for example, points to the ways in which Japan, with political determination and conscious effort, will be able to become a major constructive force for the establishment of stability in the area, and thus make a significant contribution to security in the global context as well.

NOTES
1. *U.S. Department of Defense Annual Report, FY 1979* (Washington, D.C.: GPO), p. 40.
2. This is with the one possible exception of the Korean peninsula where the north and the south are engaged in a clear confrontation, within the basic framework of East–West conflict. The Korean situation is one problem which requires a special treatment in the security framework of East Asia. On this point, see Richard L. Sneider, "Prospects for Korean Security," in Richard H. Solomon ed., *Asian Security in the 1980s* (Rand Corporation 1979), pp. 109–147.
3. Final Communique of the NATO Defense Planning Committee, M-DPC-1 (79) 10, May 16, 1979.
4. *Defense of Japan* 1979, Defense Agency, Section I, p. 21.
5. Ibid., Section I, pp. 31–32.
6. Ibid., Section I, p. 32, p. 46.
7. Ibid., Section I, p. 22.
8. Solomon, *Asian Security*, p. 45.
9. *Defense of Japan* 1979, p. 37.
10. Ibid., Section I, p. 36–37.
11. *U.S. Department of Defense Annual Report, FY 1979*, p. 37 and p. 40.
12. Figure as of the end of 1979. *Defense of Japan* 1980; Defense Agency, Section I, p. 15.
13. The three nonnuclear principles, a policy formulated by the Sato administration and followed by the successive administrations, consist of the following: the principle of not possessing nuclear weapons, the principle of not manufacturing nuclear weapons and the principle of not permitting the entry into Japan of nuclear weapons.
14. See to this effect the declaration of the government of Japan made at the time of the ratification fo the Treaty on Nuclear Non-proliferation, contained in the *Present State of Diplomacy of Japan* (*Waga Gaiko no Kinkyo*), Ministry of Foreign Affairs, vol. 22 (1977), Part 2, p. xx.
15. Obviously this is not the place to go into an analysis of the European problem in this respect, for which there is an abundance of literature. For some of the more recent representative treatment of the subject see, e.g., Gregory F. Treverton, "Nuclear Weapons and the 'Gray Area' " 57 *Foreign Affairs* (1978–79), pp. 1075–1080; Alex Gliksman, "Three Keys for Europe's Bombs" 39 *Foreign Policy* (1980), pp. 40–57.
16. See to this effect, Admiral Noel Gayler, "Security Implications of the Soviet Military Perspective in Asia," in Solomon, *Asian Security in the 1980s*, pp. 54–68.
17. Richard K. Betts, *Insecurity and Strategy in Northeast Asia: An American Perspective* (unpublished paper), p. 1
18. Article VI of the Treaty of Mutual Cooperation and Security between Japan and the United States provides as follows: "For the purpose of contributing to the security of Japan and the maintenance of international peace and security in the Far East, the United States of America is granted

the use by its land, air and naval forces of facilities and areas in Japan."
    19. For the complete text of the Outline, see *Defense of Japan* 1979, Appendix No. 10, in Documents Sections, p. 17.
    20. *Defense of Japan* 1979, pp. 221–227.
    21. The most fundamental problem is the gap being created between Japan and the United States on the basic political orientation of Japan as a result of radical shifts in U.S. policy toward the question of armament of Japan through the postwar period. Although this is not an appropriate place for discussing this issue in depth, it should not be forgotten that a too opportunistic shift in policy from one extreme position to another on such a basic question, motivated primarily by the interest of the moment, would not simply create for Japan difficult legal and technical problems to overcome; it could have the serious danger of disrupting the body politic of Japan and of creating a political climate whose long-term implications to Japan herself, to the region and to the world would have to be carefully appraised. The constraints that the Self-Defense Forces are suffering in Japan are nothing other than a reflection of such disruption in Japanese society, and therefore cannot be overcome simply through legalistic approaches.
    22. *Defense of Japan* 1979, Appendix No. 11, in Documents Section, p. 23. Also, *Washington Post*, 20 May 1980.
    23. To be more precise, the figures for respective years are as follows:

Defense Expenditure Real Increase	(GNP deflated)
FY 75	14.6
FY 76	7.6
FY 77	6.6
FY 78	8.4
FY 79	8.0

    24. Article by Michael Getler, *Washington Post*, 20 May 1980.
    25. Ibid. Also see Howard McElroy, (unpublished paper at Center for International Affairs, Harvard University, 1980), p. 40.
    26. See for the contents of the understanding, Japan–United States Joint Announcement to the Press, 6 August 1975, in *The Present State of Diplomacy of Japan* (*Waga Gaiko no Kinkyo*), Ministry of Foreign Affairs, vol. 19 (1976), part 2, p. 97.
    27. For the text of the Guildelines, see *Defense of Japan* 1979, Appendix 40, in Documents Section, p. 57.
    28. Article 9 of the Post-War Japanese Constitution contains the following provision: "Article 9. Aspiring sincerely to an international peace based on justice and order, the Japanese people forever renounce war as a sovereign right of the nation and the threat or use of force as means of settling international disputes."
    29. For Article VI of the Treaty of Mutual Cooperation and Security between Japan and the United States, see *supra* note 14.
    30. The Exchange of Notes concerning the Implementation of Article VI of the Treaty, in part, provides as follows: "Major changes in the deployment into Japan of United States armed forces, major change in the equipment, and the use of facilities and areas in Japan as bases for military combat operations to be undertaken from Japan other than those conducted under Article V of the said Treaty, shall be the subjects of prior consultation with the Government of Japan."

31. Ibid., p. 26.
32. See footnote 20.
33. For the text of the Manila Declaration, see the *Present State of Diplomacy of Japan* (*Waga Gaiko no Kinkyo*), Ministry of Foreign Affairs, vol. 22 (1978), p. 326.

16

The Regional Projection of Military Power— The Caribbean

Roger W. Fontaine

In the summer of 1825 rumors that a powerful French fleet was heading for the Caribbean touched off near panic in Washington. The rumors proved false, but the concern was justified. It had been, after all, only 10 years since British warships stationed in Havana had ravaged American commerce in the Caribbean. Our leaders were fully aware of the Caribbean's importance, commercially and militarily, and were so long before any serious discussion of a transisthmian canal emerged. Indeed, American concern for the security of that southern sea was deeply rooted in history— preceding by decades the formal declaration of our concern, the Monroe Doctrine of 1823.

Thomas Jefferson's Large Policy of 1808 had as its core concern the fate of Mexico and Cuba. As long as those Spanish possessions remained dependent on that weak power, Jefferson was not unduly alarmed. But if either Mexico or Cuba were "under subordination to either France or England, either politically or commercially"—that subordination would be met with "the strongest repugnance."[1] "Repugnance" probably meant war although Jefferson himself was profoundly a man of peace. He knew full well that the young and weak American republic could be destroyed by a major conflict with a European power.

In 1890—a quarter of a century before the Panama Canal opened—Admiral Alfred Thayer Mahan grasped the increased future importance of the Caribbean once a transisthmian canal was built. He wrote:

> If one be made, and fulfil the hopes of its builders, the Caribbean will be changed from a terminus, and place of local traffic, or at best a broken and imperfect line of travel, as it now is, into one of the great highways of the world.

Along this path a great commerce will travel, bringing the
interests of the other great nations, the European nations,
close along our shores, as they have never been before. . . .
The position of the United States with reference to this
route will resemble that of England to the Channel, and of
the Mediterranean countries to the Suez route.[2]

Having established its importance, by analogy if nothing else,
Mahan next discussed what logically followed, namely, who would
have "influence and control over it." By geography alone, it would
clearly be the United States. Or as he put it: "The positions now or
hereafter occupied by them [nations other than the U.S.] on island or
mainland, however strong, will be but outposts of their power." But
Mahan was also quick to point out that other factors were involved.
The United States was weak militarily in 1890 when Mahan was
writing, and the gulf ports provided only exposed and poor
anchorages.[3] Furthermore, if it was the new canal that made the
Caribbean vital, protection of the canal itself was crucial. In that
regard, America's geographic position was helpful, but far more was
needed. Therefore, the Admiral concluded,

. . . the United States will have to obtain in the Caribbean
stations fit for contingent, or secondary bases of operations;
which by their natural advantages, susceptibility of
defence, and nearness to the central strategic issue, will
enable her fleets to remain as near the scene as any
opponent. With ingress and egress from the Mississippi
sufficiently protected, with such outposts in her hands, and
with the communications between them and the home base
secured, in short, with proper military preparation, for
which she has all necessary means, the preponderance of
the United States on this field follows, from her geographical position and her power, with mathematical certainty.[4]

And so it was until the present time. Admiral Mahan's analysis
held absolutely true from 1890 to 1975. The United States, as our
great naval strategist outlined, built a transisthmian canal and
obtained the Caribbean stations in Panama, Cuba, and Puerto Rico
to defend it. No foreign power, not even Nazi Germany or Stalin's
Russia, had the power or position to threaten any American interests
in the region. It remained, in fact, a "mathematical certainty."

The American position in the Caribbean has deteriorated in the
last few years. Enough feuilletons have been written on this to make
even the general reader uneasy. But so far little analysis—even less

systematic analysis—has been done. My intention is plain: to do precisely that with the materials at hand.

But let us begin with definitions. Though Mahan offered none regarding the size and extent of the "Caribbean," I define the term as the waters and lands touched by that sea and the Gulf of Mexico. The area stretches from Key West on the extreme tip of the Florida peninsula up and through the United States gulf coast to Mexico's east coast, to the Central American isthmus, to the straits of Darien and Colombia, Venezuela, and the former Guianas—British, Dutch, and French—plus the islands of the Greater and Lesser Antilles with the Bahamas serving as an Atlantic forward screen.

According to Webster, the general term *force* "implies an overcoming of resistance by the exertion of strength, weight, power, stress, or duress." I therefore define "military force projection" as the exertion of military or paramilitary strength or power. By paramilitary, I mean the use of clandestine forces to achieve what von Clausewitz would have accomplished by means of an army of grenadiers. And von Clausewitz would surely have agreed that the paramilitary has become critically important in achieving one's aims in the post–World War II era.

The power equation of the Caribbean is changing and it may change radically. Nevertheless, this chapter is restricted to an assessment of what was, what is, and what is likely to be. In doing so, the military and paramilitary capabilities of the Soviets and the Cubans and their chief adversary, the United States, will be examined.

Soviet and Cuban intentions—and the consequences of those intentions—will be surmised. Finally, steps will be suggested that the United States can take in response, including the likely costs of such steps. If throughout this chapter, the reader is visited with ghosts—past, present, and future—as was Mr. Ebenezer Scrooge, perhaps what will be learned will be learned in time.

The Soviet Union has the most rapidly expanding military and paramilitary force in the Caribbean. If the build-up continues, the United States may well face the first extra-hemispheric challenge based in the region itself since the War of 1812.

Soviet strength in the Caribbean is a relatively new phenomenon. It is an ungentle irony of history that in October 1962 the Caribbean was the location of the Soviet Union's greatest postwar humiliation. The event—the Cuban missile crisis—also sparked the making of the Soviet military machine of today, one which can project force nearly anywhere on the planet. As John Collins reminds us, this is in startling contrast to the Soviet capabilities of 1962:

> Soviet nuclear capabilities at that stage featured a handful of heavy bombers and a few ballistic missiles. The Soviet Navy was suitable essentially for coastal defense. Tactical air arms were primitive by U.S. standards. A mammoth army, organized, trained, and equipped to protect Mother Russia, comprised the principal sinew. Combined arms offensive strength was strictly circumscribed, even on the Eurasian land mass.[5]

In retrospect then, the Soviet's first military challenge in the Caribbean was nothing less than a gamble. Its only chance of success was a supine American response despite the possession by the United States of an overwhelming strategic and local conventional military advantage. The Soviet adventure was secret, reckless, and unconventional—unconventional in every sense of the word—involving medium range ballistic missiles. It was meant to be a quick fix to help overcome a sizeable missile gap that existed between the United States and the Soviet Union in the early 1960s. It was not, of course, the mythical missile gap of the 1960 presidential campaign, but a real one that faced the Soviet leaders.[6] That quick fix ended in humiliation, and no doubt contributed to Khrushchev's forced retirement a little less than two years later. The USSR, in short, or at least its leader, N. S. Khrushchev, had forgotten the lessons of Mahan.

The 1962 retreat, however, was a sharp reminder of the basic elements involved in regional force projection. In the case of the Caribbean, the first rule is to proceed with caution and restraint when one is the outside power with limited means at hand. The Soviets learned the lesson and after 1962 they did precisely that. For seven years Moscow did little of a military nature in the Caribbean.[7] Indeed, the Russians scrupulously adhered to the letter of the agreement on offensive weapons worked out between Kennedy and Khrushchev. The Caribbean remained, in military terms at least, an American lake.

The second Soviet military adventure in the Caribbean came in 1969. It was open, cautious, and quite conventional. In fact, it was the cliché of military force projection, namely, a naval task force putting in at more or less friendly ports of call. In July and August 1969, nine Soviet warships steamed through the Caribbean stopping at Havana, Cuba, Port de France, Martinique, and Bridgetown, Barbados.

The entry of the Soviet navy in the Caribbean was preceded by

Soviet warships entering, for the first time on a regular basis, two other strategic bodies of water: the Mediterranean in 1964 and the Indian Ocean in 1968.

The first Caribbean task force included two Foxtrot and one November class submarines, together with a missile-equipped light cruiser and two guided missile destroyers. It was by no means an overwhelming display of military strength either in size or in length of stay—the task force remained in the Caribbean thirty-two days—but it was a significant beginning.

Since 1969, there have been a score of such visits. The exact composition of these task forces has altered, but not dramatically—with an exception shortly to be noted. Approximately a half-dozen surface warships are always included with submarines usually present, particularly in the years 1969–1975.[8]

Soviet objectives for these deployments have been widely discussed. The possibilities include showing the flag, reassuring an ally (Cuba), familiarizing themselves with the region, and taking advantage of a pleasant location for training exercises. Another purpose, extremely difficult to measure but real enough, is desensitizing American policymakers to Soviet activity in the Caribbean. Each deployment—they have occurred now for twelve years—acts as further precedent and thus legitimization of Soviet force projection in the region.

This leads us to the exception noted above. While the size of the Soviet task force has remained nearly the same,[9] one very important deviation from the past has occurred. That has been the incremental introduction of "nuclear" force. The Soviet leaders have done it in two ways. First, they introduced nuclear powered, but conventionally armed, November class submarines in 1969 and then in 1971 conventionally powered nuclear ballistic missile-equipped Golf class submarines joined the task force. The next step, of couse, is obvious.[10]

Naval task forces can and do serve a variety of objectives. But they do have one great drawback—they are ephemeral. To project force on a continuing basis, a permanent naval presence is required. That means bases or access to bases, as Admiral Mahan well knew and as both the Carter and Reagan Administration realized in their searches for facilities near the Persian Gulf. To date, Soviet leaders still lack such bases although, as we shall see, it is neither from want of trying nor their nearness to success.

Their first attempt at establishing a permanent naval base came a year after the first Soviet naval task force entered the Caribbean. In September 1970 the Soviet leaders sent their third and to date most powerful surface vessel squadron.[11] The principal elements of that force, however, ignored Havana as a port of call, and proceeded to the Cuban naval base of Cienfuegos on Cuba's southern coast. The Soviet vessel that caught the eye of intelligence officers was not the Kresta-class guided missile cruiser or the Kanin-class guided missile destroyer (both types had paid earlier visits to the Caribbean), but an Alligator-class amphibious landing ship. The Alligator (comparable to our LST) was spotted transporting two barges later identified as support barges for nuclear armed submarines.[12] Both barges were towed into Cienfuegos and they were complemented by an Ugra-class submarine which had been attached to the first several naval deployments.

Nevertheless, the appearance of that tender with the barges plus the naval construction detected in August led the Nixon Administration to conclude that a permanent Soviet nuclear submarine base was nearing completion.[13]

In late September, Henry Kissinger, then Assistant to the President for National Security Affairs, warned the Soviet Union against establishing such a base. Kissinger argued that it would be a violation of the 1962 Agreement, and then added: "The Soviet Union can be under no doubt that we would view the establishment of a strategic base in the Caribbean with the utmost seriousness."[14]

Subsequent statements from Administration officials including President Nixon reemphasized that no base would be permitted.[15] In fact, Mr. Nixon went beyond Henry Kissinger's general warning to state that no Soviet nuclear submarines could be serviced "in Cuba or from Cuba." The reference to "in Cuba" is obvious: no nuclear submarine could put in at any Cuban port; "from Cuba" apparently meant that submarine tenders based in Cuba could not service submarines on the high seas.[16]

The Soviet reaction was a categorical denial of any attempt at constructing such a base although they never explained the barges or the construction.[17]

The affair is still shrouded in mystery.[18] Clearly, the Soviets were preparing such a base. Moreover, the attempt was a low-risk probe. The facilities for a forward submarine base are, in fact, minimal. Nuclear submarines need relatively little in the way of service facilities as they are designed to be more self-reliant than their conventionally powered cousins. In any event, what had been constructed at Cienfuegos remained in place. The fate of the celebrated barges cannot be determined from the public record—that is, they may have remained there at least until their land-based equivalents were constructed. Certainly, no demands were made (at least there is no public record of such demands) for their removal.[19]

The objective for the Soviets in all of this was and is extending their ability to project strategic forces from a relatively invulnerable weapon system located in the Caribbean—thus exposing the American heartland to attack. If facilities were available in Cuba, Soviet submarine time-on-station could increase from 20 to 50 percent. And that, in effect would represent a substantial increase in the active duty Soviet underseas fleet.[20]

Before leaving entirely the question of Soviet naval force projection, it is useful to reexamine Admiral Mahan. Like the Russians, Mahan knew intimately the relations between seapower and geography. In 1897, a year before the Spanish–American War, the Admiral focused on the importance of Cuba as a geo-military factor—a factor that serves as a natural link for us to other aspects of Soviet force projection in the Caribbean.

Mahan wrote:

Cuba, though narrow throughout, is over six hundred miles long, from Cape San Antonio to Cape Maysi. It is, in short, not so much an island as a continent, susceptible, under proper development, of great resources—of self-sufficing-ness. . . .

Regarded, therefore, as a base of naval operations, as a source of supply to a fleet, Cuba presents a condition wholly unique among islands of the Caribbean. . . . Such supplies can be conveyed from one point to the other, according to the needs of the fleet, by interior lines, not exposed to the risks of maritime capture. The extent of the coast-line, the numerous harbors, and the many directions from which approach can be made, minimize the danger of total blockade to which all islands are subject.[21]

The discovery of a Soviet brigade in Cuba in the summer of 1979—precisely a decade after the first Soviet demonstration of force in the Caribbean since 1962—came as a shock to the American public. It also came as an unwelcome surprise to the Carter Administration which had striven for both Soviet–American the Cuban–American detente. In fact, the Carter White House was the first to show a dual track on detente since President Kennedy attempted it in the fall of 1963.

The controversy over the brigade, however, threw a spotlight on a variety of Soviet military and intelligence activities on the island that had little or nothing to do with the combat/training brigade or the occasional naval force projections of the past ten years. Indeed, after the 1970–1971 submarine base flap, the Soviets at the end of the 1970s were making their boldest bid yet to exploit Cuba's military potential—precisely along lines suggested by Admiral

Mahan in 1897. Cuba was to house a multipurpose set of bases and facilities available to the Soviets and scattered throughout this island "continent."

That raises once again the question of definition. Force projection embraces far more than naval deployments or even support bases for those deployments. In the Caribbean, the Soviet Union has established all three traditional services on the island—naval, air, and ground with a (potential) strategic mix that would add to overall Soviet strategic capability. In addition, force projection includes an intelligence collection capability, and that again touches on a number of key areas involving military preparedness. To be sure, information about Soviet military use of intelligence capabilities is far from complete and the following description and analysis is anything but definitive. But a picture—distorted and flattened a bit like a Gauguin portrait perhaps—nevertheless is available, and the reality it portrays is at least recognizable even to the untrained eye.

At the height of the combat brigade controversy with its maximum media attention, renewed Soviet naval activity on the island came in for quieter scrutiny. The amount of attention paid seems, in retrospect, indirectly proportional to each issue's strategic significance. Consequently, far less is known of the recent expansion of the Soviet naval capability in Cuba—but an examination is necessary nonetheless.

Two points can now be made. First, there has been new construction at Cienfuegos—the first since 1970. Second, there has been a significant upgrading of facilities designed to improve Soviet strategic submarine capability in the Caribbean.

Senator Richard Stone (D–Fla) who first warned of Soviet combat troops in Cuba in July 1979 has also commented on the Cienfuegos naval facilities:

> . . . It is a substantial and major expansion of facilities far over and above the confrontation—*far over* and *above* what it was when the Nixon and Kissinger negotiation took place with the Soviets in 1970 about Cienfuegos.[22]

The facilities which once could service submarine tenders and barges necessary for receiving radioactive wastes now appear to be considerably expanded. They include improved anchorage with the addition of two piers, a nuclear weapons handling facility, and an air strip.[23]

If this is the case, then a complete strategic submarine base has been finished and is ready for activation. The Carter Administration's denials that such base improvements are a violation of the 1962 agreement rested on a technicality. That is, the base itself would remain unimportant until used by Yankee-class Soviet submarines.

It is useful to clear up obfuscations on the problem of Soviet naval facilities. As James Theberge wisely observed, "there is still a tendency . . . to think of a 'base' in prewar terms of fixed, massive, expensive, and politically fragile complexes. . . ."[24] But, in fact, a modern forward base for strategic naval vessels needs only a deepwater anchorage and an airstrip. Support facilities are not required at the base itself—but afloat in ships kept "mobile and secure"—against attack or sabotage, and furthermore, free from the risk of on-shore political turmoil.[25] Apparently, all these elements plus back-up support facilities on shore are now available to the Soviets primarily for strategic submarines, but for conventional warships as well.

If the Soviet naval arm has been recently improved in Cuba, so has its air capability. This too has suffered from a comparative lack of publicity, and therefore of information in the public record. Let us now examine the separate Soviet air capability, and later the question of improved Cuban air strike capability.[26]

Soviet air capability has increased in two and potentially three ways. First, since early 1976, Soviet pilots have flown air defense missions in Cuba. That, of course, helped free Cuban pilots for African and Middle Eastern duty. But it has also given the Soviet Union trained airmen located within minutes of the U.S. mainland. Jack Anderson, citing a Defense Intelligence Agency report as his source, wrote that the Soviet pilots are "an independent fighter unit in Cuba," and that they now number approximately fifty.[27]

Second, one major air facility has been turned over to the Soviet Union. That base, the San Antonio de los Baños airfield, is located a few miles south of Havana. Furthermore, San Antonio's facilities have recently been improved. The chief improvement has been the lengthening of the air strip. That improvement alone raises the potential threat of Cuba being used as a forward base for Soviet bombers, principally the Backfire. An argument throughout the SALT debate has been whether the Backfire is a strategic weapon system. A principal argument against that classification is the bomber's limited range: unrefueled it cannot make a round trip to the United States and back. However, it can land in Cuba, and in the last two years, a facility has been prepared for these aircraft. San Antonio could also serve as a Backfire bomber station in the future. If so, the airfield would be another Soviet strategic arm designed to complement the sea-launched ballistic missile system of the Yankee-class submarine.

But the single best known Soviet addition to its military

presence in the Caribbean to date remains the combat/training brigade. During September and October 1979 it dominated the news—until the seizure of the American embassy in Tehran on November 4.

That tangled story cannot be recounted in a few paragraphs. In fact, the story has no end, much less a satisfactory resolution.[28] Nor is the exact nature of the problem fully understood or agreed upon today. Indeed, much of the debate—quite deliberately fostered by the Carter Administration— centered around the question of *when* the brigade or elements thereof first appeared in Cuba. Estimates have ranged from several years to as long as seventeen years ago.[29]

Nevertheless, a number of observations can be made:

First, Soviet troops were introduced in large numbers (up to 22,000)[30] on the island in 1962 to protect the land-based strategic missiles introduced by Khrushchev.

Second, these, essentially security troops, were removed in 1963 after they lost their reason for being. Throughout the 1960s and most of the 1970s, Soviet military personnel consisted of advisers who worked closely with the Cuban armed forces helping to mold a guerilla-style Rebel Army into a formidable and conventional fighting force.[31]

The brigade itself took shape in 1975 or 1976—the imprecision of its genesis is blamed, in the public record at least, on an intelligence gap. In any case, the first references to the "brigada" were intercepted by the National Security Agency. The brigade reached its present configuration in 1977 or 1978 and consisted of 2,300–3,000 men formed into three under-strength battalions— armor, artillery, and infantry.[32] At least that is one official version. Another official version is that the brigade consists of three infantry and one tank battalions plus the usual support elements.[33]

The brigade's maneuver area was located some twenty miles southwest of Havana wedged between Jose Marti international airport and the San Antonio de los Baños air base. The military equipment was stored at Lourdes military headquarters a few miles east of San Pedro while the troops were garrisoned still further east at two camps, Santiago de las Vega, and Managua.[34]

Finally, the brigade is equipped with artillery, forty tanks, and sixty armored personnel carriers.[35] The brigade, however, does not have any airlift or sealift capability—a point frequently made by the Carter Administration.[36]

At this point the consensus breaks down. There is no agreement on the brigade's purpose.[37] No less than nine reasons have been suggested. Many of these are not mutually exclusive, however. They also range from the vaguely geopolitical to the very specific—

keeping Fidel Castro in office, for example. They are listed in order of specificity.

First, the combat brigade was introduced sometime in 1976 as a test for the new American President.

Second, the brigade was meant to establish permanently a Soviet presence in the Caribbean of the most tangible kind, and in doing so to remind Central America and Caribbean states that the second superpower was neither remote nor disinterested in the political nature of their regimes.

Third, the Soviet brigade is a replacement for Cuban troops serving in Africa and the Middle East.

Fourth, the Russian troops are acting as a tripwire and thus reinforce Cuban security. They are, in short, "an insurance against retaliations from the U.S."[38]

Fifth, it is, in fact, a combat brigade which probably is now only a nucleus for a much larger force in the future. When it acquires an airlift or sealift capability it will become a force for theatre operations.

Sixth, it is a training/demonstration brigade designed to instill combat techniques in Cuban forces being prepared for duty in Africa.

Seventh, it is a praetorian guard protecting Fidel Castro against potentially unreliable Cuban military officers.

Eighth, the brigade is a special security unit designed to protect sensitive Soviet facilities, including a command center for all Soviet operations in the Caribbean.

Finally, it is a special security unit designed to protect Soviet nuclear weapons stored in Cuba.

What evidence is publicly available cannot definitively rule out any of these nine possibilities, although some are more plausible than others. For example, the praetorian guard hypothesis is perhaps the weakest for two reasons. First, Castro has other means to protect himself—means well known to chiefs of state who have a communist party to control other political groups. Second, the Soviet brigade is not particularly well positioned to protect the peripatetic Cuban leader.

On the other hand, the security unit suggestion, especially the variation dealing with the guarding of intelligence facilities or command center, has something to say for it. The brigade *is* located in or near such facilities at Lourdes and Los Palacios.[39]

But whatever its function or cluster of functions, it is a new development in the Soviet Union's changing and expanding military role in the Caribbean.

The final aspect of Soviet force projection in the region has already been alluded to—namely, intelligence. For reasons that are obvious, Soviet intelligence collection capability in Cuba is the least known component of force projection in the Caribbean. What is known, however, can be broken into two categories.

First, there is an electronic intelligence intercept complex located near Havana that can monitor American telephone and cable traffic. It may also be able to collect usable data from the encoded messages transmitted from our satellites and missiles. Moreover, there is reason to believe that additional collection capabilities may exist or will exist in the near future. The Soviet Union, in short, possesses a forward intelligence base similar in capability to the ones we once maintained in Iran and now operate in Turkey. (The bases in Turkey, however, do not have capabilities comparable to those lost by the United States in Iran.)[40]

Second, Cuba serves as a base for Soviet aerial reconnaissance. Russian Tu-95 (Bear) naval reconnaissance flights monitor U.S. naval operations in the North Atlantic. They can also sweep the U.S. seaboard on flights from Cuba to the Soviet Union.[41] This type of intelligence collection activity is not a recent development—in fact, it began in November 1972. However, there is some evidence to suggest that these flights have increased in frequency in recent years.[42]

The Soviet Union is not unaided in projecting force in the Caribbean. In the last decade, the Cubans have developed their own potential as well. One assumption must be made clear from the beginning. In 1980, separating Cuban and Soviet capability is increasingly difficult. The meshing of the two ostensibly separate military and intelligence efforts is becoming an increasingly academic exercise—witness the wholesale takeover of Cuba's foreign intelligence arm, the DGI, by the KGB in 1970–1971.[43] A second assumption is that the Cuban capability to project force on short notice cannot be underestimated. No expert, to my knowledge, predicted Cuba's move into Angola in 1975—especially on such a large scale. Few would have thought it possible at all.

Cuba's naval arm has experienced recent improvements. There is no doubt that its capability will continue to grow and that the improvements will be directly linked to Soviet strategy. In the early 1960s, the Cuban navy was a small force equipped with vintage American ships, among them, four frigates—one dating from 1911—and several escort patrol boats. The Soviets expanded this meager force by turning eighteen submarine chasers and eighteen Komar patrol boats over to Cuba in the mid-1960s. In the mid-1970s, five Osa patrol boats equipped with Styx surface-to-surface missiles were transferred from Soviet inventories.⁴⁴ The latest addition to the Cuban navy, however, has caused the most comment. In 1979, the Soviets gave the Cubans one Whiskey-class submarine, ostensibly for training purposes, and a Foxtrot submarine for active duty. A second Foxtrot was spotted in February 1980 and all three are stationed at Cienfuegos.⁴⁵

As for the airforce, Cuba's arsenal has steadily improved since a handful of American-built trainers spelled the difference between victory and defeat at the Bay of Pigs in April 1961. Later in that year the first MiG-15s and 17s arrived, and in subsequent years the newer MiG-19s and 21s were added.⁴⁶ By 1978, the Cubans had over 200 modern combat aircraft, interceptors and fighter-bombers.⁴⁷

The latest (1978) addition to the inventory, however, has caused the greatest stir over aircraft in Cuba since the Il-28 bombers were spotted in September 1962. Although this last controversy did not reach the public until November 1978, the first MiG-23/27s arrived in crates the previous April.⁴⁸ As of 1980 two squadrons (ten planes each) are operational. One squadron consists of MiG-23s (Flogger-E), and the other is a mixed group of the attack versions of the MiG-23 and MiG-27 (Flogger-D).⁴⁹

The question that preoccupied Washington for three weeks in November and December 1978 was whether the new planes constituted a breach of the 1962 agreement. In the end, the Administration decided that they were not; the critics disagreed. There was, however, no disagreement over the fact that the attack variants of the MiG-23 and the nearly similar MiG-27, both with a combat radius of 1,200 miles, were stationed in Cuba.

The question revolved around a technical point: were the attack aircraft wired to carry nuclear weapons. To answer that meant that an intensive (and resumed) aerial reconnaissance effort had to be made. Although the electronic wiring itself is internal and cannot be detected by technical (nonhuman) intelligence collectors, the bomb racks and radioactive material are observable.⁵⁰ At the end of that intelligence effort, the Administration concluded that the attack versions were not at that time carrying nuclear weapons and therefore were not in violation of the 1962 understanding.⁵¹

But a number of questions remain unanswered. First, for Cuba's MiGs to remain certifiably nonstrategic requires an ongoing intelligence effort of some magnitude—an effort which is both expensive and will divert scarce intelligence assets from other high priority problems. And the effort must be sustained with no terminal date in sight.⁵² Second, it throws open the question of what the 1962 understanding really means—and in three ways.

First, it seems to redefine "offensive" to include only strategic weapons—a nonnuclear weapons system capable of doing damage to the U.S. mainland is eliminated altogether. Second, and more importantly, it eliminates weapons systems only "capable" of becoming strategic—a very different interpretation on the matter than is found in Kennedy's October 27, 1962 understanding with Khrushchev.[53] Third, it clearly violated the precedent laid down during the missile crisis. It was, in fact, a missile and bomber crisis. Thus, President Kennedy not only insisted on the removal of the SS-4s but the Il-28s as well. This twin engine bomber was also capable of carrying nuclear weapons but was not as lethal as the attack version of the MiG-23. Nevertheless, Kennedy insisted on the removal of the Il-28s despite the advice of a number of his advisors.[54]

A final problem: the purpose of the MiG-23/27s. Again the hypotheses are more plentiful than the evidence. On a spectrum of benign to malign, they are as follows:

First, the MiGs are nothing more than a simple upgrading of the Cuban inventory—a natural progression from the MiG-15 to the first line MiG-23/27. Arguing in favor of that view is that when the first MiG-21s were introduced in 1965 no objections in public at least were made by previous administrations—even considering that the MiG-21 can be used as an attack aircraft. Arguing against the upgrading inventory argument is that the MiG-23 interceptor variant added only marginally to Cuban capabilities while the MiG-23/27 attack version represents a considerable jump in their strategic capability.

Second, the addition of the MiGs was another probe of Carter's intentions and specifically it tested the Administration's own definition of the 1962 understanding. That test, according to this hypothesis, led to further testing including the introduction of a combat brigade and further improvements in the Cienfuegos facilities, and *will* lead to the introduction of Backfire at a later date.

Third, the transfer of the MiGs to Cuba was meant to be an incremental addition to the Soviet strategic capability—an addition that perfectly matched a glaring American weakness, namely, a poor interceptor capability. If nothing else, it would force the United States to direct increasingly scarce intelligence and defense resources toward Cuba at a far greater expense than the limited threat would otherwise justify.

Fourth, the transfer of the MiGs to Cuba was primarily "an upgrading and training of Fidel Castro's expeditionary forces for use in the world of tomorrow." That world included any existing or potential conflict in Africa or the Middle East in which Cuban forces could serve Soviet geopolitical purposes.

Finally, we must look at Cuban ground force capability. It is an example of force projection, and is the most difficult to assess. As mentioned earlier, in the last decade the Cuban army has been transformed into a conventional force of considerable power. Until 1975, it was the universal assumption that the Cuban army (active duty and ready reserves) was designed for home island defense— although its sheer size should have provoked second thoughts among analysts.

The Cuban army totals approximately 90,000 active duty personnel—divided into three geographically-based armies. The army is supplemented by perhaps 180,000 reservists, many of whom are combat-ready and, in fact, have served already in Africa. In addition, the Ministry of the Interior has a special force unit which saw action against the South Africans in the first days of the Cuban intervention in Angola.[56]

What is that army's potential for projecting force in the Caribbean? The conventional assumption that ground forces will remain on the island continues to be the unshakeable belief of many—even after Angola, Ethiopia, and Yemen. The belief rests on the assumption that while projecting force (albeit with Soviet help) is "acceptable" in Africa and points east, it is not acceptable to the United States in its own backyard. This assumption rests on a presumption held by American policymakers—a presumption for which the "policy" has not been spelled out in public.

Further force projection certainly is not undercut by a lack of manpower. Even if one assumes that there are 50,000 Cuban troops abroad, 220,000 combat ready soldiers are available, a number greatly in excess of that needed for home defense.

The next question is, do the Cubans have the capacity to *project* ground forces in the Caribbean? The answer is clearly yes. Moving troops to any point in the region (Managua, for example, is 1,000 miles from Havana) is far simpler than moving troops to Angola, much less Ethiopia—Luanda is some 6,000 miles away.

Moreover, the Cubans did move their first units, totaling over a thousand men, into Angola with their own transportation; that is, they did not depend on Soviet logistical aid until later. Finally, Cuba's admittedly threadbare 1975 military transport system has been recently improved with the addition of An-24s and 26s—a present total of 30 planes with the capability to carry a maximum of 1000 men.[57] As with all recent upgradings of Cuban military capabilities, there is no reason to believe that further improvements will not be made.

In any case, Cuban conventional force projections are possible under the proper circumstances. They certainly will be done with vastly more sophistication than Castro's first attempts in 1959. These first trial runs were not the attempts to implant guerrilla *focos* which became common in the 1960s, but were primitive invasions of Panama and the Dominican Republic. In both cases, they were failures—the Dominican adventure was, in fact, a bloody fiasco.[58]

But under what circumstances would the Cubans deploy conventional forces outside their home island in the Caribbean? Such a move would probably follow the African model, at least in the latter's early stages. Small, highly specialized units (again the Ministry of Interior's special forces) would be flown in at the request of either a friendly government *in extremis* or belligerent forces close to overthrowing a hostile government (Angola). In the present day Caribbean, there are at least a half-dozen countries which fit either of the above categories. In the early 1980s at least three others could be added to the list.

Soviet forces would not necessarily be involved and the United States would therefore be denied any excuse for retaliatory countermeasures. Cuban actions under the above formula do not clearly violate any recent American warning. President Carter, for example, in his 1 October 1979 speech on the Soviet combat brigade, warned against use of that brigade "to threaten the security of the United States or any other nation in this hemisphere." He added: "The United States will act in response to a request for assistance in meeting any such threat from Soviet or Cuban forces."[59] In short, we have prepared ourselves for a remote contingency. The more immediate possibility of *Cuban* forces meeting a call for assistance remains unaddressed. Havana need take only one small step above existing precedent, in effect, to write its own Truman doctrine for the Caribbean. There can be no doubt: Cuba does have the physical capability of doing so unless the United States is prepared to use force to stop it.

Finally, a few observations on Cuban paramilitary capabilities, which may be defined as nonconventional forces to achieve desired aims.

Through the first half of the 1960s, it was precisely Havana's plan to destroy nearly all existing regimes in Latin America. The means chosen were thought to be what worked in Cuba in the struggle against Batista, namely, small groups of armed guerrillas operating in the countryside and growing in strength while the regular army became demoralized and detached from the people. The end is well known. The army collapsed, leaving the power in the hands of the *guerrilleros*.

Although it had worked in Cuba, these attempts at overthrowing other regimes were dismal failures elsewhere. The failures were most keenly felt in Venezuela, Peru, and Bolivia—the final resting place for Che Guevara. The reasons for the multiple failures were many. The regimes of Latin America were tougher than anticipated by Havana, and one suspects by Washington as well. Nearly all of them eventually had the backing of the United States, which under the Alliance for Progress summoned up the diplomatic, political, economic, and military resources needed to control the bands of guerrillas which were, in fact, getting much less aid from Cuba. At the same time, Cuba was often working alone and at cross-purposes with the Soviet Union, whose leaders never accepted the Guevara–Debray thesis of making revolution. Furthermore, the communist parties (or at least the majority of them) operating in Latin America had no desire to be thrown into an openly revolutionary situation. Their discomfiture was extreme, and the Bolivian Communist Party may have been instrumental in the betrayal of Che Guevara.[60]

By the 1970s, the Cubans had learned these lessons. But they had not learned the lesson too many analysts ascribed to them, namely, that troublemaking had no future in Latin America. Instead, the Cubans learned to be more selective, to concentrate on the more vulnerable targets—all of them in Central America—and they began with the most vulnerable of all, the Somoza regime in Nicaragua.

These targets were not only closer to home, but most of the regimes were to a greater or lesser extent dependent upon American protection—protection suddenly absent since 1977. Nevertheless, the Cuban leadership was prepared for a prolonged struggle; no quick, cheap victories were expected as they had been in 1959. The Cubans willingly supplied training, weapons, advisers, the (forged) documents and transportation necessary for a serious insurgency. They also provided propaganda support and sanctuary. Quite possibly Havana's contribution was political advice which led to the at least partial unification of the splintered guerrilla groups in Nicaragua, El Salvador, and Guatemala.

There is no doubt that Cuban paramilitary capabilities are at an all-time high. Havana has had two decades to learn through trial and error what works best in the Caribbean basin. The lessons from the past have been drawn and are now being applied. Moreover, Cuba has the support of the Soviet Union and its first visible success, the Sandinista revolution, can only strengthen Havana's resolve to continue.

Finally, the paramilitary effort is likely to continue, and this time it will be complemented by a conventional force projection capability. They will use both in tandem, first to nurture and then to protect an insurgency anywhere in the region.

The other chief actor in the Caribbean remains the United

States. And despite rapid improvements in Soviet and Cuban capabilities, the United States retains an advantage in force projection in the Caribbean. The United States has the natural advantage of geographic position, and it still has considerable conventional power available for the area. But there are two caveats.

First, capacity simply begs the questions of whether this country's leaders have the will or skill to use the available forces. Second, we cannot neglect the size of the problem involved in dealing with a hostile Cuba intimately linked with an equally hostile superpower.

Writing in *Harper's Magazine* at the end of the last century, Admiral Mahan put it quite succinctly:

Cuba has no possible rival in her command of Yucutan passage, just as she has no competitor in point of natural strength and resources, for control of Florida Strait which connects the Gulf of Mexico with the Atlantic.[61]

But before analyzing the problems that Mahan's observation entails, it is necessary to discuss those assets the U.S. still retains in the Caribbean along with their principal characteristics. Finally, we need to put our position in the region in some time-perspective.

U.S. military bases in Latin America have, in fact, been confined to the Caribbean basin, and despite an interest displayed earlier in the nineteenth century, such bases were not secured after the Spanish-American War. Even then the American military presence was not of enormous dimensions until World War II.

What remains of our base structure is designed for a conventional war. With present facilities, the United States can protect narrow sea lanes through the Caribbean—trade routes which carry strategic raw materials, petroleum and bauxite in particular. Such facilities also help in shielding the approaches to the Panama Canal. In the last decade, they have also been the base of highly technical missions, including tracking Soviet warships. In addition, they serve as superb facilities for underwater training. The old Canal Zone is still the headquarters of the Southern Command and has acted as a collection point for intelligence on Latin America. Finally, the old Zone once provided training facilities for Latin American officers at the School of the Americas—scheduled to be closed in the next few years.

The projection of American military forces in the region is widely criticized today. It was, of course, not always so. Military force was used repeatedly in the region by the United States beginning at the turn of the century and ending (apparently) in 1965. The bulk of these interventions occurred in the Caribbean and

Central America in the first quarter of this century. After the Roosevelt–Hull pledge of nonintervention in 1933, however, American forces were used extremely sparingly. Thus, only on occasion did naval forces maneuver in foreign waters, as was the case near Santo Domingo in 1961—a ploy to keep the Trujillo family from regaining power—or the better known example of that year, the Bay of Pigs.

The direct use of force that occurred earlier in the century was carried out for one of two reasons: first, to help establish "responsible," competent governments, and thus to minimize the possibility that other foreign countries would intervene in the area, or second, to protect American lives and property. (The 1965 intervention in the Dominican Republic began as a classic "lives and property" mission and ended up preventing a foreign—that is, communist—takeover.)

Since World War II, less direct instruments of military power have also been employed. Military missions, officer training programs, and arms sales have been a major part of U.S. diplomacy throughout Latin America. U.S. military officers attached to American embassies cultivated relations with their Latin American colleagues. Such contact not only elicited information, but also was an effort to improve the professional quality of the Latin American officer corps. That hope was reinforced by large-scale officer training programs available in the United States (Fort Leavenworth, for example) and more importantly in the Canal Zone at the School of the Americas. The overt purpose was to improve military skills, but the less obvious hope was that contact with "nonpolitical" North American officers would inspire their counterparts from Latin America to be the same.

Finally, the United States has used arms sales to reinforce contacts with the region's military officers. Until the last decade, the overwhelming percentage of the area's military equipment came from the United States. The aid and trade in weaponry attracted heavy criticism over the years, particularly in this country, although per capita arms purchases in Latin America were far lower than anywhere else with perhaps the exception of Africa. Again, the objective was to keep Latin American militaries relatively dependent on U.S. sources, and thus perhaps to enhance our influence on their attitudes and behavior.

Thus, even indirect military influence has also been under attack, and has therefore declined in importance. Moreover, many policies of the Carter Administration aggravated this problem. Military agreements have been cancelled by countries as diverse as Brazil and El Salvador for alleged U.S. intervention in their internal affairs. Military sales have also been restricted, resulting in increased purchases of weapons from sources outside the Western Hemisphere. Such restrictions have had the added effect of promoting a more rapid build-up of Latin America's indigenous arms industry.

Finally, the number of U.S. trained officers in Latin America will probably also decline as the School of the Americas is phased out, leaving the United States with substantially less contact and probably less influence over Latin American militaries than it once had. Moreover, the trend is not likely to reverse. The present American policy is supported by domestic opinion which tends to oppose arms transfers and training programs for Latin American states. If that continues to be the case, a reduction in American military influence will also undercut the perceived need for fixed military installations in Latin America with perhaps only a few minor exceptions in the Caribbean.

Any consideration of the future of American military facilities in the Caribbean region must examine their present capabilities and uses. It is difficult to determine in any absolute sense which facility is most important to the United States, since so much depends upon future missions, challenges, and the availability of alternatives. However, it is possible to indicate the capabilities of those bases now in existence.

The base at Guantanamo Bay, Cuba is located adjacent to what is probably the best (at a minimum among the best) anchorage in the world. The bay is some 14 miles wide, and the 120 fathoms depth at its mouth increases to 150 fathoms within a relatively short distance. These statistics are significant because it means that naval combatants can reach good operational depths rapidly and within a relatively short distance. As long as there is reliance upon the utilization of submarines, these are important factors, since they can reach their operational stations relatively easily.

Guantanamo also possesses significant potential for military operations in the event that hostilities erupt in the region. The most apparent use would be in terms of naval combatants and various fleet support functions. There are two airfields at Guantanamo which can be used for a variety of purposes. Historically, they have served mainly for training air-related personnel. In the event of conflict, however, both could perform a variety of functions—as was the case during the 1965 Dominican Republic crisis, and during the flap over the Soviet combat brigade in 1979. Depending upon the type of threat or the missions required, the airfields could be used for antisubmarine warfare, as important logistical links, for staging, and ultimately for protecting the Guantanamo base itself in the event of a

Cuban effort to disrupt operations there. Indeed, ships which arrive for training purposes are also prepared for specific combat assignments in the event hostilities erupt during their stay.

The possibility of Cuban military action against these facilities makes reliance upon Guantanamo a less than attractive option. The question becomes one of determining the cost of protecting the base so that it would remain a positive contributor to any necessary military action. For example, the Cubans could tie down U.S. forces from military bases within easy range of Guantanamo and prevent those forces from being used elsewhere in the region. In such a situation, it is likely that the Soviet Union would be the prime mover in the conflict as a whole. Indeed, short of Soviet action it is doubtful that the Cubans would launch any serious military action against Guantanamo. The Cubans are well aware that the United States possesses the capability to inflict serious punitive damage on their own military capabilities should America decide to do so.

Of course, it should also be noted that Guantanamo possesses an important peace-time capability involving early warning and surveillance functions. This is particularly the case in regard to antisubmarine surveillance and, ultimately antisubmarine warfare.

Much has been written about the importance of the Panama Canal and arguments have raged about the treaties which give Panama control and ownership of the Canal. Yet, there are more implications than just the question of the Canal itself. The United States possesses twelve military facilities in Panama ranging from those involved in support, to those at which training occurs, to those which perform communications functions. All of these facilities must be surrendered to Panama at the end of this century. Whether the United States could use them after that time would depend on the willingness of the Panamanians and on the feasibility of restoring U.S. capabilities to those bases.

The Zone is the communications hub of the area south of the continental United States, and as such, has been an important element in America's worldwide military posture. The communications facilities located in Panama have been of considerable importance in transmitting and relaying communications for thousands of miles. The facilities there have also been of significance in terms of American technical intelligence coordination efforts. More generally, the Southern Military Command of the United States has relied heavily upon the communications and other facilities located in the Zone.

The Zone facilities also provide general support facilities. These would be used during any large-scale hostilities in the Caribbean area. Key among the various facilities are: the naval

station at Rodman; the ship repair facilities located near Panama City;
and the communications station close to Balboa. Obviously, the airfields can also be of great potential assistance during crisis periods.

Yet, once again, as in Guantanamo, there is the potential for
internal disruption. However, unlike the Guantanamo situation, the
government of Panama is not an ardent enemy of the United States,
nor is it likely to develop a significant military capability of its own.
In addition, it is unlikely to receive substantial military assistance
from a major outside power like the Soviet Union. Nonetheless,
there is a danger of sabotage that could tie down some American
units for defensive purposes, and it is possible that the Canal itself
could be obstructed unless a sizeable contingent of American
resources were to be dedicated to its protection.

Another group of facilities in the Caribbean which have been of
importance to the United States are those in Bermuda, the Bahamas
region, and the eastern Caribbean islands. These facilities have
played key roles ranging from underseas surveillance to communications and long-range aviation and space tracking. The United
States has relied upon facilities in the area for a variety of missions.
The facilities in the Bahamas at Eleuthera, those in Trinidad and
Tobago, and the air station in Bermuda have been of key importance
to the U.S. Navy, and the long-range navigation station in Caicos
has been utilized in American defense efforts. The island of Andros
in the Bahamas has been the location of an Atlantic Underseas Test
and Evaluation Center. Vital oceanographic research has been
conducted from stations in Antigua, Barbados, San Salvador and
Grand Turk; and the National Aeronautics and Space Administration has relied upon facilities in Antigua and Grand Bahama. The
latter two, plus Eleuthera, Grand Turk, Mayaguana and Trinidad
and Tobago have been part of the United States Air Force's Eastern
Test Range.

More specifically, American facilities in this area of the
Caribbean have been of vital significance to the functioning of the
Sound Surveillance System (SOSUS). Not surprisingly the amount
of undersea activity is a major determinant of the number of
American air and naval units required to be available in the area.

The other major American facilities located in the Caribbean
region are those in Puerto Rico, where all three American services
have an important presence. Yet the U.S. activity there is not just
limited to Ramey Air Force Base, the naval station at Roosevelt
Roads, and the army command headquarters located in the
Commonwealth. The Marine Corps also are present in Puerto Rico
and have conducted extensive maneuvers and training exercises in
the vicinity of, and on, nearby Vieques.

Roosevelt Roads is a key naval facility for the United States and is the control center for testing weaponry ranging from sophisticated submarine and antisubmarine weapons to the use of drones in testing missiles. Facilities at St. Croix and St. Thomas are also involved in some of these tests and along with Roosevelt Roads comprise important links in the Atlantic Fleet Weapons Range. Another island associated with the test range is Culebra which, prior to 1975, was used extensively for ship gunnery practice.

Although the trend since the Vietnam War has been to reduce or dismantle U.S. facilities in the Caribbean, the combat brigade crisis of October 1979 has nevertheless added to the American military presence in the region. On October 2, President Carter announced the establishment of a "full-time Caribbean Joint Task Force Headquarters" at Key West. That inter-service task force was given the responsibility of monitoring Soviet and Cuban military activities and of planning and executing countermeasures.[62] It would be premature to assess the eventual effectiveness of this joint command—whether, in fact, action will be expedited or delayed with the addition of this extra link in the chain of command.[63]

At the same time, the actual projection of force in October left something to be desired. The sixteen ship task force had difficulty in landing 1,500 Marines on a friendly shore. Moreover, two of the troop transports were scheduled for repair rather than active duty—throwing into question America's sea and airlift capabilities in its own neighborhood. Meanwhile, the promised follow-on exercises designed to demonstrate a U.S. capacity to project military power have yet to materialize.

From this examination of Soviet, Cuban, and American power projections—potential and actual—four broad conclusions can be reached.

First, Soviet and Cuban capabilities have steadily grown, at an accelerating rate. Such capability, particularly in the paramilitary and conventional military areas is likely to continue to be employed in support of Soviet objectives.

Second, American capability is on the decline and that decline is accelerating as well. Because of its position, however, the United States still enjoys local superiority in being able to project power. The Carter Administration's reluctance to use force except *in extremis*, however, points to a fundamental asymmetry, namely a superior American capability and the unwillingness to use it.

Third, the U.S. capability is not well suited to counter the present threat. The Soviets could easily add to their strategic capabilities by an operational submarine base at Cienfuegos; MiG-

23/27s wired for nuclear weapons; and/or Backfire bombers stationed in Cuba. Moreover, the United States is not now prepared to counter Cuban ground forces invited into a Caribbean basin country by a friendly regime, and it has refused to adopt effective measures against Cuban paramilitary efforts in Central America.

Fourth, the effect of Soviet–Cuban policy on the political makeup of the region has not yet been fully assessed. But the indications are not encouraging. American friends have become cautious neutrals, neutrals have become cautious enemies, and enemies have been further emboldened in their efforts.

What is to be done? A number of measures come to mind, but again a caveat is in order. In the best of circumstances the trends disadvantageous to the United States will not soon reverse themselves, while Soviet and Cuban capabilities will continue to improve. Moreover, even if these trends are reversed, the perception in the Caribbean of waxing Soviet capabilities and waning American strength will linger. Nevertheless, some practical measures can be taken by the United States before present trends become irreversible.

First, the United States can halt further erosion of its position. Guantanamo, for example, must be retained, and its position strengthened. Marine exercises should be resumed on a regular basis.

Second, the U.S. Navy needs to be rebuilt and the Second Fleet resuscitated. It was the Second Fleet that bore the chief burden during the Cuban Missile Crisis in October 1962.

Third, the United States must reexamine the 1962 understanding. If it is found that the agreement has been stretched beyond its original meaning, it should be scrapped, leaving this country free to take whatever measures are deemed necessary to counteract the Soviet and Cuban military and intelligence threat.

Fourth, the United States should make explicit the unacceptability of any Soviet or Cuban force projection which is meant to create or protect new Marxist regimes in the Caribbean.

Fifth, the United States must make clear that it will support any regime under attack by armed minorities supported by hostile outside forces.

Last but not least, a Caribbean policy adequate to American security must be based on a coherent foreign policy and global strategy.

NOTES

1. Arthur P. Whitaker, *The United States and the Independence of Latin America* (New York: Norton, 1964), p. 42.

2. A. T. Mahan, *The Influence of Seapower Upon History* (Boston: Little, Brown, 1894), p. 29.

3. A decade earlier, Secretary of the Navy, Benjamin Tracy, stated in a secret report to the Congress that the American navy would be swept from the sea in two weeks by any one of a dozen navies.
4. Mahan, *Influence of Seapower*, p. 30.
5. John M. Collins, *American and Soviet Military Trends Since the Cuban Missile Crisis* (Washington, 1978), p. 1.
6. In land based ICBMs alone, the U.S. in 1962 held a 294 to 75 advantage. Ray S. Cline, *World Power Assessment 1977* (Boulder, CO: Westview Press, 1977), pp. 87–89.
7. The Soviets were not totally absent in the Caribbean from 1963 through 1969, but it was a limited presence at best. Oceanographic and surveying ships did research in the Caribbean, providing information useful to the Soviet navy and fishing fleets. The Russians also assigned intelligence collection ships off the southeast coast of the United States to monitor Cape Canaveral and the submarine base at Charlestown, South Carolina. James D. Theberge, *Russia in the Caribbean, Part Two* (Washington, DC: Georgetown University, 1973), p. 102.
8. Since 1975, the number of submarines has dropped according to public sources to one Foxtrot in December–January 1978. See James D. Theberge, "Soviet Naval Presence in the Caribbean Sea Area," in James L. George, *Problems of Sea Power as We Approach the Twenty-First Century* (Washington, DC: American Enterprise Institute, 1978), pp. 184–185.
9. They have ranged from three to nine ships. Smaller task forces were more typical of the late 1970s. Ibid., p. 185. Regarding recent Soviet restraint (at least for the years 1977–1978), several reasons have been offered. First, the Soviets wanted to lower their naval profile in order "to help the Panamanians secure a favorable Panama Canal Treaty." Second, the Soviet Union wanted to promote Cuban–American detente in order to lessen the economic burden on itself. One expert, James D. Theberge, favored the second explanation. My personal opinion is that neither explanation excludes the other. Furthermore, since Caribbean detente is dead and the Panama treaties are in effect, the Soviet naval activity, *ceteris paribus*, should resume at earlier levels. Quotation taken from Rear Admiral Mark Hill's remarks published in James L. George, ed., *Problems of Sea Power* (Washington, DC: American Enterprise Institute, c. 1978), p. 207.
10. According to public sources, no Soviet SLBM forces have been attached to any naval task force. Golf-class submarines are not defined as "strategic" under SALT definitions. Cline, *World Power Assessment*, pp. 104–105. Nevertheless, the diesel-powered submarine can carry three SS-N-5 solid fuel missiles which are equipped with a one megaton warhead with a range of 650 miles. Soviet strategic Yankee-class submarines have been in Caribbean waters but have not been attached to any naval task force and have not, according to public sources, visited any Caribbean ports. Meanwhile, the last Soviet task force was detected in August 1979, at the height of the Soviet brigade controversy, heading for the Caribbean.
11. James Theberge in James George, ed., *Problems of Sea Power*, p. 185.
12. The barges are designed to carry radioactive wastes taken from nuclear submarines. See James D. Theberge, *Russians in the Caribbean, Part Two* (Washington, 1973), p. 108.
13. Ibid. The facilities included barracks, communications and the famous soccer field.

14. *U.S. News and World Report*, 12 October 1970, p. 22. At first Kissinger was identified only as a "highly placed official." Later the *New York Times* identified Kissinger as that official. *New York Times*, 26 September 1971, p. A16.

15. President Nixon made his statement twice: first to John Chancellor in an NBC television interview conducted on 4 January 1971, and second in a press conference held 17 February 1971, and reprinted in the *Department of State Bulletin*, March 8, 1979, p. 284.

16. Secretary of Defense Melvin Laird made the same point on 2 December 1970. See the *New York Times*, 3 December 1970, p. 2.

17. The Soviet Union denied wrong-doing on two occasions. First in *Izvestia* on 9 October 1970, and then in *Tass* on 13 October 1970. Quoted in James D. Theberge in James L. George, ed., *Problems of Sea Power*, p. 189. At least one Kremlinological explanation of the Soviet–American exercise in cold war crisis management was the belief that "Aesopian language" used in each other's press permitted an early and peaceful resolution of the dispute. The October Soviet statements were, in fact, a coded message indicating that a "verbal agreement" had been reached "in talks for Russia to tear down the base [already completed] and that the U.S. through intelligence methods had verified this." This explanation was offered by American officials to Russell Freeburg of the *Chicago Tribune*, 17 October 1970, and reprinted in "Soviet–Cuban Sub Base An Exercise in Aesopian Diplomacy," *East–West Digest*, vol. VII, no. 1 (January 1971), p. 4.

18. Theberge, for one, has written: "The vague declarations of White House and Pentagon spokesmen over the precise meaning of the so-called U.S.–U.S.S.R. 'understanding' suggests strongly that no clearly specified limits were established concerning the placement of seaborne weapons systems in Cuba or the Hemisphere. More likely, there is a tacit understanding with a margin of uncertainty as to what the U.S. reaction might be under various contingencies. Whether the 'understanding' is oral or written, U.S. officials decline to say, and the details have been held in strict secrecy by the few top officials aside from the President and Dr. Kissinger who know the facts." Quoted from *Russia in the Caribbean, Part Two*, p. 111.

19. The mystery of the barges includes the following elements: the Defense Department announced on October 13 (the day of the second printed Soviet denial) that the two barges left Cienfuegos and had put in at Cuba's north coast naval base at Mariel. But a month later, the barges returned to Cienfuegos (one account gives the time as six weeks), but there was no subsequent U.S. comment after November 1970. *East–West Digest*, vol. VII, no. 1 (January 1971), p. 5.

20. *U.S. News and World Report*, 12 October 1970, p. 12. Also see Theberge, *Russia in the Caribbean, Part Two*, pp. 117–118.

21. Alfred T. Mahan, *The Interests of America in Sea Power, Present and Future* (Boston: Little, Brown, 1897), pp. 278–280; 288–289. Quoted in John D. Hayes, "The Soviet Navy in the Caribbean Sea and Gulf of Mexico," *Interplay*, January 1971, pp. 6-F and 7-F.

22. Stated in an interview to John McLean of the *Chicago Tribune* on 6 September 1979. Quotation taken from a transcript of that interview, pp. 8–9. Senator Stone repeated the substance but left out a number of details in a telephone interview with John Goshko of the *Washington Post*, 31 October 1979. In the *Chicago Tribune* interview Senator Stone repeated

his earlier charge that Soviet nuclear missile carrying submarines had already visited Cienfuegos in 1974, p. 4.

23. *Washington Post,* 31 October 1979, p. A6. See also Secretary of State Cyrus Vance's reference to a nuclear arms handling facility at a press conference reported in the *Washington Post,* 1 November 1979, p. A21.

24. Theberge, *Russia in the Caribbean, Part Two,* p. 114.

25. Ibid., pp. 114–115.

26. See below, p. 268.

27. *Washington Post,* 14 February 1978, p. 1, and 28 September 1979, p. B15. Additional details were later reported by Anderson in a subsequent column based on further leaks from the DIA. This second report locates the future Backfire bomber base at Cienfuegos and not San Antonio de los Baños. *Washington Post,* 26 February 1980, p. B15.

28. The brigade, of course, remains in place. In addition, the State Department disclosed in late February: "Elements of the Soviet brigade in Cuba are conducting another of their periodic training exercises." Quoted in the *New York Times,* 1 March 1980, p. 9, from an official statement.

29. The latter claim was the official Soviet position. That is to say, the brigade, according to the Soviets, consisted of military instructors who formed a training center beginning in 1962. According to *Pravda,* "neither the numerical strength nor the functions of the Soviet personnel have changed all these years." That view was echoed by Fidel Castro in a press conference given on 20 September 1979 in Havana. Reprinted in *FBIS Latin American Report,* 1 October 1979, p. Q1.

30. The exact number was never determined by American intelligence because of the inherent difficulty of the problem. Indeed, all "exact" troops counts should be greeted with skepticism.

31. Jorge I. Dominguez, *Cuba: Order and Revolution* (Cambridge, Mass.: Harvard University Press, 1978), pp. 349–353. See also the *Washington Post,* 9 September 1979, p. A18 for a detailed history based on intelligence estimates of Soviet military personnel in Cuba.

32. It was photographed in field maneuvers on 17 August 1979 by camera satellite. *New York Times,* 13 September 1979, p. A16.

33. The first version was offered to the press by Secretary of State Vance on 5 September 1979. The second version came from unnamed senior officials on September 10. See the *New York Times,* 4 October 1979, p. A3.

34. The *New York Times,* 13 September 1979, p. A16.

35. The rocket battalion was mentioned first by David Binder in the *New York Times,* 13 September 1979, p. A16. Other details given by Bernard Gwertzman in the *New York Times,* 4 October 1979, p. A3.

36. Including President Jimmy Carter in his 1 October 1979 televised address to the nation. The text is available in the *New York Times,* 2 October 1979, p. A18.

37. The brigade's configuration as a brigade has in itself caused problems. It is an unusual formation within the Soviet army—only a few are identified and the function of most of those is unknown.

38. The quote is from Senator Frank Church who supports this thesis. Quoted in *Time,* 17 September 1979, p. 14.

39. *New York Times,* 13 September 1979, p. A16.

40. William Safire, *New York Times,* 6 September 1979, p. A21.

41. Jack Anderson, 14 September 1979 and 28 September 1979, *The Washington Post.*

42. Theberge, *Russia in the Caribbean, Part Two*, p. 114.
43. Brian Crozier, "Soviet Pressures: The Satellisation of Cuba," in Robert Moss, ed., *The Stability of the Caribbean* (Washington, D.C., 1973), pp. 90–93. On a slightly less serious subject, Havana radio disclosed in December 1979 that two Cubans are in training in the USSR for a future space flight. Reported in JPRS *Latin America Report*, 18 December 1979, p. 46.
44. Dominguez, *Cuba*, p. 349. Raymond V. B. Blackman, ed., *Jane's Fighting Ships, 1969–1970* (London, 1969), pp. 68–69.
45. Horace Sutton, "Caribbean in Conflict," *Saturday Review*, 1 March 1980, p. 16.
46. Dominguez, *Cuba*, p. 349. The MiG-21s given in 1965 made Cuba the first Latin American country to be equipped with supersonic aircraft.
47. Jan Knippers Black, *Area Handbook for Cuba* (Washington, D.C.: U.S. Government Printing Office, 1976), pp. 465–466.
48. Fidel Castro's claim of November 1978 that the MiG-23s had been in Cuba for a year and that the U.S. knew it all along cannot be taken too seriously. Castro made that statement at a press conference in Havana on 22 November 1978. It is available in *FBIS Latin American Report*, 24 November 1978, Q5. Castro added: "They are tactical planes, absolutely defensive. Therefore, this pseudo-crisis, this farce, has been mounted in recent days because someone has said that history was repeating itself. Once it was a tragedy and this time it is a farce. The tragedy could have been 1962 and the contrived and artifically fabricated farce on the MiG-23s. . . . And what sort of country and what sort of moral standard can that country have when it creates a scandal and almost a crisis because of the fact that Cuba has a few MiG-23 planes which are not strategic and are tactical and defensive?" The someone who wrote that aphorism on history was, of course, Karl Marx in his *Eighteenth Brumaire of Louis Napolean*.
49. They were identified as such by IISS's *Military Balance, 1978–1979* (London, 1979), p. 79; and *Aviation Week and Space Technology*, 1 January 1979, p. 19. The interceptor squadron was put on public display on 2 December 1978. See *Latin American Political Report*, 8 December 1978.
50. *Newsweek*, 27 November 1978, p. 52.
51. *New York Times*, 8 December 1978, p. A18.
52. William Safire reported in early December 1978 that the Department of Defense had begun "drafting plans and budgets for four AWACs for "positive air defense" against the MiGs at a cost of $488 million plus a squadron of F-15s. *New York Times*, 4 December 1978, p. A 21.
53. Ibid. Also see Elie Abel, *The Missile Crisis* (Philadelphia: Lippincott, 1966), p. 199. The relevant passage is found in Kennedy's letter to Krushchev: "The first thing that needs to be done, however, is for work to cease on offensive missile bases in Cuba *and for all weapons systems in Cuba capable of offensive use to be rendered inoperable*, under effective United Nations arrangements."
54. Abel, *Missile Crisis*, pp. 214–215.
55. Rowland Evans and Robert Novack, *Washington Post*, 8 December 1978.
56. Black, *Handbook for Cuba*, p. 465, and Dominguez, *Cuba*, p. 348. That unit according to Dominguez numbers 650.

57. IISS, *Military Balance*, p. 79.
58. Andres Suarez, *Cuba: Castroism and Communism, 1959–1966* (Cambridge, MA: MIT Press, 1967), pp. 63–68.
59. President Jimmy Carter quoted in the *New York Times*, 2 October 1979, p. A18.
60. Leo Sauvage, *Che Guevara: The Failure of a Revolutionary* (Englewood Cliffs: Prentice-Hall, 1973), *Passim*.
61. Alfred T. Mahan, "Strategic Features of the Gulf of Mexico and Caribbean Sea," *Harper's New Monthly Magazine*, June 1897. Quoted in John D. Hayes, "The Soviet Navy," *Interplay*, January 1971, p. 5-F.
62. How effective the Key West command will be remains unclear. Its effectiveness has also been made suspect by the fact that U.S. naval exercises are still very much controlled by Atlantic Fleet headquarters in Norfolk, Virginia. See the *Washington Post*, 2 October 1979, p. A6.
63. The Marine landing at Guantanamo was not an encouraging beginning. What was meant to be a training exercise (suspended since 1975) rapidly turned into a media event—in the strict sense of that awful term—that is, an event staged and managed to suit the cameras (ours and unfortunately, the oposition's) rather than the military requirements of the situation.

17

Surrogate Forces and Power Projection

Gavriel D. Ra'anan

AUTHOR'S NOTE

Expanded and updated to address the issues posed by the 1980 Conference of the International Security Studies Program of The Fletcher School of Law and Diplomacy, this chapter incorporates a considerable amount of material from the author's Rand Paper P-6420 ("The Evolution of the Soviet Use of Surrogates in Military Relations with the Third World, with Particular Emphasis on Cuban Participation in Africa"). The author wishes to acknowledge with gratitude his debt to The Rand Corporation for making it possible to research this significant aspect of current international conflict.

This piece does not purport to be an exhaustive account of the Soviet use of surrogate forces in relations with the Third World, nor does it present a series of case studies of Cuba's role in Angola, the Ogaden, and Shaba. Rather, it attempts to analyze the cause, nature, and effect of "operations of indirection" (Soviet style), especially in Africa. It is hoped that this study will shed some light upon the evolution of the Soviet use of proxies in an active combat role.

OVERVIEW

In order to project power and gain influence abroad, it is not uncommon for states to use operatives that are "low-profile" or "low-cost" (in societal as well as economic terms). History is replete with examples, such as the employment of Swiss mercenaries by Italian and German princes, Britain's resort to Hessians in the Western Hemisphere, or Gurkhas in Malaya, not to mention the continued utilization by France of the Foreign Legion. The advantage of using forces whose casualty rates remain a matter of relative indifference "back home" is obvious. Indeed, one wonders if the First Lord of the Admiralty, Winston Churchill, could have recovered politically had he been fighting "to the last Englishman" rather than to the "last Anzac" at Gallipoli.

On the debit side there is the consideration that the patron state may be simply transferring such "domestic costs" to client regimes that it is eager to support in power rather than to destabilize. For instance, in connection with the current activities of the contemporary "Afrika Corps," the *Leipziger Volkszeitung* felt compelled recently to print a letter by a reader asking if it would not be "more in the interest of peace and disarmament if the G.D.R. sent no soldiers into crisis areas." It was not the newspaper's response (that socialist countries could not permit imperialism to act at will) which was significant, of course, but rather the very fact that this delicate issue had to be aired at all. Cuban ventures in the Middle East and Africa are approaching Vietnam proportions in terms of casualties and have evoked serious grumbling and unrest. As compensation for such "inconvenience," the patron state may have to satisfy certain demands by the regime acting as a surrogate; examples include the Soviet economic subsidies to Fidel Castro and the dispatch to Cuba of Soviet elements that may act as a Praetorian Guard against popular discontent, as well as of advanced weapons, such as the MiG-23, to cover an island denuded of a considerable portion of its own armed forces. Moreover, popular displeasure with a satellite regime may be aroused not only by human costs, but even by pure material expense, real or perceived. Surrogates, of course, have acted not only in a combat capacity but also as arms suppliers on behalf of a patron. Czechoslovakia "enjoyed" this role for several decades and, as long ago as the Stalinist Novotny regime, a Czechoslovak journal, *Veda A Zivot*, felt compelled to act as a pressure valve for mass grumbling concerning this fact. It expressed annoyance that, from Afro–Asian recipients, one heard "assertions to the effect that . . . arms shall not be sold to the developing countries like merchandise, but shall be supplied to them free of charge and in the amount required for their fight against the 'common enemy', etc. . . ." The journal then echoed what clearly was a popular view: "It is not the situation in the developing countries alone which must be taken into consideration, but also the possibilities which are open to the socialist states . . . the efforts made by socialist societies to raise their living standards. . . ."

As opposed to such "costs" (which, perhaps, are not widely understood or appreciated), there are obvious benefits deriving from the employment of surrogates. A major consideration, for instance, is that the use of proxies can serve, if not directly to "disinform" opponents, at least to provide them with the "ammunition" with which to deceive themselves. Thus, from 1975 onward, a Vietnam-weary United States was presented with the picture of an incursion into Angola by elements from a Caribbean island state with a population of less than ten million. Had the USSR adopted an overt combat role, instead of confining itself more discreetly to logistical tasks, could the Clark Amendment have been passed or could an American diplomat have remained in office after describing the Soviet Union as "a stabilizing force in Africa"? Yet, from the Western point of view, is the potential impact upon vital sea lines of communication really less because "only" Cubans (and, subsequently, East Germans and other East Europeans) were involved in West and East Africa and the Middle East, prior to Afghanistan, rather than the Red Army?

World reaction to the ongoing Soviet invasion of Afghanistan is indicative of the advantages of resorting to operations by indirection. It should be noted that, when the USSR utilized Cubans to achieve Soviet goals, not only did Moscow pay no price for such ventures, but the Cubans themselves were able to emerge virtually unscathed in diplomatic terms. Apparently it was "acceptable" for a "Third World" Fidel Castro (although, actually, of purely European ancestry) to become involved in military confrontations on the other side of the globe without forfeiting his role among the "nonaligned" and while garnering plaudits from an American ambassador to the United Nations. However, when Castro's closest ally, the USSR, with a population almost thirty times as large as Cuba's, engages in a military expedition, i.e., "projects power" directly and overtly "next door," it arouses deepest concern, indeed anger, on the part of the same West that benignly observed Cuban forces hopping from continent to continent (on behalf of the very same Soviet Union)! Even the membership of the United Nations suddenly awakens to the iniquity of the Red Army conferring the boon of "proletarian internationalism" upon a helpless people that happens to share a border with the USSR.

It is questionable, however, whether the effects upon the recipients of such "fraternal aid" are really very different when it emanates from Havana or Pankow, rather than from Moscow. Indeed, it may be postulated that one is dealing with a case of two-fold perception: sophisticated Western minds may be confused as to *whose* power is being projected in Angola, Ethiopia, or South Yemen, as opposed to Afghanistan; "simple" Somalis and others at the "receiving end," however, do not appear to have that much trouble identifying the real source. From the point of view of the patron state resorting to surrogates, of course, these two divergent perceptions actually confer double benefit. Global adversaries are far more constrained in their reactions to "mere" surrogates, indeed seem to have difficulty recognizing them for what they are; local and regional regimes and populations, on the other hand, quickly identify the USSR not merely as the power responsible for the logistics of such ventures, including lift, organization, and supply, but as the initiator, director and controller. Whatever anger they may feel toward Moscow is suppressed eventually by an even more potent emotion, namely, respect and naked fear (at the sight of a mighty state projecting power with such persistence, whether directly or indirectly). If such are the advantages of surrogate operations, the distinctions concretely, "on the ground," between Cubans, East Germans, or the Red Army, in a combat capacity, may be rather fine. The difference may be more apparent than real between, let us say, the injection of Soviet units (putatively) in Ethiopia, and Cuban forces operating there with Soviet logistical support (while Soviet pilots patrol Cuban skies, run the D.G.I.—the Cuban secret police— and subsidize Havana to the tune of some $7 million per diem, not to speak of propping up Castro with the aid of Soviet combat elements on the island). For that matter, similar considerations are appropriate when viewing East German military and security activities around the Red Sea and in Africa, while Soviet divisions "guard" the East German "homeland."

Another "local" advantage of surrogate operations relates to sudden and brutal "reversal of alliances." When Moscow decides to "drop" a long-term client and to switch sides in favor of the traditional adversary of that client (e.g., Somalia and Ethiopia), the shock may be cushioned (and a door left ajar in both directions) if the "culprit" actually firing upon Somalis is not the Red Army, but Cubans.

However, the balance sheet is not totally one-sided in favor of surrogate operations. Otherwise, presumably, one would have found Bulgars or North Koreans, rather than Russians, "helping the government of Afghanistan." (Interestingly enough, recent reports refer to Soviet attempts to turn this particular venture into an all-Warsaw Pact operation!) The "domestic cost" to the stability of the client regimes of being saddled with the particular burden have been mentioned already. Another significant consideration relates to the effectiveness of surrogate forces. If "equations" were not so likely to be misinterpreted, one might suggest the following proposition: surrogates tend to have political utility in inverse proportion to their technological capabilities, with Third World elements less likely to antagonize the indigenous population but also being less effective militarily. That, presumably, is the reason why East Germans increasingly have assumed roles in certain parts of Africa and the

Middle East, played previously by the Cubans. At first sight, the appearance of Europeans, not to speak of the associations evoked by the Afrika Corps, is likely to be far more conspicuous and provocative in the Third World, than the activities of Cubans, who, in most instances, tend to blend into the racial environment. The only reason for such substitutions, therefore, is likely to relate to (East) German efficiency, not to mention discipline, and, strange though this may seem, political reliability.

Of course, any temptation to defect, in view of the vast distances separating such units from the home base, is likely to be kept in check by the pervasive presence of the East German Stasi (State Security Service). This factor also produces an intelligence bonus for the Soviet Union, as does the Russian co-option of the D.G.I. (with its various Latin American and African contacts). Here, again, there are some drawbacks; the Stasi, for instance, may itself be penetrated by agents from the Federal Republic.

While the balance sheet, therefore, shows not only assets, there is little doubt but that, on the whole, surrogate operations have proven to be relatively low-cost (at least in political terms); they consititute a fairly advantageous method of projecting power over major distances.

It has to be remembered, however, that the utilization of surrogates can take numerous forms and, as far as the USSR is concerned, has done so throughout the post-War period.

TRANSFER OF WEAPONS (PRODUCED IN
EAST EUROPEAN COUNTRIES).

Probably the lowest rung on the ladder of risk in the use of surrogates involves resort to clients as conduits for the transfer of arms produced (actually or ostensibly) outside the USSR. At a time of relative Soviet weakness, Stalin made extensive use, in this mode, of "German" hardware produced at Czechoslovakia's Skoda plant to supply both sides in the 1948 Arab-Israeli conflict. The origin of these weapons was difficult to establish in the flourishing post-War black market in munitions; thus, obsolescent arms could be utilized to "project" Soviet power, since the recipients knew to whom they were beholden and became responsive to Soviet political and financial leverage. At the same time, because of the involvement of "third parties" in this surreptitious traffic, the West was not unduly alarmed. By 1954, however, a Soviet attempt to ship Czech weapons to Guatemala in Swedish-registered vessels, embarking from Szeczecin, Poland, was detected in time by the United States and produced interdiction and the overthrow of the Arbenz regime.

Despite the lesson of Guatemala, the USSR soon escalated to transferring weapons produced in the Soviet Union itself, and identifiable as such, but still using client states as conduits. In the 1955 arms deal with Egypt and the subsequent agreements on hardware with Indonesia's Sukarno, the initial contacts were made with Czechoslovak and Polish delegations, sending, in the beginning, weapons produced in these countries, but switching, very soon, to Soviet-manufactured versions of the same prototypes. However, even at that stage, Moscow remained very careful and unobtrusive; for instance, in the Indonesian case, during one period, the Soviet hardware was shipped via Rijeka, Yugoslavia; and Egyptians, rather than Warsaw Pact personnel, trained the Indonesians in the use of the newly arrived weapons. Interestingly enough, this approach served its purpose: the West became less rather than more alarmed and, eventually, was habituated to the sight of Soviet weapons in Third World countries. No other arms deal ever produced another "Guatemalan" reaction on the part of the United States. On the other hand, the Soviet "low profile" involved no costs as far as the recipients were concerned, both Nasser and Sukarno being well aware to whom they owed their growing military might.

A subdivision of the same category involved the use of regional noncommunist regimes as surrogates, rather than Warsaw Pact states. This particular approach flourished with the establishment of competing blocs in Africa, where the Casablanca group displayed willingness to play this role. At one time or another, Nkrumah, Sekou Touré, Keita, Nasser, the Algerian F.L.N., and even the King of Morocco, as well as Gizenga and Lumumba, were involved in such clandestine activities. This served the purpose not merely of obfuscating the full extent of Soviet initiatives, as far as Western eyes were concerned, but of enabling the Kremlin to continue walking an awkward political tightrope, whenever two of its African friends were using armed force against one another. For instance, the Soviet leaders, while flirting with the Gaullists (who were estranging France from its NATO allies), were also aiding the Algerian insurgency against France. In such a situation, the willingness of other Arab leaders in the Maghreb and Egypt to act as conduits for Soviet weapons to Algeria provided a neat solution. The F.L.N. knew who its benefactors were, but Paris found Soviet involvement far less obtrusive. Again, during the 1963 Algerian–Moroccan border war, Soviet material reached Algeria clandestinely (but, this time, not via Arab surrogates who, perhaps, could not be relied upon to maintain discretion vis-à-vis two fellow Arab regimes, but in Cuban vessels).

Significantly, the limitations of such subtleties were demonstrated more than a decade later, when Moscow found it impossible to support Ethiopia without "losing" Somalia.)

During the Nigerian Civil War, a new (combat) stage was reached in the utilization of regional surrogates, when the USSR permitted Egyptian pilots to fly Soviet planes with Egyptian or Nigerian markings in missions against Biafra. In this particular instance, the fact that Britain was supporting the same side openly may have emboldened the Soviet Union.

SOVIET SURROGATES IN COMBAT

Even during earlier stages, of course, Warsaw Pact personnel (including, from time to time, Soviet as well as East European officers) had been present in increasing numbers as military advisers, instructors, and maintenance crews. Inevitably, these experts had been caught up, on certain occasions, in armed conflict situations. Indeed, during Nkrumah's ouster from power, an East European Praetorian Guard had fought on his behalf at Flagstaff House.

In 1970, however, during the Egyptian–Israeli war of attrition over the Suez Canal, the USSR moved one significant step further by sending Soviet pilots to Egypt, who engaged eventually in combat, resulting in five MiG-21s being shot down with their Russian pilots by the Israelis.

This development may have had a sobering effect on the Soviet leadership. Moreover, perhaps equally importantly, the USSR, in an attempt to orchestrate the appropriate atmosphere at the height of the arms control negotiations, codified the "Basic Principles" with the United States on 29 May 1972, and subsequently, the 22 June 1973 agreement, stating that the parties undertook to "refrain from the threat or use of force against . . . the allies of the other party and against other countries." No doubt this induced the Kremlin to show a little more circumspection than in 1970. However, having lost a vast Soviet-produced arsenal in the 1967 and 1970 Middle Eastern conflicts, Moscow employed "other means" during the October 1973 War to safeguard its "investment." This took the form of the dispatch of North Korean pilots and North Vietnamese antiaircraft personnel to the battle areas; moreover, early in 1974, between the first and second Israeli–Syrian cease-fires, Cuban armored units were sent to aid the Syrians. Neither side, for very different reasons, chose to publicize this fact at the time. As far as the Soviet role during this period was concerned, it was "confined" to the massive sea and air lift to Syria and Egypt, at least officially. (Combat was left for non-Warsaw Pact units.)

The Cuban intervention in Angola (and the subsequent combat roles of the Cubans, East Germans, and others, in the Horn and on the other side of the Red Sea) constitutes a natural outgrowth, as it were, from these activities in 1973–74, during the Arab–Israeli conflict. Significantly, during the initial stages of the Cuban incursion in Angola, Havana was providing "its own" transportation; the Soviet Union became more overt subsequently about its logistics role in lift and resupply (not to mention increased defense activities in and over Cuba, to replace the "absent" Cuban combat elements).

"VANGUARD ACTIVITIES"—INTELLIGENCE AND PREPOSITIONING

Soviet "subsidiary" activities in support of surrogate combat personnel inevitably lay the groundwork for eventual direct Soviet intervention. Afghanistan, during its initial stages (like Prague in 1968), witnessed an almost classical "combined operation" of the Soviet Security Services and Airborne Divisions. The integration of G.R.U., K.G.B., D.G.I., Stasi and other "arms" in Africa and the Middle East provides one factor for such operations, with the Soviet lift of its surrogates providing the other. Moreover, the transfer of vast quantities of weapons during such ventures (as well as to Syria, Libya, etc.), means, in fact, the prepositioning in appropriate spots of the Soviet hardware (well in excess of the absorptive capacity of its clients) that would be situated ideally for use by Soviet airborne units. The latter could be transported at far greater speed if only personnel and sidearms needed to be flown in. This would appear to constitute the logical culmination of the gamut of activities that has been surveyed here.

Cuba and the USSR—A Marriage of Convenience?

EARLY CUBAN INVOLVEMENT IN AFRICA

Cuba's role in Africa is unlike that of any other Soviet surrogate to date.[1] Unlike East European states, Cuba is not subject to Soviet military occupation, as were Prague and Budapest. Nor is it a partitioned country involved in an ongoing conflict with its next door neighbor over national unification, thus requiring military aid from Moscow itself, as is the case with Pyongyang. Castro is not beholden to the Kremlin for his seizure of power and its extension by military conquest, as is Hanoi. Nevertheless, the Cubans have committed to

African ventures an armed presence of over 40,000 men, equivalent in population to an American force of over 850,000. These Cuban expeditionary units are dependent for combat upon intimate Soviet logistical support. This development is all the more remarkable inasmuch as not so very long ago, for instance in 1968, Soviet–Cuban relations were quite poor.

Serious Cuban military involvement in Africa began long before Havana decided to back Agostinho Neto's MPLA against two rival African groups, Holden Roberto's FNLA and Jonas Savimbi's UNITA.

Previous Cuban participation in African affairs was less prominent, and perhaps more sporadic, then at present—and generally less effective. Cuba first embarked upon military relations with African elements in 1961, when rebels from Zanzibar came to Cuba for paramilitary training.[2] Many of the "graduates" of the course subsequently participated in the successful January 1964 Zanzibar coup.[3] During the early 1960s, similar training was given in Cuba to Cameroonian and Senegalese revolutionaries.[4] Meanwhile, the Soviet Union was engaged in a somewhat frustrating campaign to win the allegiance of key African leaders already in power, such as Ghana's Kwame Nkrumah, Mali's Modibo Keita, and Guinea's Sekou Touré.[5] These Soviet efforts paid only limited dividends during the years that followed: Nkrumah was overthrown in 1966 and Keita in 1968, while Sekou Touré had expelled the Soviet ambassador by December of 1961.[6] Of course, Moscow's most conspicuous (short-term) failure occurred in the Congo (Zaire), where Lumumba was toppled in 1960. Nor was the Soviet-supported Gizenga regime in Stanleyville successful. However, Cuba was developing a close working relationship with Guinea during the 1960s, when Conakry was used as a contact spot and control point for African trainees taking courses in guerrilla tactics in Cuba.[7]

Thus, over a decade ago, Moscow found "Third World" Cubans more successful than overtly Soviet elements (the former proving clearly more acceptable to African sensitivities). Castro, himself very light-skinned, has referred on many occasions to Cuba's Latin *and African* roots,[8] an emphasis that presumably is intended to help legitimize his regime's African ventures. Reportedly a disproportionate number of Cuban soldiers in Africa are dark-skinned.[9]

In 1966, Sekou Touré invited Che Guevara to assist in establishing and training an elite corps to serve as the Guinean leader's Praetorian Guard.[10] Apparently at the behest of PAIGC leader A. Cabral, Guevara recently had led a Cuban mission to Brazzaville to help defeat a pro-Western regime in Leopoldville.

CUBAN–SOVIET TENSIONS

It was during this period also that Cuban–Soviet relations began to show signs of apparent strain. As Cuba became more closely involved in sub-Saharan African affairs, the Soviet Union was suffering some setbacks in relations with Havana and the non-Arab portions of Africa.

Cuba's role in the international communist movement at that juncture was fairly neutral, with Havana aligning itself clearly neither with Peking nor Moscow, but adopting a policy most readily identifiable with the tone of the January 1966 Tricontinental Conference. At that gathering, the North Vietnamese, North Koreans, and Cubans demanded support for revolutionary endeavors in the Third World.[11] A prominent spokesman at the Tricontinental Conference was Amilcar Cabral, the leader of PAIGC.[12] The Castro line with respect to Latin America (in implicit contrast to the Soviet line) was clearly stated:

> If . . . it is understood once and for all that sooner or later all or almost all peoples will have to take up arms to liberate themselves, then the hour of liberation for this continent will be advanced. What with the ones who theorize, and the ones who criticize those who theorize while beginning to theorize themselves, much energy and time is unfortunately lost; we believe that on this continent, in this case of all or almost all peoples, the battle will take on the most violent forms.[13]

The Cubans felt that the Soviet Union had indicated weakness in the 1962 Missile Crisis and demonstrated insufficient resolve during the conflict in the Dominican Republic and in Vietnam (so, for that matter, had China); thus, the best course for community leaders to adopt, according to Havana, was the sponsorship of a series of armed insurrections and incursions ("many Vietnams," as Guevara put it),[14] which would divert the United States from Vietnam and limit American efficiency by dissipating U.S. power all over the globe. Cuban moves in Africa, the resolutions of the Tricontinental Conference and the Guevara mission to Bolivia were consistent with this policy.

In 1967, Castro indicated that Cuba would act independently of the Moscow-led portion of the world communist movement in dealings with Latin American revolutionaries.[15] The issue distinguishing the position adopted by the Tricontinental Conference from the attitude of the Soviet leadership was the role of revolutionary guerrilla movements in the Third World. The Castro–Che Guevara position amounted to support for revolutionary movements (at least in Latin America) whereas the Soviet Union (and communist parties loyal to it) accommodated noncommunist Third World regimes, particularly those more friendly to the USSR than to the West or China. In some cases, local regimes were supported at the price of eliminating the indigenous communist parties; for example, in 1965, Moscow sacrificed the Egyptian Communist Party to curry favor with the Nasser regime.[16]

In 1964, at the so-called Havana Conference, it appeared that this issue had been settled by means of a comprehensive formulation, whereby the Russians supported selected guerrilla groups and the Cubans supported the mainline Muscovite communist parties (rather than pro-Chinese and other "schismatic" groups). At the time, this compromise infuriated the Chinese leadership and drove a wedge between them and Castro. Soon afterward, the Cubans deviated from the Havana compromise, much to Moscow's chagrin. A focus for new Russo–Cuban disagreements was Venezuela, where the Cubans, in a policy strongly identified with Che Guevara personally, backed the revolutionary FALN, and the Muscovite Venezuelan Communist Party assumed a quiescent role.[17] At that point, the Cubans could have made a major shift and committed themselves to the Chinese side in the Sino–Soviet rift, particularly because Cuban ideological positions, both in domestic and foreign policy (heavily influenced by Guevara), were not dissimilar to Maoism. However, Havana, probably repelled by the internal turmoil in China and aware of the limits of possible military or economic assistance from Peking, decided to remain neutral.

Following the 1966 Conference, Cuba became a main supporter of the PAIGC, operating out of Conakry and Senegal.[18] The Soviet predominance in operations and supply (dating back to 1964) was replaced by a significant Cuban presence, after Amilcar Cabral issued a request for Cuban aid at the Tricontinental Conference.[19] A few Cubans were even killed in skirmishes in Portuguese Guinea.[20]

Cabral had developed a close relationship with Sekou Touré in Guinea, and was an old friend of Neto in Angola and a founding member of the MPLA. In 1965, a Cuban mission that was to train the MPLA had been dispatched to Brazzaville. Subsequently, a Guevara-trained unit of 700 Cubans helped to suppress an attempted coup there. Only after President Massamba-Debat was deposed in the fall of 1968 were the Cubans evicted from the Congo.[21]

The divergence between the Kremlin and Cuba, although primarily over Latin American issues, possibly was exacerbated by Cuba's close relations with Sekou Touré and with the PAIGC, when

Moscow was not yet fully *persona grata* with either. For several years these African recipients accepted Soviet military aid, much of it "laundered" through Czechoslovakia, but preferred Cuban personnel (especially from 1966 onward). Because Cuba had its problems with Moscow at the time, the Cuban presence in Africa may have been a mixed blessing for the Kremlin. African participants in the struggle over the Portuguese colonies were being trained in various portions of the communist world, including the USSR, the German Democratic Republic, Czechoslovakia, Yugoslavia, and Cuba.[22] However, these Africans apparently felt strongest identification with Cuba. Members of the PAIGC even wore Cuban military jackets and hats.[23] Perhaps it was during this period that Moscow began to realize the potential advantages of a rapprochement with Cuba that would enable the Kremlin to operate through a willing Cuban surrogate in Africa.

At the August 1967 meeting of the Latin American Solidarity Organization, Castro pushed through a resolution condemning Soviet policy in Latin America as a betrayal of Latin American revolutionary movements. Although this document was not published officially, it leaked out almost immediately.[24] A serious confrontation seemed to be brewing.

Early in 1968, Cuban–Soviet relations reached their nadir. The bloody termination of Guevara's Bolivian venture in October 1967 (simultaneously provocative and ineffective) jeopardized Soviet relations with Latin American states, undermined Latin American communist parties, and even could have led to a military confrontation with the United States in an arena hardly of Russia's choosing. Furious with Havana, the USSR severely cut back oil supplies to Cuba.[25] This was followed by the revelation, early in 1968, of an alleged Soviet plot to depose Castro.

It is possible that Castro was exploiting Soviet–Cuban difficulties as a pretext for eliminating a rival, the (Muscovite) faction led by Anibal Escalante.[26] Certainly, that group otherwise would have been strengthened by the manner of Guevara's death, which vindicated previous Soviet assertions to the effect that Cuba's policies constituted adventurism (a very pejorative term in the Marxist vocabulary). In that sense, Escalante's purge probably was a sign of Castro's anxiety concerning his own position. He had not been undermined to the extent that Escalante could remove him, but the continued existence of the Muscovite faction was beginning to pose a distinct threat. Given Cuba's economic disorders, Castro could hardly afford strong adversaries in Havana. An extended oil embargo could have destroyed what remained of the Cuban economy.[27]

In exchange for an increase in oil and other economic concessions, the USSR demanded several major conditions. Included among these were complete endorsement of Soviet policies, the subservience of the Cuban intelligence network (the DGI) to the KGB, and the acceptance of 5,000 Soviet specialists to supervise the Cuban economy. Presumably, the functions of this group also were to include surveillance of Castro to ensure that he behaved himself. Thus the Cuban shift back to intimacy with the USSR was hardly voluntary, if this analysis is correct.

CUBAN-SOVIET RAPPROCHEMENT

The death of Che Guevara in 1967 may well have pointed out the futility of limited Cuban actions on behalf of revolutionary forces unsupported by the USSR. In 1968, the Soviet Union demonstrated a toughening of its foreign policy with the invasion of Czechoslovakia. Unlike Peking (which voiced support for the Czechoslovak people),[28] Havana supported the invasion. Castro emphasized that Warsaw Pact aid would be expected for Vietnam or Cuba too, if their revolutions were endangered, as Czechoslovakia was alleged to be (by "German-American collusion").[29]

The rape of Prague appears to have signaled a turning point in Cuban-Soviet relations. It is unclear whether support for the invasion was an indicator of a new Cuban policy or if the invasion helped bring about such a new policy by holding out the possibility that a more activist Soviet regime might give greater support to Cuban activism. Nevertheless, the invasion did coincide with indications that the Soviet-Cuban rift had begun to mend.

The Soviet oil embargo against Cuba must have had even greater effect than these foreign policy considerations. Apparently, the USSR had become sufficiently concerned over Cuban ideological revisionism, specifically with the provocative Guevara mission to Bolivia, to confront Havana both with the carrot of renewed Soviet activism, and the stick of Soviet restrictions on oil exports to Cuba. At the same time, the USSR began to replace some of Cuba's obsolete military equipment, after a three-year hiatus in shipments.[30]

In July of 1969, the first major Soviet naval visit to Cuba in many years took place.[31] Subsequently, such visits were institutionalized, as have been Tu-95 (Bear) reconnaissance flights from Cuba over the Caribbean[32] and the South Atlantic (in the latter case, in conjunction with flights from the USSR and Conakry).[33]

Since then, not only has Cuba cooperated closely with the USSR in Africa, the Caribbean, and the Middle East, but it has become one of the major proponents of the Soviet regime's domination of Eastern Europe. An interesting sample of Castro's ideological perspective was presented during an extended interview with Barbara Walters in 1977. He described Czechoslovakia under the Soviet subjugation as having "very close relations in the economic, political and ideological fields" with the USSR but nevertheless still being "totally independent." Although these points had been reiterated frequently by Castro in addresses to his own domestic audience, the Walters interview is significant in that there were potential gains to be made from disinforming the American viewers with regard to Cuba's military, political, economic, and ideological links to the USSR. Nevertheless, he was extremely frank, almost defiant during the interview, in asserting the strength of these ties.

Asked whether Russia was a free country, he replied, "I think it is the freest of all countries" (presumably freer than Cuba too). He condemned Solzhenitsyn as "a mediocre writer [whom] the West converted into an international hero."[34]

Of greater significance was his reaffirmation of the Cuban foreign policy line of recent years regarding the PRC, which he asserted "is carrying out a foreign policy that betrays the international revolutionary movement."[35]

In addition to backing the Soviet Union against the Chinese "revisionists" on the "left," Castro also has implicitly supported the USSR against the "Eurocommunists" on the "right." Frequently Cuban officials have referred to the importance of operating according to the dictates of "proletarian internationalism."[36] Use of this term, identified with the Soviet invasion of Czechoslovakia and the "Brezhnev Doctrine," is anathema to the Eurocommunists. Apparently, the latter made omission of this phrase a major condition for signing the communique summing up the June 1976 East Berlin meeting of European Communist Parties.[37]

1968–70 might be termed a transitional period in Soviet–Cuban relations. In 1968 Castro came out strongly in favor of the USSR over the invasion of Czechoslovakia and in 1969 the Soviet Navy initiated deployment in the Caribbean, paying a port call to the Cienfuegos naval base.[38] In spring of 1970, Soviet naval air was allowed to refuel in Cuba for the first time; by 1972, it was allowed to fly regular reconnaissance missions from the island.[39] Most important, Soviet materials for construction of a submarine base in Cienfuegos were delivered in September of 1970.[40] Perhaps not entirely coincidentally, Cuba's friend in Guinea, Sekou Touré, began to allow Soviet naval visits in February 1969, culminating in the December 1970 Conakry patrol, granted to the Soviet Union after a Portuguese-inspired coup almost eliminated the Guinean leader.[41]

Although the Soviet Union appeared to be making gains with respect to Castro, and apparently in relations with his friends or clients in West Africa, Castro still seems to have been trying to avoid an irrevocable commitment to the USSR. He continued the radical attempt, initiated in 1966, to collectivize agriculture, centralize the economy, eliminate material incentives, and even phase out the use of money, all to be accomplished in a brief period of time.[42] This Cuban version of the Great Leap Forward was likely to prove anathema to the Russians, who had just been through an ideological confrontation with Peking over the issue of whose system would lead to world communism first. As was the case with the left wing Maoist–Trotskyite Cuban foreign policy of the early and middle 1960s, this economic plan was inspired by Che Guevara and opposed by the pro-Soviet faction.[43]

By the second half of the 1970s, Castro's unqualified support for Soviet foreign policy, as expressed in the Walters interview, and in the Cuban media, hardly indicates that Soviet–Cuban policies in Africa, or elsewhere, still diverged significantly. Whether the Cubans or the Soviet Union initiated the strategy of surrogate operations is academic, because it serves the purposes of both parties. However, North Korea and North Vietnamese (and Soviet) personnel were used in the Middle East before Cuba's participation there and elsewhere, so a logical inference would be that Moscow originated the concept.[44] Moreover, the subsequent use of East Germans and other Warsaw Pact participants (who certainly cannot be viewed as independent parties) in Africa and the Middle East, to the advantage of the USSR, imply the same conclusion.

It is unclear whether Havana's favorable reaction to the Soviet invasion of Czechoslovakia was merely an indicator of a new Cuban policy with regard to Moscow or actually was a factor in changing Castro's previous approach.

By 1970, other factors came to the fore. The economic situation in Cuba, almost totally reliant on the vicissitudes of the world market for sugar, was in very poor shape after the 1970 "Great Sugar Harvest" failed to yield desired results (falling short by 15 percent).[45] Apparently labor morale was low, as indicated by a high rate of absenteeism. The situation was serious enough to merit a public *mea culpa* by Castro and a cataloging of the failures of the radical phase in Cuban economics.[46]

During the next eight years the Soviet Union was to assume the burden of carrying Cuba's financial debt (to the tune of over $5 billion),[47] while subsidizing Cuban sugar at several times the market price. Havana's failure to propel Cuba into economic self-sufficiency left the state with little choice but to adopt a traditional "path to socialism." The concomitant to this acknowledgement was complete economic dependence on the USSR. After the bold assertions of upcoming economic accomplishments during the early- and mid-1960s, Castro may have felt it necessary to assert Cuba's machismo in the international arena to galvanize the state and restore his own credibility. After the Bolivian episode, a further move in Latin America was hardly feasible; moreover, operations in Africa could meet both Cuban and Soviet needs. There, the United States would be less likely to react with a military confrontation than in a Latin American venture, and the Soviet Union could more easily assist the Cubans, particularly logistically.

Finally, the emergence in 1970 of Allende's government in Chile probably indicated to Castro that the Soviet line on Latin American "national liberation" was more likely to prevail on that continent. The fall of Allende in 1973 may have warned Castro of the precarious nature of any communist government in the Western Hemisphere (including his own) and thus reemphasized his need for greater intimacy with the Soviet Union. To guarantee Cuba's economic, and perhaps military, viability and to insure implementation of his definition of the "Brezhnev Doctrine," Castro would have to cooperate, and even collaborate closely, with the USSR.[48] To a considerable degree, of course, the outcome of the Chilean episode constituted an ex post facto vindication of the Guevara line; however, by 1973, Castro had already committed himself to the USSR, not only in terms of trade, but also ideologically. Having shifted away from a radical position, he could hardly swing back again so soon and still maintain his personal credibility.

ECONOMIC FACTORS

There is no question that, in the short run, the policy of cooperation with the USSR has benefitted the Cuban economy (although part of the problem had been caused by the Soviet oil cutback in the first place). According to one report, the USSR was paying 400 percent of world market price and buying one-half of the Cuban sugar harvest in 1976, when the world price plummeted; moreover, it was supplying Cuba with all of its oil at considerably less than world prices.[49] The USSR is buying Cuban nickel at greater than world market prices and is helping Cuba to develop its infrastructure (particularly in the Holguin area of Oriente province). However, in the long term, the Cubans may regret these practices. They are due to begin repayments in 1986, by which time they may be locked into a position of total dependence on COMECON.[50]

A good index of the change in Soviet policy toward Cuba since

1968 is the amount of oil that the USSR has been shipping to that country. Between 1966 and 1968, Soviet shipments increased from 5.1 to 5.3 million tons (m.t.) per annum, a modest increase of less than 4 percent. During the same period, Moscow increased its global oil exports from 73.6 to 86.2 million tons, over 17 percent. However, after 1968 (when Castro supported Moscow on the invasion of Czechoslovakia and the "Brezhnev Doctrine"), the situation changed dramatically. In 1969, Soviet oil shipments to Cuba increased about 9 percent, while Soviet global exports went up only 5 percent. Between 1968 and 1974, Soviet shipments to Cuba increased over 43 percent, whereas worldwide exports rose less than 35 percent. Clearly 1968 was a pivotal year in Cuban–Soviet oil relations.[51]

CUBAN INCENTIVES

The 1970s found Cuba in need of economic assistance and, perhaps, of an opportunity to reassert the Castro regime's virility. In Latin America, however, Castro stood in danger of encountering both U.S. and Soviet opposition. In Africa, the Soviet Union was seeking new points of entry without fearing a confrontation with America. Consequently, the Cuban venture in Africa, starting with Angola, constituted the natural confluence and culmination of three factors:

1. Cuban ideological predilections, as embodied in long-term policies toward Africa and Latin America;
2. Castro's need to bolster the regime's (and his own) fading image and, perhaps, the morale of the people, a decade after the revolution. After the failures of Guevara's adventures and Castro's equivalent of the Great Leap Forward, Castro could not afford another blunder. A spectacular showing abroad would bolster his image, both in Havana and in the international arena;
3. The phenomenon of increased Soviet–Cuban cooperation based on complementary needs and capabilities. Havana did not need to win a conflict in Latin America so much as a Cuban victory *somewhere*,[52] in the name of a cause compatible with the regime's ideology, such as "proletarian internationalism." The Russians needed a new entry into non-Arab Africa, as well as something concrete to offer prospective African leaders. However, Moscow had good reasons for wishing to avoid direct embroilment.

Advantages to the USSR of Use of Surrogate Forces in Africa and the Middle East

CUBAN PLUSES

It is doubtful that news of a Soviet victory over "imperialist forces" in Angola or elsewhere would accomplish much in the way of bolstering the image of Soviet leadership, or legitimizing Soviet arbitrary rule domestically. A smaller state might be able to assert itself in Africa, and even claim major victory, without appearing to be a bully boy.

A Soviet force is likely to have a far more abrasive effect upon Angolans and other Africans than, for example, Cubans, many of whom are at least partly of African ancestry. Soviet emissaries have a long history of haughty, aloof, even arrogant behavior. One observer has quoted an Angolan official to the effect that

> the Soviets . . . usually demand rooms in the best hotels or well-furnished houses with air conditioning and new stoves and refrigerators, which cost us a lot of our precious foreign exchange, whereas we can put five or six Cubans in a hot one-bedroom apartment with mattresses on the floor and we will never hear a complaint.[53]

After Che Guevara was killed in Bolivia, and the failure of the much-vaunted 1970 sugar harvest to attain predicted levels, Castro may have believed a display of machismo was necessary. With the condemnation of the Soviet invasion of Czechoslovakia by the French, Italian, and Yugoslav Communist parties (although Cuba endorsed the move), Moscow may not have been too eager to be seen sending Soviet expeditionary forces overseas. Furthermore, Soviet troops were reported to be demoralized when they encountered hostility from the Czechoslovak people whose "socialist system" they were supposed to be "saving," an additional disincentive to direct use of the Red Army abroad.

Before the 1976 East Berlin Conference of European Communist Parties, the USSR went to great lengths to include the recalcitrant PCI, PCE, and League of Communists of Yugoslavia, probably to create a unified front to the Chinese Communist Party.[54] Thus, the Russians were unlikely to go out of their way to provoke further controversies with these parties, particularly if Moscow could achieve its objectives without incurring additional problems.

In its guise as a "Cuban" operation, the Angolan incursion received Tito's support, to the point of allowing Soviet arms shipments bound for the Cubans in Angola to overfly Yugoslavia;[55]

the Italian Communist Party also gave explicit and even enthusiastic support to the Cubans and refrained from adverse comment on the Soviet logistical role in the venture.[56]

It is questionable whether the "Eurocommunists" would have been quite as supportive if Soviet rather than Cuban forces had to shoulder the bulk of the fighting in Africa. Admittedly, if Moscow were to regard a particular action as essential, the feelings of the Italians or the PCE would be given short shrift. However, *direct* Soviet intervention was *not* essential in Africa. Moreover, it is doubtful whether a Soviet overseas expedition to a primitive tropical region could be carried out without adverse effect upon the morale of Soviet fighting men (and, eventually, their dependents back home). Were the operation to bog down, the result most likely would be a disastrous decline, both in the regime's credibility and in the image of the Red Army. Thus, although Castro had little to lose from an African encounter, the Soviet Union had little to gain from direct participation in combat. Consequently, backing the Cubans held the prospect of reaping the strategic benefits of Havana's new foothold in Africa—if all went well.

In the event that the campaign proceeded less than smoothly, the Soviet leadership would not incur much of the blame; after all, inexperienced Cubans were claiming to be operating on their own accord. Moreover, joint ventures, based on Soviet logistical support, would provide an opportunity to solidify the rapprochement with Cuba that had developed after the Soviet invasion of Czechoslovakia. The Cuban intelligence network apparently is subservient to the Soviet apparatus, so presumably the Cuban presence (as well as a sprinkling of Soviet and East European elements) would net the KGB some extremely useful contacts.[57] A key Soviet consideration is probably that Cuban involvement was far less likely than direct Russian involvement, in terms of jeopardizing Moscow's ability to maintain detente in a form palatable to the United States.

THE U.S. FACTOR

If the Soviet Union were to become an overt actor in an armed overseas venture, a legal problem is the 22 June 1973 *Agreement Between the United States of America and the Union of Soviet Socialist Republics on the Prevention of Nuclear War*, which states that "the *parties* [the two signatory states] agree . . . that each party will refrain from the threat or use of force against . . . the allies of the other party and against other countries in circumstances which may endanger international peace and security."[58] This codified the "Basic Principles" endorsed by the two superpowers, acting on behalf of the two opposing blocs, on May 29, 1972, during the Moscow Summit.[59] (These "Principles" committed the parties to refrain from exploiting crisis situations, particularly in the Third World, for unilateral gains.)

Presumably the Soviet Union embarked upon the detente process believing it had something to gain from agreements on such topics as SALT. Certainly one way of jeopardizing negotiations was blatant violation of this understanding. Not only would that strengthen the influence of important circles in the West that already harbored deep suspicions of Soviet intentions, but it was bound to deprive the Western arms control lobby of its political ammunition.[60] After all, it would be hard to argue that the Soviet Union was negotiating in good faith in SALT if it were simultaneously violating the two protocols governing the general behavior of the two powers.

MIDDLE EAST PRECEDENTS

Some analysts have argued that the Soviet Union violated both the letter and the spirit of these agreements with the more covert aspects of its conduct during the period leading up to and including the October 1973 War in the Middle East, well beyond the first ceasefire.[61] When these analyses appeared, the full extent of the use of proxy forces on the side of the Arab states during this period was not widely known. It now appears that the USSR resorted to surrogates to a really significant extent during 1973–74. Although the Vietnam conflict was still in full tilt, North Vietnamese personnel reportedly were brought in to defend Syrian air space over Damascus and North Korean pilots to fly over Egypt (ultimately to engage Israeli planes in that sector).[62]

Cubans, North Koreans, and North Vietnamese, of course, do not represent members of the Warsaw Pact. East Germans, however, have been active but not as combat troops. Resort to non-Warsaw Pact elements, as viewed in Moscow, presumably would implicate the Soviet Union far less than active combat participation of forces from countries formally allied with the USSR and, in most cases, occupied by Red Army units and subordinated to Soviet military command.[63]

Four months before the outbreak of the 1973 war, Brezhnev is alleged to have requested direct Cuban military participation (particularly of armored units) in the forthcoming conflict. If this *Foreign Report* account is correct, the request took place approximately one month after the 23 June 1973 Washington accord was signed; in that case, the USSR apparently initiated resort to proxies when the agreement was still brand new and was bound to be taken into consideration in planning Soviet foreign policy. (It may be that the Cubans were intended only for special situations, as they had not yet arrived when the October War started or when the first ceasefire, on October 22, finally stopped Israeli forces a few miles from Damascus.

During the next few weeks, in a hectic campaign of reconstruction of the wrecked Syrian military machine (entirely at Soviet expense), additional North Vietnamese (pilots) were reportedly brought in and Soviet and East German engineers and officers rebuilt the Syrian artillery and antiair defenses. Two full Cuban armored brigades reportedly were airlifted from Cuba (by Cubana Aviación airliners normally used for commercial flights); the Cubans themselves unloaded tanks, trained Syrian tank corpsmen, and used the opportunity to learn new combat methods (derived from the lessons of the October War) from Soviet and East German officers.[64] During this period, members of Palestinian Arab paramilitary units, who had been (and continue to be) trained in Cuba, served as interpreters.[65]

Soon after Israel and Egypt signed a "disengagement agreement" on 18 January 1974, Cuban forces reportedly joined a Syrian armored division on Mt. Hermon. Tanks at the front carried mixed Cuban–Syrian crews (usually Syrian signalmen and drivers and Cuban commanders and gunners—apparently a precursor to the identical allocation of duties between Cubans and Ethiopians in the Ogaden). Early in the morning of 4 February 1974, the Cuban–Syrian tank forces, in conjunction with a barrage from artillery units (reportedly commanded by East German and Russian officers), began firing on Israeli forces. Thus started the "War of Attrition" on the Golan Heights (which was to last until the May 31, 1974, Syrian–Israeli "Disengagement Agreement"). Seven hours after the Cuban–Syrian offensive of 4 February started, the Israelis counterattacked. According to available reports, during the next few hours eighteen "Syrian" tanks were destroyed.

The United States, along with Israel, apparently kept secret the reports that the Israeli Army was engaged in combat with more than just Syrian forces.[66] It remains a major question whether, or to what extent, U.S. reaction might have been different had there been *Soviet* troops in the Syrian tanks.

Significant airlifts of Cuban forces reportedly were observed during late February and early March, precipitating a partial Israeli mobilization of reserves and shift of tanks to the Golan front, commanded by General Rafael Eytan. According to one unconfirmed account, during the February–May 1974 "War of Attrition," the Cubans suffered casualties of approximately 180 killed and 250 wounded, whereas the Israelis lost 68 dead and 178 wounded. If so, contrary to popular belief, the Cubans as early as 1974 had confronted a mechanized "enemy" army in combat (in addition to a subsequent brief encounter with South African forces in Angola). Apparently, Havana's forces did not conduct themselves as well as they might have hoped. Once they were withdrawn from the front, Cuban forces reportedly spent considerable time with Soviet officers (who had observed in detail the course of the February–May conflict), discussing the mistakes of the "War of Attrition" and, (in conjunction with Syrian forces) engaging in exercises based on the lessons of the fight.[67]

AFRICAN FOLLOW-UP

One night early in the spring of 1975, Cubana Aviación planes apparently were put to work again, this time ferrying Cuban soldiers from Syria to Angola. Subsequently, some Cuban officers were reported once again to be involved in the Middle East, this time aiding Palestinian Arab elements against Syrian army units in Lebanon, during that country's "civil war."[68] (It remains unclear to what extent this action meshed with Soviet policy.)

Having noted that the United States seemed willing to tolerate Cuban activities in the Middle East so soon after the 22 June 1973 agreement, Moscow must have been tempted to foster Cuban participation in combat on a grander scale (if in a less prominent environment). Consequently, the Cubans drastically augmented their previously very limited presence in Angola. Then, emboldened by success, Cuba felt free to intervene in Ethiopia in fairly large numbers where the Soviet Union's precarious balancing act between Somalia and Ethiopia proved no longer tenable in 1977–78.

A Somali Minister confided to Arnaud de Borchgrave that in 1973, five years before the Cuban expeditionary force's arrival to join the Ethiopian army in the drive against the Somali military effort to "liberate" the Ogaden, Castro had offered Somali President Muhammed Siad Barre the use of Cuban troops to help pluck the Ogaden from Ethiopia.[69] (At that time, of course, Soviet–Somali relations had been fairly intimate.)

Possible Costs to the USSR of Surrogate Operations, and Other Soviet Considerations

In the *Polemic on the General Line of the International Communist Movement*, published by Peking in 1965 to air its grievances, two of the key complaints pertained to Russian willingness to "fight to the last Chinese soldier" in Korea and to Soviet reluctance to extend a protective shield over China so that a "War of National Liberation" could be launched against Taiwan. Peking referred in the same breath to "The Korean War against the U.S. aggression in which we fought side by side with the Korean comrades and our struggle against the United States in the Taiwan Straits." (In this context, Korea could be analogized to Angola, and Taiwan to Venezuela or Bolivia.) The Chinese described their role in Korea essentially as surrogates for the USSR: "We ourselves preferred to shoulder the heavy sacrifices necessary and stood in the first line of defense of the Socialist Camp so that the Soviet Union might stay in the second line."[70]

Of course, analogies may be taken too far. It is not clear to what degree the Chinese entered the Korean conflict with genuine hope that the Kremlin would assist the PLA in a Taiwan "liberation" campaign. It would be overstating the case to define the PRC's relationship to the USSR during the early 1950s as that of a mere proxy, but the Chinese probably believed that Moscow's perception of Peking was precisely that. Russia's failure to back the Chinese adequately (as far as Peking was concerned) *followed* China's Korean sacrifices, whereas Havana's unsuccessful Bolivia venture *preceded* Cuba's surrogate role in Africa. However, should Castro, emboldened by African successes, insist on Soviet participation in future Latin American ventures in payment for favors rendered, Moscow might find itself in something of a quandary. Precisely for the reasons that render support for surrogate forces preferable to direct Soviet intervention, the Politburo might consider major Soviet operations in the Western Hemisphere too risky. Moreover, even providing Soviet logistical infrastructures for such ventures in this portion of the world would be regarded by the Kremlin as a dubious proposition because of the same considerations that have kept the USSR from probing too deeply into Latin America since 1962. Moscow well remembers U.S. reactions to the Guatemalan affair in 1952 and to the disorders in the Dominican Republic in 1965, not to mention the Cuban Missile Crisis itself and perhaps the fall of Allende. Moreover, the Kremlin does not wish to jeopardize other Soviet interests in such matters as SALT or M(B)FR.

The USSR cannot very well discourage Castro from glorifying his African successes to justify the cost in Cuban blood. However, Moscow also cannot afford to let Havana develop unrealistic perceptions either of its own military capabilities or of its political role.

One error committed by the Soviet Union in connection with the role of the Chinese forces in Korea was compelling Peking to reimburse Moscow for the weapons that the USSR sent to the Korean front. While the Chinese were shedding their blood on the Korean battlefield, the Soviet Union was war-profiteering at Peking's expense, as the *Polemic* pointed out so bitterly:

> As for the Soviet loans to China, it must be pointed out that China used them mostly for the purchase of war materiel from the Soviet Union, the greater part of which was used against U.S. aggression. The Chinese people . . . made great sacrifices and incurred vast military expenses. The Chinese Communist party has always considered that this was the Chinese people's . . . internationalist duty and that it is nothing to boast of. For many years we have been paying the principal and interest on these Soviet loans, which account for a considerable part of our yearly exports to the Soviet Union. Thus, even the war materiel supplied to China in the war to resist U.S. aggression and aid Korea, has not been given gratis.[71]

Apparently, this practice engendered no little resentment in Peking.

It is not clear whether the USSR has learned a lesson from its experiences with the PRC or has realized merely that Cuba could not conduct a successful African campaign without the Soviet Union supplying weapons and "lift" at its own expense. Regardless of the motivation for Soviet behavior, Cuba's expeditionary force has been the beneficiary of the aftermath of the Korean episode and no cause seems to have been given, at least so far, for recriminations against Moscow on Cuba's part.

Cuba's response to the invasion of Czechoslovakia was to support the doctrine of "proletarian internationalism" and to insist that Moscow should apply this "Brezhnev Doctrine" also in the event that the West attempts to undermine other existing communist regimes:[72]

> The statement by TASS explaining the decision of the governments of the Warsaw Pact says in its final paragraph: The brother nations firmly believe and resolutely oppose their unbreakable solidarity against any threat from abroad. They will never permit anyone to snatch away even a single link of the socialist community. We ask: Does this statement include Vietnam? Does this statement include Korea? Does this statement include Cuba? Does it consider Vietnam, Korea, and Cuba as links in the socialist camp that cannot be snatched away by the imperialists?

On the basis of this declaration, Warsaw Pact divisions were sent to Czechoslovakia, and we ask: Will Warsaw Pact divisions be sent to Vietnam also if the imperialists increase their aggression against the country and the people of Vietnam ask for this aid? Will Warsaw Pact divisions be sent to the Korean Democratic Republic if the Yankee imperialists attack that country? *Will Warsaw Pact divisions be sent to Cuba if, in the face of the threat of an attack by the Yankee imperialists, our country requests it?* (Emphasis added.)

This constituted an overt attempt to push the Soviet Union into an even tougher position with regard to the West. Similarly, at one stage, the PRC tried to prod Moscow to extend its nuclear shield to cover the Chinese in a confrontation with the United States in the Taiwan Straits. The PRC referred to the Communist bloc "headed by the USSR," and to the Soviet Union already "building communism," to point out both the obligation and the capability of the USSR to assert its power in support of the interests of other communist regimes.[73]

Liberal Cuban use of the term "proletarian internationalism," although supporting the Russian stand in the dispute with the Eurocommunists, could prove troublesome to Moscow if Havana attempted to apply it in an area outside of Moscow's choosing.

Regardless of whether Havana feels that it has earned rewards for its performance in Africa and the Middle East, Castro probably has little flexibility left to act independently of the Soviet Union, in view of the enormous economic debt Havana owes Moscow, Cuba's dependence on the USSR for arms[74] and raw materials and, particularly, the Soviet subsidization of the Cuban economy, and the integration of Cuba into CMEA.[75] Thus, Castro may find himself very disgruntled from time to time but with no alternative to Soviet dominance.

There has been some question as to the feasibility of the Soviet Union "turning off" the Cuban military machine now that it has been activated. For example, the Shaba incursion of 1978, resulting in massacres of civilians and the consequent entry of West European protective forces, probably distressed the Soviet leaders, who like conveying an aura of vast power and forward thrust, but not necessarily of open brutality; even less can Moscow wish to activate a Western response-mechanism through bloody incidents in Africa. Presumably, one of the Soviet reasons for using proxies is to make it awkward for the West to react on the ground, because it might seem humiliating for a developed state to have to fight with Cubans and

Africans. The political difficulties engendered by American involvement in Vietnam bear witness to that aspect.

An instance when such considerations might not apply would be a prima facie case of humanitarian assistance in the wake of the slaughter of women, children, and clergy, as occurred in the copper-rich Shaba province of Zaire, where the French felt compelled to intervene, purportedly on humanitarian grounds. Even this episode, however, did not necessarily lead to an unequivocal Soviet setback. Tanzania's Julius Nyerere, an influential African statesman not traditionally viewed as pro-Soviet, condemned the French and Belgian reaction, but did not comment on the invading forces who provoked the European response.[76] His statement, and the lack of O.A.U. consensus on the issue, minimized the damage suffered by Soviet and Cuban interests. Although the degree of Cuban involvement in the Shaba incursions has not been fully established,[77] Moscow is unlikely to have been entirely delighted at the way events unfolded there. It is unlikely that the Cubans would have assumed any major commitments in Africa without assurance of Soviet support. But that does not necessarily mean Soviet day-by-day supervision of tactical developments under battlefield conditions.

The Soviet Politburo initially may have viewed its rapprochement with Cuba not so much in terms of surrogate warfare in Africa, but rather in the context of Moscow's political/ideological struggle with China. It must be remembered that the major clashes with China along the Amur-Ussuri occurred soon after the invasion of Czechoslovakia,[78] at a point when Moscow probably was as isolated in the communist world as it had ever been.[79] At the June 1969 Moscow Conference of Communist Parties, Yugoslavia, Albania, China, North Korea, and North Vietnam were among the absentees. Cuba cagily sent only an observer delegation.[80] The message was clear—Castro is willing to back Brezhnev (as demonstrated by Cuba's general support for the invasion of Czechoslovakia), but, in return for full Cuban loyalty, the USSR must pay a price.

Although this line mirrored the P.R.C.'s in the late 1950s and early 1960s, there was a fundamental difference. As indicated by the famous episode in March 1953 of the "doctored" photograph of Mao and Malenkov in *Pravda*, once Stalin died Mao was regarded as the senior personality in the international Communist movement. Malenkov thought, presumably, that Mao was a potential kingmaker even within the USSR. Castro has never achieved comparable stature. Moreover, by virtue of its size and population, the P.R.C. commands more respect and poses a greater challenge to Soviet "hegemonism" than Cuba. During the late 1960s, Castro's policy, both domestically and in foreign affairs, had an extremely left-wing tinge, perhaps comparable to Chinese excesses in the late 1950s.

A rather backward state with a population of 9½ million, dependent economically on one or two commodities, cannot be genuinely autonomous unless it is willing to pay the extremely high social costs inherent in such a policy. The example of poverty-stricken Albania hardly invited imitation on Castro's part. The failure of Cuba's "Geat Leap Forward" was acknowledged in July of 1970, when Castro announced that the goal of a ten-million-ton sugar harvest had not been achieved.[81] This address was followed by a broadening of the government, featuring the rise of members of what was described by one analyst as the "technocratic" faction led by Carlos Raphael Rodriguez (Deputy Prime Minister responsible for Foreign Relations), who, unlike Fidel Castro or his brother Raúl, originally was a member of the Popular Socialist Party, rather than of the guerrilla element.[82]

These "pragmatists" leaned toward the USSR, hoping that Cuba could avail itself of Soviet military, industrial, and consumer goods and technology. Although some in this group were ex-members of the Muscovite PSP, others had been junior participants in the guerrilla revolution, who subsequently were trained by the USSR to assume technocratic positions.[83] The cooptation in the Cuban "establishment" of this faction, which was not identified with the turmoil of the abortive radical reforms of the late 1960s, helped to stabilize the government and reduce some of the pressures on Castro. Although this group might not have been strong enough to topple him, it certainly could damage his credibility. By promoting some of its members, Castro was giving them a stake in stabilizing the situation.

There appears to have been compromise involving all the factions. Certainly Cuba is far closer to the Soviet Union now than a decade ago, and Havana is reaping some of the short run economic and technological benefits of allegiance to the USSR. Nor can it be asserted that the F.A.R. (Cuba's military apparatus) is missing any opportunity to sharpen its claws in the name of "proletarian internationalism," even if the site of operations is chosen by Moscow. The "Fidelistas" have been able to continue "revolutionary" activity (although one might well ask just why the MPLA necessarily should be viewed as more "progressive" than may be to the taste of those still loyal to Che Guevara's theories.)

To a great extent, the three factions have apparently coalesced around a position that is neither ideal for, nor anathema to, any of them. The present "line" probably is closer to the preferences of the "Pragmatists" and "Raulistas," than of the "Fidelistas." However, Fidel Castro's problems in 1970 left him with little choice but to cooperate with the others. Given the circumstances, he has come out with his prestige intact, if not enhanced. Whether the mortgaging of his country's economy and his acquiescence in Soviet control over the security service ultimately will hurt him, is another matter.

The creation of the new "coalition" in Havana seems to have strengthened links with the USSR because many of the newly promoted personalities, most prominently Rodriguez, had developed considerably more intimate relations with the Russians than had Castro himself. This factor apparently helped to bridge the remaining gaps between Havana and Moscow, as the Cubans reorganized their political system under the slogan of "Institutionalization of the Revolution," moving toward a system resembling that of the USSR. The cult of Fidel was all but eliminated. Moreover, the Cuban economy was reoriented toward closer cooperation with the USSR, culminating in 1972 in the admission of Cuba to C.M.E.A.[84]

The cumulative cost to Castro of these various moves cannot be considered insignificant. Having "routinized" socialism and moved away from his own cult, and having planted himself firmly within the Soviet camp, his own domestic and diplomatic position and Cuba's international standing were bound to have suffered. Castro, moreover, needed Soviet aid to redress some of Cuba's economic problems (particularly the dearth of domestic energy production and the vicissitudes of the sugar market). Thus, he was shackled by serious constraints, discouraging any attempts to assert Cuban, or his own, independence with regard to Moscow. After U.S. intervention in the Dominican Republic and Guevara's death (and, ironically, at the very time when left-wing governments took over in Peru and Chile and later in Guyana and Jamaica, indicating a general upsurge in radicalism), Castro had to shelve his dreams of fostering Cuban-led guerrilla movements throughout Latin America.[85] Part of the Soviet–Cuban accommodation implicitly was that Castro should not disturb relations between the Soviet Union and existing governments (whether moderate or leftist) in the Western Hemisphere.[86]

Surrogate Activities and the Expansion of the Soviet Intelligence Network

A key component of Soviet-Cuban intimacy has been the co-option of the Cuban intelligence network (the D.G.I., or Direccion General de Intelligencia) into the KGB. This development is likely to mean not only new and expanded Soviet entries in Latin America and Africa,[87] traditional areas of Cuban influence, but even in the West, where some young radicals may find the Cuban image more appealing than that of the stereotypically stony-featured, grim KGB or East European intelligence agent.[88] Cuban agents also have been active in Hong Kong, which could facilitate Soviet intelligence functions in Asia, particularly with respect to the PRC.[89] The Cubans, moreover, have close working relations with the Basque E.T.A., the F.L.Q., the I.R.A. and the P.L.O.[90] Thus, low-key, indirect Soviet contacts with terrorist groups can be maintained through the Cubans, so that the USSR can avoid the stigma attached, at least in the West, to support of terrorism.

The Cubans, moreover, are not the only significant Soviet proxy in the Middle East and Africa. Although the USSR uses various East European and other Communist elements (e.g., North Koreans and North Vietnamese), increasingly the burden on Cubans in these regions is being eased through the employment of East Germans, particularly in the realm of intelligence.[91] Ladislav Bittman, a former leading official in the Czechoslovak intelligence network (dealing with "disinformation") who fled to the West in 1968, estimated that satellite countries augmented Soviet intelligence by about 50 percent.[92] Presumably, he did not include Cuba as a "satellite," because his role in the Czechoslovak STB terminated with the invasion of his country in 1968, before the Havana–Moscow rift had mended. With the various Warsaw Pact intelligence outfits, therefore, inclusion of the D.G.I. almost as a functional arm of the KGB should make the "Cuban connection" a major asset for Soviet intelligence.[93]

The implications for Castro of having his intelligence network subordinated to the KGB/GRU are quite deleterious. Not only does this undermine his image as an independent actor, but it gives the USSR enormous leverage over him should he deviate from the Soviet line. According to some estimates, perhaps five of the 50 or so D.G.I. agents trained annually in the USSR are intended to spy *for the KGB within the Cuban network*.[94] Regardless of whether the USSR was prepared to intervene directly against a recalcitrant Castro, Soviet agents in Cuba might well be able to give operational support of various kinds to the Muscovite elements there. Certainly, this would give Castro reason to pause, prior to defying Moscow.

Some of Russia's economic assistance involves development of the Cuban fishing industry.[95] Assuming that Cuban trawlers perform the same types of services for surveillance and ASW as do their Soviet counterparts, this program should serve to enhance Soviet naval activities in the Caribbean, and from West Africa to the Canary Islands.[96]

One of Cuba's foreign activities during past years has involved forming palace guards for insecure regimes (e.g., Sekou Touré's Guinea, Manley's Jamaica). Presumably, this enhances the Cuban influence on such leaders and could be manipulated by the KGB to Moscow's advantage. However, Sekou Touré's suspension of Soviet reconnaissance flights from Conakry in the fall of 1977 indicates the limits of such leverage.[97]

The D.G.I. is supervised currently by General Vasily Petrovich Semenov, a KGB general residing full-time in Havana. Within Cuba, reportedly, there are stationed some 4–6,000 "civilian" Soviet advisers, a permanently assigned military personnel of some 2,000, and, of course, the 3,000-man brigade which was the cause of an ephemeral crisis during the Campaign 1979–80.[98]

East German and Other Surrogates

Once it was established that Cubans, North Koreans, and North Vietnamese could assume proxy roles without serious "costs" to the Soviet Union, to detente, and to the surrogates themselves, it was apparently decided to ease the burden on the Cubans (and perhaps to test the resolve of the West) through escalation of the challenge to NATO. This took the form of significant augmentation of the number and upgrading of the role of Warsaw Pact personnel in the Third World.[99] Most notable in this respect are the East German military elements in Africa, now numbering some three thousand. The G.D.R., and not the Cubans, masterminded the 1978 incursion in Shaba, according to one source.[100] The Germans also have been quite prominent in Mozambique, where they constitute the personal bodyguard and secret police of President Machel and have been arming Zimbabwe guerrilla forces.[101] G.D.R. personnel, moreover, are very active at present in the Malagasy Republic (Madagascar), where they are attempting to create conditions that may eventually convert the island into a dependable Soviet base in the Indian Ocean.[102] Moreover, East German and Czech technicians and engineers currently are involved in a joint Soviet–Libyan venture in Chad, specifically building military facilities.[103] Such a base, if manned by a serious Warsaw Pact force, could be a threat to the Sudan and Egypt (unlikely at this time). Although less visible than the Cubans, the (estimated 300) East Germans are quite active in Ethiopia, training troops and secret police, among other functions.[104] The movement of East Germans into Angola, in various capacities, presumably has freed Cuban elements stationed there to move into Ethiopia.[105] In all likelihood, the East Europeans (and the East German Stasi in particular), like the Cubans, have assumed a significant role in intelligence and indoctrination activities within the countries to which they are assigned.[106] Specifically they are known to specialize in teaching logistics, communications and mining operations.[107]

East German and other East European countries have played important roles in Soviet policy toward the Third World by means of supply of industrial products, economic and military aid, and technical training, in addition to helping to build infrastructure.[108] At this juncture, the Warsaw Pact elements in Africa do not begin to compare in size and importance to the Cuban presence. However, should the assumption of new duties by the East Europeans continue, they too could reach the rank of full-scale proxies, marking a distinct new escalatory phase in Soviet surrogate operations in the Third World.

The position of the East Germans appears to have evolved toward its present dimensions over the course of a few years. In the latter part of the 1960s, the G.D.R. was involved primarily in a search for recognition by Third World states; it met with initial success in 1969, when Sudan and then four more Arab states recognized Pankow. Another five "Third World" states responded in this manner during the following year. The advent of Brandt's Ostpolitik brought about a slew of diplomatic recognitions of the status quo in the Germanies. After that, the G.D.R. began to operate increasingly (if not exclusively) on behalf of Moscow's interests in Africa and the Middle East.[109] According to one source, the East Germans have as many as nine thousand soldiers and military advisers in these regions, plus some six thousand others, including advisers in the realm of security, espionage, logistics and communications.[110] Furthermore, the East Germans are supporting African movements with "revolutionary potential" to the tune of some two hundred million marks annually ($60 million approximately).[111]

The intelligence apparatus (Staatssicherheit or Stasi), under Erich Mielke, is in charge of training the national security services of Angola (replacing the Cubans there),[112] Mozambique, Ethiopia and even the post–Idi Amin regime in Uganda.[113] In Mozambique, for example, it has trained the two-hundred-man personal bodyguard of President Machel (thereby, presumably, guaranteeing not only his survival, but also his cooperation). In Addis it is preparing the plans for "Socialist implementation of penalties" (presumably including execution). The presence of the Stasi has effectively guaranteed that there is no desertion among the East German regular military forces (Nationale Volksarmee or NVA) abroad, a problem the Cubans were experiencing. Moreover, the Ministry of the Interior under Friedrich Dickel serves a major role in indoctrination and training of Third World police forces, primarily within the G.D.R.[114]

There are limitations upon the East German role in Africa. The

Soviet Union reserves to itself the privilege of training staff officers. The Germans avoid signs of rank, wearing neutral khaki, while Soviet officers are clearly designated.[115] Moreover, as discussed subsequently, the G.D.R. possesses virtually no independent "airlift" capability. The main function of the G.D.R. is to train and polish effectives from Third World forces. Its ability to do so is complemented significantly by major training programs within the G.D.R., e.g., the forty Angolans learning parachute techniques in Prorva, the Libyans and Congolese being instructed in the Officers' School of the people's Navy "Karl Liebknecht," Libyans training with the NVA-Luftwaffe in Kamenz, as well as the initiation of special twenty-man police classes in the "Wilhelm Pieck" Officers' School at Aschersleben, including students from the P.D.R.Y., Ethiopia, Angola, Mozambique, and Guinea-Bissau.[116]

THE CASE OF SOUTH YEMEN

Perhaps the single most notable instance of actions by the G.D.R. on behalf of its Soviet patron has occurred in South Yemen. Reportedly, at least 1,350 East Germans are based in that country, of whom, allegedly, about 600 perform intelligence functions, and approximately 750 are military personnel. The East Germans, together with some 500 Cubans, are subordinate to a Soviet group consisting of more than 1500 military, communications, and intelligence officers. The Soviet-led elements have set up three key base facilities in that small country. Al-Mukalla is a subsidiary base, with an air field and seaport; the other two facilities are more important.[117]

Socotra Island contains a major complex of deep anchorage areas, command, control, communications, and surveillance facilities, and, it has been rumored, even a capability to house ballistic missiles.[118] The USSR is believed to have moved missiles to Somalia on a previous occasion, so this last item, if correct, may become important.

The Soviet facilities in Aden are likely to prove especially significant because of several considerations: to start with, the P.D.R.Y. has unambiguously committed itself to the 'radical' cause and sent some 3000 soldiers to Ethiopia, to help fight against South Yemen's colleague in the Arab League, Somalia, in the Ogaden.[119] This was a large contribution from a state with a total military force numbering only some 21,000 men.[120] The Russians are busily shipping military hardware to the P.D.R.Y.,[121] but it is doubtful whether all of it is in reward for South Yemen's help in Ethiopia. It is far more likely that much of this materiel will be added to the prepositioned stockpiles at the Aden base awaiting future contingencies by Cuban and perhaps East German military personnel (either operating out of S. Yemen or airlifted into the prospective battlezone from Angola or other locations).[122] The P.D.R.Y. has apparently become the central Soviet command post for the Horn of Africa and Persian Gulf region.[123] Most ominous for Saudi Arabia is that the P.D.R.Y. stockpile in the south is complemented by an Iraqi stockpile in the north. Egypt and the Sudan also must take account of the potential "squeeze play" between surrogate forces supplied from the P.D.R.Y. stockpile in the east and prepositioned weapons in Libya to the west.[124]

It is hardly necessary to add that these concentrations of materiel also make the Israelis very nervous. Indeed, one Israeli argument in favor of keeping control of the air base near Rafiah in the Sinai has been that it is one of the few air fields in the region that would be at the disposal of the United States for lifting men and materiel to potential conflict sites to counter forces operating from the Soviet-controlled facilities in South Yemen, Libya, and Iraq.

More recently, according to *Al-Anba*, published in Kuwait, the East Germans have been involved in intrigues in both South Yemen and its northern neighbor the Yemen Arab Republic. Reports regarding the assassination of the North Yemeni President, Lt. Colonel Ahmad al-Ghashmi, on June 24, 1978, indicate that the envoy carrying the package that took al-Ghashmi's life as well as his own may in fact have been an East German agent. According to this account, the assassination in part was intended as a diversion from a power struggle within the P.D.R.Y. (which had started just before the attempt), perhaps even with the aim of provoking North Yemen into a war that country was bound to lose. Primarily, however, it was designed to liquidate al-Ghashmi, because he had allegedly been cooperating with U.S. and Saudi intelligence and was permitting those two countries to develop a base at Karaman Island, located immediately across from Eritrea, and conveniently situated for intervention in ethnically divided Djibouti.[125]

Some 400 Afar students from the Djibouti region are being trained in Cuba, probably with the aim of spearheading a Cuban and Ethiopian-backed anti-Somali Afars "liberation" campaign.[126] If the French garrison in Djibouti declined to fight (not an unlikely development in view of African reactions to French assistance in Zaire), the strategically situated harbor of Djibouti could well end up under Soviet control. Soviet and surrogate elements, with S. Yemen already under their influence, then would have a firm grip on the entrance to the Red Sea.

The upshot of the turmoil within South Yemen was the death of

the country's leader, Robayi Ali, who was replaced by Ali Nasser
Mohammed Hasani. Robayi Ali apparently had become disgruntled
with the accretion of Soviet control over his state, from which
Vladimir Sharaip, a member of the Soviet security services, was
running the massive Soviet/East European/Cuban intelligence
network for the Horn and Gulf. Robayi Ali apparently tried to oust
several political opponents more intimate with Moscow than he
himself. Robayi Ali's purge attempt failed, he was killed and
replaced by Hasani, a more unequivocally pro-Moscow figure.
Hasani and P.D.R.Y. Defense Minister Lt. Colonel Ali Antar
supposedly obtained a commitment by Moscow to intervene against
any North Yemeni invasion backed by the United States and the
Saudis. Because "invasions" can be fabricated, this is an ominous
note for the future of North Yemen.[127]

LOGISTICS

The degree of coordination required for efficient operation of
the Soviet/surrogate/client network requires a great deal of effort
and even more practice.[128] In addition to such major naval
maneuvers as Okean-75, the USSR also conducted an important
exercise in December 1977 simulating airlifts of supplies and men,
including the use of prepositioned fuel (in South Yemen and
Mozambique) and weapons. Based on the demonstrated capabilities
of the Soviet air force during the exercise, using An-22 and Il-76
transports the USSR could airlift three divisions to prepositioned
stocks of materiel in Iraq and Libya in as little as eight or ten hours.
(Syria appears, at the moment, to have superseded Iraq as a Soviet
"arms cache.") Thus, before the United States had time to react, the
USSR could establish a significant "presence" (Soviet or surrogate)
in a conflict locale.[129]

For the most part, the bloc's capability to conduct major airlifts
depends on the USSR, because neither its satellites nor Cuba have
long-range heavy transports (such as the Antotav-22 and the
Ilyushin-76). However, it would be incorrect to say that these
countries have *no* airlift capacities. In addition to some obsolescent
transports, they possess commercial airliners that can and have been
used by the Russians during the prolonged airlift starting late in
1975, when a major Cuban presence was established in Angola.

From November 1977 to June 1978, it is reported that the
Soviet Air Force flew as many as 10,000 operational flights
(including many within the boundaries of the USSR). Nearly half of
these are thought to have been in support of Soviet activities in
Africa. Up to 100,000 tons of military hardware were dispatched to

Africa and the Middle East (valued at up to four billion dollars). Some 45,000 troops were shipped or flown to, or around, Africa: 25,000 Cubans were brought to Ethiopia (10,000 from Angola and another 15,000 from Cuba), 10,000 more were flown from Cuba to Angola to replenish depleted garrisons, and some 10,000 Russians, East Europeans, and South Yemenites were dispatched to Angola, Ethiopia, Mozambique and other African destinations. In addition, some of these forces were rotated or relieved, and, of course, a regular supply of food and equipment was maintained.[130]

Unquestionably, the Soviet Union has a logistical network so large and elaborate that no combination of surrogates and clients could replicate it. At the same time, the USSR can maintain a low profile (avoiding damaging implications for East–West relations) by letting its proxies conduct field operations by themselves, so far as possible. The ideal, of course, would be to equip surrogates to the point of military autarchy, but this might exceed their absorptive capacity technologically and deprive Moscow of its cherished leverage. The dispatch of Il-76s to Iraq evokes the specter of development of a major Iraqi "lift" capability which would enable Baghdad to sway the balance in a Middle Eastern or other serious military conflict, assuming that Soviet–Iraqi differences over the Eritrean issue do not lead to a rift.[131]

The USSR has sold four Il-62Ms to Cuba.[132] Although ostensibly commercial airliners, in fact these are precisely the planes the USSR used in the airlift of Cubans to Angola.[133] Each flight ferried some 150 Cuban soldiers across the Atlantic.[134] The Cubans also managed some of their own airlift, on old British-made Bristol Britannias.[135] The augmentation of the Cuban "lift" capability could ease the burden on the USSR. However, in a major conflict, four Il-62Ms probably would be insufficient to alter the situation dramatically. Moreover, Cuba itself is almost totally reliant on Soviet, or at least Soviet-controlled, materiel. An "independent" Cuban capacity could operate only with Soviet indulgence, although the USSR might prefer to represent the situation in a different light.

The Cubans have received a squadron of AN-26 "Curl" medium transports, with a 600 mile range and a capacity to lift thirty-eight combat troops, or five tons of equipment. These aircraft, which were active in Nicaragua, are of use only in a regional conflict. Altogether the USSR limits the lift capacity of its friends and allies, thereby maintaining Soviet leverage. The USSR, with some twelve-hundred transport planes, possesses about seven times as many as the rest of the Warsaw Pact put together (about two hundred and twenty-five transports). However, when necessary, Bulgaria's Balkan airlines, Czechoslovakia's C.S.A., the G.D.R.'s

Interflug, Poland's Lot, Hungary's Malev, and Cuba's Aviaçion Cubana, are available to supplement Soviet military aircraft. Reportedly, the USSR has established sub-commands in Budapest and East Berlin to run trips to the Middle East and Africa.[136]

Most Soviet transport of hardware, particularly armor, has to be dispatched by sea. During the October 1973 War, over 80 percent of arms to Egypt and Syria (as measured in tonnage) was sent by sea. Of course, this factor enhances still further the importance of prepositioning heavy materiel. In recent African campaigns, the USSR has made considerable use of sea transportation, including French-built *Akademik*-class and Finnish-built *Inzhenier*-class containerized vessels. The *Akademik*-class vessels carried armored vehicles and other weapons to the region. The *Inzhenier*-class ships, by agreement with Helsinki, could not be used to transport weapons but ran the Middle Eastern routes of other vessels, releasing them for transportation of hardware.[137]

STRUCTURE AND ORGANIZATION

A West European journal has outlined the organizational hierarchy of the Soviet–Cuban decision-making apparatus for Africa.[138] Reportedly, General Sergeii Sokolov, First Deputy Minister of Defense, is the officer in charge of coordinating the Cuban network. His representative in Africa is said to be General Vasilii Ivanovich Petrov, Deputy Chief of Staff of Soviet Army Aviation, who had commanded Soviet troops during the 1969 border clashes with the PRC (and is a member of the Central Committee of the CPSU). Petrov has assigned a number of senior Soviet officers to Cuba, where they formed a "permanent joint military organization," including the Castro brothers, the pro-Moscow Foreign Minister Rodriguez, and Vice Minister of the Interior General Enio Leyva (presumably representing Soviet and Cuban intelligence). This group communicates with Oscar Oramas Oliva, Cuban ambassador in Luanda and a political commissar of sorts. He, in turn, transmits orders to commanders at the front. Thus, although it is not clear how the division of responsibilities is allocated on the joint military organization, it must be assumed that General Sokolov's Soviet representatives have considerable say in decisions made in Havana, and, undoubtedly, prior knowledge of any policy determinations regarding Africa. In addition, the Soviet "apparat" has considerable personnel in Africa, including KGB and D.G.I. officers subordinate to Moscow, as well as (reportedly) Soviet commanders, such as General Koliyakov in Libya, General Petrov, and it is suspected, General Grigorii G. Barisov in Ethiopia.[139]

Thus, the Cubans have little, if any, opportunity to present Moscow with a fait accompli in Africa, assuming even that they would wish to do so.

It is reported also that Soviet ties in Lisbon, dating back to the period of Portuguese leftist turmoil, have expedited Soviet-surrogate operations in Africa. The Portuguese capital is said to have been a clearing house for D.G.I. and KGB officers being dispatched to Africa.[140] More important, despite official Portuguese government objections, Cuban flights, bound for Angola with troops and arms, were allowed to refuel at Santa Maria island in the azores early during the Angolan War.[141] This occurred because the Portuguese Foreign Minister at that time, Major Melo Antunes, a left-wing supporter of the MPLA, arranged with officials on the Islands to permit refueling.[142] This episode demonstrates some of the uses the USSR can make of sympathizers in areas not directly connected with the conflict in question. If Portugal has served as a useful arena for such activities, so too might Italy, with significant left-wing forces both in and out of power (including local police).

Domestic Effects of Foreign Ventures

In May of 1972, Fidel Castro stated:

> With the same love with which our fighters have been ready to fight for Cuba, they are disposed to struggle in the support of any revolutionary people, of any brother country. So, we shall be united in peace, we shall be united in struggle, we shall be united in combat and we shall be united under any circumstances.[143]

This pronouncement, which might be termed the "Castro Doctrine," has implications as wide as the Brezhnev Doctrine. Moreover, the same point has been repeated by other members of the Cuban regime:

> Our troops will go anywhere in the world and to any country with a formally established government of revolutionary character, which asks Cuba for help against imperialistic aggression.[144]

The Castro government has asserted Cuba's willingness to fight abroad, with the qualification that Cubans be allied with "revolutionary" or "anti-imperialist forces." Castro is free to attach labels as he pleases, so this leaves him with wide room for maneuver.

It is unclear to what degree the Cuban people identify with this attitude. Although the Cuban army is a volunteer force, there have been some indications of dissent concerning the necessity for Cuban military involvement in a distant continent (even if Che Guevara described Africa as potentially the most fruitful area for revolution).[145] Although casualty figures are not announced in Havana (the dead are buried abroad, and most of the wounded are treated in Warsaw Pact states), it is impossible for the Cuban regime to hide its losses. The relatives are bound to discover the truth, sooner or later. One 1978 U.S. government estimate claimed that some 1,500 Cubans have been killed in Africa and perhaps three times that number injured.[146] These statistics have to be evaluated in the context of the fact that almost 48,000 Cubans are believed to be stationed in Africa, over 40,000 of whom are thought to be military or paramilitary personnel.[147] (These figures do not include the substantial number of Cubans based in the Middle East.)

The same proportion applied to the U.S. population would be between 900,000 and one million U.S. soldiers. The Cuban casualty figures would extrapolate to some 33,000 dead and about 100,000 wounded, in terms of America's population. The Cuban venture has therefore approached Vietnam proportions. To a significant degree, Cuba has overcommitted itself in Africa; Russians are reported to have been substituted for Cuban pilots sent abroad. There are indications that the presence in Cuba of Russian military and other personnel, now estimated at about 10,000 (necessitated at least in part by the drain on Cuban military manpower) grates on many Cubans.[148]

Although Cuba is very much a closed society, nevertheless discontent has surfaced—particularly questioning why it should be necessary for Cubans to be killed or maimed in far-off lands. Reportedly, Castro has received major new shipments of arms from the USSR, including additional MiG-21s and, for the first time, MiG-23s.[149] It is not clear whether these constitute payoff for services rendered or are meant to help improve the image of the Cuban armed forces and, thus, indirectly, to raise Castro's stock at home, in view of growing disenchantment on the island with his prolonged and costly ventures abroad.

Although the East German Africa contingent of about 3,000–4,500 men amounts only to one-tenth or so of the Cuban presence on that continent, the G.D.R. has almost twice Cuba's population. Yet, East Germans too have begun to question whether a new "Afrika Korps" is appropriate for a state stigmatized internationally both for its Nazi past and its hard-line, almost Stalinist, present. Domestic grumbling on this topic appears to have been significant enough to merit a television campaign to play down the military aspects of East German activities in Africa and the Middle East. Similarly, in diplomatic contacts, Pankow has attempted to play down its overseas buildup.[150]

This study has assumed that the USSR substituted surrogates for direct Soviet intervention in the Third World because of two primary considerations; in terms of foreign policy (to avoid overt action likely to provoke direct confrontation with the United States) Moscow appears to have succeeded fairly well until now. With regard to domestic difficulties with overseas ventures, if current trends persist the Kremlin may find it has merely transferred problems on the Soviet scene to other Communist states for *their* leaders to confront. This may pose eventual foreign policy and military difficulties for the USSR as leader of the whole "camp." At the present stage, however, Cuba's and East Germany's domestic difficulties, insofar as they derive from their surrogate operations, still are marginal. Consequently, any countervailing force causing Moscow to terminate or curtail active utilization of surrogates in the near future would have to emanate from the West.

NOTES

1.   For the purpose of this study, Cuba will be termed a "proxy" or "surrogate" of the Soviet Union, as will North Korean, North Vietnamese, and (non-Soviet) Warsaw Pact forces and weapons transfers. The assumption is not that these states necessarily are operating entirely at the behest of the Soviet Union. Certainly in the case of Cuba, some of the initiative may have come from Fidel Castro. Nevertheless, the surrogate forces deployed in the Third World are working in cooperation with the Soviet Union, enjoy Soviet logistical support, their efforts are being subsidized by the Russians, and many of the benefits of their campaigns accrue to the USSR. Moreover, the Brezhnev regime can achieve almost as much in the way of strategic, diplomatic, economic, and perceptual gains by operating through its proxies as it would through direct deployment of Russian troops. However, some of the undesirable consequences of Soviet intervention in less developed states may be mitigated by the indirect (or proxy) approach. Perhaps, the key element is *leverage*, be it in the form of military occupation or reliance on military or economic aid (or any combination thereof), which the Soviet Union has over the states acting in its stead. Thus, the surrogates are compelled to cooperate with the USSR, regardless of their policy preferences. In some cases, they might wish to do so, but this does not exempt them from the label.

2.   Tad Szulc, "Cuba Began Role in Zanzibar in 1961," *New York Times*, 23 January 1964, p. 1.

3.   Robert Conley, "Cuban-trained Guerrillas Directed Zanzibar Revolt," *New York Times*, 19 January 1964, p. 1.

4.   Wolfgang Berner, "Kubanerinterventionen in Afrika und Arabien," *Aussenpolitik* 3/76, 27. Jahrgang, 3m Quartal, p. 326.

5.   Robert Legvold, *Soviet Policy in West Africa* (Cambridge: Harvard University Press, 1970), passim.

6.   Soviet relations with Guinea ebbed and flowed during the 1960s.

During 1964, Guinea was "demoted" ideologically. In August, the USSR ceased to mention the Sekou Touré regime in the same breath with Ghana and Mali, all three countries having been identified as the most "progressive" in Africa since the early 1960s. Uri Ra'anan, "Moscow and the Third World," 14 *Problems of Communism* No. 1 (January–February 1965), p. 28. Two months later, Guinea was omitted from the list of five states in Africa approaching the stage of "building socialism." Legvold, pp. 197–198. In February 1965, Guinea was elevated again, partly because of a domestic policy change in Conakry and partly because of a more receptive attitude toward Moscow by Sekou Touré, who believed Khrushchev had attempted to interfere in Guinean affairs, whereas the new Soviet leadership had not yet had an opportunity to prove itself. Ibid., pp. 235–239.

7.   Berner, "Kubanerinterventionen," p. 326.

8.   "Russia's War's by Proxy," *Foreign Reports* No. 1429 (February 25, 1975), pp. 1–3; Hugh O'Shaughnessy, "Castro's Long March to Pretoria," *London Observer*, 26 February 1978, p. 14.

9.   "What Are We Fighting For?" 267 *The Economist* No. 7026 (April 29, 1978), p. 79.

10.   Berner, "Kubanerinterventionen," p. 328.

11.   D. Bruce Jackson, *Castro, the Kremlin and Communism in Latin America* (Baltimore: Johns Hopkins Press, 1969), passim.

12.   Berner, "Kubanerinterventionen," p. 328.

13.   Castro's concluding speech at the Tricontinental Congress as cited by Jackson, p. 83.

14.   William E. Ratliff, *Castroism and Communism in Latin America, 1959–76*, American Enterprise Institute, Washington D.C.; and Hoover Institution on War, Revolution and Peace, Stanford University, Stanford, California, Policy Study No. 19, November 1976, pp. 124–144.

15.   Jackson, *Castro*, p. 5.

16.   Shimon Shamir, "Marxism in Egypt," in *The USSR and the Middle East*, Michael Confino and Shimon Shamir, eds. (New York: Halsted Press, 1973), pp. 294–303.

17.   Jackson, *Castro*, pp. 28–34.

18.   Berner, "Kubanerinterventionen," p. 328.

19.   William J. Durch, *The Cuban Military in Africa and the Middle East: From Algeria to Angola* (Arlington, VA: Center for Naval Analysis, 1977), p. 24.

20.   Ibid., p. 28.

21.   Berner, "Kubanerinterventionen," pp. 328–329; Durch, *Cuban Military*, pp. 20–21.

22.   *Communist Global Subversion and American Security*: vol. 1, *The Attempted Communist Subversion of Africa through Nkrumah's Ghana*, U.S. Senate Committee on the Judiciary, Subcommittee to Investigate the Administration of the Internal Security Act (Washington, D.C.: U.S. Government Printing Office, 1972), p. 3.

23.   Basil Davison, *The Liberation of Guiné* (Baltimore: Penguin Books, 1969), passim.

24.   Jean Huteau, "Committee Aprroves Criticism of Soviet Policy," Paris AFP in English 0135, G.M.T., 10 August 1967, in *Foreign Broadcast Information Service*, Latin America, 10 August 1967, pp. 13–14.

25.   Brian Crozier, "Soviet Pressures in the Caribbean," *Conflict Studies* 35 (May, 1973), pp. 13–14.

26. Edward Gonzalez, "Castro: The Limits of Charisma," 21 *Problems of Communism*, No. 4 (July–August 1972), p. 21. Muscovites consisted primarily of former PSP members, as opposed to Fidel's guerrilla forces. The major survivor of the 1967–1968 purge of Muscovites is Rodriguez, still in liaison with Moscow. John Barron, *KGB: The Secret Work of Soviet Secret Agents* (New York: Bantam Books, 1974), p. 205.

27. Edward Gonzalez, "Castro and Cuba's New Orthodoxy," 25 *Problems of Communism* No. 1 (January–February 1976), pp. 2, 7.

28. Harold C. Hinton, *The Bear at the Gate*, American Enterprise Institute, Washington, D.C., and Hoover Institution on War, Revolution and Peace, Stanford University, Stanford, California, 1971, Policy Study No. 1, 1971, p. 21.

29. "Castro Comments on Czechoslovak Crisis," Havana Domestic Television and Radio, 0102 G.M.T., August 24, 1968, *Foreign Broadcast Information Service*, Daily Report for Latin America, 26 August 1968, No 167/68, pp. 01–020.

30. Leon Gouré, "Cuba's Military Dependence on the USSR," in James D. Theberge, ed., *Soviet Seapower in the Caribbean: Political and Strategic Implications* (New York: Praeger, 1972), pp. 78–80.

31. James D. Theberge, "Soviet Policy in the Caribbean," *Soviet Seapower*, pp. 9–10.

32. Drew Middleton, "Soviets Reported Tracking US Ships in Caribbean," *New York Times*, 21 February 1971, p. 1.

33. John W. Finney, "Soviets Said to Use Guinea to Observe US Shipping," *New York Times*, 6 December 1973, p. 1.

34. Barbara Walters, "An Interview with Fidel Castro," *Foreign Policy*, No. 28 (Fall, 1977), pp. 46–47.

35. At the July 1978, nonaligned conference in Belgrade, Cuba's Foreign Minister, Carlos Raphael Rodriguez, expressed his "solidarity" with Albania in its differences with China. David A. Andelman, "Same Players, New Sides in Age Old Balkan Games," *New York Times*, 6 August, 1978, p. D2. Thus, Cuba appears to be wooing China's erstwhile ally. If the Cubans should play the role of intermediary between the USSR and Albania successfully, the Soviet Union would collect the dividends, both idiological and strategic. (The port of Valona is the key to control of the Straits of Otranto and thus to the Adriatic. Moreover, Soviet airbases in Albania could extend Warsaw Pact air power over the entire Mediterranean.) Finally, the implications for Yugoslav security of Soviet bases in Albania would be serious, particularly in view of the troublesome Albanian minority in the Kosovo and Macedonian regions.

36. "Commentary Reaffirms Proletarian Internationalism," 6 February 1978, *FBIS*, Latin America 78/27, p. Q2.

37. David K. Shipler, "European Reds Back Autonomy for Each Party," *New York Times*, 1 July 1976, p. 1.

38. Ernst Halperin, "Soviet Naval Power, Soviet–Cuban Relations and Politics in the Caribbean," in Theberge, ed., *Soviet Seapower*, p. 87.

39. Norman Polmar, *Soviet Naval Power* (New York: National Strategy Information Center, 1972), pp. 50–51.

40. John Finney, "Soviets Said to Use Guinea to Observe US Shipping," *New York Times*, 6 December 1973, p. 1.

41. Adm. Elmo R. Zumwalt, Jr., USN (Ret.), *On Watch* (New York: Quadrangle, 1976), pp. 332–333.

42. Carmelo Mesa-Lago, *Cuba in the 1970s* (Albuquerque: University of New Mexico Press, 1974), p. 6.

43. Ibid., pp. 6–7.

44. A distinction is drawn here between the sporadic, small-scale injections of Cuban personnel in Africa during the 1960s, usually in less than a full combat capacity (and apparently unprompted by Moscow) and massive Cuban military ventures in the second half of the 1970s, requiring major Soviet "lift" and other logistical assistance. It is the latter type of operations that deserve the heading of "surrogate" in the fullest sense.

45. Gonzalez, "The Limits of Charisma," p. 16.

46. Gonzalez, "Castro and Cuba's New Orthodoxy," pp. 5, 24.

47. Stephen Kinzer, "Report and Comment—Cuba," 239 *The Atlantic* No. 5 (May 1977), pp. 6–13.

48. Gonzalez has suggested that the development of "detente," and American dedication to the maintenance of relations with Moscow provided Castro with enough confidence in Cuba's internal security to feel safe in dispatching a quarter of the Cuban Army across the Atlantic. Thus, it can be argued that detente encourages adventurism in marginal regions, even if discouraging direct confrontation. (Personal communication.)

49. "Fidel Castro Speaks at Rally," Havana Domestic Radio and Television Service in Spanish 0235 G.M.T., in *Foreign Broadcast Information Service*, 29 September 1976 (pp. 7, 10; see also quotation on page 33).

50. Edward Gonzalez, "Cuban Foreign Policy," 26 *Problems of Communism* No. 6 (November–December 1977), p. 4.

51. These statistics have been derived from Robert W. Campbell, *Trends in Soviet Oil and Gas Industry* (Baltimore: Johns Hopkins Press, 1976), pp. 76–77.

52. In fact, in 1964, Guevara had termed Africa "one of the most important if not *the* most important, battlefields against all forms of exploitation in the world." William J. Durch, *The Cuban Military*, p. 18.

53. Gerald J. Bender, "Angola, the Cubans, and American Anxieties," *Foreign Policy*, No. 31, pp. 10–11.
There is some evidence that Cuban behavior is not always as accommodating as this Angolan official asserted. Cubans are alleged to have become involved in bar brawls, looted clothing warehouses and womanized excessively. See "Wir haben euch Waffen und Brot geschickt," *Der Spiegel*, March 3, 1980, #4. Jahrgang Nr. 10, p. 45 and "Internal Strains in Angola," *Foreign Report*, June 28, 1978, No. 1540, pp. 4–5.

54. David K. Shipler, "European Reds Back Autonomy for Each Party," *New York Times*, 1 July 1975, p. 1.

55. "Tito said to Dismiss Recent Soviet Overture," *New York Times*, 14 December 1974, p. 22.

56. Giuseppe Are, "Italy's Communists: Foreign and Defense Policies," 18 *Survival* No. 5 (September/October 1976), pp. 213–214.

57. This will be discussed in greater detail later in this paper.

58. Arms Control and Disarmament Agency, *Arms Control and Disarmament Agreements—Texts and History of Negotiation* (Washington, D.C.: U.S. Government Printing Office, 1977), pp. 151–154.

59. "Texts of Nixon–Brezhnev Declaration and of Joint Communique at End of Visit," *New York Times*, 30 May 1972, p. 18.

60. Secretary Vance's insistence that SALT is to be decoupled from

all other issues from a purely political point of view is only partly relevant. The Kremlin cannot be unaware of the significance of the question just how much political ammunition important Senatorial skeptics concerning SALT may derive from Soviet operations in various regions, if a controversial agreement should emerge from current negotiations. Bernard Gwertzman, "Vance is Assailed for Soviet Talks in Face of Trials," *New York Times,* 11 June 1978, p. 1.

61. Foy D. Kohler, Leon Gouré, and Mose L. Harvey, Eugene Rostow, Uri Ra'anan and others.

62. "Castro's First Middle East Adventure: Part I," *Foreign Report,* No. 1526, 8 March 1978, pp. 4–7; Von Gerd Linde, "Das Arsenal des Yom-Kippurs-Krieges," *Wehrforschung,* No. 4, June–July, 1975, pp. 109–113; Berner, op. cit., p. 330; "Foreign Soldiers Said to be Aiding Arabs," *The London Times,* 6 December 1973, p. 6; Eric Marsden, "Cubans New Factor in Israel–Syria Impasse," *The London Times,* 2 April 1974, p. 2.

63. Foy D. Kohler, Leon Gouré, and Mose L. Harvey, *The Soviet Union and the October 1973 Middle East War—The Implications for Détente* (Miami: University of Miami Center for Advanced International Studies, 1974); Uri Ra'anan, "The USSR and the Middle East: Some Reflections on the Soviet Decision-Making Process," 17 *Orbis* No. 3 (Fall 1973), pp. 94–97.

64. "Castro's First Middle East Adventure: Parts I and II," *Foreign Report,* Nos. 1526 and 1527, March 8 and 15, 1978. Durch, *Cuban Military,* pp. 28–30; Von Gerd Linde, "Das Arsenal," pp. 111–112; "Foreign Soldiers Said to be Aiding Arabs"; Marsden, "Cubans New Factor," p. 2.

65. Yehoshua Tadmor, "Cubans Said Active in Middle East," Tel Aviv *Davar,* in Hebrew, pp. 1–2. *Foreign Broadcast Information Service,* Daily Report–Middle East and North Africa, June 5, 1978, p. N8.

66. "Castro's First Middle East Adventure: Part I" (see note 64), p. 6.

67. "Castro's First Middle East Adventure: Part II," passim.

68. Ibid.

69. In March 1977, Castro attempted to mediate in an effort to bring about a "socialist federation," including Ethiopia, Somalia, Djibouti and South Yemen, thereby maintaining both Ethiopia and Somalia as important Soviet entry points in Africa. Approximately one month later, when this attempt had stalled, Cuban advisers were sent into Ethiopia. F. Stephen Larrabee, "Somalia and Moscow's Problems in the Horn of Africa," *Radio Liberty* 158/77, 5 July 1977, pp. 10–11.

70. "Two Different Lines on the Question of War and Peace, Comment on the Open Letter of the Central Committee of the CPSU, November 19, 1963," in *The Polemic on the General Line of the International Communist Movement* (Peking: Foreign Language Press, 1965), p. 246.

71. "Letter to CCP CC to CPSUS CC, February 29, 1964," in John Gittings, *Survey of the Sino–Soviet Dispute 1963–7* (Oxford: Royal Institute of International Affairs, 1967), p. 85.

72. "Castro Comments on Czechoslovak Crisis," Havana Domestic Television and Radio Services, in Spanish 0102 G.M.T., 24 August 1968, in *Foreign Broadcast Information Service, Daily for Latin America,* 1 September 1968, vol. VI, No. 167, p. 020.

73. Uri Ra'anan, *The USSR Arms the Third World—Case Studies*

in Foreign Policy (Cambridge, MA: MIT Press, 1969), pp. 109–113.

74. Not to mention that the USSR has been manning the Island's air defenses, because of the overextension of Cuban forces. William Beecher, "Cuba Can Easily Dispatch More Troops, US Believes," *The Boston Globe*, 15 June 1978, p. 24.

75. Cuba, which obtains 80 percent of its foreign currency earnings from sugar, was hit seriously when sugar prices on the world market plummeted from 65 cents a pound, two years ago, to 7 cents a short time later.

What prevented an economic catastrophe was the assistance provided by other communist countries. Under recent barter agreements, the Soviet Union buys about half of the Cuban sugar crop, at 30 cents a pound, while supplying Cuba with all of its oil consumption at rates well below current world market prices. "Paper Reviews Results of Cuban Link with CEMA," *Bridgetown Advocate News*, in English, 24 January 1977, in *Foreign Broadcast Information Service, Daily Report on Latin America*, 1 February 1977, vol. VI, no. 21, annex 10, pp. S1–S3.

76. "Tanzanian Leader Defends Soviet Role in Africa," *New York Times*, 9 June 1976, p. A4.

77. John Goshko, "Turner Gives Evidence on Hill," *Washington Post*, 6 June 1978, p. 1; "Rafael Rodriguez Refutes Carter Statements on Shaba," Havana Domestic Service in Spanish 1600 G.M.T., 27 May 1978, *Foreign Broadcast Information Service, Daily Report on Latin America*, 30 May 1978, vol. VI, no. 104, p. Q1; Richard Burt, "Lessons of Shaba: Carter Risked Serious Credibility Gap," *New York Times*, 11 July 1978, p. 2.

78. For a discussion of the border clash in the context of the Soviet invasion of Czechoslovakia, see Hinton, *The Bear at the Gate* (passim).

79. Henry Kamm, "Soviet Doctrine Scored by Italians," *New York Times*, 12 June 1969, p. 1; "World Reds End Moscow Parley," *New York Times*, 18 June 1969, p. 1.

80. It must be recalled that, during this period, Cuba was in the midst of an attempt to achieve a major economic breakthrough. Had Havana succeeded, Castro would have been in a far better negotiating position with respect to Moscow.

81. "Castro Speaks," Havana Domestic Television and Radio Services, in Spanish 1956 G.M.T., 26 July 1970, in *Foreign Broadcast Information Service, Daily Report for Latin America and Western Europe*, vol. VI, no. 147, supplement 19 (30 July 1970), pp. 4–33.

82. Edward Gonzalez has identified three basic factions at that stage: 1. The "pragmatist" group led by Raphael Rodriguez. This group consists mostly of ex-PSP members and technocrats, who, like some of the "modernizers" in China, see technological development through Soviet aid as a feasible path for their country, even if this implies some concessions to the USSR. 2. The "Raúlistas" led by Fidel Castro's brother, the First Vice President and Minister of the Armed Forces (FAR), have what Gonzalez calls the "military mission tendency," which asserts the need for Cuba to assert itself in favor of revolutionary elements through use of its armed forces. 3. The "Fidelistas," followers of Fidel Castro, stress the need to help foster revolution and "anti-imperialism," mostly in the Third World, by a suitable combination of means. Gonzalez, "Cuban Foreign Policy," pp. 6–10.

83. Ibid., p. 8.

84. Edward Gonzalez and David Ronfeldt, *Post Revolutionary Cuba in a Changing World* (Santa Monica: Rand Corporation), R-1844-ISA, December 1975, pp. 3–21.

85. As indicated by Soviet passivity concerning the overthrow of the Allende regime, the USSR still felt that it was not a good idea to provoke the US in the Western Hemisphere. James D. Theberge, *The Soviet Presence in Latin America*, National Strategy Information Center No. 23 (New York: Crane, Russak, 1974), p. 81.

86. Crozier, *Soviet Pressure in the Caribbean*, pp. 13, 17–18; Gonzalez and Ronfeldt, *Post Revolutionary Cuba*, pp. 20–22. In combined operations, the USSR has shown itself capable of spanning the 1950 nm-wide "choke point" between West Africa and South America, as demonstrated during the "Okean" 1975 maneuvers. Geoffrey Kemp, "The New Strategic Map," 19 *Survival* No. 2 (March/April 1977), p. 55. One of the keys to Soviet interest in the Caribbean area (quite apart from the fact that it constitutes the sensitive "southern flank" of the rival superpower) is that surveillance of the mid-Atlantic can be maintained by simultaneous Soviet flights from African and Caribbean airports (with obvious implications both for ASW and for interdiction of transatlantic reinforcements bound for NATO's "Central Front"). Although Cuba has served this function in recent years, airfields in Guyana would be better located for such a task.

87. For example, in the Caribbean, Cuban agents have been given responsibility for organizing and running the internal security apparatus of Jamaican Prime Minister Michael Manley's government. Given a very unstable Jamaican economy and Soviet control of the DGI, the USSR thus may be provided with significant leverage in dealing with a leftist government. J. Daniel O'Flaherty, "Finding Jamaica's Way," *Foreign Policy* No. 31 (Summer 1978), p. 149; Horace Sutton, "Caribbean in Conflict," *Saturday Review*, 1 March 1980, pp. 14–20.

As early as 1965 Cuban elements, working in conjunction with Kwame Nkrumah, the leader of Ghana (deposed in February 1966), reportedly trained insurgents and agents hostile to other African regimes, Sierre Leone in particular. One of the main disembarkation points for these trainees was Conakry, Guinea, where Nkrumah was later given sanctuary. Thus, at a period when Russian relations with Sekou Touré were not at their best, Cuba was deeply involved in joint plans with the West African leader to undermine other regimes. Cuba's role as a subversive element in Africa, therefore, antedates the Soviet–Cuban rapprochement by several years. *Communist Global Subversion and American Security, Vol. I, The Attempted Communist Subversion through Nkrumah's Ghana*, pp. 3, 75, 131.

88. John Barron, *KGB* (New York: Bantam Books, 1974), pp. 28–30; Brian Crozier, "The Surrogate Forces of the Soviet Union," *Conflict Studies*, No. 92 (February 1978), p. 9.

89. "Cuba's Hand in Argentina and Hong Kong," *Foreign Report*, 7 April 1976, No. 1435, p. 8; Barron, *KGB*, p. 259.

90. "Cuba Reportedly Trained Basques at Algerian Camp," *New York Times*, 7 July 1978, p. 2; Barron, *KGB*, pp. 27–30; "Castro's First Middle Eastern Adventure, Parts I and II"; "Middle East: How Much Can Castro Do?" *Foreign Report*, No. 1452 (August 18, 1976), pp. 6–7.

91. Crozier, "The Surrogate Forces of the Soviet Union," *Conflict*

Studies No. 92 (February 1978), pp. 9–10.
    92. Ladislav Bittman, *The Deception Game* (Syracuse: Syracuse University Research Corp., 1972), p. 142.
    93. In view of the closer Cuban ties to several Latin American states, and of the residual intelligence sources left over from Cuba's radical phase, when it was helping to train Peruvian, Colombian, Brazilian, Venezuelan, and Dominican guerrillas. O'Flaherty, "Finding Jamaica's Way," pp. 146–150; Gonzales, "Castro and Cuba's New Orthodoxy," p. 18; George W. Grayson, "Cuba's Developing Policies," 72 *Current History* No. 424 (February 1972), p. 51; "Cuba's Caribbean Probe," *Foreign Report*, No. 1458 (October 6, 1976), pp. 6–7.
    Cuba has somewhere in the vicinity of one-quarter of its 165,000-man army in Africa, in addition to some 3000 civilians. Angus Deming, et al., "The Cubans in Africa," 91 *Newsweek* No. 9 (March 13, 1978), p. 36. These forces are spread out over some 16 states in Africa (and there is a reported East German "presence" in Chad, bringing the total to 17). "Wenn Elefanten Kämpfen, Leidet das Gras," *Der Spiegel*, Jahrgang 32, Nr. 22, 29 May 1978, p. 130. "Qaddafi's Secret Base in Chad," *The Foreign Report*, 26 October 1977, p. 4; "Chad—Internal Security Developments—Relations with Libya," 24 *Keesing's Contemporary Archives* No. 1635 (May 12, 1978), pp. 28976–28978. Moreover, to this total can be added the Cuban and Warsaw Pact elements in South Yemen, Iraq, and, reportedly, in Lebanon, which have a bearing on the Horn and on Arab North Africa. Finally, the previous presence of Cubans and East Germans in Somalia undoubtedly enabled both to make contacts that probably were to be maintained despite the present rift with Somalia. Thus, the Soviet intelligence network for Africa and the Middle East is bound to have expanded considerably by virtue of the surrogates. *Al-Anba* (Kuwait), 14 July 1978, translated from Arabic: "Behind the Coup in Aden," *Foreign Report*, 5 July 1978, pp. 2–6. "Running Guns to Lebanon," *Foreign Report*, 11 August 1976, pp. 1–2.
    94. Barron, *KGB*, pp. 205–208; Crozier, "The Surrogate Forces of the Soviet Union," p. 9.
    95. Kravanja, "Soviet and Cuban Fisheries in the Caribbean," in Theberge, *Soviet Seapower in the Caribbean*, pp. 154–160.
    96. Carl G. Jacobsen, "The Civilian Fleets," in *Soviet Oceans Development*, U.S. Senate Committee on Commerce and National Ocean Policy Study (Washington, D.C.: U.S. Government Printing Office, 1976), pp. 257–305, passim.
    97. Graham Hovey, "Guinea's Halting of Soviet Flights Leaves US in a Quandary on Aid," *New York Times*, 19 November 1977, p. 2.
    98. Sutton, "Caribbean in Conflict," p. 17.
    99. Activists representing Warsaw Pact countries and forces in the Third World cannot but be perceived in the West as a greater challenge than Cubans or personnel from Asian communist states. Not only are they Europeans and represent more highly developed countries, but there can be no mistaking the direct Soviet control over major foreign policy decisions, particularly of a military, paramilitary, or intelligence nature, in member countries of the Warsaw Pact. Although the distinction may be more apparent than real between Cuban soldiers fighting in Ethiopia (while Soviet pilots patrol Cuban skies) and East German officers and military/intelligence experts actively engaged in Africa and the Middle East

(while 32 Soviet divisions control the GDR, Poland, Hungary, and Czechoslovakia), the effect of East European (particularly East German) military and paramilitary personnel in Africa is far more likely to jar the West than are the Cubans. Moscow cannot be sure whether such escalation will shock the West, provoking a tough reaction, or whether it will merely deepen the feeling of impotence in the face of increased Soviet boldness. In the latter case, the Kremlin would hope to see the Chinese eventually throw up their hands in exasperation at the West and reluctantly move back somewhat toward Moscow.

100. Elizabeth Pond, "East Germany's 'Afrika Korps'," *Christian Science Monitor*, 26 August 1978; "Wir haben euch Waffen und Brot geschickt," *Der Spiegel*, No. 10, 34 Jarhgang, 3 March 1980, pp. 42–61.
101. Martin McCauley, "GDR Involvement in Africa," 6 *Soviet Analyst*, No. 24 (December 8, 1977), pp. 6–7.
102. "Madagascar Footnote," *Foreign Report*, No. 1527, 15 March 1978, p. 8.
103. "Qaddafi's Secret Base in Chad," *Foreign Report*, 26 October 1977, p. 4; "Chad—Internal Security Developments—Relations with Libya," *Keesing's* No. 1635, pp. 28976–28978.
104. Martin McCauley, "Ethiopia Mourns an East German," 7 *Soviet Analyst* No. 12 (June 15, 1978), pp. 4–5.
105. To this, the fact must be added that some 1,000 Bulgarians have taken up positions as advisers and technicians in Angola. Many even have been able to bring families with them. Both Bulgarians and East Germans have been among the casualties suffered in the ongoing conflict with UNITA forces. "Bulgarian Casualties in Angola," *Foreign Report*, No. 1523, 15 February 1978, p. 8.
106. For insight into the role of satellite states in augmenting the Soviet intelligence network, see Barron, *KGB*, especially pp. 193–223; and Bittman, *The Deception Game*, passim.
107. Stephen H. Miller, "Iron Curtain Nations Reported Joining Soviet Drive in Africa," *Los Angeles Times*, 5 July 1978, p. 13.
108. John F. Burns, "East German Afrika Korps: Force to be Reckoned With," *New York Times*, 18 November 1979, p. 4; William F. Robinson, "Eastern Europe's Presence in Black Africa," *Radio Free Europe—Radio Libert RAD Background Report* No. 142 (Eastern Europe) (June 21, 1979), pp. 7–10.
109. Bernard von Plate, "GDR Foreign Policy to Africa and Arabia," 29 *Aussenpolitik* No. 1 (January 1978), pp. 75–86; "Wir haben euch Waffen und Brot geschickt," *Der Spiegel*, 3 March 1980, No. 10, 34. Jahrgang, pp. 42–61.
110. William F. Robinson, "Eastern Europe's Presence in Black Africa," *Radio Free Europe Research*, RAD Background Report No. 142 (Eastern Europe), 21 June 1979, pp. 7–10.
111. "Wir haben euch Waffen und Brot geschickt" (see note 109), p. 47.
112. Ibid., p. 45.
113. Ibid., p. 47.
114. Ibid., p. 45; John F. Burns, "Eastern German Afrika Korps: Force to be Reckoned With," *New York Times*, 18 November 1979, p. 4.
115. "Wir haben euch Waffen und Brot geschickt," passim.
116. Ibid, pp. 45–47.

117. *Al-Anba* (Kuwait), 14 July 1978, translated from Arabic: "Behind the Coup in Aden," *Foreign Report* No. 1541, 5 July 1978, p. 4.

118.   These activities are linked to the impressive network of Soviet surveillance satellites. Russia's capacity to coordinate major combined operations through the use of satellite reconnaisance was demonstrated during Okean 1975, a worldwide combined naval exercise, which made extensive use of Cosmos 723 and 724, launched especially for the occasion. (Manthorpe, p. 207.) This exercise involved coordination between bases in Cuba, Guinea, and the Indian Ocean (presumably including South Yemen). More recently, Cosmos 988 was used during Ethiopia–Somali combat in the Ogaden, both to facilitate battlefield coordination and to improve communications between the theater command and Moscow. "Chopper War in the Ogaden," *Foreign Report*, No. 1523, 15 February 1978, p. 3.

119.   Peter Vanneman and Martin James, "Soviet Thrust into the Horn of Africa: The Next Targets," 6 *Strategic Review* No. 7 (Spring 1978), pp. 38–39, note 1. Since the withdrawal of the Somalis from the Ogaden, the South Yemenite forces appear to have been removed from the conflict arena. The Cubans, too, have downgraded their participation with respect to Eritrea, possibly because of the embarrassment caused by their helping subdue a rebellion with which they had been strongly identified previously (unlike the Ogaden, where Cuba had not become involved publicly with the secession movement). "Going it Alone," *Foreign Report*, No. 1539, 21 June 1978, p. 6.

120.   *The Military Balance 1977–8* (London: International Institute for Strategic Studies, 1978), p. 42.

121.   "PDRY Major Armed Forces Buildup," 4 *Weekly Report on Strategic Middle Eastern Affairs* No. 2 (January 18, 1978), p. 1; "Saudi-PDRY: All Quiet on the Border," 4 *Weekly Report on Strategic Middle Eastern Affairs* No. 10 (March 12, 1978), p. 4. The Soviet Union and East Germany currently are engaged in a buildup of the armed forces of the PDRY and hope almost to double these forces to some 40,000 men, most of whom will serve in the army. The Air Force, however, will be flown by Yemenite, rather than Cuban pilots.

122.   Lawrence Whetten, "The Soviet–Cuban Presence in the Horn of Africa," 123 *Royal United Services Institute Journal of Defense Study* (RUSI), No. 3 (September 1978), p. 41; Edgar O'Ballance, "The Cuban Factor," Ibid., p. 49; "Russia's Airlift: Warning to the West," *Foreign Report*, No. 1517, 21 December 1977, p. 3.

123.   "Behind the Coup in Aden" (see note 117), p. 3.

124.   "Qaddafi's Secret Base in Chad," *The Foreign Report*, 26 October 1977, p. 4.

125.   "Behind the Coup in Aden," op. cit., pp. 2–5.

126.   "French Fears of Djibuti," *Foreign Report*, No. 1523 (February 15, 1978), p. 4.

127.   "Behind the Coup in Aden," op. cit., pp. 2–5. The PDRY also has been engaged in an ongoing conflict with Oman, which has close ties to Iran. However, probably because of the ambiguous relationship between Moscow and Teheran, Soviet backing of S. Yemen against Oman has not been overt. Eric Page, "Fighting Persists on Oman's Border," *New York Times*, 18 January 1976, p. 6.

128.   Surrogates may be defined, in this case, as states that have sent combat elements overseas in coordination with the USSR at least in part

because they are obligated to do so because of political or economic aspects of their relationship with Moscow or, as in the case of Eastern Europe, because they are dominated by Soviet military might. In the case of Cuba, a combination of economic, ideological, and military considerations (e.g., the need for Soviet military support) probably determines its policy. A client, presumably, would be an entity such as the MPLA or the Ethiopian Dirgue that accepts a Soviet or surrogate presence or other military and intelligence support for the achievement of its goals. South Yemen is both a surrogate (in Ethiopia) and a client with respect to its own quarrels, against Oman for example.

129.   "Soviet Test Airlift to Africa Reported," *The Boston Globe*, June 23, 1978, p. 31; O'Ballance, "The Cuban Factor," p. 49; Whetten, "The Soviet–Cuban Presence," p. 41. The Libyan stocks are said to include at least 2,000 tanks, mostly T-62s, T-64s and T-72s, which apparently are maintained by East German and other Warsaw Pact forces, operating, in some cases, out of climatized shelters. There are at present tanks equivalent to three armored divisions at least in Libya, with more coming in, at last report. At least five hundred warplanes are present there, including MiG-25s. These are flown by North Korean, Palestinian, Pakestani and other pilots. The key Soviet base in Libya is Al-Kufrah in the southeast.

Other Soviet bases are reported to be near Addis, and Kormaksar near Aden. Moreover, during the last few months, Syria is also becoming a major recipient of Soviet arms, including T-72s and MiG-25s. See: Drew Middleton, "Soviet Said to Build Arms Caches in Libya, Syria, Persian Gulf Area," *New York Times*, 14 March 1980, p. 2; "Russia's Arsenal in Libya," *Foreign Report*, No. 1576 (March 21, 1979), p. 3; "The Russians' Dilemma in Ethiopia," *Foreign Report*, 31 May 1978, pp. 2–4.

130.   Whetten, "The Soviet–Cuban Presence," p. 41; O'Ballance, "The Cuban Factor," p. 49; "Russia's Flying Armada," *Foreign Report*, No. 1537, 7 June 1978, pp. 1–3.

131.   Iraq reportedly has been offered an unannounced number of Il-76s. 6 *Defense and Foreign Affairs Digest,* no. 2 (February 1978), p. 25. Given the stockpiles of materiel in Iraq (including large numbers of T-62 and T-54 tanks, MiG-23-"Flogger B," as well as Scud and, possibly, Scaleboard surface-to-surface missiles), this could prove significant in the context of the regional balance. "Russia's Secret Deal with Iraq," *Foreign Report*, No 1459 (October 13, 1976), pp. 1–2; "More Soviet Planes for the Middle East," *Foreign Report* (March 9, 1977), p. 3; *Military Balance 1979–80*, p. 40. Iraq now has two transport squadrons, a significant force in regional terms.

132.   "Il-62M for Cuba," Havana Domestic Service in Spanish 1700 G.M.T., 10 February 1978, in *Foreign Broadcast Information Service, Daily Report for Latin America*, vol. 6, no. 31 (February 14, 1978), p. Q3.

133.   Marquez, "Operation Carlota," pp. 128–129.

134.   Il-62Ms flew via Conakry, or possibly Guinea–Bissau, for refueling purposes. Although the present status of the "Conakry Connection" is unclear, Guinea–Bissau appears still to be available for such operations. Needless to say, most Cuban soldiers and the greater portion of hardware came by sea to Angola. Durch, *Cuban Military*, p. 48.

135.   Ibid.

136.   *The Military Balance 1979–1980*; Mose L. Harvey, *Soviet Combat Troops in Cuba* (Miami, Florida: Advanced International Studies

Institute, in Association with the University of Miami, 1979), p. 30; "Russia's Flying Armada," *Foreign Report*, No. 1537 (June 7, 1978), pp. 1-3.

137.   John Fullerton, "The Strategic Power of Soviet Shipping," 6 *Defense and Foreign Affairs Digest*, no. 16 (June 1978), pp. 33, 39.

138.   "Magazine Outlines Soviet–Cuban Organization," Madrid E.F.E. in Spanish 1221 G.M.T., 26 May 1978 (review of French weekly *Vendredi, Samdi et Dimanche*), *Foreign Broadcast Information Service, Daily Report on Soviet Union*, vol. III (May 30, 1978) No. 104, p. H1; Graham Hovey, "Brzezinski Asserts that Soviet General Leads Ethiopia Units," *New York Times*, 25 February 1978, p. 1; Kim Willenson et al., "Red Stars Over Africa," 91 *Newsweek* No. 11 (March 13, 1978), p. 39.

139.   "Russian Foreign Legion in Ethiopia," *Foreign Report*, No. 1579 (January 18, 1978), p. 1; "Chopper War in the Ogaden" (see note 118), p. 3.

140.   "Magazine Outlines Soviet–Cuban Organization in Africa" (see note 138).

141.   Marvine Howe, "Cubans' Flights for Angola Fuel at Azores Despite Ban," *New York Times*, 18 January 1976, p. 1.

142.   "Portugal: Antunes on the Way Out," *Foreign Report*, 4 February 1976, pp. 5-6.

143.   "Sanoyan Address," Conakry Prela, in Spanish to Prela Havana 2031 G.M.T., 7 May 1972, in *Foreign Broadcast Information Service, Middle East and Africa*, vol. 5, no. 5 (May 9, 1972), p. 11.

144.   "Armed Support to Revolutionary Countries Reaffirmed," Paris, in Spanish 0134 G.M.T., February 21, 1976, in *Foreign Broadcast Information Service, Latin America* (February 24, 1976), p. Q1. But was the MPLA a "formally established government?"

145.   Most accounts stress that volunteers are eager to escape boredom, racism, or unemployment. Moreover, there are major incentives in the way of promotions and new job opportunities upon a volunteer's return to Cuba, as well as the glory of being viewed as a war hero.

146.   "Cuban Death Toll Put at 1,500," *Los Angeles Times*, 20 July 1976, p. 12.

147.   The distinctions between military and civilian personnel often are blurred, a factor that may account for discrepancies between various estimates of the size of Cuban military personnel in Africa. The estimate referred to most frequently is 40,000. "Africa: The Cuban Personnel Count," 2 *Defense and Foreign Affairs Weekly Report on Strategic African Affairs* no. 17 (May 4, 1978), p. 1; William Beecher, "Cuba Can Easily Dispatch More Troops, US Believes," *The Boston Globe* (June 15, 1978), p. 24.

148.   "The Moscow Connection," 112 *Time* no. 2 (July 7, 1978), p. 39.

149.   "Cuba: Threat of Forces Increase Is Passed to US," 4 *Defense and Foreign Affairs Weekly Report on Strategic Latin American Affairs*, no. 30 (August 11, 1978), pp. 1-2; *The Military Balance 1979-1980*, p. 79.

150.   Raymond Carroll, "The Afrika Korps," 91 *Newsweek* No. 25 (June 19, 1978), p. 44. *The Leipziger Volkszeitung* felt compelled to respond to a letter by a reader who asked if it would not be "more in the interest of peace and disarmament if the G.D.R. sent no soldiers into crisis

areas." Although the journal responded that socialist countries could not permit imperialism to act at will, the very fact that the issue was aired, would seem to indicate it was a significant issue. See "Wir haben euch Waffen und Brot geschickt," op. cit., p. 45. See also Ellen Lentz, "East Germans' Role in Africa Debated," *New York Times*, 2 August 1978; Elizabeth Pond, "East Germany's 'Afrika Korps'," *Christian Science Monitor*, 26 June 1978; Pond, "East Germans Look to Africa," *Washington Post*, 8 July 1978.

18

The Projection of Power: Implications for U.S. Policy in the 1980s

Robert L. Pfaltzgraff, Jr.

The United States confronts a series of formidable national security problems, of which the projection of power is both the most difficult and the most immediate. Although this volume has produced no consensus on all of the specific options that should guide American policy, there is general agreement on the proposition that the capabilities available to the Soviet Union for power projection are growing, while those of the United States, in relative and perhaps even absolute terms, have declined, especially in the last decade. Although there is no consensus on the precise relationship between military power, in its various manifestations up and down the escalatory ladder, and other forms of power, there is general agreement that those states that historically have held the rank of great power have possessed a broad range of capabilities of which the military has been prominent. Although there is by no means full agreement about all of the specific circumstances in which the United States should use military means in the projection of power, it is widely acknowledged that the United States retains a broad range of interests abroad, and especially in the Persian Gulf region, in defense of which projectible power, in some form, must be available.

In several chapters the question of the nature of power—in symbol and reality—is addressed. This includes problems inherent in an adequate conceptualization of power, of which the literature of political science and international relations is abundant. One of the enduring problems—indeed deficiencies—confronting the United States, as well as certain other great powers—notably Great Britain in historic context—has been the relationship between capabilities and objectives or interests or ideas. This remains a dilemma for the United States in the 1980s. It is inherent in the very concept of power viewed in political terms—relative to the goals on whose behalf it is to be used and relative to the means available to opponents against which power is used. This, in turn, may depend upon the extent to which power, in fact, has been utilized in the past. Under such circumsances, those who possess power in its fullest measure may not be compelled actually to use it in order to realize their objectives—an axiom that may have equal applicability in interstate or in interpersonal relationships. As Uri Ra'anan suggests, this notion of the political shadow cast by the possession of superior capabilities is not unknown to the Soviet Union. This is the perceptual element of power. In this view, the power equation contains such elements as strategic and general purpose forces, as well as geographic propinquity, mobilizable manpower, and less tangible factors such as ideological commitments and preconceptions.

The perception of power is related, first and foremost, to the dynamic dimension of power—that is to say, the perceived willingness and ability of its possessor to use power credibly in the achievement of some objective, and a calculation in advance of the hypothesized outcome of a conflict in which power is used. Thus, we are led to an empirical question of great importance in our discussion of the nature of power: how is power perceived, and what is its effect upon the behavior of those who perceive it? Stated somewhat differently, what is the nature, and level, of causality in political behavior that can be inferred from power and its perceptions? Can we evolve a theory of political behavior which contains as a principal element power as causation? Do capabilities produce interests which produce behavior which, in turn, produces conflict or accommodation?

Two of the contributors to this volume considered principally the historical dimensions of power projection. The historic and contemporary problem confronting the United States is the projection of power into the vast Eurasian land mass in support of our allies and of other interests, and, in order to counter the capabilities of adversaries in that land mass to project power into the rimlands of Eurasia and beyond.

The geopolitical thought of Admiral Mahan and Sir Halford Mackinder is relevant to a consideration of the problems of power projection: Mahan's work was focused on the British Empire and what he deemed to be its relevance to the early twentieth century maritime interests of the United States—in its own right an "island nation" of continental dimensions—and Mackinder addressed the impact of mobility on land upon power projection in the twentieth century. The problems confronting the United States and its allies in the projection of power lie, for the most part, in chokepoints and littorals once controlled by Britain and, to a lesser extent, regions controlled by other European imperial powers, and which are now the object of Soviet interest. Here, we need not repeat at length the analogies that have been drawn between Mahan and Gorshkov, as seminal naval strategists and geostrategic thinkers for their nations' respective navies. Drawing heavily upon the historic experience of Britain and other maritime powers, Geoffrey Kemp and John Maurer conclude that the capacity of the United States to project power, especially in the Persian Gulf, will depend, in the last resort, as much upon logistics and infrastructure as on firepower and tactics. In turn, logistics is related to the technology, or technologies, of the day for power projection, as considered in an examination of the implications of the shift from a coal- to an oil-based economy, and propulsion systems, and the rise to importance of new arenas of conflict—endoatmospheric and exospheric—from the age of air power to an emerging space age. It was the possession of an extensive and global network of bases and other facilities that made it possible for Britain not only to mount military operations far from home, but also to project power in peacetime to regions remote from her home islands.

Yet, as Michael Vlahos points out, there is a fundamental difference between the United States and Britain in naval force deployments. At no time did Britain, between 1815 and 1941, deploy more than 19 percent of her fleet outside the traditional European operating area. In the case of the United States, never has so much of the capital ship strength of a maritime state been routinely operated at war-readiness levels in regions so remote from the naval power's homeland. This distinction, together with the growing constraints experienced by the United States in the loss of access to much of the infrastructure once possessed by Britain, points up the formidable problems confronting the United States in the projection of maritime power in the 1980s.

As Barry Blechman reminds us, military power can be used for direct or for indirect purposes. Since World War II—between 1945 and 1975—military power has been employed far more often for indirect than for direct uses. If the past is an adequate guide for the future—by no means self-evident in this respect—we will need capabilities that will serve political–military purposes—the indirect use of military power. Naval forces, together with other war-fighting capabilities that provide for flexibility of action—perhaps strategic aircraft—that make it possible to establish a "presence" and to control an escalatory process, in order to signal intent.

Several contributions focus on the growth of Soviet power projection capabilities, especially since the 1960s. It is generally conceded that Soviet capabilities for power projection at all levels, relative to those of the United States, have increased substantially in the last decade, although there is by no means agreement about the full implications of this changed circumstance for the United States and its allies. Among other capabilities, the Soviet Union has acquired the means to project naval power on a global scale. Roger Fontaine considers the upgrading since 1970 of facilities in Cuba designed to improve Soviet strategic submarine capabilities in the Caribbean, as well as the development of bases for conventional warships and aircraft such as the controversial Backfire bomber, together with the stationing in Cuba, since 1975, of the equally controversial "brigada" and the construction by the Soviet Union of an electronic intelligence intercept complex near Havana similar to the facilities we once maintained in Iran.

Emphasis is placed on the growing capabilities of the Soviet Union, for which the United States possesses no counterpoise in being, for the projection of power by means of surrogate forces. The extension of Soviet influence, both in the Caribbean and in Africa and the Persian Gulf, has been made possible in large part by the use of Cuban proxies. Although there are historic examples of the use of surrogates to project military power, in our time no state has made more extensive and successful use of such forces for power projection than the Soviet Union. Gavriel Ra'anan suggests that surrogate forces, mounted at relatively low cost, represent an advantageous means for projecting power over major distances as, indeed, they have for the Soviet Union for at least the past thirty years. Furthermore, they provide for the Soviet Union a capability from which Moscow can disengage more easily than would be the case with direct Soviet military intervention. The growth of Soviet airlift capabilities, together with other advances in the power projection forces available to Moscow, is likely to enhance vastly the prospects for the use of such surrogate forces in the decade ahead, while the Soviet capacity for direct military intervention, as in Afghanistan, grows.

The most ominous of the trends in recent Soviet policy is represented by the use of Soviet forces themselves for direct military intervention in Afghanistan. The Soviet Union has been acquiring bases especially in states whose left-of-center governments have been replaced by even more left-of-center governments aligned with Moscow. At the same time, the Soviet Union has shipped large stocks of weapons and other equipment to client states and surrogates. Although, as Kenneth Allard suggests, most have come by sea, some have been airlifted. In fact, the Soviet Union, the first state after World War I to embrace the revolutionary concept of airborne warfare, has developed the largest standing airborne force in the world, which now possesses the means of operations at a radius of 2,000 miles from Soviet or Warsaw Pact territory without mid-air refueling—encompassing the Persian Gulf and the Middle East as well as northeastern Africa, Western Europe, and East Asia. The use of this force in Afghanistan was in accordance with Soviet doctrine providing for the execution of missions deep behind an enemy's front lines in coordination with ground troops and air force and naval units.

In Chapter One, Russell E. Dougherty places emphasis on essential requirements for the United States in power projection, credibility both to allies and adversaries, and the need for the United States to understand, in light of its historical national experience, the limits of popular support, which is an indispensable ingredient for the sustained projection of military power. In this view, the United States must prepare a total supporting environment and engage forces only if we are assured of the adequacy of our capabilities, including air and sea lift, supplies, and public support based upon the perception of a clear and present danger.

Implicit in contributions to this volume was the question of what can, and should, be done by the United States, both immediately and in the longer term, to redress asymmetries that favor the Soviet Union and its client states. Here, once again, the question of logistics and infrastructures is linked to any adequate consideration of the types of forces needed by the United States. Several general inferences may be set forth: (1) a rapid deployment force must rely heavily on airlift, but an airlift of such a force is likely to be most effective if prepositioned equipment is available or if it can be carried out in conjunction with friendly forces possessing such capabilities; (2) If local prepositioning is not possible, an amphibious force is likely to be a preferred option.

Both types of forces face severe constraints in the absence of a forward-based logistics infrastructure—the problem that increasingly confronts the United States in the 1980s. As Dov S. Zakheim concludes, airlift and amphibious deployment capabilities complement each other. The time factor in deployment defines airlift requirements, just as the size of the force defines sealift needs. Because of the time factor inherent in NATO readiness, the dicussions of recent years about the use of the Marine Corps in the European theater, especially the Northern Flank, have emphasized a change from traditional amphibious Marine Corps operations to the use of airlift, although it should be added that missions requiring rapid deployment elsewhere may be more appropriate for this type of force. Hence, the emphasis on the development of a new class of transport aircraft, the CX, and new types of cargo ships aboard which equipment could be prepositioned overseas.

Viewing rapid deployment forces, Jeffrey Record notes the need for the United States to overcome three major obstacles to the effective application of military power in regions as distant as the Persian Gulf: insufficient force, inadequate strategic mobility, and the lack of politically secure military access ashore. He stresses the need for a U.S. force based upon flexibility and uncertainty about the environment for its employment. In the projection of American military power to the Persian Gulf the United States faces far more formidable problems than in the Vietnam War, for we lack comparable logistical infrastructures in the Persian Gulf area. An essential prerequisite to an effective power projection capability lies in the development of new relationships with allies in the region— including Persian Gulf states as well as the Indian subcontinent. Indispensable to an adequate capability for rapid power projection, however, is the creation of what Dr. Record describes as a small agile intervention force based and supplied from the sea and supported by expanded seapower.

The power projection problems confronting the United States are global in nature. As a result of the numerous contingencies that could confront the United States simultaneously, we face the prospect that the rapid deployment of forces in one place may increase the incentive of other adversaries, North Korea for example, to attack an American ally—South Korea. The problem of inadequate levels of capabilities is related to a conception of deterrence that has been criticized and officially discarded, to be replaced by the Countervailing Strategy adopted by the United States in 1980. Rapid deployment forces could serve credibly as a trip wire symbolizing American resolve to escalate to the strategic–nuclear level only if we controlled the escalatory ladder at its upper reaches. Implicit in most, if not all, the chapters in this volume is the awareness of the growth of Soviet strategic forces relative to the United States. Hence, a concept of rapid deployment forces that possess, as the prerequisite for deterrence, some war-fighting capability, may constitute an urgent priority for the United States.

Although focusing especially on the Persian Gulf as a theater for power projection, the volume contains one chapter on East Asia. Hisashi Owada suggests that a war in Europe would probably be global in nature, or at least that it would be accompanied by threats in Asia. The problems of power projection in the Asian Pacific are, if anything, more complex than in Europe because of the relative lack, as he put it, of fixed boundaries determining the respective spheres of domination of the two camps. Asia has been the scene of the two greatest examples of American power projection since World War

II—Korea and Vietnam. Yet,the United States has drawn upon its power projection capabilities in the hope that a multipolar balance among states in the region will make it possible to safeguard American interests.

There was no consensus as to what military role precisely Japan should play in light of reductions in recent years in American military capabilities in East Asia, relative to those of the Soviet Union. Some analysts have posited the need for a strengthened American military relationship with China, and for Japan to play a somewhat greater military role, especially in maritime capabilities, in the Asian–Pacific region. As a result of the relative decline in American military power in the Western Pacific, it was suggested that Japan and the United States should try to redefine their joint and separate roles within the Security Treaty to restore or maintain its deterrent effect.

Increasingly there has been recognition in recent years that, in the broadest sense, the position of the United States as a vast technological base for logistics—the arsenal of democracy—is beset by a series of formidable difficulties. We face a potential problem of immediate consequence for a so-called short war, namely the inadequacy of our armaments production base. Here, the lessons of the War of October 1973 may be instructive: rates of armaments expenditure by Israel exceeded by far what had been anticipated before the conflict. Fred Iklé points out that Soviet weapons production capabilities now vastly exceed those of the United States. In the past, we had prevailed ultimately because of the production base that could be developed as a result of time available for such mobilization deficiencies, which now include oil and possibly certain raw materials, all of which should be stockpiled as part of a mobilization capability. The level of effort to be put into the development of an adequate mobilization base depends upon several variables: time; the long war versus the short war; the competing priorities within the domestic economy; and the level of political support available and necessary. In the aggregate, the United States, under good or best-case circumstances, possesses a superior potential for war mobilization, but it is unlikely that we would have the opportunity in a future conflict to maximize that potential. There is little understanding of the level of effort and of expenditure that would be needed, in the absence of agreement on the nature of the contingency, or contingencies, to be confronted.

What lessons can be derived from history for an understanding of the formidable problems already facing us in the 1980s in the projection of power? In addition to the historic experience of imperial states, together with the contemporary example of the

Soviet Union, we confront various dimensions of the American mind-set. Historically, Americans have been ambivalent about the role and use of military power as an instrument of foreign policy. In recent decades, the American decision-making process—in defense matters as in the modern social sciences—has been quantitative and programmatic in focus, rooted, as James Woolsey suggests, in the disciplines of economics and the techniques of professional business schools. We have become managers rather than strategists. Since the early 1960s, systems analysis, whatever its utility in operational planning, has introduced into the defense planning process a series of rigidities and delays. In the designing of forces, systems analysis has perhaps no more utility than the carpenter or plumber would have if called upon to provide the services of an architect in designing a vast new building.

Although planning for a war differs from fighting a war, the task that lies before us is to design a strategy within which forces for the projection of power, including its military dimension, can be cast. Of this we were reminded by Captain Roche, who saw the need for a strategy, for a conception of goals and interests. Having decided what we want, how do we do it? We must confront the formidable problems of determining the purposes and nature of military power projection capabilities within a strategic framework adequate to the needs of the years that lie ahead.

Index